Torres Strait

Arafura Sea

C. York

C. Grenville

C. Arnhem

Weipa

Groote Eylandt

Gulf of Carpentaria

Cape York Peninsula

Lakefield N.P.

Cooktown

Wellesley Is

Laura

Barkly Tableland

Karumba

Normanton

Cairns

Tully

Hinchinbrook I.

C o r a l

S e a

Burketown

Gregory Range

Townsville

THE GREAT BARRIER REEF AND THE ISLANDS

Camooweal

Cloncurry

Ayr

Mackay

Mount Isa

Hughenden

Sarina

Territory

Dajarra

Winton

Rockhampton

Boulia

Great Artesian

Basin

Emerald

Gladstone

QUEENSLAND

Tropic of Capricorn

Simpson Desert

Birdsville

Q u e e n s l a n d

Yaraka

Bundaberg

Fraser I.

Maryborough

P A C I F I C

Inke

L. Eyre North

Cooper Creek

Quilpie

Charleville

Roma

Gympie

O C E A N

Oodnadatta

Lake Eyre N.P.

Eyre

Cunnamulla

Toowoomba

Brisbane

Warwick

Murwillumbah

Gammon Ranges N.P.

Milparinka

Sturt N.P.

Walgett

Moree

Glen Innes

Lismore

SOUTH AUSTRALIA

Lake Torrens

Leigh Creek

Lake Frome

Bourke

Grafton

Woomera

Lake Gairdner

Flinders Ranges N.P.

Mutawintji N.P.

Darling

Armidale

Port Macquarie

Streaky Bay

Port Augusta

Broken Hill

N e w

Tamworth

Taree

Myall Lakes N.P.

Eyre Pen.

Port Pirie

Kinchega N.P.

Dubbo

NEW SOUTH WALES

Narromine

Wollemi N.P.

Whyalla

W a l e s

Parkes

SYDNEY

Newcastle

Port Lincoln

Adelaide

Mungo N.P.

Yorke Pen.

Kingscote

Hay

Sydney

Wollongong

Kangaroo I.

Victor Harbor

Wyperfeld N.P.

Murray

Wagga Wagga

Kosciuszko N.P.

CANBERRA

Canberra

Coorong N.P.

Albury

Cooma

Naracoorte

Mt Kosciuszko

Mount Gambier

Grampians N.P.

V i c t o r i a

Wangaratta

Wodonga

Snowy River N.P.

VICTORIA

Bendigo

C. Howe

Croajingolong N.P.

Portland

Ballarat

Geelong

MELBOURNE

Gippsland Lakes N.P.

Warrnambool

C. Otway

South East Cape

T a s m a n

Bass Strait

King I.

Furneaux Group

S e a

Marrawah

Burnie

Devonport

Launceston

Queenstown

TASMANIA

Tasmania

South West N.P.

Hobart

South West Cape

Southport

INSIGHT ○ GUIDES

AUSTRALIA

PLAN & BOOK
YOUR TAILOR-MADE TRIP

BRAZIL   **CHILE**   **ECUADOR**

TAILOR-MADE TRIPS & UNIQUE EXPERIENCES CREATED BY LOCAL TRAVEL EXPERTS AT INSIGHTGUIDES.COM/HOLIDAYS

Insight Guides has been inspiring travellers with high-quality travel content for over 45 years. As well as our popular guidebooks, we now offer the opportunity to book tailor-made private trips completely personalised to your needs and interests. By connecting with one of our local experts, you will directly benefit from their expertise and local know-how, helping you create memories that will last a lifetime.

HOW INSIGHTGUIDES.COM/HOLIDAYS WORKS

STEP 1

Pick your dream destination and submit an enquiry, or modify an existing itinerary if you prefer.

STEP 2

Fill in a short form, sharing details of your travel plans and preferences with a local expert.

STEP 3

Your local expert will create your personalised itinerary, which you can amend until you are completely satisfied.

STEP 4

Book securely online. Pack your bags and enjoy your holiday! Your local expert will be available to answer questions during your trip.

BENEFITS OF PLANNING & BOOKING AT
INSIGHTGUIDES.COM/HOLIDAYS

PLANNED BY LOCAL EXPERTS

The Insight Guides local experts are hand-picked, based on their experience in the travel industry and their impeccable standards of customer service.

SAVE TIME & MONEY

When a local expert plans your trip, you save time and money when you book, even during high season. You won't be charged for using a credit card either.

TAILOR-MADE TRIPS

Book with Insight Guides, and you will be in complete control of the planning process, from the initial selections to amending your final itinerary.

BOOK & TRAVEL STRESS-FREE

Enjoy stress-free travel when you use the Insight Guides secure online booking platform. All bookings come with a money-back guarantee.

WHAT OTHER TRAVELLERS THINK ABOUT TRIPS BOOKED AT
INSIGHTGUIDES.COM/HOLIDAYS

Trip to Portugal

Every step of the planning process and the trip itself was effortless and exceptional. Our special interests, preferences and requests were accommodated resulting in a trip that exceeded our expectations.

Corinne, USA ★★★★★

Trip to Vietnam

The organization was superb, the drivers professional, and accommodation quite comfortable. I was well taken care of! My thanks to your colleagues who helped make my trip to Vietnam such a great experience. My only regret is that I couldn't spend more time in the country.

Heather ★★★★★

DON'T MISS OUT
BOOK NOW AT
INSIGHTGUIDES.COM/HOLIDAYS

CONTENTS

Introduction

The best of Australia.......................6
Down Under 17
An ancient landscape..................19

History & features

Decisive dates 26
Dreamtime and discovery.............29
From gold rush to world war 36
The modern era 43
The urban Aussie 53
Life in the bush 58
A multicultural society.................61
Aborigines today 65
📷 Aboriginal art 68
The arts 71
Modern Australian cuisine............76
   🔍 Bush tucker meets
      the locavore movement 79
Australian wines 80
Where sport is supreme 84
📷 Surf culture 88
One-of-a-kind wildlife..................91
📷 Dangerous wildlife 94

Places

Introduction................................103
◼ SYDNEY.................................107
   🔍 Harbour-hopping 112
◼ NEW SOUTH WALES................124
   🔍 Whales and dolphins...........128
   🔍 Two pacific gems 134
◼ CANBERRA 151
◼ MELBOURNE 159
◼ VICTORIA................................171
◼ SOUTH AUSTRALIA 191
   🔍 Festival frenzy...................196
◼ QUEENSLAND 211
   🔍 Fraser Island.....................224
   🔍 The world's oldest rainforest...230
📷 The Rainforest.........................236
◼ THE GREAT BARRIER REEF
   AND THE ISLANDS..................238
   🔍 Visiting the Reef 242
📷 Protecting the Great Barrier Reef........246

■ NORTHERN TERRITORY.........................**251**
Uluru and Kata Tjuta..................................**266**
■ WESTERN AUSTRALIA **271**
◎ The wildflowers of
  Western Australia **292**
■ TASMANIA..**297**
  ♀ The Gulag Peninsula.........................**306**
  ♀ The Overland Track............................**315**
◎ Freycinet National Park.........................**316**

Travel tips

TRANSPORT
Getting there **320**
  By air **320**
Getting around **320**
  By air **320**
  From the airport......................................**321**
  By bus..**321**
  By train..**322**
  By sea..**323**
  Taxis **323**
  Motorcycles and bicycles.......................**324**
  By car **325**

A – Z
Accommodation **326**
Admission charges **326**
Budgeting for your trip **326**
Climate..**327**
Crime and safety.......................................**327**
Customs regulations **328**
Disabled travellers...................................**328**
Electricity..**328**
Embassies and consulates.......................**328**
Emergencies **329**
Health and medical care...........................**329**
Internet **329**
LGBTQ travellers......................................**330**
Maps..**330**
Media...**330**
Money...**330**
Opening hours...**331**
Postal services **331**
Public holidays **331**
Religion **331**
Student travellers **331**

Telephones...**331**
Time zones...**332**
Toilets..**332**
Tourist information **332**
Useful addresses **332**
Visas and passports..................................**333**
Weights and measures **333**
What to wear **333**
Women travellers.......................................**333**

FURTHER READING
General...**334**
History..**334**
Natural history...**334**
Travel..**334**
Aboriginal Australia **335**
Australian language...................................**335**
Fiction **335**
Children's books **336**
Other Insight Guides **3360**

Maps

Australia...**104**
Sydney **108**
Sydney and surroundings **115**
New South Wales **126**
Canberra **152**
Melbourne..**160**
Victoria...**172**
Adelaide **192**
South Australia **198**
Queensland..**212**
Brisbane...**214**
Great Barrier Reef and the islands **240**
Northern Territory **252**
Darwin...**263**
Perth...**272**
Western Australia **276**
Hobart **298**
Tasmania..**304**
Inside front cover Australia
Inside back cover Sydney

LEGEND
♀ Insight on
◎ Photo story

THE BEST OF AUSTRALIA: TOP ATTRACTIONS

△ **Sydney Harbour.** The Opera House is deservedly on everyone's list as a must-see attraction in Australia – it's on the Unesco World Heritage list, after all – and when you combine it with the iron bulk of Sydney Harbour Bridge, you have one of the great vistas of the world. See page 109.

▽ **The Great Barrier Reef.** More than 2,000km (1,240 miles) of mostly pristine coral gardens and rich aquatic life, the Reef rewards divers, snorkellers or those who simply gaze through glass-bottomed boats. See page 238.

△ **Canberra's museums and galleries.** Gathered around Lake Burley Griffin is what collectively amounts to the most impressive collection of educational and cultural showpieces in Australia. See page 151.

△ **Uluru.** Rising out of the parched red centre of the country, Uluru (Ayers Rock) is the dramatic touchstone of this ancient continent. It's a sacred site to its Aboriginal custodians, and worth travelling thousands of kilometres to see. See page 266.

◁ **Melbourne's music scene.** A host of brilliant venues large and small helps to make this the finest music city in Australia. See page 166.

△ **Australia's wineries.** In a nation rich in high-class, picturesque wineries, the Barossa, Clare and Coonawarra regions stand out as some of the finest. See page 80.

△ **Port Arthur.** Tasmania's grim penal settlement provides something of a crash course in Australia's colonial history. The setting, ironically, is stunning. See page 302.

△ **Kakadu National Park.** Of the numerous National Parks, this one is unmissable with its mixture of indigenous flora and fauna along with ancient Aboriginal culture. See page 261.

▷ **Boxing Day at the MCG.** Up to 100,000 spectators and fans turn out to this world-famous Melbourne stadium for the beginning of a five-day test match, an epic even in the cricket world. Even if you don't follow the sport, go to the stadium for the party atmosphere. See page 166.

△ **Wildflowers in Western Australia.** Springtime, beginning in September, is when the countryside around Perth and southern Western Australia is awash with technicolour blooms. See page 292.

THE BEST OF AUSTRALIA: EDITOR'S CHOICE

Fraser Island.

BEST ISLANDS

Fraser Island, Qld. There are endless beaches on this giant sand bar. See page 224.

Kangaroo Island, SA. Seals, penguins, echidnas, kangaroos, emus and koalas all live here. See page 205.

Lord Howe Island, NSW. This heavily forested isle has numerous walking trails, plus superb diving and snorkelling conditions. See page 134.

Magnetic Island, Qld. Just over the water from Townsville but a world away. See page 225.

Maria Island, Tas. Maria Island is vehicle-free, so pack walking boots or hire a mountain bike at the ferry point. See page 302.

Tiwi Islands, NT. Accessible only by boat or plane through organised tours, the islands are rich in Aboriginal culture. See page 265.

Diving off the islands of Queensland.

BEST BEACHES

Bells Beach, Vic. This beach is famed worldwide for its autumn surf contest. See page 174.

Cable Beach, WA. A ride on a camel train along the beach at sunset is a great experience for kids. See page 289.

Maslin Beach, SA. The backdrop of sandstone cliffs makes this family-oriented beach one of the most beautiful in the state. See page 197.

Noosa, Qld. As well as being an excellent surfing beach, Noosa benefits from a national park on one side and a shopping strip on the other. See page 221.

Shark Bay, WA. A World Heritage Site, Shark Bay has marine wildlife galore. Hand feed

Noosa Beach, Queensland.

dolphins at the bay's Monkey Mia. See page 285.

Whitsunday Island, Great Barrier Reef. As far as beaches go, Whitehaven is pretty unbeatable, and it's open for camping, too. See page 241.

Wineglass Bay, Freycinet NP, Tas. This is a breathtaking sweep of white sands and azure sea. The best views are from Wineglass Bay lookout. See page 302.

BEST GALLERIES

Tiled artwork decorates Melbourne.

Aboriginal rock art galleries at Kakadu, NT. The rock art galleries, particularly at Nourlangie and Ubirr rocks, display some of the earliest paintings on the planet. See page 261.

National Gallery of Australia, Canberra. Repository of many of the finest artworks in the country. See page 153.

National Gallery of Victoria, Melbourne. The gallery has been split over two sites; one houses national and one houses international works. See page 167.

South Australian Museum, Adelaide. Extensive Aboriginal and Pacific exhibits and a broad survey of regional natural history. See page 194.

BEST MARKETS

Central Market, Adelaide. A covered area packed with more than 200 shops, the main attraction is the wealth of local produce that SA is famed for. See page 195.

Queen Victoria Market, Melbourne. A buzzing place where locals after fresh produce or deli specialities mix with tourists seeking souvenir clocks in the shape of Australia. See page 168.

Bondi Markets, Sydney. The Bondi Markets have helped establish more than a few of the most successful Sydney fashion designers. See page 119.

Fish Market, Sydney. The ultimate seafood experience, Sydney's Fish Market has fish auctions, market stalls, restaurants and even a cookery school. See page 115.

Adelaide's famous covered market.

Sovereign Hill is an open air museum in Golden Point, a suburb of Ballarat, Victoria.

BEST COLONIAL TOWNS

Ballarat, Vic. An old gold-mining town. The Eureka Centre re-creates the day in 1854 when gold was discovered. See page 178.

Broome, WA. The timber dwellings of Chinatown serve as a reminder of Broome's pearl-diving days. See page 288.

Hahndorf, SA. Pretty German town established in 1839 in the Adelaide Hills. See page 197.

Richmond, Tas. One of the very best preserved Georgian towns in all of Australia. See page 301.

The Rocks, Sydney. Site of the first European settlement, today The Rocks is virtually an open-air museum. See page 110.

Charters Towers, Qld. Attractive former gold-mining town with splendid colonial buildings. See page 225.

Campbell's Cover in The Rocks, Sydney.

Federation Square, Melbourne.

Kangaroos on Esperance Beach.

DOWN UNDER

You can call it the world's largest island, or the Earth's oldest continent. Either way, Australia is a place like no other.

D.H. Lawrence once said 'Australia is like an open door with the blue beyond. You just walk out of the world and into Australia.'

Australians like to think of their country as God's own. Since the turn of the millennium this philosophy has taken on a new resonance as a whole series of travails has assailed the country. There has always been fire, but in February 2009 bushfires destroyed a great part of the state of Victoria and took scores of lives. A 2013 heatwave caused more fires across Victoria and New South Wales, and forced the Australian Bureau of Meteorology to add another colour band to its temperature chart – for temperatures over 50°C (122°F). New records were set in January 2019, with the mercury refusing to dip below 40°C (122°F) for many consecutive days. There have always been floods, but they attained a new scale when the fatal inundation in January 2011 affected 75 percent of Queensland. Again in 2019, flash floods in Townsville resulted in warnings for people to look out for crocodiles in their houses. Even plagues of locusts have been sweeping the land. They are living on the frontline of climate change, but Australians, tend to take these unique challenges in their stride.

Weano Gorge in the Karijini National Park, Western Australia.

This country of extremes is used to doing things the hard way. People have been inhabiting this daunting continent for around 50,000 years, and they know that for every down, there's an upside to living in one of the most remarkable places on Earth: Try waking up to the bush dawn, as the kookaburras begin maniacally laughing and the golden light pierces the gumtrees.

Australia is a long way from anywhere else, which makes it a unique land with a people used to standing alone. The very differences that permeate the land, culture and history here have also given the place a singular strength and durability. Australians will most likely agree with Mark Twain that Australia is full of surprises, and adventures. However, it wasn't always so colourful. When the British colonists and convicts first arrived in the 1780s, they attempted to re-create the places and cultures of their homeland, but the strangeness of the landscape, including the heat, rain or endless droughts meant that they could only ever be partially successful.

Today, Australians tend to be thankful for their distance from Europe and the United States, and embrace their (relative) proximity to Asia. The quirks of their homeland – the egg-laying mammals, the ghostly trees, the savage deserts, even the menagerie of deadly snakes – have become a source of endless fascination.

The Twelve Apostles as seen from the Great Ocean Road.

AN ANCIENT LANDSCAPE

Australia has been a continent for around 50 million years. But the history of the land can be traced back much further, to a time when the world was young.

Australia's topography, so forbidding to the first European settlers in the late 18th century and so compelling to more recent arrivals, takes us back to the earliest history of our planet. Certain rocks have been dated back 3,500 million years, while large chunks of the landscape suggest continental movements dating back more than 1,000 million years.

Whereas much of Europe and the Americas have the landscapes of youth – snow-covered peaks, rushing waterfalls, geysers, active volcanoes, giant gorges and mountain lakes – Australia's blunted, stunted, arid lands speak of an age that must be treated with respect. It is a land in which even the animals and plants, developed in isolation, are strikingly different.

FORCES OF NATURE

The last great geological shifts in Australia took place some 230 million years ago, before the Permian period. It was then that the forces of nature convulsed the Earth's crust and created alpine ranges whose peaks extended above the snow line. Since then, modest convulsions on the eastern and western fringes have created low ranges (now known as tablelands), and volcanoes have occasionally erupted – but, generally speaking, Australia was already a sleeping giant when the rest of the world's landforms came into being. Barring unforeseen geological circumstances, it will also be the first continent to achieve equilibrium, a flattening of the land to the point where rivers cease to run, there is no further erosion, and landscape becomes moonscape.

Australia began to take shape 50 million years ago when it broke away from the great continent known as Gondwanaland. This landmass at one time incorporated Africa, South America and

Hawks Head Lookout, Kalbarri National Park.

India. Australia broke free and drifted north at first, reshaping itself into a continent. The centre was rising from a shallow sea to unite what had been a series of islands. One of these islands, the Great Western Plateau, had been the only constant during much of this change, sometimes partly submerged but always the stable heart of the continent. Today that plateau spreads over almost half the continent, a dry and dramatic expanse of pristine beauty. It spreads from the west coast to beyond the West Australian border, taking in the Kimberley and Hamersley ranges, the Great Sandy Desert, Gibson Desert and the Great Victoria Desert, and, although its topography has changed greatly, it houses the artefacts of ancient times.

A rock found near Marble Bar in the far north-west yielded the remains of organisms which lived 3,500 million years ago – the oldest form of life yet discovered. A dinosaur footprint is frozen in rock near Broome, and in the Kimberley, once a coral reef in a shallow sea, landlocked ocean fish have adapted to fresh water.

While much of the west is brown and feature-less, every now and then something crops up to whet the appetite, perhaps because it is such a contrast with the surroundings. People will drive great distances to have a look at geologi-cal oddities. In the case of Wave Rock, 350km (220 miles) to the west of Perth, it's the edge of a granite outcrop, about 15 metres (50ft) high, that is curling over along a length a little over 100 metres (330ft), looking as if a giant wave had petrified mid-action. This distinctive shape derives from a process that commenced about 60 million years ago from a softening of some sections of the granite and subsequent water erosion, which eventually led to Wave Rock emerging from the ground.

Similarly, the magnificent Bungle Bungles on the southern edge of the Kimberley at the top of Western Australia are probably the most dramatic result of erosion in the country. This is a sandstone range that stretches 450km (280 miles) and occupies 640 sq km (247 sq miles) in the Purnululu National Park. The peculiar dome shapes of the peaks are dramatic enough, and when combined with the striping effect caused by alternating layers of orange and grey rock (according to the ferrous content), you have a heart-stopping site, unlike any other in the world. It was recognised as a World Heritage Site by Unesco in 1987.

Being so far from the main population cen-tres, relatively few visitors or, indeed, Austral-ians, ever get to see Bungle Bungles. Tourists are much more likely to find themselves at the country's more famous World Heritage-listed rock: Uluru. This, too, is sandstone, but just one monolithic form, the tip of a rocky equivalent of an iceberg, where the majority is hidden below the surface. The strength of Uluru lies in its homogeneity and in the absence of the flaws that have allowed the forces of erosion to eat away at the rocks that would once have surrounded it. The fact that it is surrounded by many kilometres of flat desert heightens the contrast.

THE LOWLANDS

The central eastern lowlands, stretching south from the Gulf of Carpentaria and bounded by the Great Dividing Range to the east, form a sedi-mentary basin that has often been encroached upon by the sea. Although this is a catchment area of 1.5 million sq km (600,000 sq miles) for rivers running inland off the eastern range, much of the water is lost through evaporation or into the vast chain of salt lakes and clay pans. The largest of the salt lakes, Lake Eyre, is also the lowest part of the continent at 15 metres

Wild flowers in the Hamersley Gorge, Pilbara.

⊘ FLORA AND FAUNA

Australia's vegetation is dominated by the eucalyp-tus, the humble gumtree, which can be found in more than 500 different forms. It's hard to escape the smell, feel and sight of this tree, which is most often stunted, knotted and offers little shade. Australian marsupials have developed in isolation in extraordinary ways, and into 120 different species – from the red kangaroo and the gliders that fly between trees, to tiny desert mice. The platypus and echidna are the world's only egg-laying mammals; the Queensland lungfish can breathe both above and under water. Australia has clear links to a time when the world was young.

(50ft) below sea level. For much of the time it is a lake in name only. However, with above-average rainfall in recent years, numerous tour operators have set up special sightseeing trips to see the lake with water and the concomitant surge in birdlife.

Much of the lowlands are so exceptionally harsh and inhospitable that it is difficult to imagine that beneath the surface lies the Great Artesian Basin, from which bores are tapped to provide water for livestock. The most ancient part of the basin area is the Flinders Ranges of

Once you're across the range, everything dries out and becomes desert.

Mount Kosciuszko, at 2,230 metres (7,315ft), is the highest point in the Great Dividing Range, but equally majestic are the rainforests of the north and the moors of Tasmania.

The Glass House Mountains in southern Queensland were formed by volcanoes about 20 million years ago; they are formed from plugs of hardened magma piped up the centre of peaks that have subsequently eroded away. The granite belt bridging the Queensland–New South Wales

Mungalli Falls, near the town of Atherton in Queensland.

South Australia, in which there are rocks and remains dating back 1,000 million years.

THE HIGHLANDS

Because of its immense age, Australia can no longer boast a true alpine range. The Great Dividing Range that runs parallel with the east coast for more than 2,000km (1,250 miles) is as diverse as any found on Earth, tropical at one end and subalpine at the other. It is a series of 'fold mountains', where tectonic plates have collided and buckled.

The Great Dividing Range dictates the climate of eastern Australia. The narrow strip between the range and the Pacific Ocean is where the rain falls and where the air stays relatively cool.

border and the Warrumbungle Mountains was born in similar circumstances.

Australia's last active volcano died only 6,000 years ago – just a few ticks on the geological clock. In Tasmania the effects of volcanic activity and two ice ages have created a distinctive wilderness. This can be seen in the Nut at Stanley, another of the nation's many geological oddities. This 150-metre (490ft) -high plug of volcanic rock was formed in similar fashion to the Glass House Mountains.

For a variation on the theme, make a trip out to the Undara Lava Tubes in outback Queensland, 130km (70 miles) west of the Atherton Tablelands. In this case it is the absence of volcanic rock that is significant. When the long-extinct Undara volcano erupted around 190,000 years ago, streams of lava spread across the countryside and, as the surface of the rock cooled, the lava inside flowed on, leaving hollow tubes behind, up to 20 metres (65ft) in diameter. These were soon absorbed into the landscape and remained undiscovered until some of the tubes collapsed.

THE COAST

The coastline of Australia is as spectacular and as varied as the centre. It ranges from the limestone cliffs at the edge of the Nullarbor Plain

Australia and extended drought elsewhere. The latter has caused major anguish to river systems and has accentuated the danger of bushfires in those parts of the country already susceptible to them. There's little doubt that the devastating fires that hit Victoria in February 2009 and again in 2013 were exacerbated by years of dry conditions.

Elsewhere, water is the problem. Tropical cyclones have regularly wrought havoc on the north and east coasts, most notably Cyclone Tracy, which ripped into Darwin on Christmas Eve 1974; and Cyclone Yasi, which just missed

The dramatic Tasmanian coast.

to the jagged rock formations of Tasmania and western Victoria, from the mangrove swamps of the north to the spectacular beauty of the Great Barrier Reef – a lagoon which runs almost 2,000km (1,250 miles) down the Queensland coast and contains more than 2,000 coral reefs.

AT RISK

Australia manages to avoid the major fault lines that cause such trouble for its earthquake-plagued neighbours. It's pretty short of active volcanoes, too. Although there are plenty of other natural hazards to deal with, most are climate-related.

Repeated El Niño events since 2000 caused mayhem, bringing increased rainfall over northern

Cairns in 2011, but still brought lots of rain and winds. There have been several storms in tropical Queensland, including Cyclone Larry, which hit the Innisfail and surroundings in 2006, and Cyclone Marcia, which caused A$750 million in damage and left over 60,000 homes without power in Yeppoon, Rockhampton and Bundaberg in 2015.

Further south, when droughts do break, they tend to do so with a vengeance. Rainfall at the end of 2010 and beginning of 2011 caused floods in southern Queensland that affected an area greater than France and Germany combined. Nothing happens by halves in Australia. Luckily, the Australian spirit is indomitable, and the local people work hard to recover quickly from events like these.

John Glover's painting The bath of Diana, Van Diemen's Land 1837.

DECISIVE DATES

c.50,000 BC
The first Australians arrive, overland from New Guinea.

8000 BC
Returning boomerangs are used for hunting.

9th century
Seafarers from China possibly reach Australia's north coast.

1290s
Marco Polo's journal refers to a land south of Java, rich in gold and shells.

1606
Dutchman Willem Janszoon lands on the western side of Cape York Peninsula – the first verifiable European landing.

1642
Abel Tasman names the west coast of Tasmania Van Diemen's Land.

1688
English buccaneer William Dampier lands on the northwest coast.

1770
Captain Cook lands at Botany Bay, then sails northward, charting 4,000km (2,500 miles) of coast.

1773
The first picture of a kangaroo is seen in Britain.

1788
First Fleet arrives in Sydney Cove with a cargo of convicts.

1790
Second Fleet arrives.

An Australian propaganda poster from World War I.

1793
First free immigrants arrive.

1801–3
Matthew Flinders proves Australia is a single island by circumnavigation.

1813
Australia's own currency is established. The first crossing is made of the Blue Mountains.

1817
The name Australia is adopted (instead of New Holland).

1829
First settlers land at Fremantle, and found Perth two days later. Western Australia becomes a colony.

1830
All Aborigines in Tasmania are rounded up and herded into reserves.

1831
Publication of *Quintus Servinton*, the first Australian novel, by Henry Savery, a former convict.

1838
The Myall Creek Massacre: 28 Aborigines are butchered by white farmers.

1851
Gold discovered, first in NSW and then Victoria.

1854
Battle at the Eureka Stockade between state troopers and miners protesting against licence fees.

1855
Van Diemen's Land becomes Tasmania.

1860
First south–north crossing (Melbourne to Gulf of Carpentaria), by the Burke and Wills Expedition.

1861
The first Melbourne Cup horse race is watched by 4,000 people.

1868
The transportation of British convicts ends.

1880
Bushranger Ned Kelly is captured and hanged.

1883
Silver is discovered at Broken Hill, NSW.

1891
Delegates from the six colonies meet in Sydney to draft a constitution.

1893
Gold rush in Kalgoorlie, Western Australia.

1895
Banjo Paterson writes *Waltzing Matilda*.

1896
Athlete Edwin Flack represents Australia at the first modern Olympic Games.

1901
The six colonies join together to become a federation, the Commonwealth of Australia.

1914–18
330,000 Australians serve in World War I; 60,000 are killed, 165,000 wounded.

1915
Australian troops take a major part in the Gallipoli siege; more than 8,000 are killed.

1923
Chemist Cyril Callister creates Vegemite.

1928
Royal Flying Doctor Service is founded by Rev. John Flynn in Cloncurry, Queensland.

1932
Sydney Harbour Bridge opens.

1942
15,000 Australians are captured when Singapore falls to Japan. Japanese bomb Darwin.

1950
Immigration peaks at 150,000 new arrivals.

Sydney Opera House under construction, 1966.

1954
Elizabeth II is the first reigning monarch to visit Australia.

1959
Danish architect Jørn Utzon wins the competition to design Sydney Opera House.

1967
Aborigines are finally granted Australian citizenship and the right to vote.

1973
Sydney Opera House is completed. Australian Patrick White wins Nobel Prize for Literature.

1974
Darwin is flattened by Cyclone Tracy.

1985
Uluru, Kata Tjuta and the surrounding desert (now a National Park) are returned to Aboriginal control.

1995
Australians protest strongly over French nuclear testing in the South Pacific.

1999
Australians vote against becoming a republic.

2000
Sydney hosts the Summer Olympic Games.

2002
A bombing in Bali by Islamist extremists kills 88 Australians.

2006
Melbourne hosts the Commonwealth Games.

2008
Prime Minister Kevin Rudd apologises to the Stolen Generations (Aboriginal children forcibly taken from their families to be raised by whites).

2009
Bushfires in Victoria claim 173 lives.

2010
Julia Gillard is the first woman to be elected Prime Minister.

2011
Queensland is devastated by floods over 1 million sq km (386,000 sq miles).

2012
Australia wins a seat on the United Nations Security Council.

2013
Heatwave causes more devastating bushfires across Victoria and New South Wales. Sydney records its hottest day on record – 45.8°C (114°F).

2014
Lindt café siege in Sydney claims three lives.

2015
Malcolm Turnbull becomes 29th Prime Minister.

2018
Scott Morrison replaces Malcolm Turnbull as Liberal Party leader and Prime Minister.

2019
Record-breaking heatwave sees large parts of Australia sweating in temperatures well above 40°C (144°F) for many consecutive days. Townsville in Queensland suffers terrible flooding.

Australian aboriginal, from Ebenezer Sibly's 'Universal System of Natural History'.

J. Ihle Del.t

J. Chapman Sculp.t

An exact Portrait of
A Savage of Botany Bay.

DREAMTIME AND DISCOVERY

Living in harmony with the land, Australia's Aborigines developed a culture rich and complex in its customs, religions and lifestyles, which was abruptly interrupted by the arrival of the British in 1788.

Long before the ancient civilisations in the Middle East, Europe and the Americas flourished, and more than 50,000 years before European, Asian or Middle Eastern navigators recorded visits to the shores of 'the Great South Land', Australian Aborigines occupied this continent – its arid deserts and tropical rainforests, and especially its major river systems and coastal plains and mountains. Estimates by anthropologists put the population of Aborigines, prior to 1770, at more than 300,000.

The ancient traditions of these people are based on a close spiritual bond with every living thing and with the land as represented in rocks, rivers and other geographical features.

THE DAWN OF CREATION

Dreamtime is the basis of all traditional Aboriginal thought and practice, informing their cultural, historical and ancestral heritage. Dreamtime was the dawn of all creation, when

A cave painting of a turtle on Ubirr Rock at Kakadu in the Northern Territory.

⊘ EARLY EXPLORERS

The Ancient Greeks, the Hindus and Marco Polo had all speculated upon the location and nature of the 'Great South Land'. The Arabs, Chinese and the Malays had probably come and gone, as had the Portuguese. The Dutch came, looked and left, disappointed at not finding 'uncommonly large profit'. At the end of the 17th century, the English ex-pirate-turned-explorer William Dampier was appalled by the bleak landscape of the northwestern coast, inhabited by 'the miserablest people on earth'. The fertile east coast was missed by just a few kilometres by both the French explorer Louis Antoine de Bougainville and the Spaniard Luis Vaez de Torres.

the land, the rivers, the rain, the wind and all living things were generated. The individual exists within an eternal Dreaming, only attaining physical embodiment through a mother and briefly existing on Earth before returning to the Dreamtime continuum. The place of birth is key in relating an individual to a specific region or clan.

Tribal elders are responsible for maintaining the clan's group identity through its totemistic belief system. Each clan forms special bonds with a totem, usually an animal or a plant that acts as a protector and a symbol of group identity. Through special ceremonies and other social and religious practices, the elders transmit their knowledge to younger generations.

Aborigines have always celebrated the adventures of their Dreamtime spirit heroes through paintings, songs and sacred dances. Rock paintings are of special significance, bearing the strongest psychological and ritual values. As Aboriginal language was not written, these paintings, along with the oration of legends by tribal leaders, were the main media for passing Dreamtime stories from one generation to the next.

The Aboriginal ceremony of celebrating with song and dance is called *corroboree*. For centuries the male dancers have been experts at mimicking the movements of animals; with these skills they reconstructed legends, heroic deeds or famous hunts. Bodies were elaborately painted, and songs were chanted to the accompaniment of music sticks and boomerangs clapped together.

Basic dance themes deal with hunting and food gathering, or sex and fertility; sometimes they take a humorous vein, but more often they deal seriously with the business of life. Some tribes use a long, hollow piece of wood which, when blown, emits a droning sound. This is the

An engraving depicting a night-time Aboriginal corroboree.

⊘ CAPTAIN JAMES COOK

James Cook was stern and hot-tempered; physically, he was tall, dark and handsome. He was also, in the parlance of his time, a 'tarpaulin', an officer who had prospered without the boost of an aristocratic birth.

Born in 1728, the son of a Yorkshire farm labourer, at age 18 he was apprenticed into the North Sea colliers. Enlisting in the Royal Navy in 1755, he distinguished himself as a navigator and a master, particularly on the St Lawrence River in Quebec, Canada, during the Seven Years' War with France.

A courageous and proud man, Cook was driven more by a sense of duty and personal excellence than by greed or God. All supplies of fresh food obtained by his crew he

'caused to be equally divided among the whole company generally by weight, so the meanest person in the Ship had an equal share with myself [Cook] or anyone on board'. As for the soul-snatching men of the cloth, he would never permit a parson to sail on any of his ships. Reflecting during his homeward journey upon the state of the Australian Aborigine, he took a remarkably enlightened view, writing the classic description of the noble savage: 'In reality they are far more happier than we European; being wholly unacquainted with not only the superfluous but the necessary Conveniences so much sought after in Europe... the Earth and sea of their own accord furnishes them with all things necessary for life.'

didgeridoo, whose sound is said to resemble the calling of the spirits.

Aborigines believe that a person's spirit does not die with their last breath, and that ceremonies are essential to ensure that the spirit leaves the body and becomes re-embodied elsewhere – in a rock, a tree, an animal, or perhaps another human form. This explains why such significance has been attached to the retrieval of cadavers or body parts from museums around the world, returning them to the country of their birth and performing the ceremonies to finally bring the spirit to peace.

Each person is the centre of an intricate web of relationships, which give order to the entire world. In the late 18th century, this delicate relationship with the land was thrown out of kilter with the arrival of the Europeans. Aboriginal culture had prepared the people for many things they might expect to face in life – except the coming of the white man.

THE IMPACT OF CAPTAIN COOK

When James Cook, a 41-year-old Royal Navy lieutenant, dropped anchor in 1770 in an east-coast bay that so teemed with exotic new life forms he decided to call it Botany Bay, he verified by flag and map an idea that Europe had long suspected.

Cook had been sent by the Admiralty to Tahiti, at the request of the Royal Society, to observe a transit of the planet Venus. Among the company of 94 on his second-hand coal ship *Endeavour* were Daniel Carl Solander and Joseph Banks, two great botanists of the age.

After leaving Tahiti, Cook opened a second set of secret orders, sailed southwest to New Zealand and spent six months charting both islands. He was then free to return to England by either the Cape or the Horn. Instead, he and his officers decided upon a route leading via the largely unknown southern land called New Holland.

On 28 April 1770, *Endeavour* anchored in Botany Bay for one week. No naturalists before or since Solander and Banks have ever collected in such a short time so many new specimens of plant, bird and animal life. Meanwhile, the sailors ate their fill of seafoods, causing Cook at first to name the place Stingray Harbour Bay. He later changed it to Botany Bay because of Solander and Banks' discoveries.

A CLAIM FOR THE KING

Sailing north, Cook sighted and named (but did not enter) Port Jackson, Sydney's great harbour-to-be. After stopping at a place now known as Seventeen Seventy, the *Endeavour* collided with the Great Barrier Reef on 11 June 1770, almost sinking and forcing the crew to camp where modern-day Cooktown stands for seven weeks while repairs were made. On 22 August, at Possession Island off the tip of Cape York, Cook hoisted the flag and claimed the eastern side of the continent under 'the name of New South Wales' for George III.

Captain James Cook.

⊙ THE NEW SETTLERS

The transportation of convicts was phased out between 1840 and 1868. By 1860, the continent had been divided into five separate colonies, with each exhibiting (at times) more loyalty to London than to any neighbouring siblings. A major force within the colonies was the 'squatocracy', the rich officers, emancipated convicts and free settlers who had followed the explorers into the fertile hinterlands. They had simply laid claim to or squatted upon enormous tracts of land, often 8,000 hectares (20,000 acres) or more. Like the merino sheep they introduced to their stations, the squatters both lived off and were the fat of the land.

Reaching London in 1771, Cook told the Admiralty he'd found the east coast of New Holland, but not the fabled Great South Land. During his second voyage 1772–75, he destroyed the myth of the Great South Land by circumnavigating the Antarctic. In 1779, he died at the hands of Polynesians in the Hawaiian islands.

THE FIRST FLEET

In May 1787, 11 small ships of the First Fleet under Captain (later Governor) Arthur Phillip sailed from Portsmouth. Eight months later,

A painting of ships of the First Fleet in Sydney Cove.

⊘ HUNTERS AND GATHERERS

Aborigines lived in clans of 10 to 50 or more people. To survive the harsh Australian landscape, men hunted and women were fishers and gatherers. A good hunter knew intimately the habits of the creatures he stalked, was an expert tracker and understood the seasons and the winds. Each tribe recognised the local landmarks and their links with the rich mythology of Dreamtime. Various geological aspects were sacred sites with their own personality and significance. The Aborigine considered himself, nature and the land inseparably bound and interdependent. In this state of unity, he (and she) achieved a balance with the environment.

the 1,000 passengers and prisoners arrived at Botany Bay. Three-quarters of them were convicts, since Britain had been forced to find a new dumping ground for rebels, poachers, prostitutes and murderers after it lost the New World colonies in the American War of Independence. The auguries for Australia's future were not those of the Promised Land.

A quick survey showed two things: Cook's description of the place was far too generous; and two ships of the Comte de la Pérouse expedition were also there, possibly shopping for a new continent on behalf of France's Louis XVI. Phillip hurriedly sailed 20km (12 miles) up the coast to Port Jackson and raised the flag for George III on 26 January 1788.

After 30 months of isolation, locked in by the natural prison of the alien bush and suffering from a lack of decent supplies, the settlement was down to half rations. When a ship finally appeared, to their despair, it was carrying not supplies but 222 elderly and ill female convicts. Fortunately, the supply ships of the Second Fleet were close behind.

THE BIRTH OF SYDNEY

The tents at Sydney Cove were eventually replaced by brick and timber huts. Phillip tried to lay out a town along orderly lines, but conformity was not in the nature of its inhabitants. Short cuts soon became streets and, despite later attempts at order, the convenient jigsaw that resulted can still be observed today as the ground plan of Sydney's high-rise pile-up.

Sydney Town expanded west towards the fertile farming lands of Parramatta, but was still hemmed in by the impenetrable escarpment of the Blue Mountains. Explorers fanned out by land and sea to open new pastures and farms, and to establish even more isolated and savage prisons, such as Norfolk Island. This small piece of land in the Pacific originally figured in British strategy as a potential source for flax, needed to create sails. Unfortunately, the island became known as a hellhole of corporal punishment.

Conditions weren't that much better in Sydney. In 1804, prisoners at Castle Hill Reserve rose against the government. Some 200 convicts set out to capture Parramatta, then tried to seize the ships in Sydney Harbour. Troops swiftly quelled the rebellion at what became known as the Battle of Vinegar Hill. Nine of the ringleaders were hanged and another nine received between 200 and 500 lashes from the whip.

New South Wales was still costing London dearly (£1 million in the first 12 years), but it was turning a profit for its local landowners and the officers of the NSW Corps, otherwise known as 'the Rum Corps'. The Corps resisted the extortionate demands of trading-vessel masters, and developed its own monopolies. The colony had become such a vat of drunkenness, and the demand for Bengal rum (which the Corps controlled) was so great that rum almost became the currency.

CAPTAIN BLIGH FAILS AGAIN

Governor William Bligh (of *Bounty* fame) was despatched to clean up the Rum Corps' act, and to encourage free settlers to come to Sydney. However, the Corps, at the bidding of farmer and officer John Macarthur, pulled the second of the famous mutinies in Bligh's career, and in 1808 deposed him.

New South Wales and its penal settlements at Moreton Bay (now Brisbane), Norfolk Island and Van Diemen's Land (Tasmania) entered the 19th century with a reputation as 'hell on Earth' – a reputation that the British hoped would serve as a deterrent to crime.

Forgers, union members, and petty thieves caught stealing bits of muslin or loaves of bread were thrown together in Australia, when death at the end of a noose would often have been more merciful. In attempting to escape, some inadvertently became the interior's first explorers. They fled into the bush; some believed that China lay beyond the Blue Mountains or that a colony of free men dwelt inland. On Norfolk Island, the only guaranteed method of escape from the inhuman conditions was to commit murder in the hope of being hanged.

Transportation to Australia's penal settlements ceased by 1868. By then, 160,000 convicts had arrived; only 25,000 were women, a distortion which left its stamp on the harsh, frontier

A painting of the view of Parramatta, showing the barracks and Sydney Cove.

society for decades. These pioneers made few concessions to each other and none to the original inhabitants of the land.

NO MAN'S LAND

When the First Fleet arrived, no war was declared against the indigenous people. The British government simply declared the land *terra nullius* – literally, land belonging to nobody – based on the notion that the territory lacked human habitation and could therefore be obtained for free. The first settlers to arrive on Australia's remote shores could not understand the Aboriginal people's nomadic lifestyle or their profound connection to their tribal lands. It

⊘ A TOUGH BEGINNING

Officers, marines, transportees, sheep, goats and cattle were disgorged in 1788 into a cove that is now overlooked by the Sydney Opera House. The surgeon-general to the fleet rhapsodised that Port Jackson was 'the finest and most extensive harbour in the Universe'. It is said that even the convicts raised a cheer of joy. It is also noted that two Aborigines shouted 'Warra! Warra!' (Go away!); no one heeded. Thus the colony stumbled to life. It was a rough beginning. The English authorities did not provision the expedition well; many of the tools were next to useless, and their crops failed to thrive in the unusually sandy soil.

seemed that they came and went without reason across the sparse landscape.

European settlers occupied the land; Aboriginal resistance was met with savage reprisals. Those living in the vicinity of Port Jackson were the first to lose their lands, and, as settlement expanded, so began the cycle of attack and reprisal. Previously unknown European diseases brought death and misery to the Aboriginal people, while survivors were reduced to living in abject squalor around the periphery of the settlements. An ugly war of attrition prevailed, and

The list of convicts on the ship Merchantman from Portland to Western Australia, June 1864.

massacres were exacted upon people who often had taken no part in any transgressions.

As the spread of settlement advanced, Aboriginal people ejected from their tribal lands were forced into territory belonging to their neighbours – adding internal conflict to an already difficult predicament. Either way, spears stood no chance against bullets.

DOMESTIC EXPLORATION

A continent of 7.7 million sq km (3 million sq miles), much of it searing desert or dense scrub, could not be explored easily. Before the crossing of the Blue Mountains in 1813, most significant exploration took place by sea. Two British

sailors, Bass and Flinders, guessed correctly at the separation of Tasmania from the mainland. The French ships of Baudin in 1802, and later of Dumont d'Urville in 1826, scared the colonial authorities into establishing settlements in Tasmania and Western Australia respectively. Once the Great Dividing Range was penetrated in 1813, the drive for new lands, minerals and the glory of being 'first there' – wherever 'there' happened to be – lured men and women on.

Early explorers believed that the westward-flowing rivers of the NSW interior led towards a vast inland sea. In 1830 Charles Sturt and his party set out on the Murrumbidgee River, following its current into the Lachlan and Murray rivers, finally reaching Lake Alexandrina near the South Australia coast. After travelling more than 1,000km (600 miles), they were within sight of the sea, but were unable to reach it. Instead, they had to row back against the current toward their starting point. Their 47 days' rowing, on meagre rations and against flood tides, left Sturt temporarily blind, but it is one of the most heroic journeys in Australian exploration.

By 1836, the vast river systems were charted. Tasmania had been explored, and the genocide of its natives had begun. A decade later, most of New South Wales, half of Queensland, and the southern and northern coasts had been thoroughly explored.

However, as late as the 1870s and 1880s, explorers were still having first-contact encounters, often with surprising results.

⊘ LACHLAN MACQUARIE

The initial brutality shown to convicts was tempered by the reforms of Governor Lachlan Macquarie (1810–21), by the influence of some emancipists (freed convicts), and by a growing prosperity through trade. Macquarie, a paternalistic autocrat, stifled the Rum Corps' monopoly on the import of spirit, established the colony's own currency (1813) and first bank (1817), and encouraged the first crossing of the Blue Mountains (1813). His programme of public works and town planning (265 projects in 11 years) owes much to Francis Greenway, an emancipist transported to Sydney for forgery, who became the colony's leading architect.

In 1869, South Australia's surveyor-general, G.W. Goyder, surveying the land that was eventually to become Darwin, was invited to a corroboree by the local Larrakia people, who performed word-perfect renditions of 'John Brown's Body', 'The Glory, Hallelujah' and 'The Old Virginia Shore'.

They had learned the words not from 'white-fellas' but from the Woolna people who, in turn, had memorised the tunes spying on surveyors working near the Adelaide River.

HEROES AND VILLAINS

The 19th century is rich in tales of intrepid adventurers. Some of them were driven by the urge to explore unknown territory, but most were motivated by dreams of finding riches. One such tale of misadventures is now deeply ingrained in Australian folklore.

In August 1860, Robert O'Hara Burke and W.J. Wills left Melbourne with a well-equipped team and a camel train (imported from Afghanistan). Their intention was to be the first party to cross the continent from coast to coast.

Burke was brash, inexperienced, supremely confident. Too impatient to wait for the supply camels to keep up, he took Wills and other team members, Grey and King, with him; from Innamincka on Cooper's Creek, he forged ahead in 60°C (140°F) heat. They reached the Gulf of Carpentaria in February 1861 and immediately began retracing their footsteps. Grey died along the way. The three emaciated survivors finally reached their earlier camp at Innamincka where they had left another companion, William Brahe. But Brahe, who had waited four months for them, had departed only seven hours earlier. After rejecting the assistance of local Aborigines, Burke and Wills died in the Stony Desert. Only King, cared for by Aborigines, survived to tell the story. The Dig Tree is so called because when Brahe's party left camp, they left instructions carved into a tree that provisions were buried nearby. The tree still attracts tourists to this remote pocket of southwest Queensland.

A depiction of farm life.

⊘ LUDWIG LEICHHARDT

Many early explorers blended courage and folly, but few as spectacularly as Ludwig Leichhardt. In 1844, Leichhardt, a 31-year-old Prussian draft dodger, launched an ambitious expedition heading northwest, despite the fact that he could neither shoot nor see very well; he also had a poor sense of direction. His expedition ran into innumerable difficulties, with provisions lost, and three men speared (one fatally) by natives. Fourteen months after their departure, and long after being given up for dead, Leichhardt and his party staggered into their destination, Port Essington (Darwin). These 'men from the grave' were fêted as national heroes; the Prussian government even pardoned Leichhardt for his military desertion.

In April 1848, Leichhardt set out again, this time aiming to trek from Roma in southern Queensland to the Indian Ocean. His party of seven men and 77 beasts was never seen again. The search continued for years, spurred on by finds of skeletons, relics and pack horses. Stories of a wild white man living among Queensland Aborigines in the 1860s suggested that one member, Adolf Classen, might have survived for some time. In all, nine major searches were conducted for survivors or evidence of Leichhardt's party. The desert has never relinquished the tale of their fate; however, the city of Sydney has named one of its suburbs after him.

FROM GOLD RUSH TO WORLD WAR

After gold was discovered in the 1850s, a sudden influx of immigrants set out to make their fortune. A similar boom of outlaws set out to relieve them of it. Then, in 1901, the six quarrelling colonies became a nation.

In 1851, Edward Hargraves, an Australian forty-niner (a fortune seeker in the 1849 California gold rush) returned home. He was certain, given the geological similarities he had observed between California and Australia, that gold must exist in New South Wales. Unbeknown to him, gold had been found 10 years earlier by a Rev. W.B. Clarke, but news of the discovery was suppressed. Upon seeing the gold, the Governor, Sir George Gipps, had said: 'Put it away, Mr Clarke, or we shall all have our throats cut!'

The announcement on 15 May 1851 of 'Gold Discovered!' near Bathurst, 170km (106 miles) west of Sydney, sent shock waves through the Australian colonies. The rush of prospectors to Bathurst was so great that the population of Victoria immediately nosedived. Melbourne employers offered a £200 reward for the discovery of gold near *their* city.

By July the prize had been claimed, and before the end of the year incredibly rich fields were in production in Victoria at Ballarat, Bendigo and Castlemaine. For the businessmen of Melbourne, the finds were a mixed blessing. While the prices of flour, blankets, bread, shovels and mining gear doubled and tripled, there was often no one to sell them. Melbourne and Geelong were almost emptied of able-bodied men.

THE ROARING DAYS

The scene in the goldfields was one of frantic activity, where teams of four or six men worked a claim, digging, shovelling, washing and cradling from dawn to dusk. When the miners hit town, they careened around the streets on horseback or in cabs. At one

Painting depicting gold panning in Australia.

Melbourne theatre, reported an eyewitness, the actors 'were obliged to appear before the footlights to bear a pelting shower of nuggets – a substitute for bouquets – many over half an ounce, and several of which fell short of the mark into the orchestra.'

Gold rushes flared like bushfire around the continent during the next two decades, and then sporadically for the rest of the century. The last great find was the Kalgoorlie-Coolgardie field in Western Australia in 1892–93.

It was not only the shop assistants of Sydney and the sailors of Port Phillip who caught gold fever. In 1852 alone, 95,000 hopefuls from around the world flooded into New South Wales and Victoria.

THE EUREKA STOCKADE

At Ballarat, near Melbourne, the early gold diggers smarted under the imposition, whether they struck gold or not, of a £1-a-month licence fee. Raids by thuggish police who enforced the licence fee *and* collected half the fine from defaulters added to their rancour.

In October 1854 a miner was kicked to death by a local publican, who (despite strong evidence against him) was cleared of the crime. Mass meetings attended by up to 5,000 miners railed against these injustices. The men demanded the granting of universal franchise and the abolition of licence fees. They formed the Ballarat Reform League and on 29 November made a bonfire of their mining licences.

The lieutenant-governor of Victoria, Sir Charles Hotham, sent in the 'traps' (policemen) and troopers. Five hundred diggers built a stockade and swore to 'fight to defend our rights and liberties'. In the early hours of 3 December 1854, a force of 300 infantry, cavalry and mounted police savagely attacked

The site of the 'Eureka Stockade'.

⊘ BUSHRANGERS AND REBELS

The gold rush created a new boom in bushranging, or highway robbery. Many an 'old lag' (ex-convict), as well as poor settlers, saw that gold need not necessarily be dug from the ground. The proceeds from holding up a stagecoach or gold wagon could be good, and the work was a lot cleaner than digging. In 1853, one Victorian gang relieved the gold escort of 70,000g (more than 2,400oz) of gold and £700 in cash; three gang members were sent to the gallows.

In the 1860s the most famous of the 'Wild Colonial Boys' were the bushrangers Ben Hall, Frank Gardiner and John Gilbert. Well-armed and superbly mounted – often on stolen racehorses – they pulled off audacious raids. In November 1864, Hall's gang of three, working the Sydney–Melbourne road, rounded up 60 travellers at once. Then came the prize they were waiting for: the armed mail coach. While one bushranger covered the 60 captives, Hall and Gilbert shot the police guard and robbed the coach. Several of the captives came out of the bush, not to aid the police, but to watch the shoot-out.

From their first appearance, bushrangers were often sheltered by the rural poor, many of whom were descendants of political transportees. Their strong republican sentiments led them to regard some of the outlaws as rebels against the same enemy – the British, Protestant landlords and civil authorities.

the sleeping stockade, whose defenders had dwindled to 150. Within 15 minutes it was all over. Six soldiers and 24 miners were dead.

Eventually an amnesty was proclaimed for the rebels, and the licence fee was abolished. While the incident is replete with tragedy and some farce, the Eureka Stockade and its flag continue to evoke the ideals of revolt against colonialism and bourgeois authority. As Mark Twain commented, Eureka was: 'the finest thing in Australian history... another instance of a victory won by a lost battle'.

Strong box used by gold commissioners for storage and carriage of gold in the 19th century.

THE FEDERATION IS BORN

In September 1900, Queen Victoria regally proclaimed that, on 1 January 1901, not only a new century but also a new nation would be born.

A federal government for the six Australian colonies was generally welcomed. Under the new Constitution the Queen remained head of state, retaining power over all foreign affairs. British parliamentary legislation could overrule any laws passed by the Commonwealth, and legal appeals ultimately were settled in London. Few Australians objected to this arrangement, for each of the six colonies felt more at ease in its dealings with the motherland than with the other colonies.

For her part, Britain did not let the new nation escape the interests of imperialism. She expected, and got, continuing support in her military involvements, and ample returns on her substantial investments in Australia.

THE QUEST FOR A CAPITAL

The new nation needed a capital. Bitter rivals, Sydney and Melbourne both coveted the honour. Melbourne was made temporary capital but in 1908, after considerable back-biting, it was decided a separate Australian Capital Territory would established at a point between the two cities, 320km (200 miles) from Sydney on the beautiful Monaro Tablelands. Some suggested naming the capital Shakespeare, but in 1913 the Aboriginal word 'Canberra', meaning 'meeting place', was chosen instead.

THE GREAT WAR

When Britain declared war on Germany on 4 August 1914, Australia, as a member of the British Empire, was automatically at war, too. The response by both Labor and Liberal parties was immediate. By the end of October the First Australian Infantry Force of 20,000 volunteers had been despatched to Europe via Egypt. Many would die at Gallipoli.

Australian 'Diggers' (soldiers) were deployed in France, on the Western Front, from April 1916. In the grisly attacks, through mustard gas and frozen winters, their losses were appalling – 23,000 dead in nine weeks in the First Battle of the Somme, 38,000 at Ypres, 10,000 at Bullecourt. The new nation was being cut down. Indeed, so was some of the old nation; more than 420 Aboriginal soldiers served in the war, largely from Tasmania's Bass Strait islands.

Many Australians were now questioning the sense of supporting Britain in what they saw as a 'sordid trade war'. But a deciding factor was the presence at Australia's helm of a feisty and dogged little man who was loved and loathed with equal passion: William Morris ('Billy') Hughes, or 'the Little Digger'.

In 1916, Hughes pledged a supply of 16,500 Australian troops a month. Such a number could be raised only through conscription – previously, recruitment was voluntary. The proposal was defeated narrowly in a referendum, and Hughes was expelled from the Labor Party. He set about forming a national coalition government and held a second referendum in December 1917. He was defeated but bounced back, winning a seat at the Versailles Peace Conference.

From a total population of less than 5 million, 416,809 Australian men enlisted to fight in the war. By the end, 62,000 had been killed and 156,000 wounded, gassed, or taken prisoner.

THE GREAT DEPRESSION

Between 1929 and 1933, every government in Australia, both state and federal, was thrown out of office by an unimpressed electorate. But unfortunately their replacements could do no better, for the Great Depression had arrived. Thirty percent of the country's breadwinners were on 'Susso' (sustenance benefits). Wearing World War I surplus greatcoats, hundreds were tramping the Outback roads as 'swagmen' looking for rural work.

Ned Kelly surrounded by police.

⊘ THE KELLY GANG

Ned Kelly was born in 1854 and grew up among impoverished Irish farmers near Benalla, northern Victoria. He first ran foul of the law in 1877, when he shot a constable in the wrist. Teaming up with his brother Dan and two friends, Joe Byrne and Steve Hart, he fled to the bush and turned outlaw. The following year, in a shoot-out at Stringybark Creek, Ned killed three of a party of four police who were hunting him. From then on, the Kellys became part of Australian folklore. Ned saw himself as a Robin Hood, a defender of the free against the oppressive British overlords. Instead of robbing coaches, his gang bailed-up whole towns, cutting the telegraph and robbing the bank before escaping.

The gang hid out in the Wombat Ranges, but in June 1880, on hearing that a train-load of police was on the way to arrest them, they captured the town of Glenrowan, Victoria, and held the townsfolk prisoner in the hotel. A furious shoot-out erupted between the Kellys and the cops. Wounded, Ned donned his suit of home-made armour and attempted to escape. Instead, he stumbled into the police who at first thought they were seeing a ghostly apparition. Ned was shot down but not killed. The police torched the hotel and the other three members of the Kelly Gang died within rather than surrender. Four months later in Melbourne, Kelly was sentenced to death. He was hanged on 11 November 1880.

Australia's economy was based heavily on the export of wheat and wool, and upon continued borrowings from Britain. When world prices for primary products slumped by 50 percent, and when Britain withdrew £30 million from the Australian economy, the result was traumatic, especially for the poor.

Sir Otto Niemeyer of the Bank of England was despatched to scold Australians for living at an unsustainably high standard, to advise wage cuts and retrenchments, and to make sure that the interest was still paid on the loans.

Australian and New Zealand troops on the way to Gallipoli in 1915.

WORLD WAR II

When Britain again went to war against Germany in September 1939, Australia once more automatically entered the conflict. A Second Australian Infantry Force was raised and despatched to the Middle East.

In 1939 Australia's prime minister, the leader of the United Australia Party, was Robert Gordon Menzies, a clever, witty barrister and a deeply conservative Anglophile. He had earned the nickname 'Pig-Iron Bob' by selling pig iron to the re-arming Japanese, of whom Australia had become increasingly nervous.

While Australian air, land and sea forces fought in Britain, the Mediterranean, North Africa, Greece and the Middle East, Japan began to move south, first into French Indochina. Australian forces were sent to Malaya, the Dutch East Indies, Darwin and Rabaul (New Guinea) to try to stem the tide of the Japanese invasion forces.

In Canberra, Pig-Iron Bob was reviled for his Chamberlain-like pre-war appeasement of the Axis powers. By October 1941 a Labor Government under John Curtin was in power.

A NATION COMES OF AGE

The Japanese attack on the United States at Pearl Harbor confirmed Australia's great fear: to be isolated in an Asia at war. When Singapore fell on 15 February 1942, 15,000 of the 130,000 captured troops were Australian. The country was faced with the fact that a distant and beleaguered Britain could be of no real assistance against an imminent Japanese invasion.

Japanese planes bombed Darwin on 19 February and Broome on 3 March. Arms and food caches were established in the northern regions of the continent. Australia faced the very real threat of invasion by Japanese troops.

The Australian war cabinet outraged Prime Minister Winston Churchill by diverting the 7th Australian Division from the defence of British Burma to the New Guinea and Pacific theatres. If it is true, as is commonly said, that the Australian nation was born at Gallipoli, it

⊘ THE CHINESE INFLUX

The vast majority of gold-diggers were British, but the Chinese were also numerous. In the five years from 1854, more than 40,000 flocked to the Victorian fields. The Chinese lived in their own communities, were diligent labourers, and produced only one Chinese bushranger, San Poo.

By 1887, Asian immigration was stifled. Australia inaugurated 'the White Australia Policy' with federation and nationhood in 1901. The Immigration Act allowed an impossibly tough dictation test in any European language to be given to all non-European arrivals. It was not until 1966 that there was any genuine reversal of this race-based exclusion.

is no less true that with the fall of Singapore, Australia finally came of age.

THE END OF THE WAR

The tide began to turn against Japan in May 1942, when a combined fleet of American and Australian forces checked the Japanese at the Battle of the Coral Sea. The US victory at Midway in June assured Allied control of the Pacific, but on New Guinea, Japanese foot soldiers were closing in on Australia's main base at Port Moresby. After months of guerrilla combat and hand-to-hand jungle fighting, the Australian troops finally pushed them back.

Of the 1 million Australian servicemen and women who enlisted, almost 10,000 died in Europe and more than 17,000 in the Pacific. Over 22,000 were taken as POW by the Japanese. Of those taken prisoner, 8,000 did not survive the Japanese camps. An Aboriginal complement of more than 3,000 bravely served in the forces, despite official discouragement early in the war.

A wrecked Japanese plane after the Battle of the Coral Sea, 1942.

⊘ THE DEATH TOLL OF GALLIPOLI

While Australia's troops trained in Egypt, Winston Churchill (then First Lord of the Admiralty in London) conceived a plan to relieve Turkish pressure on Russia's troops by forcing an entrance to the Black Sea. He wanted to capture the Dardanelles, and ordered the waiting Australian, New Zealand, French, British, Indian and Gurkha divisions to attack from the sea. The Turks, warned of British intentions, entrenched themselves in fortified positions along the ridges of the Gallipoli Peninsula. Their commanders (Mustafa Kemal and the German Liman von Sanders) were able to direct their fire upon the exposed beaches below without exposing their own troops to much risk.

From 25 April 1915, when they landed, until 20 December, when they withdrew, the Allied forces were pinned down to the near-vertical cliffs and narrow coves. There was both horrendous carnage and epic heroism. During the eight months of fighting at Gallipoli, 78,000 were wounded and 33,500 killed on the side of Britain and its allies. Of the dead, 8,587 were ANZACs (belonging to the Australian and New Zealand Army Corps). Almost as many French died at Gallipoli, and twice as many Britons, Indians and Nepalis fell. On the other side, 250,000 Turks died in battle. Nevertheless, out of this baptism by mud, blood, shrapnel and gallantry came Australia's first coherent nation-based narrative.

Sculpture at the National Gallery of Victoria.

THE MODERN ERA

Over the past 60 years, Australia's population has trebled, against a background of industrial booms and economic slumps, rigid conservatism and progressive liberalism.

Australian history since World War II has been an up-and-down saga – a rise to undreamed-of affluence in the 1950s and 60s when the wool prices boomed, followed by unexpected cracks in the great suburban dream. Today the image of the country as a conservative, Anglo-Saxon society somehow finding itself lost in Asia has been completely recast. But the road towards a cosmopolitan, liberal, middle-class Australia has been tumultuous. For a relatively young and small country – in terms of population – it has endured dramatic successions of booms, recessions, political crises, wars, culture shocks and social changes.

The 1940s were the most difficult years in Australia's history, the long war against Japan emphasising the country's vulnerability. The war also shook up Australian society internally; many women served in the armed forces, or worked in factories or office jobs that had previously been reserved for men, and were reluctant to go back to purely domestic duties.

Migrants sail into Sydney Harbour in 1949.

RADICAL POST-WAR CHANGES

In 1946, Australians voted an activist Labor government, led by Ben Chifley, into power with plans for an expanded social welfare programme. In quick succession, Chifley nationalised the country's biggest airline (Qantas), took initiatives in housing and education (the Australian National University was opened in Canberra), and ordered massive work projects such as the Snowy Mountains Scheme, which provided hydroelectric power for southeast Australia.

The most radical and revitalising change, however, occurred in immigration. The spectre of a Japanese invasion in World War II convinced

⊘ GOVERNMENT AND POLITICS

Australians are triple-governed – by local councils, and at the state and federal levels. According to polls, most people feel that politics is the least trustworthy of professions. Many people believe that a nation of nearly 24 million people can't produce enough talent to run three levels of government. Judging by the acres of newsprint and airspace devoted to the topic, the nation is obsessed with politics, though no more than a few thousand people are members of political parties. Everyone votes because they have to: federal law made it compulsory in 1924; unless you have a good excuse, you will receive a small fine for not voting.

Australians that the country's population must increase. Labor's immigration minister, Arthur Calwell, embarked upon one of the most spectacular migration programmes of the 20th century. Half of the assisted migrants were to be British, but the other half could come from anywhere – as long as they were white. More than 2 million migrants arrived between 1945 and 1965, helping Australia's population to leap from 7 to 11 million.

The nation still clung to its White Australia policy, and Calwell himself was a racist. (He

Queen Elizabeth II and Australian Prime Minister Robert Gordon Menzies arrive at a state banquet in Canberra during the Queen's tour of Australia in 1954.

made the infamous wisecrack, when asked whether he would permit Asian immigration, 'Two Wongs don't make a white'.) The policy was modified slowly in later years until it was formally abolished in 1973. So rapid has been the overturning of these anachronistic attitudes that at the present time one-third of all immigrants are Asian.

THE 'BORING' 1950S

Still, mainstream Australian culture changed slowly. In the 1950s, Australia remained a rigid society, one which had grown up in comparative isolation and was complacent and illiberal. It

was still dominated by men, despite the post-war challenge from women, and male rituals like sport, drinking and brawling predominated; homosexuals were persecuted as 'poofters' and anyone with a beard or long hair was dubbed a 'weirdo'. Male values such as 'mateship' were extolled, while 'the missus' was expected to stay at home and look after the kids. It was a very working-class society, a land of boots and felt hats, of men in dank pubs calling each other 'mate' or 'sport'.

The churches, especially the Roman Catholic Church, dictated morality; divorce was legal, but it was condemned and hard to obtain. Abortion remained illegal, the province of backstreet doctors. The nation was burdened with a suffocating puritanism which Australians labelled 'wowserism'. Censorship was strict: James Joyce's *Ulysses* and D.H. Lawrence's *Lady Chatterley's Lover* were banned, and had to be smuggled into the country. The language was stamped with prejudices, many directed at migrants and refugees ('reffos').

Politically, the decade is referred to as the 'Boring Fifties'. A revived conservative party – known as the Liberal Party (although it was formally and ideologically unrelated to its British namesake and often far from liberal in the word's literal sense) – was led by the rabid Anglophile Robert Menzies. He proclaimed himself 'British to his boot-straps' and was able to tap into the growing Cold War hysteria, attacking the Labor Party for being riddled with Communists.

When rising unemployment threatened to turn the Liberals out of office, Menzies decided to plump for safe, middle-of-the-road policies that would disturb neither extreme of the electorate. The Labor Party split in 1955 on ideological lines and effectively kept itself out of power for another 17 years.

'Development' became the national slogan; there were posters everywhere stressing peace, prosperity and progress, and even the arrival of rock'n'roll from the United States didn't seem to disturb the social equanimity. There were a few rebel groups, such as the bodgies (male) and widgies (female), who did such radical things as ride motorcycles and listen to Elvis, but it was hardly more than a milk-bar menace. Another nonconformist group was the Sydney 'Push', a group of freethinkers and libertarians who gathered at pubs and coffee shops and scorned the suburban coma ward that surrounded them. They wrote poetry and bawdy songs and, though mainly a male group, produced two remarkable women – Germaine Greer, author of *The Female Eunuch*, and the late Lillian Roxon, author of the first *Rock Encyclopedia*.

THE AFFLUENT 1960S

Meanwhile, Australia had begun turning itself from a nation of primary industry (sheep, wheat and cattle) to one of manufacturing. Between 1940 and 1960 the number of factories doubled; fridges, washing machines, vacuum cleaners and cars became available to the great mass of the population for the first time.

By the mid-1960s, Australians were enjoying (after the Americans) the highest standard of living in the world. They were also living in the most urbanised nation on Earth, with three-quarters of the population in cities – more than half of that on the eastern seaboard.

Barry Humphries as Dame Edna Everage, 1976.

⊘ THE FLIGHT OF THE FREE SPIRITS

Every year from the late 1950s onward, thousands of young Australians left on their equivalent of the Grand Tour of London and other cities in Europe, seeking excitement and the sort of mind-broadening experiences that were unavailable at home.

They could hardly be blamed. Newsreels of Australia at the time, seen now, are embarrassingly nationalistic, racist and sexist. The pubs closed at 6pm sharp each weekday, producing the infamous 'six o'clock swill', when men crammed into bars and guzzled as much as they could between the end of work and closing time (women wouldn't have been allowed in even if they'd wanted to). Off-course

betting was illegal, so SP (starting price) bookmakers flourished alongside sly-grog joints, where liquor could be bought after hours. There is another side to the story, too. During the prosperous 1950s Australia enjoyed the most even income distribution of any Western industrialised nation.

Well into the 1960s, the district of Earls Court in London became an Aussie ghetto; unique talents like Barry Humphries, Clive James and Robert Hughes all fled Australia. The nation's best artists and writers – Patrick White, Germaine Greer and Sidney Nolan among them – turned themselves into expatriates.

Links with the Old Country were weakened when Britain joined the European Economic Community; trade with the US and Japan grew to fill the gap. The 1951 ANZUS security treaty brought Australia and New Zealand securely within the USA's sphere.

In the meantime, the shape of Australian society was being entirely changed. In the early 1960s the number of white-collar workers exceeded, for the first time, the number of blue-collar workers, and then streaked far ahead. This booming group typically lived in

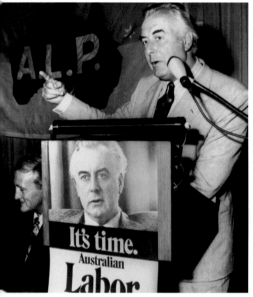

Gough Whitlam, Australian politician, campaigning in 1972.

comfortable suburban homes, owned cars and TVs, had bank accounts, and voted Liberal (Australia's conservative party). Australia, regarded for so long as an egalitarian paradise, had transformed itself (almost unnoticed) into one of the most middle-class nations in the world.

But, amid the prosperity, many were dejected over the fate of Australia and the consequences of its new-found wealth. Donald Horne wrote a book called, with heavy irony, *The Lucky Country* – a land that had squandered its opportunities and abandoned its best egalitarian traditions to wallow in complacency. The Australian social ideal of

communality was changing and with it, apparently, the Australian character.

Cracks began to appear in the bland facade of Australian contentment. In 1962 Australia became involved in the Vietnam War; in the next 10 years, some 49,000 conscripts, chosen by lottery, were sent off to the jungles of Southeast Asia – where 499 were killed and 2,069 wounded. As in the United States, the anti-war movement breathed life into all forms of liberalisation, pushing Australia into an era of crisis and questioning.

POLITICAL CHANGE IN THE 1970S

When the Labor Party, led by Gough Whitlam, finally won office in 1972 under the slogan 'It's Time', it seemed to many that a clean break with the past had occurred and a promising new, progressive era was about to begin.

Labor moved quickly to abolish military conscription, to end Australia's involvement in Vietnam, to recognise communist China and to begin the long process of reconstructing the social welfare system. Everything appeared to happen at once, with plans under way for a universal health-care system, increased support for the arts (resulting in a spate of Australian films), and the formal end of the White Australia policy.

But Whitlam didn't reckon on the economic and social impacts of big government spending. He managed to win another election in 1974 but was confronted with a sudden and unexpected world recession provoked by an oil price hike. Australians suddenly faced growing inflation and unemployment, and the government was beset by a series of damaging scandals.

Labor was hobbled in its programme by a conservative majority vote in the Senate. In 1975 the Liberal-National Country Party opposition, led by Malcolm Fraser, used this power to deny the government its money supply. Whitlam refused to resign, and the nation was thrust into a grave political and constitutional crisis. This was resolved in a controversial manner: the governor-general, Sir John Kerr, as the Queen's representative in Australia, dismissed Whitlam and called another election. It was an act that many considered illegal – in spirit, if not in the letter of the Constitution. Fraser won the subsequent election, consolidated his power and swore he would take politics off the front page.

STABILITY UNDER LABOR – THE 1980S AND 90S

In 1983 a new Labor era began when Australians voted in a government led by Bob Hawke, an ex-union leader, ex-Rhodes scholar at Oxford and one-time world-record-holding beer drinker (2.5 pints in 11 seconds). Hawke later wrote that this feat did most for his political career in a country with a strong beer culture. The Labor Party became more right-wing, economically liberal and in closer touch with the increasingly powerful white-collar unions and business.

For the next 13 years, Labor ruled with little challenge (with Paul Keating taking over the prime ministership in 1991). Consensus became the catchword, with the government brokering historic accords between business and unions, promising unprecedented industrial peace, and finally introducing a national health-care system for all, Medicare.

Germaine Greer at a women's liberation march in Sydney's Hyde Park, 1972.

⊘ THE SPIRIT OF THE 1960S

Student power, the women's movement, black power and sexual liberation groups began challenging the conservative consensus. The rigid censorship of books and films was slowly dismantled, allowing Australians the opportunity to pore over previously forbidden classics of literature such as *Lolita* and *Portnoy's Complaint*. Aborigines had been allowed to vote in federal elections in 1967, but a 'freedom bus' drove through Queensland and New South Wales in protest against the deep-rooted, systematic discrimination against black people. At the same time, it was found that 10 percent of Australians were living in chronic poverty; they included Aborigines, single parents, and the sick, disabled and jobless.

At the same time, migrants began transforming the staid British social customs of their host country. At an obvious level there was the introduction of delicatessens, continental European food, open-air cafés, new varieties of music and a hectic sort of cosmopolitanism hardly imaginable before World War II. More profoundly, the migrants also opened Australians up to fresh ideas and new ways of looking at the world that have gradually altered the national character. Spurred on by this spirit, a revived Labor Party argued for new policies on a grand scale, and was led by its most inspiring politician for years, the towering, bushy-browed, charismatic Gough Whitlam.

This new-look Labor government had to deal with an ever-sliding Australian economy, starting off with a series of devaluations of the Aussie dollar (the 'Pacific peso', as it wryly became known). Under Keating, Labor presided over a push towards free-market policies, yet was able to maintain some degree of social justice by keeping Australia's welfare system intact.

Diplomatically and economically, Australia linked itself much more closely to Asia, while on the home front Asian immigration was stepped up, shifting the emphasis away from European profile. Australians also began talking seriously about becoming a republic at last – an initiative driven by the news that Sydney would host the Olympic Games in 2000.

Despite the steady achievements of these years, Australian voters wearied of Labor and in 1996 voted in a Liberal-National coalition government, led by the determinedly conservative John Howard. In economic matters, Howard advocated a freer market and smaller government. Conservatism also held out in the 1999 referendum, in which Australia voted against becoming

Sydney Harbour Bridge decorated with the Olympic rings, 2000.

immigration. Women were admitted to more positions of power, and Aboriginal land rights (control over their native homelands) was put on the national agenda. The celebration of the Bicentennial of British settlement in 1988 was a landmark of Australian self-confidence, but also a cause for some national soul-searching. In 1992, a High Court ruling, known as the Mabo case, finally abolished the historical fiction of *terra nullius* – the colonial doctrine that said Australia was uninhabited when the British colonists and convicts first arrived – and opened the way to Aboriginal land claims.

The 1980s and 1990s saw a flowering of the Australian arts, with local film-makers and writers increasingly taking on an international a republic and (by the narrowest of majorities) opted to keep the Queen as head of state.

THE NEW MILLENNIUM

Australia's economic outlook has improved steadily with the globalisation initiatives of successive recent governments, a booming resources industry and the often-controversial privatisation of the transport, energy and communications monoliths. In recent years the Australian dollar regained considerable ground against the US greenback, reaching parity in 2010. The country celebrated its new-found confidence in the euphoria of Sydney's staging of the 2000 Olympics. Dubbed the 'best Games ever' by the IOC president, the Games were an unequivocal success, both as a mark of

Australia's sporting prowess and as the ultimate high-profile evidence of Australia as an attractive travel destination.

There were clouds on the horizon, however. Howard championed a foreign policy more closely aligned with that of the United Kingdom and the United States. He then committed troops to the war in Iraq despite widespread public disquiet. A perceived connection of this presence to a spate of terrorist attacks across the Western world was reinforced by the 2002 Bali bombings, in which 202 people died, including 88 young Australians.

have been too high. Rudd was helming one of the few countries to escape largely undamaged in the global financial crisis, and while prudent financial management was to be expected, the aversion to reform was not. As the 2010 election loomed, the party's power brokers did the numbers and ousted Rudd as leader in favour of Julia Gillard. In a knife-edge result, and only with the help of a handful of independents, Julia Gillard became Australia's first female prime minister in September 2010 – nicely coinciding with the tenure of Australia's first female Gover-

Former Australian Prime Minister Michael Turnball.

John Howard went on to become Australia's second longest-serving prime minister after Robert Menzies. A buoyant economy and a disorganised Labor party helped keep him in office; however, an increasing disillusionment among the electorate, exacerbated by the government's treatment of refugees and its refusal to sign the Kyoto Agreement on climate change despite overwhelming evidence of global warming, finally saw Howard and his Liberal-National coalition ousted in 2007. Howard suffered the ultimate ignominy of losing his own seat after 11 years as prime minister.

The Labor Party, led by centre-left Kevin Rudd, took power, surfing a wave of expectation of change. In retrospect, these expectations may

nor General, Quentin Bryce. Despite Australia's ongoing economic strength, Gillard's minority government struggled to maintain support (and a nasty level of misogyny entered politics). However, she can be proud of a number of successes, including Australia's appointment to the UN Security Council in 2012.

In 2013, the Liberal/National Coalition, led by Tony Abbott of the Liberal Party, won the federal election. In 2015, after a leadership spill, Malcolm Turnbull became prime minister and lead the Coalition to victory by a single seat the next election in 2016. Yet another leadership spill took place in 2018, however, which resulted in Turnbull resigning as PM, to be replaced by former treasurer Scott Morrison.

Centre Place, Melbourne.

Lifeguards on the Sunshine Coast, Queensland.

THE URBAN AUSSIE

Most of the population live in cities and suburbs, and most of them on the coast. But that doesn't stop Australians dreaming of the wide-open Outback.

According to myth, the 'true blue Aussie' is a sun-bronzed stockman or jillaroo, riding the Outback range with a trusty sheepdog – which is like imagining all Americans to be tobacco-chewing cowboys, and Frenchmen going about in berets and striped shirts. Truth be told, Australia is the most urbanised country on Earth, with 80 percent of the population living in cities (66 percent in the state capitals). The Great Australian Dream, still enjoyed by a huge portion of the population, was to live on your own plot of land, with a brick house with a red-tile roof, and host a 'barbie' in the backyard. The dream was founded on the belief that home ownership leads to a better life and is an expression of success and security. However, today's rising property prices are dashing this dream for many. Not willing to let dreams pass them by, many an Australian is happy to simply adapt and be content with an inner-city apartment and to travel the world instead.

Family enjoying a barbie in their backyard.

CLINGING TO THE COAST

Most Australians now work in office jobs, and wouldn't recognise a trough of sheep dip if they fell in it. And although many still see the Outback as somehow embodying the most distinctive part of the country, relatively few have visited it, let alone considered living there. Even Patrick White, who set famous novels such as *Voss* in the furthest red-sand-and-spinifex deserts, never actually saw them (he got his images from his friend Sidney Nolan's paintings). White settled in Sydney's eastern suburbs, thousands of kilometres from the Red Centre.

The fact is that Australians have clung to the coast rather naturally, shrugging off the

⊘ RISING TENSIONS

Events like the Bali bombings of 2002, the 2014 Lindt Cafe siege in Sydney and the terror attack on Bourke Street in Melbourne in 2018 have caused racial and religious tensions to shift. Where previously Aboriginal groups were the scapegoats for the ills of urban Australia, now the sizeable Muslim communities are being targeted as troublemakers, despite living peacefully in Australian cities for decades. Racially motivated beach riots erupted in the Sydney suburb of Cronulla in 2005 and, in 2009, Indian students protested against racist attacks. For a place built on immigration, which professes to be an idyllic sun-splashed paradise full of opportunity for all, it is a worrying development.

priggish, cramped and tight-lipped spirit of the first British settlers and openly embracing the more sensual and hedonistic spirit of their Mediterranean environment. At least in the 21st century, the coast – and specifically the beach – has a far more powerful claim on Australian souls than the Outback. 'How shall I put this delicately?' asks Australian writer Robert Drewe. 'Most Australians of the past three generations have had their first sexual experience on the coast. So is it surprising that for the rest of their lives the sexual and litto-

Sydney's Gay and Lesbian Mardi Gras.

ral experiences are entwined in their memories; that most Australians thereafter see the beach in a pleasurable light?' It is to the sea that Australians return at each crucial stage of their lives: as young kids, on honeymoon, as parents. It is to the sea that they were taken as children, and to the sea that they return in old age, to the endless retirement villages of the Queensland shores.

How could it really be otherwise, in a country with such a climate and geography? It would take a serious effort of will not to lap up the perfect skies, the sea breeze, the glorious mounds of prawns and oysters, the bodies laid out on the sands and saturated in SPF 30+. Under the antipodean sun, more austere

national traits succumb to the easy-going, tolerant, obsessively casual Australian manner. It's no surprise to see a first-generation immigrant from Glasgow turn into a surfie overnight, or the daughters of conservative religious families lolling bikini-clad in the outdoor beer garden of a pub.

Leisure has become crucial to the Australian way of life – while working from 9 to 5 provides the means, it is at the weekends when Aussies truly come into their own, and few other places give people such opportunities to use their leisure well. Nature is close in Australia as nowhere else: in Sydney, with its 70 metropolitan beaches; in Melbourne, with one-third of its area devoted to parkland; or in Darwin, where 4-metre (13ft) crocodiles are regularly fished from the harbour. Some visitors still arrive expecting kangaroos to hop across the tarmac. This may not be so, but even in the red-brick back blocks of suburbia a national park might begin at the end of the road, and residents may keep an eye out for funnel-web spiders, possums in the roof and snakes in the garden.

Despite the occasional natural menaces, relaxation is part of the territory in Australia. It takes something truly grim to rouse most people to anger – and there's always a swim, or a beer, or a crisp Chardonnay to calm them down. From railway workers to restaurant waiters, the most common response to questions these days is a breezy 'No worries', 'Too easy' or 'Not a problem' – the latest incarnations of the 1950s slogan 'She'll be right, mate'. Politics is a matter to shake your head at ('The bastards are all the same' is the common refrain at election time). Economics, however, has become a matter of fascination, and taxi drivers and supermarket clerks can talk with authority on economic rationalism and exchange rates.

FROM CONVICTS TO DEMOCRATS

Every country is shaped by its past, and few have had a stranger start than Australia's, as the dumping ground for Britain's petty criminals. As Robert Hughes remarked in *The Fatal Shore*, it's one of the great ironies of history that a land founded by felons should evolve into one of the world's most law-abiding societies. Few cities of equal size around the world are as safe, tidy and downright civil as Australia's.

Social commentators have tried to draw conclusions from the country's awkward origins: that the convict legacy instilled a disdain for authority, leading to its powerful union movement, or that it led to a blunt conformism, accepting serious curtailments of civil liberties for most of the 20th century. Hughes comes up with the formula 'skeptical conformists': Australians like to think of themselves as rowdy rebels, talking big at the pub or behind authority's back, but obey with little question when it comes to the crunch. Other (more jaded) social commentators might say that Australia's beginnings as a penal colony have made it a corrupt place from day one.

As diverting as such theories are, the truth is that few modern Australians can really trace their lineages to convict times; most are the descendants of free English, Scottish and Irish settlers after the 1850s, or the wave of immigrants from the rest of the world a century later. Although the convict stain was once a matter of horror – an ignoble memory that any respectable society would excise, particularly from school books – the opposite is true in Australia today. Anyone who can dig up a convict ancestor now wears the fact as a badge of honour. In Sydney's Hyde Park Barracks Museum, schoolchildren eagerly type their names into a computer bank to see if they too bear the felon's mark.

Sydneysiders, of course, are more likely to come up trumps in this game of ancestral rivalry, since theirs was the original convict settlement. Melbourne, being established by free settlers, has always seen itself as having a more respectable and cosmopolitan flavour.

There lies another of the great Australian stories: the antagonism between the two major habitats of the urban Aussie: Sydney and Melbourne. Both have their distinctive character, both have world-leading attractions, and both are worth a lingering visit.

COLONIAL MACHISMO

The traditional image of Australians as sturdy bush workers may have little to do with modern life, but it has been a robust stereotype. It's the local version of the great frontier myth that crops up in the United States, parts of South America and South Africa. By the 1890s, writers, poets and painters were suggesting that a distinctive national spirit had been forged in the great empty wilderness, and that this 'New Man' was typified by a Kiplingesque mishmash of colonial values: naturally democratic, excelling at sports, blunt in his language, sardonic, self-reliant, independent, and not over-educated or burdened by musty traditions. Above all, an Aussie trusted his mates, who were bound to one another by an

Shoppers at Rundle Mall, Adelaide.

⊘ THE RISE OF GAY CULTURE

Visitors hoping to find the 'last refuge of unselfconscious masculinity' – as Ocker Aussies term it – may be disappointed. In recent times, gay culture has exploded in the country – especially in Sydney, which now has a higher concentration of gay residents than San Francisco.

At the first Gay Mardi Gras parade in 1978, police blockades were set up and 53 marchers were taken into custody. Today, the annual LGBT pride parade is the highest-attended event in the country, luring 300,000 people from across the country and abroad to watch floats of fabulously attired folk having fun.

almost mystical bond. This image transmuted over the years from the miners of the gold rushes to the Outback drover and the ANZAC Diggers of Gallipoli.

The one obvious drawback of this stereotype was that it did not include women. The contribution of women on the frontier, in the arts, or in the factories during wars, tended to be brushed aside, so that by the 1950s Australia had earned a reputation as one of the most sexist societies in the developed world. The worst manifestation of the crass male spirit was known as the 'Ocker Aussie' – the beer-swilling, pot-bellied, narrow-minded, gay-hating, provincial redneck, who watched footie at the pub while the Sheila stayed at home minding the kids. Barry Humphries satirised the type with Bazza MacKenzie, the simple-minded tourist who was always ready for a schooner and a chunder. Paul Hogan, as Crocodile Dundee, refined and introduced the persona to the New World.

Like the long-ingrained racism, sexism abated with the general loosening-up of society in the 1970s. Aussie women have always been strong characters – perhaps even more blunt, independent and self-reliant than the men so loudly proclaimed themselves to be, out of sheer necessity – so in recent years they have easily taken the lead in many fields. Still, as in other Western nations, women remain sadly under-represented in politics and top management positions. When Julia Gillard became Australia's first female prime minister, misogyny infected the national debate and was all too apparent in the country's mainstream media.

AUSTRALIAN DREAMS

Perhaps the myth dearest to the Australian heart is that theirs is the most naturally democratic of societies – the frontier past, and distance from the Old World, have naturally levelled Aussies to equals.

Certainly the outward signs are there: waiters may still call you 'mate'; taxi drivers can still get cranky if you sit in the back seat instead of up front (as a social equal would); and public officials, even prime ministers, are often known by their first names. The other side of the egalitarian coin is known as the 'tall-poppy syndrome': a national resentment

of high achievers and an inescapable urge to bring them down.

But is Australia a classless society? Patently not. There may be none of the rigid divisions evident in Britain, or the gross inequalities of the American system, but there are serious divisions of wealth and opportunity – and many believe that the gaps are increasing. At both social events and interviews certain people will ask loaded questions like 'So...what school did you go to?' – a reference to private education. According to pessimists, the great settler's dream of Aus-

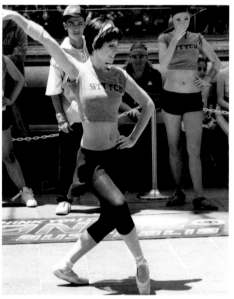

Street dancing in Perth.

tralia as the 'millennial Eden' is being eroded. In a haphazard way, Australians have committed themselves to avoiding the errors of Europe and the US, and guaranteeing an unusual measure of social justice. But Australians are becoming increasingly materialistic, and less generous in their vision of society as a place where the weaker are protected. Australia's great narrative historian, Manning Clark, had a bleak vision of his compatriots before he died in the 1990s: 'Mammon had infected the ancient continent of Australia,' he intoned, in the manner of an Old Testament prophet. 'The dreams of humanity had ended in an age of ruins.'

Just don't try telling that to any Aussies on a sunny day. They'll already be at the beach.

Surfing off the Queensland coast.

LIFE IN THE BUSH

The old stereotypes of rural Australia are disappearing quickly, but there's still a distinct attitude of mind among those who live 'out bush'.

Ten-year droughts, dramatic floods, bushfires whistling through the scrub – the same natural processes that allowed the Aborigines to eke out an existence from the land have made life unpredictable for most farmers. Yet despite constant threats of bankruptcy, few give up. They stick to the land, aided by their own brand of black humour and the solace of Saturday night at the pub.

Rural Australia – sometimes referred to as 'West of the Divide', 'The Bush', 'Back o'Bourke', 'Beyond the Black Stump' or 'The Mulga' – is, in some respects, an antipodean myth. Most Australians rise each morning to spend another day at the factory or office, a far cry from the days when men tramped 'the Wallaby Track' (the old sheep station shearing circuit), with belongings in a 'swag' on the shoulder and a faithful blue-heeler cattle dog padding alongside.

CHANGING ATTITUDES

The image of a roving jackaroo is a romantic one, straight from the work of one of the country's literary folk heroes, Andrew Barton 'Banjo' Paterson. His poem, *The Man From Snowy River*, is a tale of derring-do in the Victorian high country that still resonates with Australians and visitors today.

The other great turn-of-the-20th-century bush writer, author and poet Henry Lawson, had a more nuanced and, arguably, grounded view of the bush. After a wretched childhood on the western New South Wales goldfields, Lawson kept returning to the bush to reinforce his dislike of it. He hated the unrelenting grey-green of the eucalyptus, the monotony and hopelessness (his word) of the countryside. Lawson railed against the heat on the track to Hungerford, the 'bloody

Mustering cattle on Delta Downs, north Queensland.

flies', the thieving publicans, the greedy bosses, the arrogant squatters and the brutal police. He did, however, love the 'bush battlers', the staunch early unionists and the great Outback tradition of mateship – male-bonding in the wild. These tough men often reciprocated his admiration, and many felt that Lawson, through his writing, was speaking for them.

Perhaps because of the residual influence of Lawson's writings, many visitors and even some urban Australians seem to believe that the Outback and its 170,000 farmers and graziers are stuck in an 1890s time warp. In fact, Aussie farmers are highly mechanised agribusiness people, mustering cattle by helicopter and trail bike, flying their own planes, and adept at using the internet to run their businesses. It's true, however, that workers on the stations put in long hours day in, day out, and often live in difficult conditions.

Another blind spot commonly found concerns the colour of cowboys. The best stockmen have always been black, although until the 1960s they were often paid half of what white workers received. As jackaroos, boundary riders, shearers and trackers, Aborigines have contributed skill and labour to Australia's rural prosperity, particularly in the Northern Territory and Western Australia. Furthermore, with the granting of land rights, Aborigines have taken over some of the cattle stations and found a degree of independence.

Despite all the changes of the past 100 years, it is still another world outside the Australian cities. But you don't need to trek all the way to the Outback to find a country mentality; it can be found in any small rural town where the architecture is at least semi-colonial and which services a broad rural area.

BUSH MISCHIEF

Many of the old clichés about laconic, resourceful, friendly country people still have a good deal of truth in them. And there's a helpfulness in the bush that is not always immediately apparent to the visitor, thanks to a little bush mischief on the side. Any enquiry for directions, for instance, can be met with a slow 'buggered-if-I-know' reply, followed almost immediately with an entertaining series of precise directions. Australians would never deliberately misdirect visitors, for, in the Outback, misdirection may result in death, by either starvation or thirst.

Visitors from overseas wanting to 'go bush' will find many specialised tourism opera-

Jackeroos still manage the herds with the help of a horse and hound.

Driving in the Outback is best accomplished with a 4-wheel-drive vehicle.

tors catering for just that urge. Everything's available, from luxury air, bus and rail tours to motorised four-wheel-drive backpacker parties.

The Outback has resorts ranging from remote fishing camps to the accommodation conglomerates at Uluru (Ayers Rock) offering everything from campsites to five-star luxury.

For extra authenticity it's worth seeking out one of the stations that accepts guests and gives them a flavour of what it's like to muster cattle or round up sheep in the sometimes inhospitable land of the Outback. The official tourism site for Queensland, for example, offers a range of options (www.myqldholiday.com.au).

A MULTICULTURAL SOCIETY

In the past 50 years the population has doubled and diversified. Immigrants have not always found it easy, but today's rich ethnic mix is seen as one of Australia's assets.

When a survey in 1939 showed that the Australian population was comprised of 98 percent Anglo-Celtic stock, local newspapers proudly proclaimed that Australia was the most British country on Earth. In this monochromatic society, the only unusual accents were those of the new chums from corners of Ireland or the Scottish highlands. On the dinner table, foods were rarely more exotic than Yorkshire pudding, and Christmas was a time for huge Dickensian meals of roast beef or pork, no matter how brutally hot and tropical the weather.

All that changed after 1945, when Australia embarked on one of the most ambitious and successful immigration programmes of the modern era. The migrants were drawn first from the Mediterranean and Baltic countries of Europe, but since the 1970s immigrants have come from around the world. Since the programme began after World War II, more than 6 million settlers from almost 200 countries have chosen to make Australia their home.

A group of young Muslim women wear hijabs made from the national flag on Harmony Day.

IMMENSE DIVERSITY

Almost one-quarter of the population was born overseas; 15 percent speak a language other than English at home. In recent years, more than 40 percent of settler arrivals have come from Asia, with the British and Irish down to 14 percent. The humanitarian programme is gradually adding even more diversity to the population. In the 1990s, most of these arrivals came from the Balkans; lately African and Asian arrivals far outnumber Europeans, with people from India topping the list, followed by Chinese.

Just as the United States and Argentina were transformed by immigration in the 1890s, so the post-war influx has radically changed the structure and habits of Australian society. Take a seat on the Manly ferry or a Melbourne tram and you're as likely to be sitting next to the daughter of a builder from Athens as you are to a journalist from Dakar or a car salesman from Thailand. There is a wonderful sense of cultural diversity to be had across Australia. Multiculturalism was clearly missing entirely from the 'White Australia' immigration policy of 1949–73, and some governments have been more welcoming than others even since that racially discriminatory policy was scrapped, but it's firmly established in modern Australian society, and most Aussies prize tolerance and respect for all cultures and races.

Although a multicultural society is a *fait accompli*, balancing the demands of such a heterogeneous population can be a delicate task. There have been missteps along the way, but since so many people have chosen Australia as their homeland, there is a strong motivation to work together and find solutions to ethnic or racial problems. Ethnic traditions and loyalties are respected and encouraged, but the first loyalty must be to the Australian legal and parliamentary system; multiple languages are promoted, but English is the official tongue of the country; coercive cultural practices, such as arranged marriages, are illegal.

Dancers at an Indian wedding in Sydney.

THE CLOSING DOOR

With a small populations bouncing around in a massive continent-sized country, Australia once welcomed almost anyone who applied as an immigrant. These days, more emphasis is laid on skills, with targets set each year for migrants with skills in areas where there are gaps. Sometimes, however, events overseas do influence this – as a result of taking an additional 12,000 people from Syria and Iraq in 2015–16, for example, Australia's humanitarian intake for that period (over 25,000) was the largest since World War II.

If the statistics are cold, the issue isn't. Despite being a country where almost 97 percent of families' recent roots lie overseas (just 3.3 percent of Australia's population identifies

as Aboriginal), immigration is still a major point of debate within Australian society. Scarcely a week goes by without a politician, academic, or public personality adding to the discussion.

The immigration process can be laborious. Applicants are tested for their suitability to settle successfully, assimilate into the community and find work. Points are allocated for such categories as age, employability, English-language skill and so on, although concessions are sometimes made for immigrants willing to move to less popular states or far-distant country regions. Employability usually gets the highest weighting because of the greater contribution skilled migrants make to the economy.

THE NEW AUSTRALIANS

When Australia became a nation in 1901, racial purity was top of the agenda; the notorious White Australia policy, instituted by the *Immigration Restriction Bill*, was one of the first measures to be passed by the new parliament. It would govern migration for decades, and was not formally overturned until 1973.

Thus the first wave of non-British immigrants, brought over in the 1950s and 1960s, was drawn from Europe – mostly from Greece and Italy. Some 275,000 of these 'New Australians' arrived in those years – although now, of course, they are Old Australians. Some 5 percent of the population is now of Italian descent, while Melbourne is often touted as the second-largest Greek city in the world (after Athens).

THE POLYGLOT NATION

Even during the 19th century, there had been some exceptions to Australia's monoculture. A large Chinese population came to Australia during the gold rushes of the 1850s (and survived the bitter resentment of Anglo miners, which occasionally erupted into violent attacks).

Several wine-growing valleys of South Australia, settled by Silesians in the 1840s, are still Teutonic in ethos. Remote Broome at the top of Western Australia was once full of Japanese pearl divers. But these areas remained exceptions to the rule until the boom in different cultures that Australia received in the 1970s, once it truly opened its doors to the rest of the world, particularly to Asia. By the 1990s, one-third of all immigration was from Asian countries, and the proportion has increased steadily. The new arrivals do not always find it easy to adapt, but their cultural influence is increasingly obvious in all regions of the country.

Around 2 million Australians speak a language other than English when they are at home. An ethnic radio and television broadcasting network – Special Broadcasting Service (SBS) – began in the 1980s to transmit in many languages (with television programmes subtitled in English), and SBS Television's evening news has the most wide-ranging foreign coverage of all the stations in Australia.

archipelago – including Kurds from Iraq, Afghanis, Syrians, Iranians or Sri Lankan Tamils – are a major concern. Introduced by the strongly anglophile Howard government, the Pacific Solution, whereby asylum-seekers are processed offshore, is still contentious and skirts the edge of the country's obligations under international law. Labor has essentially followed the same policy since 2007, as have the following Liberal governments.

Just like in the US and the UK, over the last decade rightwing politicians have chased the votes of an aging population who often express con-

Greek parade for Australia Day.

OTHER WAYS OF SETTLING

For those for whom all legal avenues have failed, or who are too desperate to go through the lengthy process, there is illegal immigration – often by arriving as a tourist and then overstaying the visa. It is estimated that there are about 60,000 people living like this, many of whom remain undetected for years. When apprehended, they face the choice of rapid departure or mandatory deportation (with digital black marks on their passports that could cause them problems for many years). The single biggest group of offenders in this category is British tourists overstaying their visas.

If media coverage is any indication, asylum-seekers arriving by boat from the Indonesian

cerns about diversity. Although Australia accepted only 162,417 permanent migrants in 2017–18, a decrease of more than 10 percent on the previous year and the lowest level in a decade, in November 2018, Prime Minister Scott Morrison announced a populist policy of reducing the intake even more.

But, overall, the Australian experience of immigration has been massively successful, with newcomers being absorbed into society with comparatively little friction. Indeed, many people see this diversity as the key to the country's vitality, with new ideas and fresh talent flowing in, and even the most conservative commentators don't seem to object when immigrants and their offspring contribute to the country's considerable sporting successes.

A rock painting in Kakadu
National Park.

ABORIGINES TODAY

Captain Arthur Phillip reported that the first words the Australian Aborigines said to his men in 1788 were 'Warra! Warra!' (Go away!). Given the subsequent cultural attrition, their first reaction was remarkably prescient.

Interest in the Aborigines is often piqued by modern Aboriginal art. The symbolism found within these paintings has helped generate interest in learning about a culture that is vastly different from any other.

In much of Aboriginal art, it all comes back to the land. For Aboriginal groups, land rights have always been a top priority. The land is a crucial part of their being and their culture, and the responsibility for protecting significant sites is central to their spiritual life. Yet the Aborigines have been forced from their traditional homes, and have seen sacred sites mined, built on, flooded or destroyed.

There have been a few attempts at partial restitution. The *Northern Territory Land Rights Act* (passed in 1975) allowed Aborigines to make claims to swathes of the Outback on the basis of traditional ownership. The act also gave them significant control over mining and other activities. Royalties from mining activities were distributed to various Aboriginal groups, and land rights acts have been passed in various states in an attempt to right the wrongs of history.

Creating Aboriginal crafts.

GROWING RESENTMENT

There is a perception that Aboriginal dissent did not surface until the 1960s and 1970s, but in fact an Aboriginal rights association existed in Sydney as early as 1924. The Melbourne-based Australian Aborigines Advancement League petitioned King George V for special indigenous electorates in 1932. If colonial Australians believed (as many did) that Aboriginal people owed them a debt of gratitude for having brought civilisation to *terra nullius*, they were disabused by the Aboriginal Progressive Association manifesto of 1938. Issued on the 150th anniversary of the landing of the First Fleet in Botany Bay, this document declared 26 January

⊘ HOW ABORIGINES LOSE OUT

Aboriginal Australians are the country's most disadvantaged group. Statistics tell the sad story: the average life expectancy for Aborigines is 10 years shorter than that for other Australians; they have three times the infant mortality rate and a far higher incidence of both communicable diseases, such as hepatitis B, and lifestyle diseases such as heart failure; an unemployment rate six times the national average; half the average income level; and a large proportion living in sub-standard housing or temporary shelters. Aborigines are also 16 times more likely to be imprisoned than other Australians.

a day of mourning. 'You took our land away from us by force,' the manifesto said. 'You have almost exterminated our people, but there are enough of us remaining to expose the humbug of your claim as white Australians to be a civilised, progressive, kindly and humane nation. By your cruelty and callousness towards the Aborigines you stand condemned in the eyes of the civilised world.'

Political awareness grew steadily from the 1930s, culminating in the Freedom Rides of the mid-1960s, when activists rode in buses through Outback Queensland and New South Wales

Aboriginal boy.

⊘ THE STOLEN GENERATION

Between 1910 and 1970, police and welfare officers forcibly removed up to 100,000 children from their parents. The idea was to assimilate mixed-blood Aboriginal children into European society. They were fostered into white homes and forbidden to speak their own languages. Most were given physically demanding or menial jobs, many suffered abuse, and nearly all experienced psychological damage. The stories of these sad children, known as the Stolen Generations, were brought to public awareness by a 1997 government report, 'Bringing Them Home'. Prime Minister Kevin Rudd formally apologised to the Stolen Generations in 2008.

bringing their message to remote communities. Demonstrations resulted in violent clashes with police, pushing the Aboriginal plight on to the front pages and into middle-class homes.

Various lobby groups began to champion Aboriginal political rights. The first positive step came in 1949, when the Chifley government passed an act confirming that those who could vote in their states could vote for the Commonwealth. Aboriginal people in all states (except Queensland and Western Australia) had been entitled to vote in state elections since the 1850s; they didn't vote because no one told them they could.

By the early 1970s, this newfound political consciousness forced the government, led by Gough Whitlam, to develop a new policy of self-determination. This allowed indigenous Australians to make decisions affecting their future, retain their cultural identity and values, and achieve greater economic and social equality.

The Department of Aboriginal Affairs was established in 1972, followed by the Aboriginal Development Commission (ADC) in 1980. The underlying concept was to bring economic independence to indigenous people by fostering business enterprises, but it didn't happen overnight. In 1988, while the rest of Australia celebrated 200 years of settlement at the Bicentennial, Aboriginal activists staged peaceful protest marches. White Australians were forced to admit that, for the Aborigines, the colonial invasion had been an unmitigated disaster.

RIGHTS AND WRONGS

The public agenda changed in 1992, when the High Court of Australia overturned the legal fiction of *terra nullius*. The judges agreed that native title had always existed for land that had been continuously occupied by Aborigines; in 1993 the government set up a Native Title Tribunal to regulate claims. However, because 19th-century missionaries moved Aboriginal peoples around, often splitting up clans by force, few Aboriginal groups could prove continuous occupation of their lands.

Aboriginal industry has been promoted by politicians, community activists and Aboriginal leaders. Most promising has been the creation of successful Aboriginal businesses, from shopping centres and cattle stations to craft shops.

The problems facing the Aborigines who live in remote communities – illiteracy, unemployment, low wages, ill health, alcohol and drug abuse – resist simple solutions. A strong interventionist policy of cracking down on alcohol and delinquency in the Northern Territory, which was introduced by the Howard government, has not improved this complex situation and arguably worsened relations and elevated resentment.

Perhaps the biggest step towards some type of reconciliation occurred on 13 February 2008, when, amidst a national outpouring of emotion, Prime Minister Kevin Rudd issued a formal

the 2000 Olympics; boxer Anthony Mundine, who started his professional sporting life as a rugby league player; and numerous Aussie Rules footballers, such as Adam Goodes.

Music has always been central to Aboriginal culture and there has been a steady flow of acts who have crossed over into the commercial mainstream, from Jimmy Little in the 1960s to Yothu Yindi in the 1980s, on through Kev Carmody, Tiddas, Archie Roach, Geoffrey Gurrumul Yunupingu, Jessica Mauboy, Ziggy, Emily Wurramara and Dhapanbal Yunupingu.

Geoffrey Gurrumul Yunupingu entertains the crowd.

apology to the Stolen Generations in a speech broadcast live around the nation.

SUCCESS STORIES

Many Aborigines have successfully entered Australian society on their own terms. Neville Bonner became a senator of the Commonwealth Parliament and pastor Sir Doug Nichols was appointed Governor of South Australia. Oodgeroo Noonuccal (formerly Kath Walker) was a prominent artist and author, while writers such as Herb Wharton and Evelyn Crawford are immensely popular.

Sport has seen several outstanding performers, including Evonne Goolagong-Cawley, who became a Wimbledon tennis champion; track-and-field athlete Cathy Freeman, who won a gold medal in

TV presenter and actor Ernie Dingo is a household favourite in Australia, and other critically acclaimed indigenous actors include David Gulpilil (*Rabbit-Proof Fence, Crocodile Dundee, Australia*), Deborah Mailman (*Rabbit-Proof Fence, Oddball, The Sapphires, The Secret Life of Us, Offspring*), Yasmin Honeychurch (*Life Of Jess, Back of The Net*), Everlyn Sampi (*Rabbit-Proof Fence*), Jamie Gulpilil (*Australia, 10 Canoes*), Peter Minygululu (*10 Canoes, Charlie's Country, Crocodile Dreaming*), Frances Djulibing (*Charlie's Country, Ten Canoes*), Crusoe Kurddal (*Ten Canoes, Mad Max: Fury Road, Australia*), Aaron Pedersen (*Mystery Road*), Miah Madden (*The Sapphires, Australia Day, The Darkside*), Meyne Wyatt (*The Sapphires, Neighbours*) and Brandon Walters (*Australia, Bushwhacked!*).

📷 ABORIGINAL ART

From Dreamtime to polymer paints, the artworks being created by modern Aborigines carry the symbolism of thousands of years of myth and tradition.

It's contemporary yet traditional. It's today but it's timeless. Attaching a single label to modern Aboriginal art can be as difficult as establishing the meanings behind the symbols. But it does provide us with a unique cultural vision of Australia. The explosion in indigenous Australian art began in the early 1970s as a spark in Northern Territory, first in various groups in Arnhem Land and in the desert community of Papunya, west of Alice Springs. In Arnhem Land, missionaries encouraged tribal people to paint their designs, derived from traditional rock art and body decoration, on bark panels stripped from trees. Meanwhile in central Australia, teacher Geoffrey Bardon introduced polymer paints, producing an entirely new genre of art: the strongly symbolic dot style was born. Today the National Gallery in Canberra, all the state galleries, and many private galleries in all the major cities feature desert and Top End art.

Other Aboriginal communities have also earned distinguished reputations for their artisans: Tiwi islanders for their carving and distinctive painting; representations of WA's Kimberley region, as characterised by artists Rover Thomas and Paddy Carlton; and the blazing acrylics from Eubana Nampitjin of Balgo Hills. Works by the late Emily Kngwarreye put the central Australian community of Utopia on the map; her niece Kathleen Petyarre continues that tradition with her intricately detailed paintings, prints and batiks, which can be viewed at numerous galleries throughout Australia.

The Aboriginal Memorial, created by artists from Ramingining in the Northern Territory, is constructed of 200 hollow log bone coffins and can be seen in the National Gallery of Australia.

A Tiwi Island man creates a bold artwork. With its strong patterns and use of colour, Tiwi art is recognised as being very attractive and highly collectable.

An Aboriginal bark painting of a funeral ceremony with kangaroos on Croker Island, painted by Melangi de Milingibi. The image is used on Australian banknotes.

Inside Art Mob, an Aboriginal art gallery and shop in Hobart, Tasmania.

Buying the art

In an industry with a turnover in the millions of dollars, the Aboriginal art market is rife with opportunists trying to rip off the buyers and/or the artists. As a buyer, you can take a few simple steps to avoid the common pitfalls. Prime amongst them is establishing the authenticity of the work. Ideally, buy direct from the artist or their community, an Aboriginal art and craft centre or a reputable dealer – look for membership of the Indigenous Art Trade Association or the Australian Commercial Galleries Association – and always ask for a certificate of authenticity and/or photographic provenance of the work. That way you can establish the title, the artist's name, community and language, the date of the work and the story behind it. After that, consider (with reference to the quality and price of other works by the artist) whether you are getting value for money. In recent years there have

Modern Aboriginal art is often created to evoke the culture of the Dreaming, without any strong connection to a particular Dreaming story or song.

Detail of Aboriginal bowl bearing an intricate pattern, burnt into wood.

been several instances of exploitation of artists by unscrupulous traders, so enquire whether the dealer subscribes to an industry ethical code, such as the Australian Indigenous Art Code of Conduct (www. indigenousartcode.org).

A potter at work in Nguiu, Bathurst Island, Northern Territory.

THE ARTS

In music, drama, literature, film and the visual arts, Australia has absorbed influences from around the world and now has its own distinctive voice.

There's good reason to believe that a fair number of visitors enjoy the opera or an orchestral concert whilst in Australia. This isn't to argue that Opera Australia is the best company in the world or that the Sydney Symphony has that something extra to get musical celibates across the line. Or perhaps it is, at least in the latter case, because what both these companies have is the Sydney Opera House as a home base. It's a Unesco World Heritage Site and dominates the harbour. It's the place all first-time visitors want to see, many going on the guided tour. The logical next step is to see a performance.

So what will you see? With both companies it will be work fit to grace any stage. In 2014, an American, David Robertson, became a chief conductor of the Sydney Symphony Orchestra (SSO). That same year he conducted the controversial but highly acclaimed MET premiere of John Adams' *Death of Klinghoffer*. In 2015, his projects with SSO included a Schumann's symphony cycle and Beethoven's *Missa Solemnis* among others.

Opera Australia splits its time between Sydney and Melbourne and tours with the odd production further afield. It stages everything from high-profile and popular shows, such as Britten's *Midsummer Night's Dream* directed by Baz Luhrmann, through to chamber productions of challenging new Australian work. In 2016, Opera Australia celebrated 60 years. Queensland, Adelaide, West Australia and Victoria all have their own opera companies, while every state has its own orchestra.

Classical music is, of course, very much part of the Western tradition – indeed, many of the pieces performed today predate the European discovery of Australia. When those first settlers arrived, almost all their cultural pleasures were transplanted from the mother country, much

The award-winning author Peter Carey.

like their language, skills and crops. Indigenous Aboriginal culture, which dates back at least 50,000 years, was largely ignored.

The first stirrings of a specifically Australian cultural identity came in the 1890s and coincided with an upsurge in Australian nationalism. This was reflected initially in literature. It was the period when *The Bulletin* magazine's school of poets and short-story writers was founded, spearheaded by balladeers such as Banjo Paterson, who wrote *The Man From Snowy River* and *Waltzing Matilda*, and Henry Lawson, Australia's revered short-story writer. Their work celebrates the bush, mateship, Aussie nationalism and the triumph of the underdog, usually at the expense of the ruling Anglophile 'bunyip aristocracy'. Joseph Furphy wrote his novel *Such Is Life* at this time, capturing the world of rural dwellers in a style not dissimilar to Mark Twain's. Marcus Clarke's *For the Term of his Natural Life* was more of a potboiler, but did provide a gripping portrait of convict life in 1830s Van Diemen's Land (Tasmania).

LITERATURE

Steele Rudd began his *On Our Selection* series in 1899, about life on poverty-stricken bush properties and featuring the characters Dad and Dave, who lived on for years in the wider world of radio

Malouf (*The Great World, Remembering Babylon*). Australians are some of the most voracious book buyers in the world, and they flock to the many literary festivals in Australia.

THEATRE

In theatre, Louis Esson began writing plays in a self-consciously Australian idiom in the 1890s, but it took a long time before any groundswell of home-grown drama could be detected. Ray Lawlor's *Summer of the Seventeenth Doll* (1955) was the first portrayal of clearly Australian char-

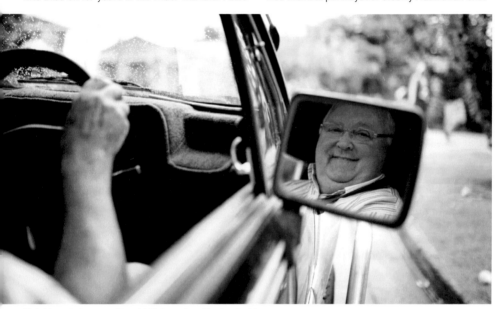

'Neighbours' character Harrold Bishop, played by Ian Smith

and cinema. A little after Rudd, C.J. Dennis started celebrating city larrikins in his poems about Ginger Mick and The Sentimental Bloke (1915).

This creative leap was the start of a distinctive Australian literature, which continued strongly in the 20th century through the novels of Henry Handel Richardson, Miles Franklin, Christina Stead, Ruth Park and the towering, Nobel-prize-winning Patrick White. Today's high fliers include Peter Carey (*True History of the Kelly Gang, Oscar and Lucinda*), Kate Grenville (*The Secret River, The Lieutenant, Sarah Thornhill*), Richard Flanagan (*Death of a River Guide, The Sound of One Hand Clapping, The Narrow Road to the Deep North*), Tim Winton (*Breath, Dirt Music, The Riders, Cloudstreet, The Shepherd's Hut*) and David

acters to break out internationally and is still revived periodically. The 1970s saw an exponential expansion of Australian theatre as a wave of politically active writers filled the fringe theatres in the main cities. These writers inexorably moved into, and became, the mainstream. David Williamson is the best known of these and is still writing today. Of the next generation, Louis Nowra, Hannie Rayson and Joanna Murray Smith are consistently producing interesting work.

All the big cities have theatre companies, usually with a state-funded flagship accompanied by a range of smaller fringe enterprises. The Sydney Theatre Company is currently run by Kip Williams, but previous directors have included playwright Andrew Upton, who in 2008–13 held the role jointly with his wife, actor Cate Blanchett, before going solo at the helm for another two years.

The large commercial theatres tend to be clogged up with clone musicals from Broadway or London's West End, with the odd home-grown production, such as *Priscilla Queen of the Desert*, going the other way.

The great anomaly of the Australian stage is the Bell Shakespeare Company. In 1990 John Bell effectively revived the role of the actor/manager, which had died out as a concept everywhere else, by setting up a company to tour Shakespeare

Melbourne-based Australian Ballet, which presents both classical and contemporary repertoire. Cutting-edge smaller companies include Chunky Move, which leads the way in harnessing modern technology to complement its performers.

PAINTING

A recognisable school of landscape painting in Australia emerged in the late 19th century, personified by Sir Arthur Streeton, Tom Roberts and the Heidelberg School (named after the Melbourne suburb, not the German town), which

Actors from Belgium's Theatre Royal de la Monnaie perform 'Babel' as part of the annual Sydney Festival.

around the country. It's still going and producing three shows a year. In 2015, Bell stood down after 25 years as the company artistic director.

DANCE

Dance was one of the first disciplines in which colonial Australian culture began to reconnect with the country's indigenous population. Composer John Antill wrote *Corroboree*, a ballet suite, in 1946; it was performed as such in 1950, touring the country over the next decade. It combined Aboriginal and Western forms to great acclaim. Today the Bangarra Dance Company does the same thing; the company is directed and run by Aboriginal people. The company tours extensively in Australia and overseas, as does the

⊘ THE SOAPS

Recently, locally produced television has been finding its way beyond the shores of Australia – from *The Secret Life of Us* and *Offspring* to the unsettling serialised remake of *Picnic at Hanging Rock* and the four-part drama *The Cry*. And then, of course, there are the soap operas, which have consistently found an audience in the UK, from *Wentworth* to *Home and Away* (set in Sydney since 1987) and the perennially popular *Neighbours*. Such is the level of its following that an entire industry has evolved to serve the legions of fans who visit Melbourne. Various organised tours run to 'Ramsay Street', and there's even a weekly Neighbours-themed pub quiz in a St Kilda hotel.

pioneered Australian impressionism. Today there is an art trail in the vicinity and, nearby, the Heide Museum of Modern Art. This property was, for a spell, the haunt of Albert Tucker, Joy Hester and probably Australia's best-known painter, Sidney Nolan. Nolan was one of a group of figurative painters working after World War II, identified as part of the Australian School. His series of paintings on Ned Kelly, the outlaw bushranger, became national icons.

In the early 1970s Sydney became the centre for an abstract expressionist movement that drew upon earlier painters such as Ian Fairweather and Godfrey Miller. Local artists were soon experimenting with hard edge, colour field and lyrical expressionist modes. A new breed of younger painters looked up to Brett Whiteley as the poster boy for artists living the rock'n'roll lifestyle.

In Melbourne, painter and printmaker Fred Williams established himself as the most important landscape artist of the post-war years with his haunting, semi-abstract depictions of the Outback.

Perhaps the best-known contemporary Australian artist is Tracey Moffatt, born in Brisbane in

Mandawuy Yunupingu of Aboriginal band Yothu Yindi.

Ⓞ ANTIPODEAN RHYTHMS

Australia has become as well known for its rock bands as its films; the pub music scene is extraordinarily healthy. Performers such as Nick Cave, Courtney Barnett, Tame Impala, King Gizzard & The Lizard Wizard, Wolfmother and the Temper Trap started off on the pub circuit and now enjoy international success. Others that made it big overseas include the Seekers, the Bee Gees, AC/DC, Midnight Oil and INXS. The Aboriginal band Yothu Yindi, with didgeridoos and tribal dancers, is unmistakably Northern Territory. One of Australia's best-known exports (in Europe, at least) is Kylie Minogue, a former teenage soap star and now pop icon. At home the dance scene is pumping, and acts such as Pendulum have taken off overseas.

There are two particular musical fields in which Australians have twisted the popular American styles into something distinctly antipodean. Bush ballads may have died out, but American country and western music took off in the rural areas of Australia in the 1940s and 50s. Local singers adopted names like Tex Morton and Slim Dusty and began writing songs about outlaws, pubs, and the country myths of girlfriends past. Slim Dusty's The Pub with No Beer was a huge hit. More recently, Keith Urban has become a global star, while Kasey Chambers is the biggest name locally. Meanwhile, a hip-hop scene is blossoming, with Adelaide's Hilltop Hoods and Sydney's Bliss 'n' Eso leading the charge.

1960. Her painterly films and photographic works have won international critical acclaim and been widely exhibited. She is symptomatic of a whole wave of artists working across various media who set out to challenge not just with the message, but also with the medium.

Brisbane's impressive new Gallery of Modern Art leads the way in this field, but Sydney's Museum of Contemporary Art and Melbourne's Australian Centre for Contemporary Art have consistently supported adventurous work. The multimillion-dollar Museum of Old and New Art, just

(Gillian Armstrong's 1979 version of the Miles Franklin classic, *My Brilliant Career*) to George Miller's 1996 talking pig, *Babe*; to Baz Luhrmann's dazzling dance comedy *Strictly Ballroom* (1992), and David Michôd's crime thriller *Animal Kingdom* (2010). Miller's *Mad Max Fury Road*, scooped up six Oscars at the 2016 Academy Awards, and other critically acclaimed Australian films include *Lion*, and *The Proposition*.

Australian actors including Nicole Kidman, Cate Blanchett, Heath Ledger, Toni Collette, Guy Pearce, Hugh Jackman, Hugo Weaving, Naomi

A still from 'Rabbit-Proof Fence'.

north of Hobart, opened with a bang at the beginning of 2011.

FILM

Soldiers of the Cross (1899) is said to be the world's first feature film and, like the more famous *The Story of the Kelly Gang* (1906), was made in Australia. It took several more decades, however, for local cinema to find its voice; it wasn't until the 1970s that films emerged onto the world stage with the likes of *Mad Max* and *Picnic at Hanging Rock*. Progress was swift thereafter, and, with a burst of dramatic talent and new government incentives, the film industry became Australia's biggest cultural export. The most celebrated films to come from Australia range from period pieces

Watts, Sam Worthington, Margot Robbie and Bryan Brown have all become big names in Hollywood.

Some actors and directors prefer to create work that reflects the realities of modern Australia. Since 2000, for instance, a spate of indigenous-themed films has been released, including *Rabbit-Proof Fence*, *The Sapphires* and *The Tracker*, whose director, Rolf de Heer, won international praise for *Ten Canoes* – the first Australian film to feature an entirely indigenous cast and to be spoken entirely in indigenous languages – which he directed with Peter Djigirr. *Samson and Delilah* (2008) portrayed the desperation of Aboriginal youth in central Australia; the film won the Caméra d'Or (Gold Camera Award) for best first feature film at the 2009 Cannes Film Festival.

MODERN AUSTRALIAN CUISINE

It took a long time to happen, but food in Australia is now distinguished for its quality, imagination and a truly multinational diversity.

Not so long ago, the term 'Australian cuisine' conjured grisly images of meat pies, Vegemite sandwiches and sausage rolls. Not anymore; Australia is now a trendy paradise for foodies. Few places in the world have restaurants with such variety, quality and sheer inventiveness. From formal dining rooms to tiny beach-side cafés, menus explore the merging of Australia's bounty of native ingredients with international culinary traditions. Even the most basic corner diners, which once served up hamburgers and chips, now dish up focaccia with fresh King Island cheeses and exotic fruits. And Australia's artisan coffee culture is legendary around the globe.

In fact, Australia's culinary establishment may be the most adventurous in the world. Nearly every city has seen a swarm of 'Mod Oz' restaurants with inventive chefs at the helm and an audience of willing epicures. This renaissance is due to two factors: the wealth of superlative Australian produce – including native foods – and the plethora of international cuisines brought to Australia by its immigrants. The mix of traditional flavours from around the world has inspired a flurry of innovation.

The Australian palate, like the nation, is relatively young, and the current sophistication belies a bleak culinary history. The early settlers struggled to maintain their stolid British or Irish diets, subsisting on salted meats – either roasted, stewed or baked into pies. Various early recipes indicate that native animals were eaten but, apart from kangaroo (whose tails make a fine soup), were rarely appreciated. The unfamiliar harshness of the Australian bush bred tough bellies used to tinned beef and damper (the most basic bread of flour, water and a pinch of salt).

Oysters for sale at Sydney Fish Market.

During the gold rush days of the 1850s, Chinese immigrants recognised the potential for cultivation and grew a great variety of herbs and vegetables. On some occasions, their industry saved white mining camps from starvation. Even the tiniest country town still has its Chinese restaurant, which for decades saved the citizens from complete culinary deprivation.

Even in the 1960s, the only things approaching an Australian cuisine were a couple of sweet confections – pavlova (a meringue pie shell, filled with fruit and cream), and lamingtons – sponge cubes covered with chocolate and coconut. Of course, there was always Vegemite – the black, salty yeast spread that most Aussies were weaned on, generally abhorred by others (including, famously, Barack Obama). Thanks to the climate, the 'barbie' (barbecue) did become an Australian institution, but British roast dinners were turned out every Sunday; and on Christmas Day, in steaming hot summers, the hot roast turkey graced every table.

CULINARY IMMIGRATION

The massive migration from Mediterranean countries after World War II made the first real dent on Australia's palate. Italians in particular helped revolutionise cooking, introducing wary

almost as often as in major cities. Diners enjoy pristine teppanyaki Japanese dining rooms, and take-away lakhsa stalls. Singapore-style food courts have sprung up everywhere; even local supermarkets now stock Thai and Indian ingredients. Lemongrass, chilli, coriander and cardamom give new depth and flavour to many essentially European dishes.

Not that Australia has tossed off its British culinary heritage altogether. Your fish'n'chips might still come in folded newspaper, but inside is fresh-grilled barramundi instead of

An upmarket restaurant in Melbourne.

Aussies to the wonders of pasta, garlic and olive oil. Today, each capital city has its share of Italian restaurants serving authentic, well-priced food: in Melbourne, Lygon Street is the heart of Little Italy; in Sydney, it's Norton Street in the Leichhardt neighbourhood.

This was only the beginning. The extension of immigration in the 1970s added myriad new cuisines. The great melting pot – or perhaps more appropriately, salad bowl – of Australian society meant that restaurants were suddenly opened by Lebanese, Turkish, Balkan, Hungarian and Spanish chefs. But the biggest impact by far has been made by the Asians. Restaurants featuring the cuisine of every country in the Pacific Rim are found in rural villages

deep-fried cod. And although pies'n'peas are now thankfully low on the food chain, you can still get the Australian version at the occasional retro-chic diner.

GOING LOCAL IN THE KITCHEN

The foundation of Australian cuisine is the quality and variety of its ingredients. Without them, all of the exotic spices and exciting recipes in the world would still result in dismal dining. Locally sourced produce, meats and fish are highly sought after. Aussies were slow to recognise the wealth of seafood in their waters, but now a range of fresh fish is on every menu. Small farms devote themselves to gourmet beef and poultry, while the quality of everyday vegetables rivals that grown on organic farms in Europe or the United States. Far from pining for imports of French cheese, Greek olives or Italian wine, Australians produce their own, which are often rated superior to the imports.

Australia can be divided into regions that are known for particular produce: King Island cream, Sydney rock oysters, Bowen mangoes, Coffin Bay scallops, Tasmanian salmon, Illabo milk-fed lamb. Each state has its acknowledged specialities. Tropical Queensland produces a wealth of exotic fruits, like Bowen mangoes

Western Australia has received rave reviews for its superb new wines from the southwest and for goat cheeses.

TOWARDS A FLAVOURFUL FUTURE

Established chefs who pioneered the Australian culinary adventure are being joined by a new generation of emerging talent eager to further explore gustatory possibilities. At top restaurants such as Sydney's Quay, customers make reservations months in advance. But kitchens throughout Australia are being taken over by

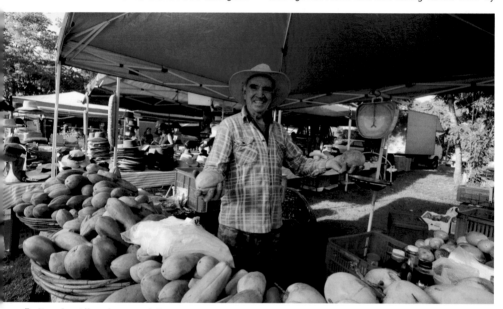

Fruit vendor at Yungabarra markets.

and papaya, succulent reef fish, mudcrabs and Moreton Bay Bugs (shellfish, not insects). From The Northern Territory come the white-fleshed barramundi and Mangrove Jack, while in Darwin, sample buffalo burgers and crocodile steaks. New South Wales has Hunter Valley wines, Balmain Bugs and perfect Sydney rock oysters. Victoria produces some of the tenderest meats, such as Gippsland beef and Meredith lamb, Mallee squab and corn-fed chicken. Tasmania is one of the least-polluted corners of the globe, and has gained national attention for its salmon, trout, cheeses, oysters and raspberries. South Australia is home to the Barossa Valley wine industry, Coffin Bay scallops, olive oils, tuna and cultivated native foods. Finally,

chefs in their 20s who are rated as highly as those far senior in both age and experience.

There is much flavour and excitement to be found in unpretentious neighbourhood restaurants, as well. Pub grub is as often spring rolls with satay dipping sauce or bruschetta with tomatoes, feta and basil as it is a meat pie or hamburger. Australians have a passion for pizza and will top a thin crust with everything from emu to pineapples to tandoori chicken. Local restaurants offer Moroccan-spiced chicken breast, chicken parmigiana, and lamb shank with red cabbage on the same menu. The wine and beer list at even the most humble restaurant will be more than adequate. Non-licensed establishments usually welcome BYO customers.

BUSH TUCKER MEETS THE LOCAVORE MOVEMENT

As Australia's culinary consciousness matured, it looked inward to the foods native to its shores.

The phrase 'bush tucker' has become the buzz word for truly Australian ingredients, referring to edible flora and fauna found in the great storehouse of the Outback. Possum, quandong fruit, eels, bush tomatoes, emu and even witchetty grubs were common items on the Aborigine menu. The natives thrived on these foods for 50,000 years, but the arriving Europeans dismissed them as uncivilised.

When the restaurant scene exploded in Australia in the 1990s, many restaurants began to incorporate native elements into their elegant recipes. Chefs happily experimented with riberries, bunya nuts, wild rosellas and Kakadu plums. High-end restaurants featured main courses which used ingredients from the Outback in ways the Aborigines never imagined (and not just because they did not own Cuisinarts).

Much of that frenetic energy has simmered down. Modern Australian cuisine ('Mod Oz') has been tempered to mean appreciating and incorporating indigenous ingredients without ignoring the conventional pantry. There is still an obvious delight in using the more unusual ingredients in ways to satisfy the curious gourmand. Every major city has at least one restaurant with distinctive Bush Tucker courses. Along with standard offerings like lamb short loin with spinach soufflé, fine-dining menus will feature roasted emu wrapped in prosciutto and seared kangaroo rump with seasonal vegetables. Sweet potato mash is served alongside salads of warrigal and samphire greens. Wattle seed, pepper leaf and lemon myrtle join thyme and oregano as seasonings. Meanwhile, pubs serve deep-fried crocodile bites and pizza with kangaroo topping along with the expected meat pies or fish and chips.

The change in the concept of bush tucker reflects an evolution in the Australian attitude towards food. Culinary writers and food industry analysts see an increasing interest in nutrition and in ways of using local ingredients and simple preparation techniques in cooking both at home and in restaurants. Those incorporate Australian ingredients, but that now often means foods from other cultures and traditions, which have taken root in Oz.

The emphasis now is as much on how and where foods are grown as on what they are. 'grow and buy Australian' is the new movement. Chefs and home cooks seek out locally sourced ingredients grown by sustainable methods. Consumers want to know that their produce was grown without pesticides and that their beef was grass-fed, their chickens free-range and their fish wild-caught. Farmers' markets are springing up like mushrooms after a heavy rain in

Kangaroo steaks.

city centres as well as country towns. Increasingly, consumers want to meet the person who planted the lettuce, made the cheese or picked the fruit. Websites supply consumers with links to Australian raised, grown or produced food and drink that aren't available in local shops.

Chefs are responding to diners' interests for healthier menu items. 'hyper-local' is the new restaurant buzz-phrase for a chef who maintains his or her own garden for produce and herbs. Others have arrangements with farmers for regular purchases of fresh produce, cheeses and meats. For restaurants, with their notoriously slim profit margin, buying locally is usually more economical. For their customers, it means fresher, healthier food.

AUSTRALIAN WINES

The Australian wine scene might be a late bloomer, but it has quickly earned the respect of the wine world's cognoscenti for the consistent quality delivered by the major labels and the mature treatment of varietals by the smaller producers.

When Australian wines first appeared on the international scene, they were considered a novelty. But now, each of the six states and both territories boast vineyards and wineries. The great differences in climates and soils, often even within a few kilometres, create conditions for a range of wines as vast as the continent.

Although more than 140 varieties of grapes are cultivated Down Under, Europeans found no native grapes. Cuttings of plants from the Cape of Good Hope arrived with the First Fleet in 1788. By the 1850s, grapes were being grown in most Australian states. When the phylloxera epidemic (which decimated Europe's vineyards in the 1870s) spread to Australia, strict regulations and quarantine limited the damage. As a result, vines that were planted in Australia before the epidemic are some of the oldest in the world. That said, most of the nearly 2,500 wineries in Australia are less than 30 years old.

The most popular red grapes are shiraz, cabernet sauvignon and merlot, while chardonnay, semillon and riesling are the most popular whites. Once a mainstay of the industry, fortified wines – largely muscats – still have a small but loyal following. 'Stickies' is the name for golden sweet dessert wines made from grapes deliberately affected by Noble Rot, which concentrates their flavours and sweetness.

Australia is the sixth-largest producer of wine in the world and the fourth-largest exporter, selling to more than 100 countries and contributing about A$5.5 billion to the nation's economy. The largest export market by volume is the UK, which imports more than 250 million litres (66 million gallons) of Australian wine annually. While the value of wine export to the US fell by 8 percent in 2014, the US and Canada are still the most lucrative markets

Early morning sun on the vines, Barossa Valley.

for Australian wine. Coming up fast is China; an expanding economy has turned China into the fastest-growing wine market in the world and the fourth-largest export market for Australia.

ECONOMIC AND CLIMATIC CHALLENGES

The Australian wine industry faces challenges from an oversupply of wine and grapes, the global economic downturn and a strong Australian dollar. There's also another obstacle not so easily dealt with: global warming. The continent is already at the edge of the sustainable grape-growing environment and most of Australia's 62 wine-growing regions are highly susceptible to climate change.

Australians thrive on challenges and, with the fate of one of their favourite luxuries and one of their most important exports at stake, this is one they take on with exceptional energy and enthusiasm. Wineries like Henschke in the Barossa and d'Arenberg in McClaren Vale, Tyrrell's in the Hunter Valley north of Sydney and Sandalford in West Australia draw on up to six generations of experience.

One advantage for Australian wine makers is the lack of the regulations that define so much of European wine-making. This leaves them free

elevations of 2,200 metres (7,000ft), it's the highest land in Australia. As conditions throughout the rest of the grape-growing world deteriorate, the microclimate in the Snowys should develop as one of the best for grape cultivation. Growers think this will give them up to a century of compensation for predicted climate change.

FLYING VINTNERS

Since the harvest in Australia is six months earlier than in the northern hemisphere, wine makers and grape growers can visit other wine

Wine barrels.

to innovate with flexible wine-making practices. Growers lead the way in 'canopy management', artificially controlling the heat and humidity of vineyards. Organic and sustainable viticulture and planting drought-resistant varieties are popular.

Mother Nature may be playing a role in climatic adaptation. Cleggert Wines in Langhorne Creek in South Australia has cultivated Australia's first indigenous grapes. Malian and shalistan are both the result of natural genetic variations of cabernet sauvignon grapes, which were noticed and propagated by the wine maker. Whether this was a genetic accident or an evolutionary response to conditions is a matter of debate.

Growers are buying property in the Snowy Mountains in southern New South Wales. With

regions internationally when those areas are busy with production. The passing on of proven techniques elsewhere to Australia's 'flying wine makers' is evened out by the introduction of Australian ideas and innovations, particularly in France, Spain and Italy.

The 2018 harvest was 1.79 million tonnes with some modest and patchy strengthening in average winegrape prices and exports. That still leaves an enormous inventory of existing vintages. Most of that consists of wines for which Australia is well known, particularly shiraz, cabernet and chardonnay. However, those are wines that are produced equally well in many other places and create a marketing challenge for the Australian wine makers.

EXPANDING THE MARKET

To avoid becoming stereotyped as producers of a limited range of wines, Australians are exploring the potential of other grapes. They are planting European varieties like barbera and chenin blanc, and some exotic varieties only a true oenophile would recognise, like saperavi from Southern Russia and Spain's doradillo, both of which are being cultivated in Victoria.

In the Granite Belt in Southeast Queensland, wine makers use the 'Strange Bird Wine Trail' to market unfamiliar European varietals. The map

shiraz. This area was not affected by the phylloxera epidemic, and as a result, it has some of the oldest vines in the world. It's fitting then that the National Wine Centre of Australia is in Adelaide (Corner of Hackney & Botanic roads; www.wineaustralia.com.au). The multimedia exhibits, demonstration vineyard and tasting room present an overview of the wine-making process and the delectable results. Nine distinct regions are within 90 minutes' drive of the Centre. Barossa Valley, Adelaide Hills and McLaren Vale are the best known, but Langhorne Creek is

Enjoying a wine tour in the Barossa Valley.

points out wineries which bottle alternative varietal wines like tempranillo, malbec and silvaner, which are rarely found on bottleshop shelves. While the immediate goal is to develop a domestic market for these wines, the long-range plan is to create wines fine enough to challenge their historic producers.

THE GRAND TOUR

Wine tourism is a major industry, with each wine region uncorking new initiatives to attract visitors. Wine-lovers will have far more tasting rooms (also called cellar doors) to visit than the time or fortitude to do them justice.

South Australia produces more than half of the nation's wine, and focuses on cabernet and

considered a hidden gem. It is home to about 20 wineries, including Bleasdale, where the Potts family has been making wine since 1860, and Zontes Footsteps, where enthusiastic newcomers produced their first vintage in 2003.

Victoria boasts five diverse wine regions within an hour of Melbourne. Most of the wineries offer amenities beyond their liquid attractions. Cafés, spas, fine dining, luxury accommodation, even art galleries are part of the experience. The Yarra Valley has the oldest vineyards and there is a definite Mediterranean influence which reflects the approach by Italian wine makers who arrived in the 1860s. Meanwhile, the Geelong region along the Great Ocean Road in the southwest corner of Victoria takes advantage of climate and soil similar to Bordeaux and Burgundy.

New South Wales has the broadest range of climates in Australia, from the Alpine conditions of the Snowy Mountains to the coastal breezes of Shoalhaven Coast and the cool conditions of the Southern Highlands. With over 130 wineries, Hunter Valley, a two-hour drive north of Sydney, is the most established region, with a reputation for exquisite semillon and shiraz and acclaimed chardonnay and verdelho. Tourists can visit the Visitors' Information Centre in Pokolbin for

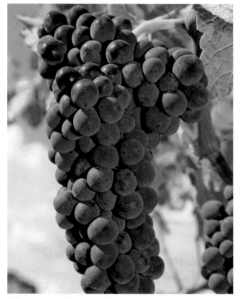

Shiraz grapes from the Barossa Valley.

maps, information and a chance to sample a few wines. It's also possible to sample many of the region's wines at the many tasting centres in and around Pokolbin. The Small Winemakers Centre, Boutique Wine Centre, Hermitage Road Cellars and the Hunter Valley Winegrowers are cellar doors showcasing smaller wineries which emphasise their individual approach to their art. South of Sydney, the Shoalhaven Coast is home to Coolangatta Estate, which was started in 1822. Nearby Kladis Estate is a relative newcomer, just 25 years old. Australian wine guru James Halliday ranks both as 5-star wineries.

The Australian Capital Region, while technically and politically independent, is physically within New South Wales. Clonakilla Estate at Murrumbateman routinely produces the finest shiraz-viognier red blend (like Côte de Rotie) made in Australia.

For many years wine aficionados ignored Queensland's wines. The region produced well-respected wines until the 1930s when the domestic market turned to the southern states. Not until Ballandean Estate near Stanthorpe in the Granite Belt started producing wine commercially in 1970 did attention once again shift northward. Queensland wines are considered lighter, crisper and fruitier than varietals from other states. The most established region is the Granite Belt. Three hours west of Brisbane and the Gold Coast, it is 1,000 metres (3,000ft) above sea level and is the only area in Queensland with four distinct seasons. The crescent of higher ground from the Sunshine Coast Hinterlands to Brisbane's Scenic Rim and the Gold Coast Hinterland is home to several dozen new, small wineries. For a completely different experience, wineries near Cairns make wines from tropical fruits like mango, passionfruit and bush lime.

The southwest corner of Western Australia is home to more than 170 wineries in nine distinct regions. It is known for its cabernet sauvignon but it also has a reputation for sauvignon blanc and zinfandel. With vines planted as early as 1829, viticulture in the Swan District, which stretches from the east side of Perth northward, predates both Victoria and South Australia. The headliner region is Margaret River. Surrounded on three sides by the Indian and Great Southern Oceans, it has a distinctly Mediterranean climate and powerful cabernet and merlot. It also has the most well-developed and comprehensive tourism industry.

The island of Tasmania has a cool climate which lends itself to producing excellent sparkling wines. The sometimes-fickle pinot noir enjoys the maritime influence and thrives here. Most of the 60 or so wineries are very small operations run by passionate vintners. The Jansz Vineyard, with its connection to the French Champagne house Roederer, is credited with bringing attention to Tasmania's sparkling potential. Wineries are clustered around Hobart on the Tasman Sea on the eastern side of the island and Launceston and the Tamar River to the west. On the east coast, Frogmore Creek is noted for its sustainable, organic viticulture techniques, while its wines have won awards for their compatibility with Asian cuisine.

WHERE SPORT IS SUPREME

If you want to join the locals for a pint and a chat, you'll need to know how the local team is getting on.

Arguably, sport was the language in which Australians first shouted: 'Hey world, here we are!' Wherever people gather – in pubs, clubs, the workplace or around the barbecue – sport tends to be the major topic of conversation. They bet on it and brag about it, they eulogise or verbally flay its performers, analyse its conduct and speculate about its future. One thing they never do is tire of it.

THE GOLDEN 1950S

The sports fixation reached its apogee in the 1950s, a period when Australia dominated in world swimming and tennis, and arrived as a force to reckon with in track and field, cycling, boxing, sculling and golf. The climax came in 1956: Australia dusted the United States 5–0 in the Davis Cup tennis final, while at the Melbourne Olympic Games, Aussie athletes won 35 medals – 13 gold, eight silver and 14 bronze – an astonishing number for the small population.

Australia has always punched above its weight at the Olympics, and continues to produce track and field stars. For many proud Aussies it all culminated in Cathy Freeman's gold-medal-winning run in the 400 metres at the Sydney Olympics in 2000.

THE CRICKET MANIA

It's only in summer, when cricket grabs the public's imagination, that Australians are more or less united in their sporting focus. Spectator interest settles squarely on the national team in its test match encounters with the West Indies, India, Pakistan, New Zealand, South Africa and, most crucially, England.

A test match takes up to five days to complete; even then it frequently finishes in a draw. Yet the game is followed with religious zeal. Radios blare out the ball-by-ball commentary at the beach; pub

Aaron Finch bats at the Manuka Oval, Canberra.

discussions focus on the diving catch in the slips; and cricket is on TV, day in, day out. In the more than 100 years since Australia played its first Test series against England, nobody has been better at the game than a slightly built fellow by the name of Donald Bradman. 'The Don' was to cricket what Pelé was to football or Babe Ruth was to baseball.

A Test series is played over three to five matches, with the battlegrounds moving between Sydney, Melbourne, Adelaide, Brisbane and Perth. Ground capacities range from 30,000 to 100,000; lovers of the game say there are few greater sporting moments than to experience the opening over of an England v Australia Test before a capacity crowd. The Australian team was the top-ranking team for most of the 1990s and 2000s but has recently slipped in the rankings. Probably nothing hurt quite so much as the thrashing the England team handed out when they toured Australia in 2010, although, the 2018 ball-tampering controversy – when three players and the head coach were all implicated in cheating during a Test against South Africa – was the real low point for the national team.

If a five-day Test sounds too much to take in, consider watching a 'limited-over' or one-day game. As the name implies, these are quick affairs that come and go in a heated rush and

most popular football leagues in the world. It is estimated that each winter weekend in Melbourne, one person in 16 attends an Australian Football League (AFL) game; thousands more

The uncompromising style of defence in rugby (and lack of protective gear) prompted one American football coach to observe: 'Our guys could never stand up to that sort of constant punishment'.

The Queensland Maroons take on the New South Wales Blues in Brisbane.

often wring participants and spectators dry with tension and drama. A standard one-day game gives each side 50 overs to bat and 50 to bowl, while the much newer T20 format gives each side 20 overs and usually lasts about 3 hours.

AUSSIE RULES FOOTIE

On the surface it seems incongruous that a country so fond of cricket, with all its esoteric customs and traditions, could have given birth to a game as apparently anarchic as Australian Rules football. The sport may be virtually unknown beyond Australia's shores, but in the southern states it's a passion, particularly in Melbourne: the city may have only 4 million inhabitants, yet Aussie Rules ranks among the

follow on TV. September's AFL grand final is one of the great sporting experiences.

RUGBY LEAGUE

In Sydney and points north, footie of a different kind is the winter preoccupation. Rugby League started as a professional alternative to Rugby Union. It's played in a half-dozen provinces of a half-dozen countries, and to that degree qualifies as an international sport. League attendances are nothing like as large as those of the AFL, but the Sydney clubs – such as St George, the Western Suburbs, Manly and Parramatta – keep their players fabulously well paid through the revenue from their slot machines and licensed clubs. In Brisbane and Sydney, the game found its roots in the working-class inner suburbs and, despite media overkill, hasn't significantly broadened its social base.

Rugby League is a physical rather than cerebral game. You don't have to play this game to feel how much it hurts. The game's appeal rests in its strong gladiatorial image and macho confrontations as pairs of teams slam into one another – although fans believe that a dazzling backline movement resulting in a try (touchdown) is one of the real joys in sporting life.

Two or three times a year in the State of Origin series, the New South Wales and Queens-

Jockey Michelle Payne on Prince of Penzance.

land teams engage in a brutal battle. The Aussie national side, known as the Kangaroos, regularly hops through tours of France and Great Britain unbeaten.

RUGBY UNION

According to its devotees, Rugby Union is 'the game they play in heaven' – which is remarkable considering its relative popularity in New South Wales and Queensland, where angels are in short supply. If you enjoy rugby, watch the Wallabies (the national side) in action, especially if there's a spare ticket for a Bledisloe Cup match, which sees the Wallabies face up to the mighty All Blacks from New Zealand.

At club level, Rugby Union projects a social spirit often lacking in the professional codes.

The game has a 'silvertail' (upper-crust) image based partly on its strength in the universities and private schools. The 'flying Ella brothers' of the 1970s were a contradiction to the class rule, three gifted Aboriginal athletes from Sydney's inner southern suburbs who all wound up wearing the gold shirts of the Australian team.

SOCCER

The history of soccer in Australia bears little comparison to other forms of football. The game first kicked off more than a century ago among British migrants, then more or less stagnated until post-World War II, with the arrival of migrants from Southern Europe. Now most clubs in the National Soccer competition – the A League – are dominated by players from the Italian, Greek, Croatian, Slavic, Maltese, Dutch and Macedonian communities. The national team, the Socceroos, continue to edge their way up the international ladder, and their success in the 2006 World Cup – the first World Cup they qualified for since 1978 – consolidated by their performance in South Africa in 2010, has helped revive the sport's popularity at home. While Australia's 2014 and 2018 World Cup performances were far from successful, soccer remains popular.

GREAT INDIVIDUALISTS

The 1950s and 60s brought forth a rash of tennis talents, including Rod Laver, John Newcombe, Evonne Goolagong-Cawley and Pat Cash. Recent hopes, including Adelaide's Lleyton Hewitt, have not managed to reach the same heights consistently.

Australian golfers have generally kept their end up, and Greg Norman, 'the Great White Shark', was a phenomenon. Today Jason Day is the pick of the bunch.

But it has been those sports that pit the individual against the elements which have brought out the best in Australians. It's not surprising that swimming has been a top sport: kids are tossed into the pool almost as soon as they can walk. In the 1950s, Dawn Fraser became Australia's darling as much for her cheeky anti-establishment attitude as her victories. In the 1970s, Shane Gould followed in her wake, with a slew of Olympic medals. Australia's most recent swimming superstar is Ian Thorpe, who won three gold and two silver medals in the 2000 Olympics, and in 2003 became the first swimmer ever to win three consecutive world titles in one event, the 400 metres freestyle. At the 2004 Olympics, 'the Thorpedo' added four medals to his Olympic tally: two gold, one silver and one bronze. By contrast, the swim team performed poorly at the 2012 London Olympics, with a total of only 10 medals (including one gold) derided as the worst result in more than 30 years, and although they did better in Rio in 2016, they have a way to go to recapture former glory.

By contrast, on the track Sally Pearson won gold in the 100 metres hurdles in 2012, setting

up with the best of them. Yet the real local heroes of the track are the V8 touring car drivers. The class attracts heavy sponsorship for its championship series, the highlight of which is the Bathurst 1000 held in October, an endurance event that attracts an international field of drivers. The Formula 1 Grand Prix is held on Melbourne's Albert Park circuit in early March.

A NATION OF PUNTERS

It is often said that Aussies would gamble on just about anything, but there's only one race that cap-

Christopher Ikonomidis celebrates with fans after Australia wins the 2018 World Cup qualifying match at Allianz Stadium, Sydney.

a new Olympic record time of 12.35s (the medal sits with her 2011 and 2017 World championship golds, and silver medals from the 2008 Summer Olympics and the 2013 World Championships).

Aussies have ruled the waves almost since surfing's inception as a competitive sport, with Mark Richards' four world titles marking him as one of the world's greatest-ever surfers. Names like Nat Young and Tom Carroll have permanent niches in a national surfing hall of fame, and Mick Fanning is a living legend.

Australian motor racing has produced Formula 1 world champions in Jack Brabham (three-times winner) and Alan Jones, while recently retired driver Mark Webber was right

tures everyone's imagination and puts millions of dollars through the bookmakers and the agencies of the Totalizator Agency Board (TAB). That race is the Melbourne Cup.

At 3.30pm Melbourne time on the first Tuesday in November, the whole of Australia stops for the running of this classic horse race. The 3,200-metre (2-mile) event has become an international thoroughbred classic since it was first held at Melbourne's Flemington course in 1861. It's a public holiday in Victoria, and even the process of government is suspended so that the nation's decision-makers can watch the race. In 2015, Michelle Payne, riding Prince of Penzance, was the first woman to win Australia's greatest race.

📷 SURF CULTURE

Introduced to Australia in 1912 by Duke Kahanamoku of Honolulu, surfing has become a way of life for many of Australia's coastal dwellers.

On a good day at Noosa Heads, Manly or countless other Australian beaches, thousands of surfers of all ages and on all kinds of equipment clog the line-ups. Surfing today is as mainstream as tennis, golf, cricket or football, and kids on the coast grow up riding every kind of surf craft imaginable. If you come across a Saturday-morning 'nippers' (junior surf life-saving) session, with kids who look as if they're barely out of nappies charging in and out of the waves, you would swear they're breeding a new, genetically modified amphibious race here.

The old surf clubs with their prime beachfront positions are still the social hubs of the Australian coast, where you can enjoy a cheap meal or cold beer, or succumb to the dreaded 'pokies' (fruit machines), all with unmatched ocean views. The old, framed black-and-white photos of past surf champions peer down, echoing earlier, simpler times. The worldwide boom of the surf industry means that professional surfers have the opportunity to set themselves up financially for life. Young surfers barely out of their teens drive luxury 4WD vehicles and buy mansions.

For a real surf experience, take a lesson, sit under a pandanus tree with a pie and a chocolate milk, go for another surf, then retreat to the surf club for a steak and a beer. Just see if you don't feel strangely good about the world again. Then go to bed, wake up and do it all over again.

Contemplating the waves on Main Beach, along the Gold Coast in Queensland.

King's Beach, at Caloundra, is the perfect place to learn to surf; the waves are typically small and the locals are friendly. Take your board up near the headland on the northern edge.

The northern end of Bondi Beach has been rated a gentle 4 (with 10 as the most hazardous); the southern side is rated as a 7 due to a rather strong and consistent rip current.

The SLSA has over 150,000 members, of whom more than 40,000 actively patrol 400 Australian beaches. That makes it one of the largest volunteer organisations in the country.

A brief history of surfing

Australian surfing as we know it began at Sydney's Freshwater Beach, when visiting Hawaiian champion Duke Kahanamoku put on his historic display in 1914. However, there is some evidence of a surf culture among indigenous Australians. The foundation meeting of the Greenmount Surf Club in 1908 paid tribute to a local Aboriginal man, named Churaki, for the many daring rescues he carried out in the surf prior to the club's formation. Surf life-saving clubs were formed in the early 1900s to protect public safety, and quickly grew as social hubs for the emerging beach culture. Surfboards were built for ocean rescues and manned by teams of earnest paddlers, but proved poorly designed for rough ocean conditions.

Surf clubs remained unchallenged as the pinnacle of beach culture until the 1950s, when a group of Americans visited Australia to coincide with the 1956 Melbourne Olympics. Their surf-riding displays on revolutionary, short, light Malibu boards reverberated around the country. Freshly inspired surfers rejected the conservatism of the surf clubs for the freewheeling lifestyle of the wave-chasing surfie.

In the late 1960s and early 1970s, surfing's image reached an all-time low, associated as it was with laziness, drug use and antisocial behaviour. Beneath the hippy trappings, however, surfer rivalry was pushing the sport to greater heights. In the late 1970s, Australia's success in the first ever international competitions made the dream of pro-surfing a distinct possibility. Today, lucrative careers with million-dollar salaries and worldwide superstardom beckon the most successful surfers, whose ranks include legendary Australian Mick Fanning, who was attacked by a great white while competing at Jeffreys Bay in South Africa in 2015, on live TV, and escaped by punching the shark.

The mission of Surf Life Saving Australia (SLSA) is to provide a safe beach environment throughout Australia. They patrol beaches and educate the public about safety.

Olympic swimming champion and pioneer surfer Duke Kahanamoku (1890 - 1968), a Hawaiian hero, poses for a photograph in 1935.

A koala relaxes at Lone Pine Sanctuary in Brisbane.

ONE-OF-A-KIND WILDLIFE

Australia has been a separate island long enough for evolution to take a unique path. The result is a range of plants and animals that are found nowhere else on Earth.

Research findings are thin as to just how many people around the world actually believe that kangaroos are a regular sight on the city streets of Australia. It has become one of those stereotypical notions or urban legends, alongside the idea that most Aussie men are like Crocodile Dundee. Both ideas are popular, and both are almost entirely false. And yet, if you just wander down past the National War Memorial in Canberra, the nation's capital, at dusk, there's a very good chance that you'll find a mob of kangaroos grazing on the lawn.

In smaller towns and settlements, many of which appear to have only a toehold on the harsh antipodean landscape, the bush is often just over the back fence. The proximity of the wild means there's a fair likelihood of encountering a smattering of mammals, birds or reptiles that will surprise and delight a visitor from overseas. Even in the big cities, bereft of kangaroos as they may be, there will be possums to intrigue the tourist and frustrate the locals, whose fruit they eat and whose eaves they burrow into.

Visitors can feed and pet the kangaroos at Lone Pine Sanctuary.

Of the unique animals Down Under, possums, at least, have their counterparts in the Americas (the Virginia opossum); but the Australian kangaroo stands alone. There is nothing like it anywhere else in the world, and there's a reason for that. The sheer age of the Australian landmass and its isolation from other continents allowed its animals and plants to adapt to their unique environment and evolve independently of the rest of the world, unchallenged until the arrival of the European colonists and the onset of the technological age.

ECCENTRIC MAMMALS

For the perfect example of a uniquely evolved animal, take the Australian mammal. Warm-blooded and furred, mammals almost all give birth to live young and suckle them. There are three groups: placentals, marsupials and monotremes.

Elsewhere on Earth the placental group proliferates. However, very few examples of this group can be found among the native Australian fauna. The native dog, the dingo, is one, but they were introduced into Australia from South-East Asia sometime within the last 12,000 years (we know this because there are no dingo remains on Tasmania, which split from the mainland then); latest evidence suggests they arrived with migrants between 10,000 and 5,000 years ago.

In Australia, marsupials are by far the most prominent group. Marsupials give birth to partially formed embryos, which remain secure in a pouch until they are strong enough to survive independently. Most marsupials are herbivorous, but there are some that eat insects, small reptiles or smaller mammals. The larger members of the carnivorous group include the Tasmanian devil and the Tasmanian tiger (thylacine); the latter, however, is now thought extinct (except in the minds of a handful of people who believe that a few survive in the Tasmanian wilderness). Killed on the mainland by dingoes, and hunted into oblivion in Tasmania by sheep-farming settlers, the last-known live thylacine died in captivity in 1936.

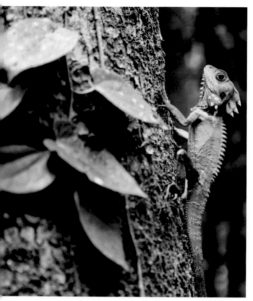

A Boyd forest dragon perches on a tree near Kuranda.

Ⓞ SAVING AUSTRALIA

A coordinated conservation movement emerged in Australia in the late 1970s, around the time of the nationwide campaign to protect Tasmania's Franklin River from being dammed. The eco-movement gathered impetus during the 1980s, and is now well known. Environmental activists have managed to ensure many wild places are now safe for future generations to enjoy. Notable victories include the protection of such landmark destinations as Fraser Island, Kakadu, the Daintree Rainforest and Tasmania's Southwest National Park. The battle to save the Great Barrier Reef continues.

It is the herbivores that abound in Australia, including the shy koala, which is not even remotely related to the bear family; many varieties of possum, including the ringtail and the sugar glider; the wombat; and the macropods, or hopping marsupials, such as the kangaroo, wallaby and potoroo. Sadly for visitors just passing through, these species tend to be most active at dawn and dusk. Unfortunately, the typical Australian visitor is most likely to encounter these crepuscular creatures on the road, as a fleeting glimpse in the headlights of a vehicle.

The koala's habit of sleeping openly in the forks of gum (eucalyptus) trees made it an easy target for colonial hunters seeking koala fur. So great was the slaughter that urgent steps were taken to save the koala in the 1920s. This laid-back marsupial is now a completely protected animal. The wombat is related to the koala, but instead of making its home up a tree and dining on gum leaves, it uses its powerful digging paws to make burrows under stumps, logs or in creek banks. It lives on roots, leaves and bark.

Monotremes are a unique and extraordinary group of animals. Rather than giving birth to live young, they lay eggs. However, they then suckle their young and display many other mammalian traits. The amphibious duck-billed platypus is a monotreme, as is the echidna (also known as the spiny anteater). These two species are the only examples of living monotremes, although the fossil record suggests that monotremes were once widespread.

SNAKES AND LIZARDS

Reptiles figure prominently in Aboriginal legend, particularly the venomous snakes such as the taipan, tiger snake, death adder and brown snake. Non-venomous species are also plentiful, as are lizards, which range from the tiniest of skinks to goannas more than 2 metres (6ft) long. Among the more exotic is the frill-necked lizard, which erects a frock of skin around its neck when confronted with danger. Don't confuse the frill-necked lizard with the bearded dragon, which has a mane of prickly spines. The blue-tongued lizard hunts snails and insects, often in city gardens. The eponymous blue tongue is often displayed as a bluff against danger. Australia also has more than its share of frogs and toads.

SEA LIFE

Queensland's Great Barrier Reef is a wonderland blessed with numerous fish, shell and polyp species peculiar to Australian waters. But you don't have to go snorkelling on the reef to sample the coastal wildlife; a scramble over any coastal rock platform will reveal shellfish, starfish, anemones and crabs. Raising your eyes to the open sea may reward you with sightings of dolphins and whales. The latter follow migratory paths along the west, south and east coasts according to season. Sharks and lethal box jellyfish are the ones to avoid.

BIRD LIFE

Australia's early explorers were as intrigued by the birdlife they saw in the skies as they were by the kangaroos and koalas found on the ground. Flocks of raucous parrots and cockatoos can be found plundering the fruit trees. They include brilliantly plumed rosellas and lorikeets.

Eagles, hawks, crows and cuckoos of native origin all thrive, while the variety of habitats allows for many species of waterfowl. Some were hunted by the early settlers, and development has consumed many coastal habitats. Luckily, protective measures have saved many species from extinction.

NATURE RESERVES

If you don't have time to spend weeks in the bush spotting creatures in their natural environment, a suitable compromise is a visit to any of the larger nature reserves that exist on the fringes of the cities. Otherwise you can go to any of the city zoos, such as Sydney's Taronga Park or the Melbourne Zoo and see most forms of local wildlife.

PLANT LIFE

From Queensland's steamy jungles to the delicate blossoms of New South Wales, there is no end to the variety of plant life. Like many animals, Australian flora has been affected by the introduction of foreign plants. Some of these have flourished, completely altering the ecological balance. In the cities, the replanting of native trees has encouraged bird and insect life to return to these areas.

Scuba diving in Cairns.

Ø TREES OF LIFE

From a stroll through the leafy outer suburbs of Sydney to a bushwalk in the jarrah forests of Western Australia, you can easily expose your senses to the great Aussie bush. Just the range of eucalypts is immense, from a low, stunted, scrub-like bush to the towering species of the highland woodlands. The mountain ash eucalyptus, found in the forests of Victoria and Tasmania, is the tallest flowering plant on Earth, growing to 70–90 metres (230–300ft) or more. Ghost gums appear silvery-white under the light of the moon, while rock-hard ironbarks are capable of blunting the toughest timber saws. Australia draws its national colours from the gold and green of the hardy acacia, or wattle – it is usually one of the first species to rejuvenate after bushfires.

Most Australian trees have very hard timber, which made clearing the land an extremely arduous task for the early settlers. In Tasmania, the Huon pine was found to be one of the best building timbers ever, and was especially prized by boat-builders. Western Australia's jarrah and the tough karri are also superb construction timbers. The jarrah forests are currently under threat from mining and foresters, and scientists are exploring ways to combat a disease called 'die-back' that has affected the forests. A concerted effort to replant some of the tree life laid waste in the name of agricultural development is currently in process.

📷 DANGEROUS WILDLIFE

Australia has many creatures that are hazardous to humans, but it's a two-way street. Humankind has been responsible for wiping out countless species, and we're only now realising the destruction we've caused.

The second most famous interlopers onto the Australian mainland (after the First Fleet) were the cane toads. These giants were introduced in Queensland in 1935 to eradicate beetles that were attacking the key sugar-cane crop. The toads were unsuccessful in their official goal, and unfortunately they also wreaked havoc on local insect species. Even worse, the cane toad is toxic to anything that tries to eat it, giving it a privileged location on the food chain.

The cane toad is now spreading relentlessly across the country. Its story highlights the dangers of introduced species. Rabbits, foxes and cats have caused untold damage over the last 200 years, as have starlings and mynah birds. One stowaway starfish is estimated to have spawned 100 million descendants in Victoria's Port Phillip Bay.

The problem is that most introduced species thrive in an environment where they lack natural predators but enjoy a ready supply of food. Foxes and feral cats prey on small native mammals, rabbits destroy crops, wild pigs destroy vegetation around watercourses, and starlings, introduced to control caterpillars that were eating fruit crops in the Melbourne hinterland in 1857, began to feast on the fruit themselves.

When an adult cane toad is threatened, it secretes a milky-white fluid known as bufotoxin from glands behind the eye. This toxin is a Class 1 drug under Australian law there have been human deaths due to the consumption o licking of cane toads.

The starling is a threat to the native flora and fauna of Australia. WA has gone to great lengths to limit the bird's territory.

Although cute, rabbits are an invasive species and a serious threat to crops.

A saltwater crocodile.

Australia's natural-born killers

Australia is a land where lethal killers abound...or crawl or slither or float or dive. Scorpions hide beneath rocks across the continent, great white sharks attack the occasional surfer in South Australia and WA, saltwater crocodiles stalk fishermen (as do box jellyfish) in the Northern Territory, the venomous blue-ringed octopus waits on the reefs, and the funnel-web spider lurks in the gardens of suburban Sydney.

And as if that wasn't enough, Australia possesses more species of venomous snakes than any other country on Earth. It is home to 40 snake species, and 12 of them, like the stunning copperhead, can inflict a fatal wound. The inland taipan, or 'fierce snake', takes the prize as the world's most venomous land snake: it is 50 times more venomous than the cobra (although it is far from the deadliest – as, despite its name it is relatively placid – although obviously don't touch one if you encounter it). This rich reptilian diversity is not limited to the mainland: 32 known species of venomous sea snakes reside offshore.

However, dangerous liaisons between humans and these creatures are rare, with most sightings of killer animals confined to city zoos. In the wild, most animals prefer escape to confrontation with potentially lethal human beings.

the past 100 years, bites from Sydney funnel-web spiders have caused 13 deaths, and seven of those were children. Luckily, since an anti-venom was developed in 1981, there have been no casualties. If you are bitten by any large, black spider while in Australia, seek medical attention immediately.

An inland taipan (Oxyuranus microlepidotus), the most venomous snake in the world, is almost never photographed due to its extremely shy nature.

Bouddi National Park.

The Big Red sand dune on the edge of the Simpson Desert.

A glorious jacaranda tree, a common sight along the Central Coast in spring.

INTRODUCTION

A detailed guide to the entire country, with main sights cross-referenced by number to the maps.

The vast Australian landscape.

Australia boasts fantastic cities: Sydney, with its glorious harbour and the twin icons of the Opera House and the Harbour Bridge; Melbourne, famed for its laneways, cosmopolitan café culture and plethora of sporting arenas; Brisbane, characterised by its subtropical colonial architecture; Canberra, full of museums and galleries, and surrounded by incredible bushwalking trails; Adelaide, and its great churches and parks; Perth, with its river and atmospheric old port; Hobart, and its colonial heart and mountain backdrop; Darwin, known for its frontier town flavour.

Every country has cities, but no other country has a vast Outback with Uluru at its parched red centre. Nowhere else has the Great Barrier Reef, the stunning Kimberley, the pristine wilderness of Tasmania, or the alpine splendour of the Great Dividing Range.

So make the most of the cities and enjoy the coast. The popular image of Aussies as surf-loving beach dwellers is grounded in truth – there are, after all, tens of thousands of kilometres of unspoilt beaches here – but the rewards for those who dig a little deeper are rich. Australia's Aboriginal population thrived for 50,000 years without the need for cities, and they spread across this entire continent, leaving tantalising fragments of rock art as their only record. You shouldn't limit your Australian experience to the well-trodden path.

Great Barrier Reef.

So visit Sydney, but go to the Blue Mountains as well, or get right out to the isolated old mining town of Broken Hill. Visit Melbourne, but don't forget to go up into the high country and drive along the Great Ocean Road. See Brisbane and then head north to the Great Barrier Reef, the islands and Daintree's tropical rainforest. From Canberra, head into the Snowy Mountains. After Adelaide, visit Barossa wine country or the underground desert dwellings of Coober Pedy. Perth has the Kimberley to the north and the ancient forests and wineries of Margaret River to the south. Hobart gives access to the wonders of Freycinet National Park or Cradle Mountain, and the remarkable Port Arthur Penal Settlement. Darwin is the jumping-off point for Kakadu, with its rich Aboriginal culture, tropical wetlands and saltwater crocodiles.

And always, so far from all of these, but essential for anyone really wanting to taste the difference of this ancient land, is Uluru, the rock at the heart of the real Australia.

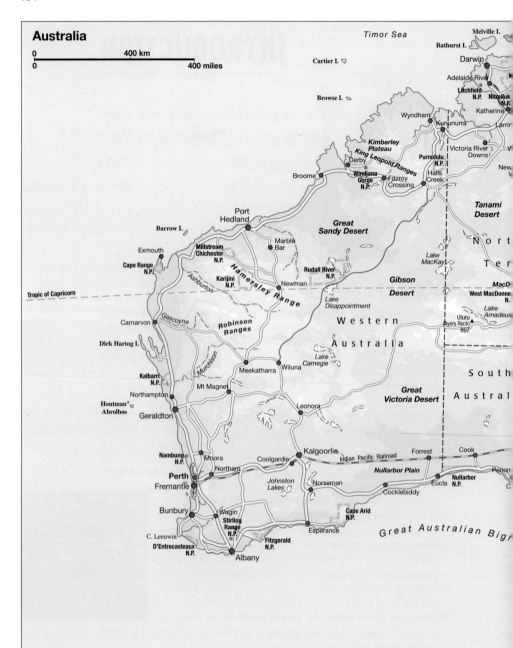

Australia

0   400 km
0   400 miles

Timor Sea

Melville I.
Bathurst I.
Cartier I.
Darwin
Adelaide River
Litchfield N.P.
Browse I.
Nitmiluk N.P.
Katherine
Wyndham
Larrir
Kununurra
Kimberley Plateau
King Leopold Ranges
Derby
Victoria River Downs
Purnululu N.P.
New
Windjana Gorge N.P.
Broome
Fitzroy Crossing
Halls Creek
Tanami Desert
Port Hedland
Great Sandy Desert
Nort
Barrow I.
Marble Bar
Ter
Exmouth
Millstream Chichester N.P.
Lake MacKay
Cape Range N.P.
Rudall River N.P.
Ashburton
Karijini N.P.
Hamersley Range
Newman
Gibson Desert
MacD
West MacDonne N.
Tropic of Capricorn
Lake Disappointment
Uluru (Ayers Rock) 867
Lake Amadeus
Carnarvon
Gascoyne
Robinson Ranges
Western
Australia
South
Dirk Hartog I.
Lake Carnegie
Austral
Murchison
Meekatharra
Wiluna
Kalbarri N.P.
Mt Magnet
Great Victoria Desert
Northampton
Houtman Abrolhos
Leonora
Geraldton
Nambung N.P.
Moora
Kalgoorlie
Coolgardie
Forrest
Cook
Perth
Northam
Indian Pacific Railroad
Penon
Fremantle
Johnston Lakes
Norseman
Nullarbor Plain
Nullarbor N.P.
Eucla
C
Bunbury
Cocklebiddy
Wagin
Stirling Range N.P.
Cape Arid N.P.
C. Leeuwin
Esperance
Great Australian Bigl
D'Entrecasteaux N.P.
Fitzgerald N.P.
Albany

I N D I A N   O C E A N

The Opera House.

SYDNEY

The glittering harbour with its coat-hanger bridge, the pearly sails of the Opera House, the bronzed life-savers at Bondi Beach... most of the symbols that define Australia are located in Sydney.

Sydney is where Australian indulgence finds its most spectacular backdrop, a city where leisure has been elevated to an art form. Yet Australia's largest metropolis, with four-and-a-half million people, can still baffle expectations. The natural beauty of the harbour and beaches often stands in stark relief to the man-made landscape: the narrow, traffic-clogged streets, the lacklustre architecture of its inner city, the endless orange-roofed expanse of its suburbia. However, if this is your first stop in Australia and the flight path of your aircraft takes you in a loop west of the city, with the Opera House and the Harbour Bridge cast in miniature against the harbour, chances are you'll be quickly smitten.

SYDNEY'S ORIGINS

To its critics – who mostly live in its traditional rival, Melbourne – Sydney is all glitz, obsessed with superficial show and appearance above substance. But none of this seems to matter to most Sydneysiders, and even less to visitors. The city continually lures many of the wealthiest, smartest and most artistically talented from the rest of Australia, and increasingly, the world, while real-estate values go through the roof. To many people, this is the capital of the Pacific Rim.

Yet few of the world's great cities have had such an unpromising start. On 26 January 1788, a fleet of 11 ships under

the command of Captain Arthur Phillip landed a seasick gaggle of male convicts while the local Aborigines threw stones in a vain attempt to drive them away. The officers pitched their tents east of the freshwater Tank Stream at Sydney Cove, with the prisoners and their guards to the west (creating a social division that lasts to this day, with the wealthier suburbs of the east versus the have-nots of the west). Two weeks later, the women convicts disembarked, with a few children in tow (some of whom had been born during the 11-month voyage).

Main attractions
Harbour Bridge
Opera House
Botanic Gardens
Sydney Tower
Bondi Market
Blue Mountains

North Sydney Olympic Pool.

Maps on pages 108, 115

Sydney

0   500 m
0   500 yds

Light rail

Today the site of these early landings is one of the most visited spots in Sydney: **Circular Quay** . This is the gateway to **Sydney Harbour** and the place where everyone should begin a visit. Ferries, water taxis and tour boats of every stripe plough in and out of its docks, taking passengers up and down the grand waterway of Port Jackson, described by Phillip as: 'The finest harbour in the world, where a thousand ships of the line may ride with the most perfect security.'

To get a feel for Sydney, hop on a ferry, take a seat outside and don't get off at all; all ferries eventually return home to the quay. There's a great view of Sydney's two familiar icons.

THE HARBOUR BRIDGE

The first of Sydney's icons to be constructed was the **Harbour Bridge** . The world's largest steel-arch bridge, it was erected during the depths of the 1930s Depression as a symbol of hope in the future. It became dubbed the Coat Hanger, the Toast Rack and the Iron Lung (the latter for the number of people given work on its construction, which kept Sydney breathing). These days, despite dire predictions that rust is rotting it away from the inside, the bridge is still the major link between Sydney's northern and southern suburbs (there's also an underground tunnel).

The southeastern pylon on the Harbour Bridge is home to the **Pylon Lookout** museum (tel: 02-9240 1100; www.pylonlookout.com.au; daily 10am–5pm), which leads up to a viewing platform with superb views of the harbour and city. Small-group guided climbs to the bridge's summit, each lasting 3.5 hours, can be booked through BridgeClimb (tel: 02-8274 7777; www.bridgeclimb.com; daily). Unless you're seriously scared of heights, spend the cash and do the climb. You'll forget all about the deeply unattractive jumpsuits that are compulsory for safety once you see the priceless view from the top.

THE OPERA HOUSE

The city's second symbol began construction in 1959, and today is the most-photographed site in Sydney. The **Opera House** (tel: 02-9250 7777; www.sydney-operahouse.com; guided one-hour tours daily between 9am–5pm; a two-hour backstage tour including breakfast is limited to 12 visitors, daily at 7am) is without a doubt one of the world's most spectacular buildings (or, as art critic Robert Hughes would have it, 'the biggest environmental site-specific sculpture south of the Equator'). It was designed by Jørn Utzon, a Dane, after an international competition – although nobody at the time quite knew how it would be built. It was the first large-scale project to make extensive use of computer technology, but, even so, the construction was fraught with difficulties. Costs escalated. Utzon became caught up in the petty-minded moneygrubbing of Australian politics, and resigned in disgust in 1966. A state lottery raised the necessary cash, and by the time the completed building was opened by the Queen in 1973, it cost A$102 million – 15 times its initial

 Tip

Take a ferry from Circular Quay to Cockatoo Island. It's a 20-minute journey out towards Parramatta and the reward is a jumble of 19th-century prison buildings – part of the Unesco World Heritage-listed Australian Convict Sites – and the remnants of a massive 20th-century shipyard. Bring a picnic with you and wander at leisure.

View of Sydney Harbour.

Bunting flutters on the old warehouses at The Rocks to celebrate Australia Day on 26th January.

Weekend market, The Rocks.

budget. But few have ever complained about the price since. The Opera House became an immediate icon for Australia's new-found cultural independence.

Also overlooking the harbour, the Gothic Revival style is exemplified by **Government House** (entry via Conservatorium Road; tel: 02-9228 4111; www.governor.nsw.gov.au; 10am–3pm), the state governor's residence which is also open to the public. The ground-floor state rooms have some beautiful 19th- and 20th-century furniture and decoration.

Apart from the docking ferries, Circular Quay is a lively place, packed with buskers, pedlars and office workers relaxing on their lunch breaks during the day, and busy with after-work drinkers and dining tourists at night. Just around the waterline lies the **Museum of Contemporary Art** D (MCA; tel: 02-9245 2400; www.mca.com.au; daily 10am–5pm, Thu till 9pm), its squat form enlivened by a new extension. The ground-floor restaurant, and the café and sculpture terrace on the fourth floor, both offer spectacular harbour views.

Those interested in Australian art might enjoy Daniel Boyd's work featuring reinterpretations of Aboriginal and Australian-European history or that of Rosalie Gascoigne who uses mostly found materials. But even if the contemporary art scene isn't your thing, the museum won't disappoint: there's always a mix of fresh styles and interesting new exhibitions.

THE ROCKS

Behind the MCA sits Sydney's most historic district, known as **The Rocks** E (www.therocks.com) after the sandstone bluffs from which the first convicts cut golden bricks for public buildings (take a look up the **Argyle Cut**, slicing straight through the cliffs – the pick marks are still easily identifiable). Almost immediately the area became the colony's main port, and warehouses grew up along the waterfront, backed by merchants' shops, offices, hotels, banks, bars and brothels that went along with the seafaring trade of the 19th century. Respectability always eluded The Rocks, and by the 1960s the area had long outlived its original mercantile function.

Today The Rocks is virtually an open-air museum, where you can absorb Australia's early history with a leisurely stroll – although the entire area is now unashamedly devoted to tourism. Be warned, at the popular markets on a Saturday you may spend hours jostling with crowds. During evening excursions you'll be spoilt for choice in over-priced but top-notch restaurants.

SYDNEY'S OLDEST BUILDINGS

Next to the MCA is the tiny stone **Cadman's Cottage** (daily 9am–5pm), built in 1816 and believed to be Sydney's oldest building, now housing a museum. Only a small number of buildings remain from the first half of the 19th century. Many more date from the Victorian era, when cargoes of wool, wheat and gold provided a rich source of income that allowed architectural flourishes of the period to blossom. The contrast between these ornate buildings and the simple, embellished stonework of the Georgian era is striking.

The Argyle Cut passes the **Argyle Centre** (a convict-era storehouse that is now a boutique shopping centre) and the **Garrison Church**, and eventually leads up a steep path to **Observatory Hill**. Although a fort was built on the hilltop in 1803 for officers in case of a convict uprising, the oldest building still standing is the Signal Station, which was erected in 1848. In 1855 the hill became the site for the **Sydney Observatory** (tel: 02-9271 0222; www.sydneyobservatory.com.au; daily 10am–5pm, night sessions also available, bookings essential), which began as a time-keeping device. Since 1982 the Observatory has been a museum of astronomy, with an imaginative **3-D Space Theatre** (daily, check times). Observatory Hill has fine harbour vistas, making it a favourite viewing point for tourists and locals to watch the fireworks on New Year's Eve.

Further towards Millers Point lies a network of narrow streets, once home to wharf workers. The **Hero of Waterloo** (Lower Fort Street; www.heroofwaterloo.com.au) and **Fortune of War** (George Street; www.fortuneofwar.com.au) compete for the honour of being Sydney's oldest pub, with the **Palisade** (Bettington Street; www.hotelpalisade.com.au) one of the most atmospheric. By Miller's Point is the newly beautified Barangaroo Reserve (www.barangaroo.com), once an industrial area but now a lovely spot for walking and picnicking with views to the Harbour Bridge and North Sydney in one direction, and across Darling Harbour in the other.

THE BOTANIC GARDENS

Following the waterline in the opposite direction from the quay leads you past the Opera House to the **Royal Botanic Gardens** (tel: 02-9231 8111; www.rbgsyd.nsw.gov.au; daily sunrise–sunset) – a vast, voluptuous collection of antipodean flora, including some truly majestic Moreton Bay figs. Hidden among the sculpted lakes and exotic fronds is an excellent café-restaurant. If you decide to picnic on the lawns, be warned – the strutting, long-beaked ibis are notorious lunch burglars.

From **Mrs Macquarie's Point** one gazes out at the tiny island of Fort Denison. This is also the site of the summer Open Air Cinema (one month every year; tel: 1300-366 649; www.stgeorgeopenair.com.au), where you can sip champagne and watch a recent film from a screen that seems to rise out of the harbour. You'd be hard-pressed to find a more beautiful backdrop to a cinema, but get in quick because tickets sell out fast.

Paths continue through the gardens to the **Art Gallery of New South Wales** (tel: 1800-679 278; www.artgallery.nsw.gov.au; daily 10am–5pm, until 9pm Wed; general admission free). This imposing edifice is crowned with the celestial names of Leonardo da Vinci, Michelangelo, Botticelli and the like, although not one of these artists is represented in the

Ken Done (pronounced as in bone) is a popular local artist and designer who has a gallery in The Rocks exhibiting his paintings. A shop sells clothes, ceramics and other items featuring his work.

View of Sydney Harbour and the Bridge taken from Observatory Hill.

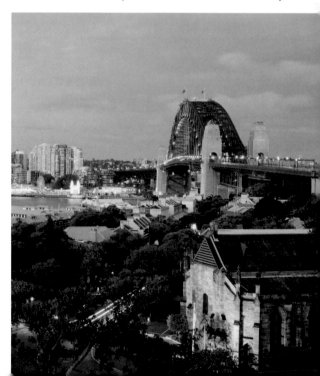

HARBOUR-HOPPING

Sydney's green-and-yellow harbour ferries are perhaps one of the city's most pleasant forms of public transport.

A surprising amount of the city can be seen by hopping from wharf to wharf. A five-minute ride directly opposite Circular Quay (the main ferry terminal) leads to the North Shore suburb of **Kirribilli**, where the prime minister and governor-general have official residences (and both are known to pop in to the legendary Kirribilli fish-and-chip shop for a meal beneath the bridge pylons).

On the other side of the bridge, **McMahons Point** is believed to have the best view in Sydney; running up to North Sydney, **Blues Point Road** has a string of much-favoured cafés. Only a bit longer is the ride to **Cremorne Point**, a dramatic promontory with a harbourside walk to Mosman (considered to be one of the best hikes in Sydney), where a ferry can be caught back to the quay.

Also accessible by ferry is **Taronga Park Zoo** (tel: 02-9969 2777; www.taronga.org.au; daily 9.30am–5pm). Surrounded by virgin bush, this must be one of the most beautiful zoo sites on Earth, with another

A harbour ferry approaches Circular Quay.

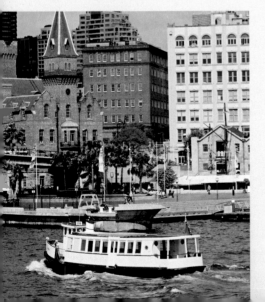

heart-stopping panorama of the city (taronga is an Aboriginal word for 'view across the water'). The collection of more than 5,000 animals includes all the local critters (this is your best chance to see a platypus, and many a snake that you would rather not encounter in the wild). In summer, classical, jazz and swing concerts are held in the zoo's gardens.

Around half of Sydney's beaches are within the harbour (some have shark nets set up). One of the best is **Balmoral**, which also has the famous Bathers' Pavilion restaurant on its shores. **Nielsen Park** at Vaucluse is a favoured picnic spot, while **Lady Jane** allows nude bathing. **Camp Cove**, on the southern side near the harbour entrance, permits topless bathing and is popular with families.

The most famous ferry ride of all is to **Manly**; it crosses through the open sea between the Heads, and on a rough day waves can dwarf the boats. The name was given by Captain Phillip in 1788 when he was struck by the 'manly' bearing of the Aborigines he met there. In the 1930s, the isthmus became Australia's favourite holiday resort 'seven miles from Sydney and a thousand miles from care'. The family atmosphere has lingered. There is an 11km (8-mile) harbourside walk to the Spit from here (catch a bus back). On West Esplanade are **Manly Art Gallery and Museum** (tel: 02-9976 1419; www.mgnsw.org.au; Tue–Sun 10am–5pm), with a good selection of Australian paintings, and **Oceanworld** (tel: 02-8251 7878; www.manlysealifesanctu ary.com.au; daily 10am–5.30pm) where visitors can watch sharks and stingrays being fed.

From Circular Quay a high-speed catamaran, the RiverCat, speeds down the river to **Parramatta** ('where the eels lie down' in the indigenous tongue) – technically a city in its own right, although Sydneysiders persist in calling it a suburb. Parramatta still has several colonial buildings scattered around, including Old Government House (tel: 02-9635 8149; www.national trust.org.au/places/old-government-house; Tue–Sun 10am–4pm); an Explorer bus meets the RiverCat at the docks and transports passengers to the attractions.

Acting as a tourist attraction and famous Sydney icon, the harbour ferries transport more than 38,000 Sydneysiders into the city every day for work, and they provide the quickest route to some seriously popular suburbs.

collection. What the gallery does contain is the country's finest grouping of Australian art, and the garden setting makes it perfect for an afternoon of browsing.

Sydney's **Central Business District** (CBD) is an oddly anonymous hodgepodge of glass skyscrapers and architectural styles from the past two centuries, all squeezed onto a street plan drawn up in Georgian times. It is best seen by strolling up Young Street from the quay, past the 1846 classical revival **Customs House** (tel: 02-9242 8551; www.sydneycustomshouse.com.au; Mon–Fri 8am–midnight, Sat 10am–midnight, Sun 11am–5pm) – now a cultural forum with an on-site lending library, a city model of Sydney and a rooftop restaurant – evoking Sydney's early days as a great imperial port.

MUSEUM OF SYDNEY AND MACQUARIE STREET

You then pass the **Museum of Sydney** (tel: 02-9251 5988; www.sydneylivingmuseums.com.au; daily 10am–5pm), which has entertaining sight-and-sound exhibits from the city's earliest days to today. Built on the site of the original Government House, remnants of the foundations (unearthed by accident in 1983) can now be seen inside the museum.

Cut over to Macquarie Street for a view of official Sydney: in quick succession come the **State Library** (tel: 02-9273 1414; www.sl.nsw.gov.au; Mon–Thu 9am–8pm, Fri 9am–5pm; Sat 11am–5pm), which contains some of the most important archives of Australiana; **Parliament House** (tel: 02-9230 2111; www.parliament.nsw.gov.au; Mon–Fri 9am–5pm, guided tour Mon & Fri 1:30pm) – seat of the NSW state government, housed in the former 'Rum Hospital'; **Sydney Mint** (Mon–Fri 9.30am–5pm); and **Hyde Park Barracks**, which houses one of Sydney's most popular museums (tel: 02-8239 2311; www.sydneylivingmuseums.com.au; daily 10am–5pm; currently undergoing a major refurbishment, reopening late 2019).

Designed in 1817 by convict architect Francis Greenway and completed in 1819, the building was first used to house hundreds of prisoners. Exhibits relating to the convict system include a re-creation of the prisoners' cramped canvas-hammock sleeping quarters. Look out for new interactive exhibits when the museum reopens.

At the end of Macquarie Street lies **Hyde Park**, with the powerful Art Deco **Anzac War Memorial**. To the east of the park on College Street stands the **Australian Museum** (tel: 02-9320 6000; australianmuseum.net.au; daily 9.30am–5pm), the oldest (1827) and one of the largest in the country. It contains the country's best collection showcasing Australian natural history, and also includes an extensive Aboriginal section. Only a fraction of its collections is ever displayed, but the museum mounts ever-changing exhibitions designed to captivate visitors (and children in particular).

SYDNEY TOWER

Cut back across Hyde Park towards Pitt and George streets, the two main

An installation at the Museum of Sydney symbolises links between Aboriginal and European cultures.

The clock tower of the Sydney Central Railway.

arteries of the CBD, and where you'll find some very respectable shopping. The controversial needle of **Sydney Tower** (www.sydneytowereye.com.au; daily 9am–10.30pm) is regarded as a phallic eyesore by many, but it has great views from the summit, and your ticket includes a 4D film about Sydney. The Skywalk, where you walk on the tower's exterior, is a must for thrill-seekers (currently closed until further notice).

Covering an entire city block is the **Queen Victoria Building** (tel: 02-9265 6800; www.qvb.com.au; Mon–Sat 9am–6pm, Thu until 9pm, Sun 11am–5pm). Built during the 1890s Depression as Sydney's main market, the arcade was lovingly restored in the 1980s. The stained-glass windows, Byzantine arches and plaster ornamentation have made the QVB, according to Pierre Cardin, 'the most beautiful shopping centre in the world'. For comparison, cross George Street and drop into the Strand Arcade (tel: 02-9265 6800; www.strandarcade.com.au; Mon–Wed, Fri 9am–5.30pm, Thu 9am–9pm; Sat 9am–4pm; Sun 11am–4pm), a

Sharks circle above at the Darling Harbour Aquarium.

smaller but, arguably, just as exquisite Victorian arcade.

DARLING HARBOUR

The controversial monorail that once ran through here is no longer in operation, so you'll have to make the 10-minute walk on foot to ever-evolving **Darling Harbour** (www.darlingharbour.com). In the 1800s, this was the back door to Sydney, where most trading ships docked. For the last couple of decades it's been a collection of shops, restaurants and family attractions, but along with neighbouring Barangaroo (www.barangaroo. com), billed as Sydney's new foreshore playground, it is currently undergoing a period of major redevelopment, which should be complete by the end of 2020. The new-look site will feature a mixture of public spaces, retail outlets, residential units, experiences and tourist attractions – including The Ribbon, an ultra-modern building which will house a new IMAX cinema (www.imax.com.au). The **Maritime Museum** (daily 9.30am–5pm, Jan until 6pm; tel: 02-9298 3777; www.sea.museum; permanent collections

Sydney and Surroundings

Wollemi National Park

0   10 km
0   10 miles

Kurrajong Heights

Mount Wilson

Panorama Lookout

Waratah Native Gardens

Mount Tomah Botanic Garden

Bowen Mountain

59

Blue Mountains

Victoria Falls

Mt King George

National Park

Faulconbridge Pt Lookout

Mt Victoria

Perry's Lookdown

Lithgow, Jenolan Caves

Govett's Leap

The Pinnacles

Norman Lindsay Gallery and Museum

Faulconbridge

Haw

7

Evans Lookout

Wentworth Creek

Linden

Springwood

Blackheath

32

Medlow Bath

Lawson

Hazelbrook

32

6

Katoomba

Leura

Explorers Tree

Echo Point

5

Leuralla

Bedford Ck

Woodford

Gle

Megalong Valley

Scenic World

Three Sisters

Everglades Gardens

Giants Stairway

Blue Mountains National Park

Mt Solitary

Cedar Ck

Jamison Valley

Kedumba

Erskine Ck

Wild Dog Mountains

free) and the **Chinese Garden of Friendship** were joined in 2012 by **Madame Tussaud's** (tel: 02-9333 9240; www.madametussauds.com.au; daily 9am–8pm), where Kylie Minogue, Nicole Kidman, Wolverine and others are on display. Another new arrival is the **ARA** Darling Quarter Theatre (www.monkeybaa.com.au), focusing on introducing young people to the arts.

One of the most popular harbourside attractions is Wild Life Sydney Zoo (tel: 1800-206-158; www.wildlifesydney.com.au; daily 10am–5pm), where you can see animals such as koalas and kangaroos, venomous spiders and snakes. The tropical rainforest enclosure, where you can walk amid thousands of brightly coloured butterflies, is a highlight.

Right next door is the **Sea Life Sydney Aquarium** (tel: 02-8251 7800; www.sydneyaquarium.com.au; daily 10am–6pm). Emerging fresh from a $10 million renovation, with 14 new themed zones, this is the best place to see Australia's extraordinary aquatic life without getting wet – or eaten. As well as crocodiles and tanks full of

multicoloured tropical fish, the Aquarium has transparent tunnels that take you underwater for a spectacular, fish-eye journey through various habitats teeming with sea creatures – the Great Barrier Reef, a seal sanctuary and the Open Oceanarium – where sharks, sea turtles and stingrays glide alongside.

For years, Sydney's casino, not far from the Maritime Museum in Pyrmont, was regarded by many Sydneysiders as an embarrassment. Since a redevelopment and rebranding unveiled in 2011, **The Star** (tel: 02-9777 9000; www.star.com.au/sydney; 24 hours), as it is now known, has been embraced by locals, not least for its clutch of fine restaurants, which include an outpost of über-hip New York restaurant chain, Momofuku.

Transfer to the Light Rail at the casino and get off two stops later at the **Fish Market** in Pyrmont (tel: 02-9004 1100; www.sydneyfishmarket.com.au). The ultimate seafood experience, Sydney's vast Fish Market mixes fish auctions, market stalls, restaurants and a seafood cooking school. Behind-the-scenes tours run every weekday, leaving at 6.40am

⊙ Tip

Sydney's main visitors centre (Shop 1–2, The Rocks Centre; tel: 02-8273 0000; www.australianvisitorcentres.com.au) is located on the corner of Playfair and Argyle streets in the Rocks. It is open 9am–5.30pm for general advice, free leaflets, maps and brochures and information about tickets for a variety of city attractions. It also sells a range of Australian-made souvenirs.

Sydney Tower is often referred to by locals as Centrepoint Tower.

from the wooden tables inside the main hall, just next to Christie's, and lasting 90 minutes to two hours (A$45/20 per adult/child 10–13 years old).

From here you can take the Light Rail back to Paddy's Markets (www.paddysmarkets.com.au), a bustling collection of stalls and food outlets, which leads to the **Powerhouse Museum** ® (tel: 02-9217 0111; www.maas.museum/powerhouse-museum; daily 10am–5pm), a huge space devoted to science and technology, with lots of interactive displays. From there, it is a short stroll back into Sydney's **Chinatown** ⑤, with its wall-to-wall Asian food.

AWAY FROM THE CENTRE

In many ways, it is the assortment of inner-city suburbs (as they are oddly called) that shows Sydney at its most genuine. In the late 19th century, row after row of terraced houses were thrown up as cheap accommodation for workers – usually with small gardens, tight porches and elaborate iron-lace decorations. In the early 20th century several families at a time

would squeeze into these places, but as soon as they could, most moved out to the more spacious outer suburbs in search of the Aussie dream. But from the 1970s gentrification began apace.

In the inner west lies **Glebe** ❶, whose main thoroughfare, Glebe Point Road, is lined with boutiques and cafés – many catering to students from the nearby **University of Sydney**, a leafy haven built in a self-conscious Oxbridge style. Harbourside **Balmain** was once the raunchiest of working-class suburbs, with industrial dockworks and 41 pubs, one for every 366 residents. There are now some 20 pubs, and the leafy ambience is decidedly more up-market. It can be reached by regular ferry from Circular Quay, and is an ideal spot for a Sunday stroll (the 19th-century waterfront residences are particularly impressive – they featured in Peter Carey's novel *Oscar and Lucinda*).

KINGS CROSS

The inner east is more of a mixed bag. In Victorian times, **Kings Cross** ❷ was an elegant, tree-lined suburb; in the 1920s and 1930s 'The Cross' was Sydney's bohemia, but the Vietnam War and the drug boom turned it into the city's sleazy red-light strip. This is still evident, with adult bookshops and dark doorways leading to some pretty seedy looking joints, all punctuated by the odd backpacker hostel and hangout, but there is a certain risqué charm to the place, which sprawls behind an iconic Coca-Cola billboard at the top of William Street.

Despite the gritty backdrop, The Cross also houses some of the city's most popular nightspots and best restaurants, not to mention a smattering of exclusive members-only (unless you're a gorgeous blonde, model or musician) bars. You'll witness weirdness in the Cross, without doubt, and should be mindful of your safety after dark, but don't be too wary of the area. It is worth exploring, and a bit of common sense will keep you safe. The southern side of Darlinghurst

The less salubrious side of Kings Cross.

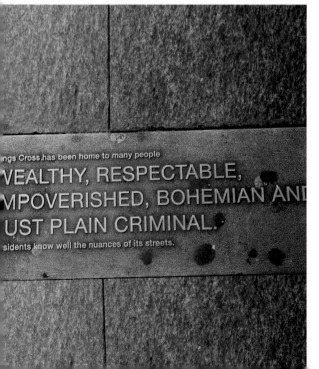

ngs Cross has been home to many people

WEALTHY, RESPECTABLE, IMPOVERISHED, BOHEMIAN AND JUST PLAIN CRIMINAL.

sidents know well the nuances of its streets.

Road is much more appealing than the main drag, and the side streets and neighbouring suburbs of **Potts Point** and **Elizabeth Bay** are filled with grand old mansions and pretty, well-maintained homes. **Victoria Street** houses more great eateries, fashionable bars and chic fashion stops.

Oxford Street is one of Sydney's most famous thoroughfares, although the Darlinghurst end in particular has seen better times. Traditionally this is the heart of gay Sydney, particularly where Oxford Street meets Taylor Square. Gay-friendly clubs, bars and shops snuggle happily together here, and every February/March the area hosts the **Sydney Gay and Lesbian Mardi Gras** (www.mardigras.org.au). Thousands of Sydneysiders line the street, peek over balconies and try and nab a spot on a roof terrace while the flamboyant floats, processions, dancers and acts sashay past. A million more watch the event on TV from the comfort of their living rooms. This is all the more remarkable, given that homosexuality was illegal in NSW until 1982. Prejudices seem to have been swept aside and locals of all backgrounds come out to applaud the efforts of the carefully constructed, but very wild party.

PADDINGTON

As Oxford Street enters **Paddington ❸**, the change in atmosphere is quite palpable. For many years now 'Paddo' has been a popular address for young Sydneysiders. The colonial-style housing is chic (although not cheap) and the boutiques, bars and restaurants that line Oxford are a weekend opportunity for the well-heeled and even better-dressed to show off their trendy tastes. It is not unusual to see the Paddo elite rummaging around the **Paddington Bazaar**, Sydney's oldest market, held in the grounds of the Uniting Church on a Saturday (10am–4pm), dressed in head-to-toe labels, straight from the covers of Vogue. However, the addition of Bondi

Junction's huge shopping mall in 2004 hit Paddo hard. The Sydney faves of Sass & Bide and Scanlon & Theodore survive, but more and more owners of small businesses are paying their last month's rent and closing up shop as they struggle to compete with the convenience of Bondi Junction or meet the ludicrously high rent rates. But if you love to people-watch almost as much as you love shopping for shoes, you will appreciate the community feel of Oxford Street – and it beats being stuck in an air-conditioned mall when there is sunny Sydney weather to soak up.

As you reach the summit of Oxford Street, before it heads along the dual carriageway to Bondi, you hit **Centennial Park** (www.centennialparklands.com. au). A favourite spot all year round for those seeking some greenery, whether you want to run, rollerblade, picnic, cycle, horse ride or just relax in a café with a coffee in the company of some very yummy eastern suburbs mummies, you can do it here. Great all year round, in midsummer the Centennial is also home to the Moonlight Cinema

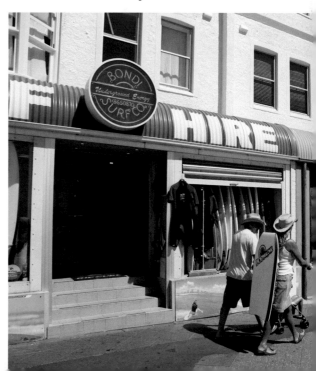

Surf shop on Campbell Parade.

Children learn to surf and swim from a very young age.

(Belvedere Amphitheatre; www.moonlight. com.au), a delightful opportunity to watch new blockbusters and old classics while lounging on a comfy beanbag in the park. Take a picnic (there are some great delis on Oxford) and a bottle of wine and relax in the great outdoors. It's an unmissable treat for a Sydney summer night.

BONDI BEACH

From Paddington, it's a short bus or taxi ride to any of the eastern beaches – of which the most famous is certainly **Bondi ❹** (pronounced Bond-eye). It was from this great arc of sand in the late 1880s that the first Sydney 'cranks' braved the ocean – breaking an old law that forbade swimming during daylight hours as indecent. The breakthrough allegedly came in 1902, when Manly newspaper proprietor William Gocher noisily defied the ban and invited arrest, although in truth this was a bit of self-promotion from a media man, overinflated in the retelling, and at the time the police were completely disinterested. Crowds of Sydneysiders were soon openly swimming. In 1906, the

world's first life-saving club was set up, and 20 years later, crowds of up to 100,000 people were reported at Bondi on summer days. With its wide golden sands, ragged sandstone headlands and reliably fine rollers, Bondi had become another potent Sydney icon. Its status was further enhanced during the 2000 Olympics, when Bondi played host to the beach volleyball competition.

The beach is at its best, not surprisingly, in summer. Activity kicks off at dawn, with the joggers on the promenade, bodybuilders by the shore and surfers catching a few waves before work. Sun-worshippers arrive early, closely followed by busloads of tourists. The Bondi Pavilion opens up, selling ice creams and souvenirs; picnickers arrive with their fish and chips; and the activity continues until well after dark, when lovers take over the sands.

Bondi is also a suburb. **Campbell Parade**, the main beachfront thoroughfare, is a motley string of 1930s-era storefronts that seems to resist all improvement ('one of the great disappointments of Sydney,' according to the

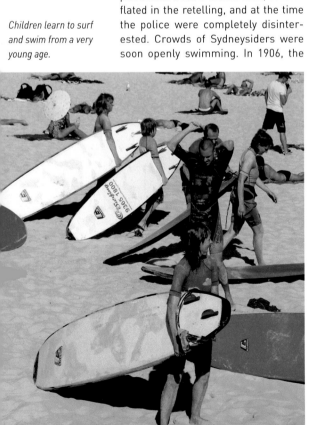

writer Jan Morris). In the mid-1990s, talk of a Bondi Renaissance began as the suburb leapt to new heights of fashionability, and strings of New Australian restaurants opened on the North Bondi end. But still, the parade hangs on to its raffish, sand-gritted personality – and most Sydneysiders really would have it no other way.

Bondi Markets (Bondi Beach Public School; www.bondimarkets.com.au; 9am–4pm) held each weekend (Farmers Market with fresh produce on Saturday, stalls selling clothes and curiosities on a Sunday), have helped establish many successful Sydney designers, and young hopefuls set up stalls each week in hope of being discovered. As if to emphasise the link, the streets behind the busy tourist trap of the parade are now lined with the fashionistas' boutiques, and are a great place to bag an expensive one-off.

BEACHES OF THE EASTERN SUBURBS

Despite its historic and iconic status, however, the face of Bondi is changing. Slightly further away from the city than is comfortable – especially in summer when the 40-minute bus ride can take twice that time thanks to the throngs of tourists – Bondi is being eclipsed by some of the other eastern suburbs beaches, which are just as beautiful (some arguably more so, although all much smaller than Bondi), but don't attract the crowds. The easiest way to see them all in a day is to walk the coastal path. **Coogee** is the best place to start from, especially in summer, because it is quicker to get to from the city on a bus.

After a face-lift, Coogee (once known as a poor cousin to trendy Bondi) is coming into its own with great restaurants and bars popping up all the time. The beach itself is flanked by the historic Wylie's Baths, and although the waves are not for surfers, there's many a boogie boarder to be found at the weekend.

Following the coast along, you'll see the small beach of **Gordon's Bay**, after which you will hit **Clovelly**. With a salt-water swimming pool and one of the best kiosks on the strip (try their milkshakes), Clovelly is popular with families because it is sheltered from the big waves and is also great for snorkelling. The Clovelly Hotel (www.clovellyhotel.com.au) is also well known for its fantastic lunch and dinner menu – best served on one of their two decks – and if there is a big sports game on, it will be on one of their massive screens.

Continue on through the stunning Waverly Cemetery until you come to **Bronte**. As well as being home to Aussie director Baz Luhrmann (and the late Heath Ledger), Bronte attracts parties of people throughout summer thanks to a crowd of free gas barbecues and some killer surf.

Next up is **Tamarama** beach, before you turn the corner to find yourself at Bondi, by the iconic Icebergs (www.icebergs.com.au) club and pool. The walk is best in summer when there is little wind and before the sun hits its peak but, there are plenty of cafés and kiosks along the way to sustain

Australia has more than 11,000 beaches; if you look hard enough, you'll find one all to yourself.

The picturesque town of Leura.

Leura's Everglades gardens integrate local and European trees and plants.

The three sisters rock formation in the Blue Mountains National Park.

you. If you are here in November, do not miss Sculpture by the Sea, a free exhibition of contemporary sculpture, which starts at Bondi and runs all the way to Bronte.

WATSONS BAY

North of Bondi, New South Head Road runs to **Watsons Bay**, where the pub/hotel (www.watsonsbayhotel.com.au) has the finest outdoor beer garden in Sydney, with views across the bobbing yachts to the city skyline. Next door is Doyle's, Sydney's oldest and best-known fish restaurant. It is a bit of a hike up to **South Head** at the mouth of Port Jackson, but well worth it.

The route back to the city goes through one of Sydney's most exclusive suburbs, **Vaucluse**. At its centre is a magnificent mansion, **Vaucluse House** (www.sydneylivingmuseums.com.au; Fri–Sun 10am–4pm), built in 1827 for the statesman, poet and explorer William Charles Wentworth. The tearooms are charming, as are the garden picnic grounds. Swanky **Double Bay** is synonymous with cashed-up long-term residents.

THE BLUE MOUNTAINS

Just 65km (40 miles) west of Sydney lie the **Blue Mountains**, the range that divides the populous, beach-fringed coastal plain from Australia's notoriously flat, harsh interior. It was an effective barrier to the colony's first explorers, whose efforts to conquer this section of the Great Dividing Range were thwarted by the rugged sandstone cliffs. The footsteps of the trio who (in 1813) successfully found the narrow passes are now followed westwards by the main route out of Sydney, the **Great Western Highway**. Today those three pioneers – Blaxland, Wentworth and Lawson – are remembered in the names of towns along the highway as it winds up into the mountains. It was not until the 1920s that this 'rude peculiar country' took off as a holiday destination for fashionable Sydneysiders. Small European-style guesthouses sprang up, catering to honeymooners and families escaping the summer heat. In 1932, a group of bushwalkers came across a farmer about to cut down a gorgeous blue gum forest in the Grose Valley. They begged him to stop, and in the end offered to buy the land. It was the beginning of a movement that has since protected almost 1 million hectares (2.5 million acres) of Australia's most magnificent wilderness.

Despite the almost impenetrable barrier the Blue Mountains presented to early travellers, they are a sandstone plateau reaching a height of only 1,100 metres (3,600ft). Erosion has caused the stone to fall away to form sheer cliff faces punctuated by picturesque waterfalls. The **Blue Mountains National Park** (tel: 02-4782 3653; www.nationalparks.nsw.gov.au; vehicle charges apply), totalling 247,000 hectares (610,400 acres), is well served by bushwalking tracks and picnic and camping spots. Small towns are riddled with fine restaurants, old-style cafés and antiques stores catering to weekenders.

LEURA

As you drive up from Sydney, the first stop should be **Leura ❺**, a classic Blue Mountains hamlet; it's a tidy, picturesque railway town that makes an ideal lunch break. The region's main town, **Katoomba ❻**, is perched on the edge of the Jamison Valley, and shows off its natural wonders to the best advantage at **Echo Point**, which overlooks one of the state's most photogenic rock formations, the **Three Sisters**. Always busy with tourists, Echo Point has a well-equipped tourist information centre. A great place to take a breather before or after a hike, it might also be wise to take a picnic.

High on the list of breathtaking experiences is the **Scenic Railway** (www.scenicworld.com.au) that winds down into a tree-clad gorge and is claimed to be the world's steepest. There are many footpaths for one-day walks in the area – an excellent choice is hiking down the Golden Stairs to the rock formations known as the **Ruined Castle**.

Katoomba has a cinema (www.unitedcinemas.com.au) with a large screen; its feature on the Blue Mountains, The Edge, is quite stunning.

Some 10 minutes' drive further west along the highway looms the **Hydro Majestic Hotel** (www.hydromajestic.com.au), an Art Deco–style former casino that catered to high society in the 1920s and was recently restored. **Blackheath ❼** has some of the best guesthouses and restaurants, along with rewarding walks and the unmissable **Govett's Leap**, a spectacular lookout over the Grose Valley.

The village of **Mount Victoria** is the highest in the Blue Mountains. As in so many of the surrounding settlements, the preservation of historic buildings, especially along Station Street, makes this spot a pleasure to wander through, or bed down for the night in one of the beautiful cottages – priceless views guaranteed.

JENOLAN CAVES

As the road drops from the mountains down the steep Victoria Pass, it narrows to cross a convict-built bridge that was part of the first road through to the rich wool, wheat, cattle and sheep country to the west. A little way on, and 46km (29 miles) south of the highway, the magnificent **Jenolan Caves** (tel: 1300-763 311; www.jenolancaves.org.au; daily, times vary) is a mighty series of underground limestone halls encrusted with stalactites and stalagmites. In the 1920s this was the premier honeymoon spot for young Australians, who regarded the arduous journey and difficult conditions as a badge of honour.

On the highway, 12km (7.5 miles) past the Jenolan Caves turn-off, signposts point to a monument to the ingenuity used in solving one of the 19th century's greatest engineering problems at **Lithgow**. It is the railway line that originally conquered the steep descent out of the Blue Mountains, known as the **Zig-Zag Railway** – so named for its unique method of overcoming the almost sheer mountain side. The zig-zag line was finished in 1869, but was abandoned in 1910 for a more modern descent. Dedicated train buffs restored the line to give day

Many beach hotels offer swimming pools right next to the ocean, just in case you prefer your water without salt and waves.

excursions travelling back into railway history; trains have been temporarily suspended, but are due to be running again in late 2019 – check the website or ring for updates (tel: 02-6355 2955; www.zigzagrailway.com.au).

COLONIAL TOWNS AROUND SYDNEY

Picturesque colonial towns also cluster on the eastern edge of the Blue Mountains. Peppered with historic buildings, the atmosphere of these hidden settlements is truly unique. Acting like a kind of time capsule of Australian colonial history, the **Hawkesbury** area was established in 1794 when settlers arrived to farm their 12 hectares (30 acres). Many of the descendants from these pioneers still work and live in the district, giving it a truly rustic Aussie atmosphere.

There are countless bushwalking and camping opportunities in the town of **Windsor**, as well as the new Hawkesbury Regional Gallery (The Deerubbin Centre; tel: 02-4560 4441; www.hawkesbury.nsw.gov.au/gallery; Mon, Wed–Fri 10am–4pm, Sat–Sun 10am–3pm), but its main appeal

An old farmstead in the Hawkesbury area.

is the atmospheric colonial architecture, the venerable Macquarie Arms Hotel and a lively Sunday street market. **Richmond** has a handful of fine Georgian streetscapes and offers camping, canoeing and swimming.

Closer to Sydney, on the southwestern edge of the conurbation, lie several more historic towns. In 1805 John Macarthur was granted nearly 2,000 hectares (5,000 acres) to raise sheep in **Camden**, the beginning of the nation's wool industry. The Camden-Campbelltown-Picton region is still known as Macarthur Country, and **Camden Park House** (1835) is owned by descendants of John Macarthur; it is open to groups by appointment (tel: 02-4655 8466; www.camdenparkhouse.com.au) – with an open day in the third week of September. Camden (pop. 8,000) is the centre of a dairy region focused on the Nepean River Valley.

Lying 16km (10 miles) southwest of Camden, tiny **Picton** also has numerous remnants of 19th-century settlement. Upper Menangle Street is listed by the National Trust as 'representing a typical country town street' of 100 years ago. It is a fine base from which to explore the scenic surrounding region.

NORTH OF SYDNEY

An hour's drive north of Sydney lies one of New South Wales' most beautiful national parklands, **Ku-ring-gai Chase National Park** ⑧ (tel: 02-9472 8949; www.nationalparks.nsw.gov.au). Hundreds of Aboriginal carvings dot the cliffs here, which often give sweeping views of the countryside and Cowan Creek: the easiest to reach are on the **Basin Trail** off West Head Road. At the mouth of the Hawkesbury River is **Broken Bay** ⑨, a favourite recreational area.

Palm Beach, home of the Aussie TV soap *Home and Away*, is one of Greater Sydney's smarter neighbourhoods, and its beach is rated highly by surfers. If you're short of time, you can visit this area by seaplane; these leave from Rose Bay in the city, landing in Pittwater.

NEW SOUTH WALES

The greatest asset of New South Wales is its diversity. From Sydney you can head north for tropical banana plantations, south for snowcapped mountains, and west into the expansive Outback.

⊙ Main attractions
Port Stephens
Bellingen
Byron Bay
Southern Highlands
Snowy Mountains
Jervis Bay
Bathurst
Mungo National Park
Broken Hill

Map on page 126

There's a lot more to Australia's most populous state than its capital city. While Sydneysiders may have the harbour as their playground, elsewhere in the state you can unwind by hiking in the rainforest, diving on a coral reef, or just counting the cattle as they come in for the muster. Similarly, while Sydney may be enjoying a balmy day, there might be snow on the southern Alps and dust storms sweeping across the sunbaked towns in the western Outback, even as monsoons flood the lush farming country of the northeast.

THE PACIFIC HIGHWAY

For generations, the Pacific Highway has been Sydney's escape route to the sun. Generations of Sydneysiders have made the regular pilgrimage up the coast, fleeing the winter chill, the big-city hustle, or just the tedium of the everyday. Not so long ago, the road passed through country that was still largely undeveloped: after the outskirts of Sydney thinned out into nothingness, you were in a place where the bush and the breezes did most of the talking.

These days, the Pacific Highway has been transformed into a traffic-laden artery that cuts through expanding coastal towns and seafront subdivisions. However, motorists may still enjoy a flickering parade of gum-trees in the late afternoon light, along with occasional glimpses of the Pacific Ocean's white-lace hems – despite its name, the Pacific Highway generally runs several kilometres from the coast, and the newer Pacific Motorway (M1), which has superseded parts of the old route and offers a faster drive to Newcastle, is even more direct. The route is currently being upgraded, with work due to be complete in 2020 (for details see www.pacifichighway.nsw.gov.au).

At a pinch, you can make the drive to Queensland in 12 hours, but it's much better to take some time to explore the unpredictable patchwork

The Hunter Valley at dawn.

of boutique wineries and old-fashioned milk bars, country pubs and fish-and-chips shops, surf spots and vast tropical plantations. Three days is the bare minimum needed to sample at least some of the coast, but if you want to do some serious exploring, five days is recommended.

The trip north starts at Sydney Harbour Bridge. Northbound traffic soon throttles down into the four lanes of the Pacific Highway; at peak hours, this artery is clotted every few minutes at stoplights and suburban intersections, although at other times it flows freely. After negotiating past the cars of the well-heeled upper North Shore, you finally hit the beginning of the motorway at **Wahroonga**.

North-bound cars cross the **Hawkesbury River** at **Brooklyn**, a vista of ridges, valleys and arms of open water spreads east and west. This is a popular weekend playground for many Sydneysiders, who rent cabin cruisers and drift among the bays and inlets. Many companies offer cruises; a highlight is the Hawkesbury Cruises, the local service departing from Brooklyn (www.hawkesburycruises.com.au).

Upstream lies **Wiseman's Ferry**, where former convict Solomon Wiseman opened the first ferry across the river in 1827. A free car ferry (operating 24 hours a day) takes you to the rugged bush-clad sandstone cliffs of **Dharug National Park** (tel: 02-6574 5555; www.nationalparks.nsw.gov.au). Walkers, cyclists and horse riders can travel a stretch of the Great North Road, literally carved out of the rock by convicts in the 1830s.

The hub of this central coast region (populated by retirees, Sydney commuters and new industries) is the not-terribly-alluring **Gosford**. But beyond the urban sprawl are the orchards and forests of the **Mangrove Mountain** area, plus a string of beautiful beaches. Nearby is the **Australian Reptile Park** (tel: 02-4340 1022; www.reptilepark.com.au; daily 9am–5pm).

Past Gosford, the Pacific Motorway (M1) heads directly north to the western outskirts of Newcastle, while the older Pacific Highway goes via **Doyalson** and traces a ridge between the ocean and **Lake Macquarie**. Frequently overlooked by tourists, the lake (particularly its western shore) is a fascinating relic of a past age, when working folk could afford water frontages. The mining village of **Wangi Wangi** (accessed via the motorway, turning off onto the B53), for many years the retreat of the artist Sir William Dobell, is a classic example of lake-shore charm.

THE HUNTER VALLEY

The second-largest city in New South Wales, **Newcastle** (www.visitnewcastle.com.au), was long burdened with a reputation as an unsophisticated industrial hub. But when steel production stopped in 2000, the town worked hard to reinvent itself as a cultural centre. Helped by a lively waterfront development, beautifully preserved heritage buildings and a large student population to liven things up, it is developing

The Redback spider is the most venomous in all of Australia. Luckily the antivenom is commercially available.

The coastal road.

New South Wales

as a destination in its own right. Newcastle also makes a great base to explore the region, with easy access to the boating and bushlands of Lake Macquarie to the south and expansive, wild Myall Lakes to the north, not to mention its own impressive surf beaches. As a bonus, there are the prosperous wineries of the lower **Hunter Valley ❶**, one of Australia's premier wine-growing districts.

Many of the area's hillsides were originally settled in the pursuit of coal. Mining is still a thriving local industry, along with aluminium smelters, giant open-cut mines and power stations, providing a surprising flipside to the area's famed wine industry. Turning inland from Newcastle, you reach **Maitland**, a city rich in historic buildings. From there, the road leads through one winery after another, with most of them gathered around **Pokolbin**.

As the highway heads deeper into the valley, the pace of life slows down. **Singleton** is an appealing mixture of modern and old civic buildings and private homes.

The town of **Scone** (rhymes with *own*) is pretty but unremarkable save for its horsiness. This is the home of thoroughbred stud farms, horse shows and the sport of polo. Much of New England is squatter territory, where the sons and daughters of the landed gentry (or those aspiring to it) continue the traditions of Mother England: good riding skills, political conservatism and bad dress sense. Scone hosts several major polo tournaments, of course.

While the Hunter Valley is very pleasant to visit, the scenery isn't particularly spectacular and in high summer the low hills can become unbearably hot. Many wine buffs now prefer to head an hour's drive further east to visit the lesser-known vineyards around **Mudgee**. The picturesque village of **Gulgong** makes an ideal base. The **Henry Lawson Centre** (tel: 02-6374 2049; www.henrylawsongulgong. org.au; Mon–Sat 10am–3.30pm, Sun 10am–1pm) celebrates the poet, who grew up here, and there's also a **pioneer museum** (tel: 02-6374 1513; www. gulgongmuseum.com).

Milking a tiger snake.

Segenhoe Stud Farm, Scone.

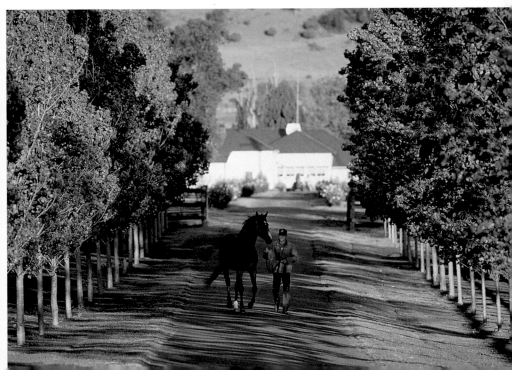

🔍 WHALES AND DOLPHINS

Watching a pod of dolphins splashing just beyond the breakers turns a day at the beach into something very special.

The coast of New South Wales is one of the best places to see whales and dolphins in the wild. While dolphins frolic near the beach, the whales' winter migration takes them along the length of the state's coastline. Over the past few years, stray whales have spent several days in Sydney Harbour, to the delight of ferry passengers.

Humpbacks travel north along the coast from about May, heading into the warm waters off the Queensland coast and returning south between September and November. Other species that are sighted less frequently include southern right whales, false killer whales, orcas, minke and, very occasionally, blue whales, the biggest creatures on the planet.

All the major holiday towns along the coast offer whale- and dolphin-watch cruises. Whale tours at Eden, deep on the state's south coast, have a fascinating edge to them, a little like visiting the scene of a crime with the criminal who did the deed. Until the

A pod of dolphins off the New South Wales coast.

1930s, the town of Eden was a whaling station, and the various species of whales were all hunted in a gruesome alliance between killer whales and whaling boats. Eden was one of the first towns in the state to develop a whale-watching industry, however, and its whaling history, the depth of knowledge that these operators bring to their task and their obvious affection for 'their' whales make this more than just a wildlife tour.

A two-hour drive south of Sydney, Jervis Bay has a pod of resident dolphins, and the relatively placid waters of the bay make this a prime viewing spot. To the north of Sydney, Port Stephens, Coffs Harbour and Byron Bay all offer their own whale- and dolphin-watching cruises.

Unlike the fast, acrobatic dolphins that never seem to idle for long, whales move slowly. On a whale-watch trip, the vessel will probably venture out into the open sea, where it will spend a good deal of time stopped and pitching in the waves while watching the whales. For anyone who suffers from motion sickness, this is not an ideal situation. If you are subject to seasickness, take medication well before you set foot on the boat.

An excursion is typically full of competitive anticipation, as children and adults alike vie to be the first to catch a glimpse of the quarry. However, once a whale is sighted, vessels are not allowed to approach closer than 100 metres (330ft). Whales are curious creatures and they will often swim closer to a stationary vessel, but you can't count on a close-up look. Larger vessels with an upper deck will usually give you a better vantage point; the best place to stand is usually forward of the bridge.

Unfortunately, much of the action with whales and dolphins takes place below the water, and out of sight if you're standing on the deck of a boat. But if the vessel is properly equipped with the right equipment, you can tune in and listen to what's happening below. Whales and dolphins communicate via high-pitched squeaks and whistles. Whales, in particular, are known for their beautiful songs, and the humpback is one of the most vocal of all the whales. If your vessel has a hydrophone, an underwater microphone, you can listen to them talking over the public-address system.

PORT STEPHENS

Back on the Pacific Highway, north of Newcastle the road crosses the Hunter River at Hexham and skirts the western shore of **Port Stephens**. Two-and-a-half times the size of Sydney Harbour and blessed with both calm swimming coves and ocean beaches perfect for surfing, Port Stephens is home to a number of popular resorts such as the sophisticated **Nelson Bay**, and quieter settlements such as **Tea Gardens** and **Hawks Nest**. The bay's most famous attraction is its large population of bottlenose dolphins. Between May and November it also offers whale-watching opportunities. The aquatic reserves at **Fly Point** and **Halifax Point** are popular with divers, and the surrounding bush offers ample walking trails.

MYALL LAKES TO MACKSVILLE

About 40km (25 miles) north of Port Stephens you reach Bulahdelah, the gateway to the beautiful **Myall Lakes ❷**. Preserving these aquatic pearls as a National Park was an early victory for conservationists. Paperbarks, palms and other wetland vegetation crowd the shores, while the waterways are filled with bird life. Surrounding the chain of lakes is national parkland where nature-lovers may camp in the wild. The beaches at the tiny community of **Seal Rocks** are some of the most scenically exquisite along the whole NSW coast, and benefit from different outlooks, so there's always one to suit the prevailing winds.

Seal Rocks offers the first of a string of beaches at the northern end of the lakes leading to the holiday resort of **Forster**, the southernmost of the North Coast beach towns. Travelling north also entails crossing numerous rivers, for the NSW coast is crenellated with the mouths of waterways, carrying runoff from the Great Dividing Range. The further north you go, the more romantic the rivers become,

their shores wilder, their bars and tides more spectacular.

Taree, about a two-hour drive from Newcastle, is a thriving market town in the dairy-rich **Manning Valley**. The beautiful Manning River runs through the middle of town and, if you follow it west to **Elands**, after an hour's drive you find yourself at **Ellenborough Falls**, one of the highest single-drop waterfalls in Australia.

The Manning and other valleys of the mid-North Coast are timber centres providing native woods and pine from vast forests, which stretch westwards onto the New England Plateau. Here the highway winds through many kilometres of forest, and for a change of scene it is worth a detour along the well-made coast road from Kew to **Port Macquarie**. These are some of the prettiest beaches in the state, with rocky outcrops and golden sands. On the western side of the road there is yet another chain of ocean lakes, ideal for fishing and boating.

However, tourism has taken its toll on the landscape at Port Macquarie (a former penal settlement, founded in

⊙ Tip

The views from the lookout tower at Cape Hawke in Booti Booti National Park (20km/12 miles south of Forster; tel: 02-6591 0300; www.environment.nsw.gov.au/nationalparks) are spectacular. You can see south to the foot of Barrington Tops. The park has walking trails, a picnic area and camping facilities, but only Elizabeth Beach is patrolled by volunteer life-savers during the swimming season.

To lessen the impact of walkers, national parks in New South Wales provide boardwalks over fragile terrain.

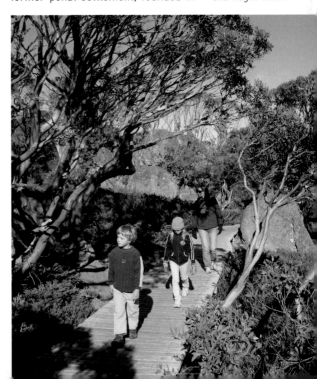

1821, and still full of historic sandstone buildings). Garish motels, retirement villages and timeshare resorts dot the headlands, and red-brick suburbia has taken over the flatlands to the west. But for all its superannuated qualities, there is still much to like about Port, including good restaurants, top-quality accommodation and easy access to uncrowded beaches. **Wauchope**, a few kilometres up the Hastings River, is worth a visit for **Timbertown**, an award-winning replica of an old sawmilling village.

The highway again snakes inland and through the forests. It is worth making the 24km (15-mile) detour to take in the resort of **Crescent Head** – a pretty, peaceful town with fine surf and good golf. For a real escape, head south from Crescent on the old dirt coast road for 10km (6 miles) to a grassy headland and beach known as **Racecourse**. There's no sign, but a ranger will appear from nowhere after a day or two to collect a modest camping fee. Given the joys of an empty beach, uncrowded waves and occasional dolphin sightings, the minimal fee is a gift.

Nearby is the town of **South West Rocks**, perched on a picturesque headland, and the famous **Trial Bay Gaol**, which held convicts and, later, German war internees.

Continuing northwards, a distinctly tropical feel begins to permeate the air and, from **Macksville** on, banana plantations are a common sight and a good proportion of houses are built on stilts, Queensland-style, in order to catch the cooling breeze and keep things dry. Everywhere the dominant colour is a lush green, and the roadside signs tell you this is paradise. It isn't, but it's a step in the right direction. While you're filling the tank in Macksville, pop around to The Star pub, which sits right on the banks of the Nambucca River, as pretty and profane an ale house as you'll find anywhere.

Just south of Macksville, the small town of **Scotts Head** presents a long, clean beach and a caravan park.

COFFS HARBOUR AND BELLINGEN

The timber port of **Coffs Harbour ❸** is reputed to have Australia's best

A rainforest waterfall in Dorrigo.

climate, and has developed into a major centre of North Coast tourism. Unfortunately, many motorists know Coffs only as the city of the Big Banana, another manifestation of Australia's bizarre gigantism trend. Those with a taste for adventure can join whitewater professionals for a day of rafting action on the nearby **Nymboida River**.

Coffs is more or less the midway point between Sydney and Brisbane – around seven and six hours' driving distance, respectively. Travellers often plan to stop here overnight only, but end up staying a week. The town is alive with restaurants and pubs, particularly in the strip from the jetty to Park Beach. Parasailing, four-wheel-drive tours, the beach, golf and galleries fill the days.

Inland, the Bellingen Valley offers scenic pleasures quite different from the coast. Some parts of this valley, particularly the pebbled riverbanks, look more like parts of temperate Europe than east-coast Australia.

The beautiful village of **Bellingen** (which features dramatically in the climax of Peter Carey's novel *Oscar and Lucinda*) is, along with Nimbin to the north, the heart of alternative culture in NSW, although concessions have been made to capitalism since the real-estate boom hit and idyllic communal farms became worth millions. Bellingen retains a relaxed atmosphere and a strong alternative bent. Browse the local arts and crafts at the Old Butter Factory or the beautifully restored Hammond and Wheatley Emporium department store. If you're in the area in August/September/October you can take in the local jazz, bluegrass or global music festivals.

BELLINGEN TO BALLINA

From Bellingen, take the Dorrigo Road to the small town of **Dorrigo**, a great base for exploring the **Dorrigo National Park** (tel: 02-6657 2309; www.nationalparks.nsw. gov.au). The park is a fragment of the massive rainforest that covered the area until the 1920s, when loggers clear-felled in their search for Australian cedar, a timber so valuable it was known as red gold. From the Dorrigo Rainforest Centre (daily 9am–4.30pm), you can take a number of walks, including the Skywalk, a wooden walkway stretched high over the forest canopy that is also open for nocturnal excursions.

The Pacific Highway swings inland yet again through the forests, this time emerging at **Grafton**, a lovely old town shaded with jacaranda trees (a wonderful sight in late October and early November) and situated on a bend of the Clarence River, 65km (40 miles) from its mouth. Grafton has some delightful 19th century architecture enhanced by its wide, tree-lined streets. This is flood country, and the houses close to the river are tropical bungalows on stilts. Like several towns away from the coast, Grafton has been bypassed in the tourist boom, and prices for food and lodging are still reasonable.

North of Grafton, the highway follows the line of the Clarence River across flatlands to the coast, with

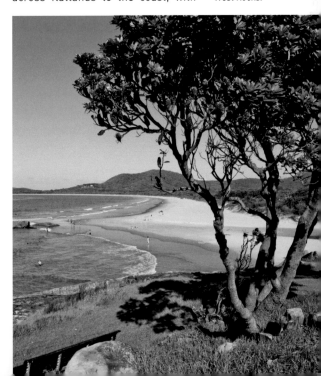

The beach at South West Rocks.

⊘ Fact

The strife of Byron: Coastal erosion has long been a problem in Byron Bay and continues to threaten beach-front properties in Byron Bay and pit homeowners against the local council, who favour a policy of a 'planned retreat' from those structures that tumble into the water rather than maintaining protective sea walls.

The lighthouse at Cape Byron, the easternmost point of Australia.

rambling old houses peering out from behind fields of sugar cane. The village of **Maclean**, built on several hills a few kilometres upriver from Yamba, is quaint, quiet, and a great spot from which to view the workings of the Clarence with its fishermen and cane haulers. Fifteen minutes down a straight bitumen road is the resort of **Yamba**, once a sleepy hollow and now filled with shoddily built weekenders and more garish motels. But the pub on the headland and the beaches spread below are first-rate. Down the coast a few kilometres from Yamba, the village and famous surf point of **Angourie** is renowned for its rocky coastline and Blue Pools.

After a stretch of alternating river and cane scenery, the Pacific Highway clips the coast again at **Ballina**, the southernmost beach town in a string reaching to the Queensland border, collectively known as the Summerland Coast. Ballina, the scene of a minor gold rush in the 19th century, has now found more consistent treasure as a bustling tourist centre and fishing port.

The highway now heads due north through magnificent rolling hills, but the alternative coastal route takes in some equally breathtaking coastal scenery, including the village of **Lennox Head**, ranked as one of the top 10 surfing spots in the world (the big waves come from May to July).

BYRON BAY

The area's big tourist pull is **Byron Bay ❹**, the easternmost town in Australia and a popular tourist destination.

In the 1960s, Byron was still a quiet rural community with an alternative bent. Today, its magnificent setting, with almost 30km (19 miles) of sandy beaches fringed by a fertile hinterland, has made it a magnet for the rich and the famous. Some, like global music star Jack Johnson, own property here; others ensconce themselves in the area's impressive array of luxury retreats.

The town is just as popular with the less well-off, who spend their time bodysurfing or relaxing in the sun, a laid-back lifestyle that has made the

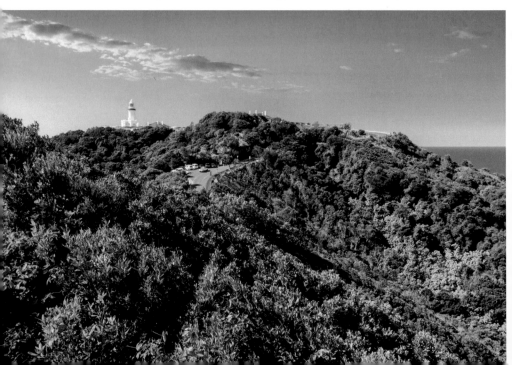

town a hub for unemployed youths. In a classic case of biting the hand that feeds it, the local council has been battling to limit the number of visitors, but thus far without success.

Come to town on a crowded festival weekend and you may even sympathise with the council. Byron has a packed roster of events, devoted variously to blues, writers, films, jazz, and many more besides, during which times the town can get uncomfortably full.

However, the town's growth has not marred its natural beauty. While the beaches are a major attraction, the hinterland features a number of national parks and nature reserves, including **Tyagarah** and **Broken Head** nature reserves, **Arakwal National Park** (tel: 02-6639 8300; www.nationalparks.nsw.gov. au) and **Cape Byron Headland**. Then of course there's the underwater world. Byron's most famous dive spot, the **Julian Rocks Aquatic Reserve**, is considered second only to the Great Barrier Reef on the east coast. This is where temperate and tropical waters meet, giving divers (and even snorkellers) the opportunity to view an astonishing array of marine wildlife, including a number of species of sharks.

The best-known attraction in Byron's hinterland is **Nimbin**, Australia's original alternative community, the town where the 1973 Aquarius Festival launched Australia's hippy culture. While much of the town is still caught in a 1970s time warp, with luridly painted houses and shops and the scent of patchouli in the air, elements of its drug community has moved on from marijuana to hard-core heroin. The overt drug peddling makes many visitors uncomfortable, and they tend not to linger.

A better option is to spend some time exploring the local area. The winding roads between Nimbin and Lismore, through undulating landscape covered in lush rainforest, offer some of the most scenic drives in the state. These pockets of rainforest, left untouched by the early settlers, were the focus of Australia's first anti-logging protest in the late 1970s.

MOUNT WARNING

The rich soil in the area is a legacy of the giant, shield-shaped volcano that once covered the entire area. The remnant of its central vent is a 1,157-metre (3,780ft) peak called **Mount Warning** in English, **Wollumbin** (Cloud Catcher) in the local Bandjalung language. Its peak is the first spot in Australia to feel the rays of the rising sun, and offers dazzling views over the district. Also worth exploring are the **Border Ranges National Park** (tel: 02-6632 0000; vehicle entry fee) and the **Nightcap National Park** (tel: 02-6627 0200), including the 100-metre (328ft) -high Minyon Falls.

The border town of **Tweed Heads** has only recently emerged from the shadow of its flashier sister across the Queensland border, Coolangatta, but the tourist boom now proceeds apace. The end of one journey is the

Surf school will teach you all the moves.

TWO PACIFIC GEMS

Norfolk Island and Lord Howe Island are lush green specks on the vastness of the Pacific Ocean.

Two of Australia's tiniest tourist areas are also among the most attractive. Although Norfolk and Lord Howe are South Pacific islands, these are not atolls of palm trees and corals.

The sea life around the islands is quite phenomenal. In the surrounding waters, warm and cool currents collide, spawning a wealth of marine creatures including giant clams, sea turtles, clownfish, lionfish, tuna, butterfly fish and a wrasse known as the doubleheader, a species that is unique to the islands' waters. It's not surprising that diving is a major draw to the islands.

A rich and fascinating cultural heritage, relaxed lifestyle and rolling green pastures characterise **Norfolk Island** (www.norfolkisland.com.au), 1,700km (1,050 miles) northeast of Sydney and covering about 35 sq km (13.5 sq miles). No one lived here until a British penal settlement was established in 1788. The prison island became known for its harsh and cruel conditions.

The most bizarre event in Norfolk's history occurred after the British Government decided, in 1852, that the settlement was too expensive to

Lord Howe Island.

maintain and evacuated all the inhabitants. At about the same time, on remote Pitcairn Island the descendants of the *Bounty* mutineers and the Polynesian women they took with them from Tahiti in 1789 (after dumping Captain William Bligh) were finding it difficult to grow enough food for their increasing population. So they were relocated to Norfolk Island in 1856, although a few later returned to Pitcairn.

Today there are about 2,000 people on the 3,500-hectare (8,750-acre) island, but many of them share the same set of Bounty surnames. Indeed, so many Christians, Quintals, Youngs, McCoys, Adamses, Buffetts, Nobbses and Evanses crowd the telephone book that it's the only one in the world to publish subscribers' nicknames.

Norfolk is a self-governing territory within Australia. The tourist clutter of **Kingston** is the island's only town. Tax-free shopping here is very cheap, especially for fashionable wool and cashmere sweaters.

Down by the waterfront, the buildings of the early settlements are still in good condition – some are still used as government offices. The evening sound-and-light show along these buildings, which are remnants from a savage time, is well worth your while.

Norfolk Island doesn't promise a wild time. However, you feel close to history here, and there is enough to do to warrant several days' stay. Diving is a popular activity. Until 2016, Fletcher Christian's descendant Karlene Christian owned the Bounty Dive Shop – she has moved on, but you can still join daily diving groups.

LORD HOWE ISLAND

About 900km (560 miles) to the west, crescent-shaped **Lord Howe Island** (www.lordhoweisland.info) is only 11km (7 miles) long and 2km (1.25 miles) wide, with a population of about 300. Visitors usually travel on bicycles.

This heavily forested and partially mountainous isle often has a cap of cloud on Mount Gower (875 metres/2,870ft), at the southern end. There are numerous walking trails, many birds and some unique vegetation. It is advisable to take a tour with a local guide, since it takes a resident expert to decipher the island's rich botany and bird life.

beginning of the next. As you cross the Tweed River, the North Coast of NSW falls behind, and what opens ahead is a very different beast: the Gold Coast of Queensland.

NEW ENGLAND

At **Murrurundi** the New England Highway climbs up, leaving the Hunter Valley to enter the Great Dividing Range, the vast upheaval which separates the coastal plains from the tablelands along the entire length of New South Wales. The town itself is set in a valley of the Liverpool Ranges, and seems constantly shrouded in mist.

The road winds into the ranges and onto the New England Plateau, eventually reaching the city of **Tamworth ⑤**. This pretty town is the largest in the northwest, with a thriving economy based on sheep and cattle. Tamworth's role as a commercial centre for outlying farms and ranches prompted a local radio announcer to establish a promotion on the cowboy theme. In the early 1970s he organised a country music festival and started calling

Tamworth 'the country music capital of Australia'. At first, residents were wary of being stereotyped, but the annual **Tamworth Country Music Festival** (tel: 02 6767 5300; www.tcmf.com.au) is now the town's major draw, attracting thousands of fans every January.

Not far from Tamworth, along a road that follows the bends of the Peel River, is the old gold-mining town of **Nundle**. Abandoned diggings and the ghostly town make it worth a detour. North of Tamworth, the New England Highway passes through spectacular country with rugged peaks and long plains dotted with quaint old mining towns. In **Uralla** you'll find the grave of the legendary bushranger Captain Thunderbolt, shot during a battle with police at nearby Kentucky Creek in 1870.

As its name suggests, the **New England Tableland** bears striking similarities, in both topography and climate, to the old country: England. Its altitude gives it frosty mornings nine months of the year, occasional snow and a year-round freshness.

⊘ Tip

Follow Scenic Drive 19 for about 11km (7 miles) east out of Uralla, until you reach the privately owned village of Gostwyck, known for its merino wool. Beautiful little Gostwyck Chapel, set on the banks of a willow-edged stream, is covered with trailing vines that blaze red around April.

Thunderbolt Rock.

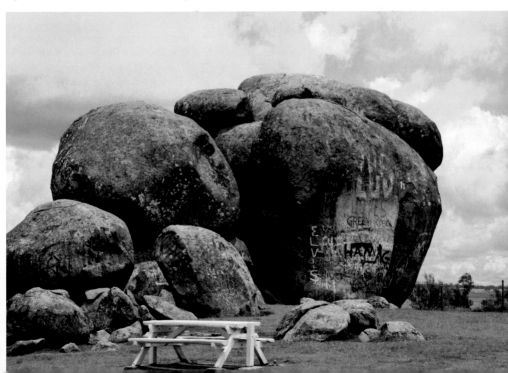

Nowhere is this more evident than in the city of **Armidale ❻**, a scholarly town greened by parks and gardens, with two cathedrals and tree-lined streets. As well as the University of New England, Armidale has one other college and three boarding schools, establishing it as the major NSW seat of learning outside Sydney. The student population has given Armidale an air of youthfulness in contrast to its stately Victorian architecture.

The highway out of Armidale leads along a ridge to the watershed of the Great Dividing Range, 1,320 metres (4,330ft) above sea level, at **Guyra**, then on to the junction with the Gwydir Highway at **Glen Innes**, famous for its fine gemstones. Almost a third of the world's sapphires are mined in this area and, although most of the good spots are on commercial lease, you can search for sapphires, garnets, jasper, agate and numerous other stones at many places. The town itself has magnificent ornate buildings and is fringed by five lovely parks. The mist-shrouded **New England National Park** (tel: 02-6657 2309), east of Armidale, is beautiful.

Tenterfield ❼ is the next major town along the route, once chiefly famous as 'the birthplace of Federation' (because Sir Henry Parkes first called for the Australian colonies to unite in a speech made in the School of Arts here in 1889), but now better known as the birthplace of Peter Allen's grandfather. The late, expatriate Aussie singer topped the charts in the early 1980s with a soppy eulogy to his grandfather called *Tenterfield Saddler*. For all that, it is a rather ordinary country town in which there is not a great deal except memories.

THE SOUTHERN HIGHLANDS

The Hume Highway is the main road from Sydney to Melbourne, along the inland route. En route, **Mount Gibraltar**, a denuded volcanic plug known locally as the Gib, rises above Mittagong and the surrounding terrain, marking the gateway to the Southern Highlands. Few people take the time to stop in Mittagong; they're heading either for the limestone Wombeyan Caves nearby, or the collection of picturesque country towns that have made the Southern Highlands a favourite weekend getaway for Sydneysiders.

The first town you'll come to is **Bowral**, 5km (3 miles) from **Mittagong**, which combines wide small-town streets with elegant big-city-style boutiques. A fashionable resort for well-to-do Sydneysiders in the 1880s, it is still favoured by a similar crowd today, which explains why the town has one of the most sophisticated dining scenes outside Sydney. Other attractions include the **Tulip Festival** in September–October and the **Bradman Museum and International Cricket Hall of Fame** (St Jude Street; tel: 02-4862 1247; www.internationalcrickethall.com; daily 10am–5pm), which includes a permanent exhibition dedicated to Australia's most revered sportsman, cricketer

⊙ SIR DONALD BRADMAN

Australia's finest cricketer and batsman, Donald George Bradman, affectionately known as 'the Don', was born in Bowral in the Southern Highlands in 1908.

Bradman attracted attention at an early age, batting golf balls against a local water tank with only a thin strip of wood. He made his Test cricket debut in 1928, at the relatively young age of 20. Two years later, he scored a record 334 not out in a Test against England and, in a match against Queensland, the highest first-class innings ever achieved (452 not out) – a record he would continue to hold until 1959.

Bradman's international career spanned 20 years, during which he played in 52 Tests and captained the Australian team for more than a decade. His unequalled reputation stems from his unique batting average of 99.94 runs per innings – he made more than 35,000 runs throughout his career. Sadly, in his final Test, he famously needed only a further four runs to reach an average of 100, but was dismissed for a duck (zero runs) on the second ball.

Bradman retired from the game in 1948 and continued to work as a stockbroker as well as serving as a selector for the Australian cricket team. He died in 2001 in Adelaide at the age of 92; eight years later he was inducted into the ICC Hall of Fame.

Don Bradman, who died in 2001. The nearby **Mount Gibraltar Reserve** offers the chance to spot wombats and brush-tailed possums.

The gem of the Southern Highlands is **Berrima ❽**, a small village preserved just as it was in the first half of the 19th century. It is off the Hume Highway, about 8km (5 miles) west of Bowral, and most of it is protected by historic trusts. The township was established in 1831, and today many of its impressive old sandstone buildings have been converted to antique and craft galleries; most of those with historical artefacts are open from 10am to 5pm daily. These include the Surveyor General Inn (1834), said to be the oldest continuously licensed pub in Australia; the Court House (1839), now the information centre and museum (tel: 02-4877 1505; www.berrimacourt house.org.au; daily 10am–4pm); the Gaol (1839), now a prison rehabilitation training centre; the Church of Holy Trinity (1849); and St Francis Xavier's Roman Catholic Church (1851).

GOULBURN

The big country town of **Goulburn** is located 200km (120 miles) southwest of Sydney, about midway between the Southern Highlands and the national capital of Canberra. For most of its life Goulburn has been a staging post for travellers along the Hume Highway. In 1992 a bypass ended all that, and Goulburn today is a much more relaxed place without the trucks rumbling through. Its Georgian homes and two classical cathedrals belie its history as a centre of police action against the bushrangers who plagued the surrounding roads in the 19th century. **Towrang Stockade**, 10km (6 miles) to the north, is sparse ruins today; outlaws like Ben Hall and Frank Gardiner gave this once-formidable penal settlement a wide berth.

Iron hitching posts still stand outside some of the graceful commercial buildings on the main street of **Yass**. Hamilton Hume, the explorer after whom the Hume Highway is named, spent the last 40 years of his life here; his **Cooma Cottage** can be inspected (tel: 0414-774 686; www.coomacottage.com.au; Thu–Sun 10am–4pm) and his tombstone can be visited in the local cemetery.

Gundagai, where the Hume crosses the Murrumbidgee River, has one of those quintessentially Australian names that songwriters find irresistible – it features in a number of tunes, from the classic *Road to Gundagai* to *When a Boy from Alabama meets a Girl from Gundagai*. The town has a colourful history – it was moved from its original site after one of Australia's worst flood disasters in 1852, when 89 people died – and was the favoured hunting ground for the bushranger Captain Moonlight, who was tried at the courthouse in 1879. The town's most famous attraction is the statue of the **dog on the tuckerbox**, a statue that has retained Aussie icon status long after the poem that inspired it has been forgotten.

Donald Bradman's statue at the eponymous museum.

A stained-glass window in Penrose Park.

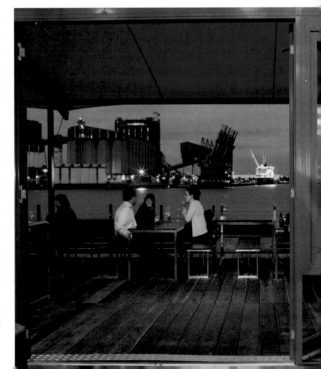

Tip

On an average day, you'll have to wait your turn for a photo opportunity by the cairn that marks the busy summit of Mount Kosciuszko. But there's a grassy knoll a little further down where you can sit on the granite rocks and enjoy the view.

Thredbo village before the snow arrives.

THE SNOWY MOUNTAINS

Some might argue that the Snowy Mountains don't really live up to their name. They're not particularly snowy, at least by international standards – the ski resorts at **Perisher Blue**, **Thredbo** and **Charlotte Pass** often rely on snow-making machines for backup during the short ski season. Nor are the peaks particularly impressive. Although it dominates the skyline, Australia's highest mountain, **Mount Kosciuszko** (pronounced *koz-ee-oss-ko*) is a not-quite-soaring 2,230 metres (7,315ft) high and can usually be climbed on a gentle hike. However, **Kosciuszko National Park** ❾ (tel: 02-6450 5600; vehicle entry), the largest protected area in the state, is well worth a visit, with a number of beautiful walks, some of which can be accessed by the Thredbo ski lifts.

Whether you're coming down the Monaro Highway from Canberra or along the Snowy Mountains Highway from the coast, the town of **Cooma**, at the intersection of the two highways, makes a good base and has a number of nice heritage buildings.

Some prefer to base themselves at **Jindabyne**, 60km (37 miles) west of Cooma on the shores of the lake of the same name. The original town of Jindabyne is buried under the lake – a picturesque history that made it the perfect setting for Ray Lawrence's acclaimed film, *Jindabyne* (2006). Intrepid divers explore lake-bed remnants, including abandoned trucks and the few homesteads that weren't relocated before flooding.

The creation of Lake Jindabyne was part of the Snow River Hydroelectric Project, a 25-year, A$820-million scheme to provide energy for Sydney, Melbourne and the rest of southeastern Australia while diverting water to irrigate vast stretches of the Riverina district west of the mountains. Regarded as one of the great achievements of civil engineering, 100,000 people worked on the scheme, mainly immigrants from 30 different countries.

The timber town of **Tumut** on the Snowy Mountains Highway is known for its autumn colours and it's May Festival of the Falling Leaves (www. fallingleaffestival.com.au).

South of Tumut, the highway enters the Kosciuszko National Park and skirts the eastern shore of **Blowering Reservoir**, venue of numerous water-ski and speed-boat records, including the fastest (510kph/317mph) and longest (1,673km/1,040 miles) runs.

Further on, the **Yarrangobilly Caves** (tel: 02-6454 9597; www.nationalparks. nsw.gov.au) have become one of the Snowy Mountains' leading attractions. About 260 caves have been discovered in a 2.5km by 12km (1.5 by 7.5-mile) limestone belt around the 300-metre (1,000ft) -deep Yarrangobilly River valley. Few caverns anywhere can rival the variety and beauty of their calcite formations. Six caves are open to the public for inspection, five of them by guided tour only.

The road climbs rapidly into **Kiandra**, 90km (56 miles) from Tumut. Now a desolate road junction, it has two 19th-century claims to fame: it was the site of Australia's highest goldfield (1,414 metres/4,639ft), and the location of its first ski club. In fact, the 15,000 miners who lived in tents and shanties on these slopes around 1860 were holding competitive ski races before anyone in Europe. They strapped fence palings – 'butter pads' – to their boots, to move around the surrounding countryside in the winter months.

Travellers proceeding towards Melbourne should turn west at the Kiandra junction. The road climbs to **Cabramurra**, the highest town (about 1,500 metres/4,900ft) in Australia. From this point, it's downhill 63km (39 miles) to the park's western gateway of **Khancoban**. From January to April, this road is a delightful trail through fields of wild flowers, forest stands of mountain ash and snow gum, a number of lovely blue lakes, and frequent herds of kangaroos.

THE SOUTH COAST

NSW's South Coast remains less developed than its northern counterpart. The occasional boutique winery and eco-resort are more subtle, but amid its authentic mix of fishing ports and vacation towns, steel mills and cheese factories, primal forest and coal works, there's plenty to justify the journey. Those travelling **Highway 1** (the Princes Highway) are at times only a short detour away from a windswept peninsular national park or an island whose best-known denizens are little penguins. Furthermore, because the highway south stays close to the coast, it is more scenic than the better-known Pacific Highway north from Sydney.

Departing the metropolis, the Princes Highway spectacularly skirts the rim of the **Illawarra Plateau** until descending suddenly to **Wollongong**, a major industrial city in an impressive natural setting. Some may argue that the smokestacks of the nation's largest steel works provide an unsightly backdrop to the otherwise pristine scene of surf and sandstone cliffs, but the

A monument in Jindabyne to Sir Paul Edmund Strzelecki (1797–1873), the Polish explorer.

Thredbo, Snowy Mountains.

The bridge leading to Kangaroo Valley.

Northeys Store at Hill End, built in 1873, is still an active retail outlet.

heavy industry is the bread and butter for around 10 percent of Wollongong district's population of over 290,000.

That population is spread along 48km (30 miles) of coastline from Stanwell Park in the north to Shellharbour in the south, but is mostly concentrated in the southern Wollongong and **Port Kembla** townships, which have a steel works, a copper smelter and an artificial harbour.

Back in 1797 explorer George Bass anchored in tiny **Kiama Bay** and remarked on a 'tremendous noise' emanating from a rocky headland. Today, the **Blowhole** is the most popular attraction of the fishing and market town of **Kiama ⑩**. When seas are sufficiently high to force water geyser-like through a rock fissure, the spout can reach an amazing 60 metres (200ft) in height. Beware – visitors have been swept to their death off these rocks.

KANGAROO VALLEY

Southwards, about 20km (12 miles) west of **Berry** (the Town of Trees), is **Kangaroo Valley**, a lovely historic township set in an isolated vale among heavily forested slopes. Established in 1829, today it is a favourite haunt of picnickers, bushwalkers and spring wildflower lovers. The **Pioneer Museum Park** (tel: 0421-930 214; www.kangaroovalleymuseum.com) at Hampden Bridge contains a reconstructed 1880s dairy farm, a settler's hut and pioneering farm equipment. Kangaroo Valley is also the gateway to the magnificent **Morton National Park** (tel: 02-4887 7270; vehicle entry), which encompasses a large part of the Shoalhaven escarpment.

Nowra ⑪ is the hub of the Shoalhaven district, 162km (101 miles) south of Sydney. A regional farming centre and an increasingly popular focus of tourism, this riverbank city is 13km (8 miles) from the mouth of the Shoalhaven River. Regional attractions include HMAS *Albatross*, Australia's last naval air training station and host to the Fleet Air Arm Museum (tel: 02-4424 1920; www.navy.gov.au; daily 10am–4pm), which, as well as housing a fine collection of military treasures,

⊘ HYAMS BEACH

The best-known of all the Jervis Bay beaches is Hyams, on the southern shores of the bay, which has the whitest sand in the world (according to the *Guinness Book of Records*). The bay's sparkling waters, its underwater topography of arches, caves and rock stacks, and a marine population that includes groupers, wrasses, sharks, cuttlefish and sea dragons, also make this one of the state's finest dive sites.

Most of the dive sites are located on the seaward faces of the northern and southern headlands that guard the approaches to the bay. Shore diving is possible from Hyams Beach and Green Patch, but the best sites require a boat.

Dive operators in Huskisson can usually supply all the gear, as well as providing regular boat trips.

offers views across the working base from its verandah; **Greenwell Point**, where fresh oysters can be purchased from local growers at the cooperative; and the **Nowra Raceways**, three separate modern tracks for horse racing, trotting and greyhounds. The horse-racing track is known as Archer Raceway after the home-bred winner of the first two Melbourne Cups (1861 and 1862). Archer's stall is maintained as a veritable shrine at Terrara House, now operating as a functions venue east of the town.

JERVIS BAY

Surrounded on all sides except the southeast by 50km (30 miles) of headland and beaches, **Jervis Bay** (pronounced *Jar-vis*) is one of the South Coast's idyllic holiday spots. Once a port that rivalled Sydney Harbour (Port Jackson) as the colony's most important harbour, these days it's home to the Royal Australian Naval College, HMAS *Creswell*. Technically, this is part of the Australian Capital Territory – co-opted under an act that stipulated

the capital must have access to the sea – but that matters not a jot to tourists who are drawn here by the bay's blindingly white, tranquil beaches, the rugged cliff-side landscapes, and the heaths, wetlands and forests that fringe the bay. Picnic in the **Booderee Botanic Gardens** (tel: 02-4443 0977; daily Oct–Apr 9am–5pm, May–Sept 9am–4pm, Dec and Jan holidays 8am–6pm), Green Patch or Illuka beaches, or sign up for a bush-tucker tour with the Wreck Bay Aboriginal Community (www.wbacc.gov.au). The clear waters and varied marine life, including soft corals, sponge gardens and giant cuttlefish, also make it a popular destination for scuba divers.

Ulladulla is a rapidly growing beach resort and fishing port which supplies much of Sydney's fresh fish daily, but hurry on through to allow time to visit Murramarang National Park and Pebbly Beach. At dawn and dusk you are almost certain to be joined by a mob of kangaroos bouncing around on the foreshore, charming food out of visitors and posing for photos.

⊘ Tip

One of the finest vistas in Australia is to be had from Cambewarra Lookout (650 metres/2,120ft up) in Morton National Park, just past the village of Kangaroo Valley, where a sweeping landscape of escarpment rainforest interspersed with tracts of dairy farmland greet the eye. There is also a tearoom here for refreshment while you gaze.

Many people enjoy the water by boat.

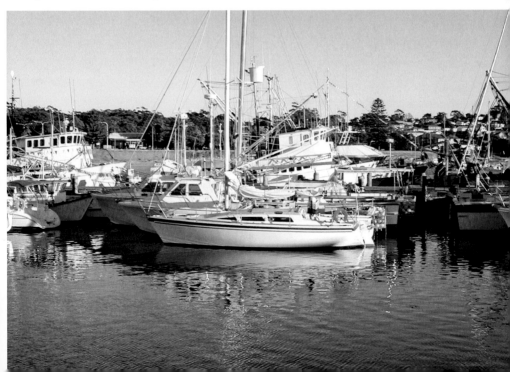

Batemans Bay is a popular tourist, crayfishing and oystering centre at the mouth of the Clyde River. The wildlife refuge on the Tollgate Islands, just offshore, is frequented by penguins. At **Old Mogo Town**, east of the Princes Highway near Mogo, 12km (7.5 miles) south of Batemans Bay, an old mine, a steam engine and a century-old stamper battery (ore crusher) attract modern-day fortune-seekers to this compact gold-rush theme park. Kids will love **Mogo Zoo** (tel: 02-4474 4930; www.mogozoo.com.au; daily 9am–5pm), a privately owned zoo specialising in endangered animals, including snow leopards, jaguars, Bengal and Sumatran tigers, and a pride of white lions.

Moruya ⑫, like Nowra to the north, is established several kilometres inland on the tidal waters of a river mouth. Its first home, Francis Flanagan's Shannon View (1828), is still occupied, and the Uniting Church (or Wesleyan, as it was known in the past) was built in 1864 of local granite. The 130-year-old granite quarry on the north side of the Moruya River once supported a town of its own. Among its notable clients has been Sydney Harbour Bridge.

As the Princes Highway winds through the hills into **Bodalla**, 38km (23 miles) south of Moruya, it's hard to miss the little town's **Big Cheese**. Some 4.5 metres (15ft) high and equally wide, it was sculpted from metal in early 1984 to bolster the community's image as a cheesemaking centre. The region's two largest cheese manufacturers produce almost 10,000 tonnes of fancy and cheddar cheese annually.

The waters off the Eurobodalla area, around the small coastal resort towns of **Narooma** and **Bermagui** – especially those around **Montague Island**, 8km (5 miles) off Narooma – yield record tuna, shark and kingfish catches. **Central Tilba**, 29km (18 miles) southwest of Narooma, is a beautifully preserved hamlet. Each of the village's two-dozen wooden buildings, classified and protected by the National Trust, is as it was in the late 19th century. The ABC Cheese Factory is open (tel: 02-4473 7387; www.

One of the beaches at Narooma.

tilbarealdairy.com; daily 9am–5pm) for cheese tasting, and ancient equipment is on display. Central Tilba was established in the 1870s when gold was discovered on Mount Dromedary. There are fine coastal views from the 825-metre (2,700ft) mountaintop, reached by a walking track.

BEGA

The lush dairy country continues around **Bega**, the far South Coast's biggest town, and famous for its eponymous cheese. There's probably a bylaw that forbids visitors to leave without sampling the local product: play it safe and take in a factory tour and cheese tasting at the Bega Cheese Heritage Centre (tel: 02-6491 7777; www.bega cheese.com.au; daily 9am–5pm).

Merimbula and its sister town of **Pambula**, on the so-called Sapphire Coast, offer fine surfing, boating, fishing and oystering. Crucially, there is also a choice of unspoilt safe beaches, which makes this a prime summer destination for families, many of them from across the border in Victoria. **Eden**, the last sizeable town before you cross the Victoria state border, is located on **Twofold Bay**, once a thriving whaling port and now host to whale-watching tours. The **Eden Killer Whale Museum** (tel: 02-6496 2094; www.killerwhalemuseum.com.au; Mon–Sat 9.15am–3.45pm, Sun 11.15am–3.45pm) on Imlay Street recalls those 19th-century days.

During its whaling era, Eden had stiff competition as a port from **Boydtown** ⑬, established in 1842 by the banker-adventurer Ben Boyd on the south side of Twofold Bay. Boyd dreamed aloud that his settlement would one day become the capital of Australia. He established a steamship service to Sydney and erected many buildings, but in 1850 his empire collapsed. Boyd went bankrupt, fled Australia to the Solomon Islands, and was never heard from again.

All that remains of the grand scheme today are the **Seahorse Inn** – a magnificent building with stone walls a metre (3ft) thick, Gothic arches and hand-carved doors and windows – and **Boyd's Tower**, a 31-metre (102ft) sandstone lighthouse built in 1846 but never lit. The 8,950-hectare (22,110-acre) **Ben Boyd National Park** (tel: 02-6495 5000; vehicle entry charge) encompasses the coastal headlands north and south of Twofold Bay. Its highlights include stunning red sandstone cliffs, rich animal- and birdlife, and lovely wild flowers.

WESTERN SLOPES AND PLAINS

The route due west from Sydney, along the Great Western Highway, passes through the Blue Mountains and enters the vast grazing land beyond. **Bathurst** ⑭, Australia's oldest inland city, was a major pastoral centre even before the heady gold rush of the 1850s, although its elegant 19th-century buildings and its lively student population, courtesy of the local

Bathurst Courthouse is home to the Bathurst Historical Museum.

campus of Charles Sturt University (split between Bathurst and Wagga Wagga), give it a more sophisticated ambience than one might expect.

There's a packaged gold-rush experience at **Bathurst Goldfields** on the city's scenic **Mount Panorama**, where old-time diggings have been set up, and gold-panning demonstrations are given. A bit more authentic is do-it-yourself panning at **Hill End** or **Sofala**, ghost towns north of Bathurst. Take a drive around the town and inner suburbs to see the civic buildings and grand mansions built from the profits of Australia's first gold rush.

In Bathurst, the scenic drive around Mount Panorama becomes a world-class motor-racing circuit for the 1,000km (600-mile) touring car and V8 race in October. Just over 50km (30 miles) west of Bathurst is the intensively photographed village of **Carcoar**, where more than 20 restored colonial buildings nestle in a picturesque little valley.

The highway runs through mainly sheep and wheat country to **Cowra**, a prosperous agricultural centre on the Lachlan River, which has a remarkable link with Japan. During World War II, Japanese prisoners of war interned in a camp there attempted a mass breakout, during which nearly 231 of them were killed. The care local people gave to the graves of the prisoners so impressed the Japanese that they repaid them with the gift of a classical garden. The **Cowra Japanese Garden** (tel: 02-6341 2233; www.cowragarden.com.au; daily 8.30am–5pm) is a colourful showpiece in the gold-brown central west of New South Wales.

WAGGA WAGGA

South of Cowra lies **Wagga Wagga**, shortened to Wagga (rhyming with *logger*) by just about everyone. Although it may seem like a sleepy country town, Australia's most populous inland city has several attractions, including the impressive Botanic Gardens, which have a walk-through aviary with over 300 bird species; the **Wagga Wagga Art Gallery** (tel: 02-6926 9660; www. waggawaggaaustralia.com.au; Tue–Sat

The Wagga Wagga railway station.

10am–4pm, Sun 10am–2pm), which houses the National Art Glass Collection; Charles Sturt University, which runs a prestigious wine course from its on-campus winery; and even a sandy river beach, on the banks of the Murrumbidgee close to the town's main street.

From either Cowra or Wagga the highway westwards becomes a basic two-lane blacktop, running fairly straight for 1,000km (600 miles) or so, until the approaches to Adelaide. Here you enter the true 'sunburnt country', the 'land of sweeping plains' of Dorothea Mackellar's famous poem, *My Country*. If you've yet to see any kangaroos, you'll probably spot them here – although they're likely to be caught in the glare of your headlights. Those cute warning signs have a serious purpose: 'roos are a dangerous hazard on these roads, particularly at night.

The harshness of the elements is burnt into the wild-west appearance of **West Wyalong** ⑮, 161km (100 miles) west of Cowra. Motorists should spurn the bypass and drive down the main street of the former gold-mining town. The quaint town of **Orange** is, predictably, a fruit-growing centre – but, not so predictably, the crops are apples, cherries and grapes that are made into quality wines (the town was named after the Duke of Orange). The extinct volcano **Mount Canobolas**, 14km (9 miles) southwest of Orange, has become a 1,500-hectare (600-acre) flora and fauna reserve with walking trails, picnic areas, waterfalls and a 360-degree view of the countryside from the summit.

Classic 2000 film comedy *The Dish* put **Parkes** on the map, or at least reminded us of a key episode in its history. The town, 93km (58 miles) west of Orange, is famous for its Observatory, housing a 64-metre (210ft) radio telescope which played a crucial cameo role in the 1969 moon landing. The Visitor Centre (tel: 02-6862 6000; visit parkes.com.au; daily 8.30am-4.15pm), on Newell Highway, north of town, explains all.

The **Ophir Goldfields**, 27km (17 miles) northeast of Orange, were

Taronga Park Zoo was officially opened in 1916.

The Japanese Garden at Cowra.

⊙ HOW THE HILL BEGAN

It all began in 1883 when boundary rider and amateur geologist Charles Rasp stumbled across a lump of silver ore on a rocky outcrop he described as a 'broken hill'. From the claim that he and his syndicate pegged, grew the nation's largest company, the Broken Hill Proprietary Co. Ltd (now multi-national giant BHP Billiton).

Although it diversified widely and had completely moved out of Broken Hill by 1939, BHP is still spoken of with distaste in the city for its abrasive attitude to the workforce – the stuff of legend. 'The Hill' turned out to be the world's largest silver, lead and zinc lode, and, while other mining towns have tended to peter out over the years, is still going strong. It has yielded more than 147 million tonnes of ore from its 8km (5-mile) -long lode.

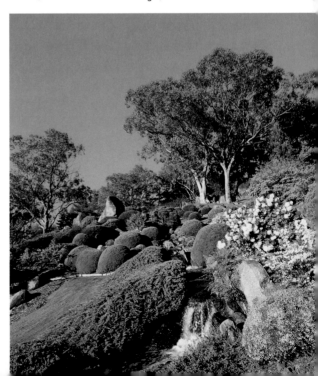

where Australia's first payable gold was discovered in 1851 and are now an official fossicking area. Banjo Paterson's birthplace is marked by a memorial 3km (2 miles) off the highway on the Ophir Road.

DUBBO

The Mitchell Highway runs through undulating terrain around **Wellington**. The **Wellington Caves**, 8km (5 miles) southwest of the town, have huge stalagmite formations in their limestone caverns. The last truly productive agricultural area is around the thriving city of **Dubbo** ⑯, in the middle of the wheat belt, with large sheep and cattle properties and irrigated farms.

Dubbo's main attraction for tourists is the **Western Plains Zoo** (tel: 02-6881 1400; www.taronga.org.au; daily 9am–4pm), which is an excellent wildlife park partnered with Sydney's Taronga Zoo. Animals are placed in settings as near as possible to their native conditions, and penned by moats rather than cages or fences. Australia has an inordinate number of jails as tourist

attractions, and Dubbo is no exception: the **Old Dubbo Gaol** (tel: 02-6801 4460; www.olddubbogaol.com.au; daily 9am–4pm), which was closed in 1966 after almost 80 years, has been restored (complete with gallows) and is open for guided tours.

Narromine, 39km (24 miles) on from Dubbo and on the edge of the western plains, is a major citrus-growing area, and the local Citrus Packers Co-operative will let visitors have a look around. The terrain here provides thermal airlifts, making the area ideal for gliding. In the **Macquarie Valley Irrigation Area**, the town of **Trangie** is the centre of a large cotton-growing industry, and visits can be arranged to the nearby Auscott Cotton Farm. Harvesting and ginning take place from late April to June, the best time to visit.

The scenery starts to turn dry at **Nyngan** on the Bogan River, where the Barrier Highway begins. Here motorists should start keeping an eagle eye on the fuel gauge. There's only one fuel supply (at Hermidale) over the 128km (80 miles) to Cobar; only one stop (at Topar) between Wilcannia and Broken Hill; and few service stations from there to Yunta in South Australia.

HAY AND WILLANDRA

It's a desolate drive on to **Hay** ⑰. Banjo Paterson's bitter poem *'Hay, Hell and Booligal'* was inspired by the almost treeless horizons and the sun-parched tedium, broken only by the sight of an occasional emu, goanna or flock of budgerigars. The town, about halfway from Sydney to Adelaide, is a well-watered oasis on the banks of the Murrumbidgee River. For many years it was an important river crossing on the stock route to Victoria; it also served as a major link in the legendary Cobb and Co. passenger coach network and is now the centre of an extensive horticultural and wool-producing area. An old Cobb and Co. coach, used until 1901, is on display at the coach-house,

The Walls of China in Mungo National Park.

corner of Lachlan and Moppett streets, and Hay's Gaol Museum has a great array of pioneering memorabilia.

Balranald is another spot of green on the Murrumbidgee. Head north to visit the **Willandra Lakes World Heritage Site**, a 370,000-hectare (950,000-acre) system of Pleistocene lakes that contains evidence of Aboriginal habitation in Australia, stretching back 50,000 years. The dry lakes contain ancient hearths and middens, and the world's oldest cremation remains – a first sign of civilisation. The most accessible part of Willandra is **Mungo National Park** ⑱ (tel: 03-5021 8900; www.visit-mungo.com.au; vehicle entry fee), about 150km (93 miles) north of Balranald. Its star attraction is the **Walls of China**, a geological phenomenon of 30-metre (100ft) -high walls of variegated sand running for 30km (19 miles).

A good base for visiting the park is the sleepy town of **Wentworth**, once one of the interior's most important towns. Its position at the confluence of the Murray and Darling rivers meant it controlled the river trade between NSW, Victoria and South Australia until it was superseded by the coming of the railways. It is a pleasant enough base, although most of the so-called attractions, such as Old Wentworth Gaol and Pioneer World, can easily be skipped.

BROKEN HILL

Head north from Wentworth for 265km (165 miles) and you'll reach New South Wales' most remote outpost: **Broken Hill** ⑲ (www.brokenhill.nsw.gov.au). In this far corner, locals set their watches to South Australian time, half an hour behind. Although it belongs to NSW geographically and administratively, most of Broken Hill's trade and communication is conducted through Adelaide, which lies much nearer than faraway Sydney.

The city looms large in Australia's industrial history, with legendary unions eventually dominating the city by means of the Barrier Industrial

Council. Its mineral wealth played the largest part in changing the nation from a strictly pastoral outpost to a more industrial base. With most of the streets named after minerals, it's impossible to escape the town's mining past. You can even see reproductions of mine workings at **White's Mining Museum** (tel: 08-8087 2878; daily 9am–5pm), off the Silverton Road.

But not everything in Broken Hill is related to the great black hill. This Outback town has become an unlikely font of the arts, renowned for several locally famous painters including the late Pro Hart, Jack Absalom and Hugh Schulz. Among the 27 galleries in the city, **Pro Hart's** (tel: 08-8087 2441; www.prohart.com.au; Mon–Sat 9am–5pm, Sun 10am–5pm) is the most quixotic. Besides a wide range of paintings by Hart himself, it also houses much of his private collection, which includes works by Monet, Rembrandt, Dalí, Picasso, Dobell, Drysdale and Tom Roberts.

An extraordinary art experience is located 45 minutes' drive from town at

Cooling-off time in Bell's Milk Bar, Broken Hill.

Broken Hill's redundant Junction Mine.

the Living Desert Reserve. A collection of sandstone sculptures is arrayed in the evocative landscape, with a trail winding between them. The reserve closes at sunset.

Broken Hill has also become a centre for one of Australia's unique institutions – the **Flying Doctor Service**, which transports medical care across the vast distances of the Outback by aircraft.

After dark, the city's social life revolves around the Musicians, Sturt, Legion and Social Democratic clubs, which welcome visitors and have good facilities.

Camels cope well in the Outback's harsh conditions.

In red, rocky country it may be, but Broken Hill still has its beach resort at **Menindee Lake**, 110km (68 miles) away. This is the city's part-natural and part-artificial water-supply system, or at least it is when long-term drought hasn't dried it up. The lake and a system of other lakes and channels cater for boating and swimming; it combines with the adjacent **Kinchega National Park** (tel: 08-8080 3200; vehicle entry fee), home to many water birds.

Sunset over a lake in Kinchega National Park.

The restored ghost town of **Silverton**, a mining centre 23km (14 miles)

from Broken Hill, is not just an attraction for tourists; it's becoming a regular star in Outback film epics. With repainted shop and hotel signs, it has appeared in *A Town Like Alice*, *Mad Max 2* and *Razorback*. Also in the Silverton area is the 100-year-old **Daydream Mine** (tel: 08-8088 5682; tours daily 10am, 11.30am), where visitors can walk down into the old workings.

For the brave traveller with a bit more time (and a 4WD vehicle), it's possible to drive right off the beaten track from Wilcannia to Broken Hill, with a detour through the opal fields. It's a rewarding diversion, but not one to be taken lightly because of its lack of sealed roads and limited fuel and water.

MUTAWINTJI NATIONAL PARK

From Broken Hill, it's about 265km (165 miles) northeast to **Mutawintji National Park** (tel: 08-8080 3200), a surprising patch of greenness in the barren Bynguano Ranges. Strange and colourful rock formations surround ancient Aboriginal campsites, tools, engravings and paintings, which are explained in films shown at the visitor centre. Visitors must check in with the resident ranger on arrival. There are camping facilities, but no power. Ranger-guided tours are available during the cooler months.

White Cliffs, 297km (185 miles) from Broken Hill, is a lunar landscape of craters created by opal diggings, and where fossickers with permits can scrounge. Many residents live underground to escape the winds and extreme temperatures; some of them don't mind showing off the interiors of their white-walled subterranean settlements, which can be surprisingly luxurious. The best accommodation at White Cliffs is an underground motel or subterranean bed-and-breakfast.

The historic buildings and wharf remnants at **Wilcannia** ❷⓿, 98km (61 miles) south of White Cliffs, are reminders of the days when its position on the Darling River made it a major inland port and earned it the title of Queen City of the West.

Take the highway from Wilcannia to Cobar, and about 40km (25 miles) before town, you'll find the turn-off to the **Mount Grenfell Aboriginal cave paintings** (tel: 02-6841 7100). Drive 30km (19 miles) along a good dirt road to the cave, a shallow overhanging rock shelter, for rare examples of techniques and pigments applied by fingers of the Ngiyampaa, in human, bird and animal outlines, and hand stencils.

COBAR

Cobar ㉑ typifies the resilience of the area's people as well as its hardy flora and fauna. From being a rip-roaring town of 10,000 people and 14 hotels not long after copper mining began there in the 1870s, its fortunes have fluctuated: 100 years later its population was less than 4,000 and only one mine was operating; today the figures are 7,000 people and four mines. The Eleura lead, zinc and silver mine

(which was opened in 1983) boosted the town's population and economy. The **Great Cobar Heritage Centre** (tel: 02-6836 2448; Mon–Fri 8.30am–5pm, Sat–Sun 9am–5pm), in an old two-storey mining company office, gives a fascinating insight into the area and its people.

Cobar's Great Western Hotel is the epitome of country hotels, with its massive first-floor verandah. Classification by the National Trust means that the exterior retains its original timberwork and iron lace but, on the inside, accommodation has been transformed into modern, motel-style units.

North of Cobar, the Mitchell Highway meets the Darling River at the small and pleasant township of **Bourke** ㉒. Once an important port, Bourke has become immortalised in the colloquial expression, 'out the back o' Bourke', signifying a place so remote that it is exceeded only by going 'beyond the black stump'. Take in the emptiness that surrounds Bourke, and you'll get a sense of what the Outback really means.

The Mad Max 2 Museum, Silverton.

Aerial view of Parliament House.

CANBERRA

The capital of Australia is a place conceived by accident, built by bureaucrats and located on a compromise. Considering all that, it's a remarkably pleasant place to visit.

During one of his visits to Australia's national capital, the Duke of Edinburgh declared that **Canberra** ㉓ (pop. about 410,000) was 'a city without a soul' – a royal snub Canberra's citizens have never forgotten. In January 2003, raging bush fires spread into the city, destroying 530 homes and 30 farms, and killing four residents. The community spirit in the aftermath demonstrated that even if Canberra lacked soul, its residents still had hearts. But it's not a dearth of soul that troubles Canberra – it just has a faint pulse sometimes. Like many administrative capitals it's an artificial city, constructed not around any existing settlement, but simply out of thin Monaro air, and at times it can feel like you've wandered into the The Truman Show. During term time though, when uni students abound, the place can be very lively. And if you're looking for bushwalking, mountain-biking or skiing trails, this is the place to come.

PURPOSE-BUILT CITY

The reason Canberra was built at all can be traced to colonial jealousy: in 1901, at the time of the federation of the six Australian colonies, there was intense rivalry (which still exists) between Sydney and Melbourne, over which was the chief city of Australia.

The founding fathers solved the problem by the deciding to build a new capital. The search for a site lasted from 1902 to 1908, and is known as The Battle of the Sites. Ultimately a small and hitherto undistinguished valley in the southern tablelands of New South Wales was selected as the site.

Visitors often complain that they can never find the centre – even when they are actually standing in it. Canberra, the political, diplomatic and administrative capital of the Commonwealth, is

⊘ **Main attractions**
Parliament House
Old Parliament House
Questacon
National Gallery
National Museum of Australia
Australian War Memorial Museum

Maps on pages 126, 152

The facade of Parliament House.

Free guided tours of Parliament House take about 45 minutes and include both Houses, the Great Hall and the roof.

simply not built as a commercial city, and so far it has stubbornly refused to look or act like one. In fact, what it looks most like, apart from a spread of pleasantly wooded suburbs, is a kind of semi-dignified Disneyland, complete with a **Captain Cook Memorial Water Jet Ⓐ** which flings water 140 metres (460ft) into the air. Visitors are either impressed or bemused by the city's uncluttered, roundabout-heavy road system that tends to lead the unwary around in circles. Of equal wonder is the absence of external TV antennae and the lack of front fences – both decreed aesthetically incompatible with Canberra's image.

Similarly, new homes are supplied with young native trees in order to promote the city's reputation as a leafy suburbia. In contrast to the absence of urban planning in other Australian cities, Canberra's character does impress. As a result, the capital is a city of showcase architecture. The main attractions are clustered in close proximity to **Lake Burley Griffin**, and a walk around the

lake will provide great views of the city and parliaments.

Although the city is Australia's capital, it can seem surprisingly casual, with low-key security. The best times to visit are spring, when it's green and covered with blossom and wattle, and autumn, when the weather is balmy and the yellowing leaves of the deciduous trees are strikingly beautiful.

Parliament House Ⓑ (www.aph.gov.au/Visit_Parliament; daily 9am–5pm), which cost more than A$1 billion and is adorned with many art and craft works. Completed in 1988, just in time for the bicentennial celebrations, it is built into the side of Capital Hill on the lakeside, its roof grassed in order to blend in, and to allow Australians to walk over their representatives. Free public tours are offered at 10am, 1pm and 3pm. You can also view the transcript of the National Apology speech delivered in 2008 by then Prime Minister Kevin Rudd to the Aboriginal Stolen Generations.

When parliament is sitting, anyone can watch the action from the Public

Galleries. The livelier of the two chambers is the House of Representatives, and the best time to be there is Question Time. This is generally held at 2pm, for which you'll need to book by calling Visitor Services 02-6277 5399 by 12.30pm on the day required.

MUSEUM OF AUSTRALIAN DEMOCRACY

Its predecessor, **Old Parliament House G** on King George Terrace, now houses the **Museum of Australian Democracy** (tel: 02-6270 8222; www.moadoph.gov.au; daily 9am–5pm) where a guided tour of the old chambers is combined with an insight into salient moments of political history.

When visitors step outside, they are confronted by contemporary politics. At the side of the glass-like pond at the front of the building sits the **Aboriginal Tent Embassy**, a collection of signs and structures first set up in the 1970s to focus attention on the Aboriginal land-rights campaign. It has been a semi-permanent fixture since 1992. Depending on your point of view, it's either an icon or an eyesore, but it does serve to remind visitors of the frequently shocking treatment of Aboriginal people in recent history, and their current situation in modern Australian society.

NATIONAL INSTITUTIONS

Also on the lake front, from west to east, are the **National Library D** (tel: 02-6262 1111; www.nla.gov.au; Mon–Thu 10am–8pm, Fri–Sat 10am–5pm, Sun 1.30–5pm), which has 10 million items and displays including a model of Captain Cook's *Endeavour* (visit the everchanging display in the Treasures Gallery); **Questacon – The National Science and Technology Centre E** (tel: 02-6270 2800; www.questacon. edu.au; daily 9am–5pm), which has many enjoyable hands-on displays; the **National Portrait Gallery F** (tel: 02-6102 7000; www.portrait.gov.au; daily 10am–5pm), which presents permanent and temporary exhibitions; the **High Court G**, grandiose enough to echo a Moghul palace; and the **National Gallery H** (tel: 02-6240 6411; www.nga.gov.au; daily 10am–5pm), which

The National Gallery's Sculpture Garden is freely accessible from the path around Lake Burley Griffin.

The National Museum of Australia.

has the world's largest collection of Aboriginal art, a Sculpture Garden and renowned American artist James Turrell's *Within without* Skyspace, an immersive work that people can walk through 24-hours a day, best viewed at dawn or dusk.

On the Acton Peninsula jutting out of the north bank is one of Canberra's more dramatic structures. The **National Museum of Australia ❶** (tel: 1800-026 132; www.nma.gov.au; daily 9am–5pm; general admission free, charge for some temporary exhibitions) houses an eclectic collection of artefacts. Highlights include the world's largest collection of Aboriginal bark paintings, convict clothing and leg irons. Perhaps the oddest exhibit is the oversized heart of the racehorse Phar Lap, whose record-breaking achievements captured the country's imagination during the Great Depression until his premature death, apparently due to arsenic poisoning. Children have their own gallery, **KSpace FutureWorld**, at the National Museum. Here kids can use touchscreen computers to design

The Australian War Memorial Museum.

cities and vehicles, then watch their designs come to life on a 3D screen.

On Aspen Island, the **Carillon** tower, a 50-metre-high, 53-bell gift from Britain, plays musical recitals on Wednesdays and Sundays from 12.30pm to 1.20pm.

North of the lake, the **Australian War Memorial Museum ❶** (tel: 02-6243 4211; www.awm.gov.au; daily 10am–5pm) has a collection of relics, weapons, documents and photographs.

The city has acquired an impressive range of restaurants and several international-class hotels (such as the fabulous Art Deco Hyatt). Nightlife is improving, too, and is especially lively when students are in town. There are 300 cafés, restaurants and bars, a variety of cinemas and theatres, a casino, and some good music venues, playing everything from classical to rock.

NATIONAL BOTANIC GARDENS

The **Australian National Botanic Gardens ❸** (tel: 02-6250 9540; www.anbg.gov.au; daily 9.30am–5pm) at Black Mountain Reserve, contain a huge range of Australian plants over 40 hectares (100 acres), the best of its kind in the country. The surrounding bush is one of the city's great attractions.

West of the lake, the **National Arboretum Canberra** (Tuggeranong Parkway; tel: 02-6207 8484; www.nationalarboretum. act.gov.au; daily Oct–Mar 6am–8.30pm, Apr–Sept 7am–5.30pm) features 100 forests and 100 gardens of threatened and iconic trees from around Australia and the world. There is an impressive nature-themed playground for families and an outdoor amphitheatre.

The **National Zoo and Aquarium** on Lady Denman Drive (tel: 02-6287 8400; www.nationalzoo.com.au; daily 9.30am–5pm) includes a wildlife sanctuary.

In the midst of all the high-minded architectural efforts, Canberra retains considerable charm. It remains one of the few full-size cities in Australia where it's still possible to see kangaroos in the streets. For those who miss out on this spectacle, the nearby **Tidbinbilla Nature Reserve** offers a range of Australian flora and fauna.

AROUND CANBERRA

Canberra is a good jumping-off place for outdoor entertainment and recreation. There are easy day trips to old mining and farming towns such as **Captains Flat** and **Bungendore**, and bushwalking and mountain-biking trails abound in the ACT, including places such as Majura Pines and Sparrow Hill.

A few hours' drive to the south is the **Snowy Mountains ski area**, which offers spectacular bushwalking in summer. About the same distance east is the south coast of New South Wales, with some of the prettiest beaches.

The **Deep Space Communications Complex** at **Tidbinbilla** (www.cdscc. nasa.gov; daily 9am–5pm) is active in the command, tracking and recording of a number of NASA space exploration projects, and is open to visitors.

Foodies will want to explore the **Poachers Way**, a food and wine trail that takes in the region's best restaurants, provedores, artists and wineries – Clonakilla winery is the pick of the bunch.

Deep Space Communications Complex at Tidbinbilla.

Melbourne at night.

MELBOURNE

The capital of Victoria is Australia's most 'European' city, a 21st-century metropolis with an abundance of 19th-century charm and a passion for culture and sport.

That Melbourne continues to feature at or near the top of *The Economist*'s 'most liveable city' table never surprises its residents, even if denizens of the harbour city across the border affect disbelief. **Melbourne ❶** doesn't compete on brash big-ticket items like a beautiful harbour or amazing opera house, but simply and quietly gets on with being the sporting, cultural and dining capital of Australia. It's also a shopping magnet for many Australians, lured by boutiques known for their one-off designs. For visitors, that combination justifies an extended stay.

Newcomers will not find the most picturesque city. The Yarra River isn't the sparkling focal point that rivers are in some cities. Novelist Anthony Trollope considered the Yarra (or Yarra Yarra as it was then) during a visit in 1871: 'It seems to have but little to do with the city. But it is popular with rowers, and it waters the Botanical Gardens.'

RIVER DEVELOPMENT

Attitudes toward the Yarra River are changing, though slowly. There has been extensive work over the past few years, with the Southgate development, Federation Square and a massive revitalisation programme at Docklands.

Trollope also complained that: 'there are no hills to produce scenery, or scenic effect. Though you go up and down the streets, the country around is flat – and for the most part uninteresting. I know no great town in the neighbourhood of which there is less to see in the way of landscape beauty.' Well, say locals, if he'd looked up, he'd have seen the Dandenong Mountains. But Melbourne is more about hidden charms. It has copious parks and gardens to linger in, and leafy suburbs proliferate.

Main attractions
Federation Square
Block Arcade
Old Melbourne Gaol
Melbourne Museum
Royal Botanic Gardens
National Gallery of Victoria
St Kilda

Maps on pages 160, 172

Flinders Street Station.

Indeed, suburbs are intrinsic to an understanding of the city. One of Melbourne's most famous exports, Dame Edna Everage, may skewer them mercilessly but this city is the sum of its neighbourhoods. And when Edna was born out of Barry Humphries' appalled fascination with the monocultural suburbia he grew up in, with its 'politics of niceness', nobody could have anticipated that by 2006 the city he scorned would have so thoroughly embraced his creation as to approve the naming of a city laneway Dame Edna Place.

Rowers on the Yarra River. Melbourne has a strong sporting history and hosted the 1956 Olympics and the Commonwealth Games in 2006.

MELBOURNE VERSUS SYDNEY

Melbourne now is not the city it was in the 1950s. At that time the majority of Australia's biggest companies were based in the Victorian capital and most overseas enterprises followed suit. Here was the seat of the establishment where background and connections determined your entry to the corridors of power. There is still some residue of those times; stockbrokers, lawyers, bankers and company directors are more often than not the product of the city's elite grammar schools and colleges. Pitch up at the wrong barbecue and you'll still find men bragging about their private school and casually dropping the names of their more successful classmates.

But the balance of power between the rivals has shifted. Sydney now has the majority of major company headquarters and, with the exception of the mining companies and banks, the trend is in that direction. So Melbourne has reinvented itself.

Much of the impetus for this adjustment has come from changes in the population. Migration has always influenced the growth of the city, and the Anglo-Celtic dominance that lasted up to World War II has diminished with consecutive waves of migrants from Italy, Greece, the Balkans, Lebanon, Turkey, China, Vietnam and Eastern Europe. The genteel, refined European tastes of the past are still there, but they have been spiced by a more vibrant and outgoing approach to life.

The Melbourne that Ava Gardner described in the 1960s, while shooting an adaptation of Nevil Shute's *On The Beach*, as the perfect place to make a film about the end of the world, is now a city of cool bars, radical architecture and sophisticated inhabitants.

MELBOURNE'S EARLY HISTORY

Unlike Sydney, Melbourne was not founded as a penal colony. Instead, early settlers were free men intent on building a new and prosperous life for themselves. In June 1835, John Batman, a land speculator from Tasmania, sailed his schooner into Port Phillip Bay, rowed up a broad river and declared: 'This will be the place for a village'. With a payment of goods including blankets, mirrors and axes, he persuaded the local Aborigines to 'sell' him 600,000 acres (240,000 hectares) of prime land and drew up a document to legalise the purchase. This was later dismissed by the British Government, which accused Batman of trespassing on Crown Land.

A year later, the settlement beside the Yarra was named in honour of Lord Melbourne, Britain's prime minister. The first land sales took place soon after, and small properties at the centre of the settlement sold for £150. Two years later, the same properties were changing hands for £10,000.

It was the discovery of gold in nearby Ballarat in 1851 that propelled the sudden growth in population and prosperity which determined Melbourne's true character. This was also when its role as Australia's financial centre was established. The finds drew thousands of fortune-seekers from Europe, the USA and China; gold fever swept the country. But in time the alluvial gold ran out, and thousands of diggers left the goldfields to make Melbourne their home. The population more than quadrupled in 10 years, and the gold revenue financed new development in a rapidly expanding city determined to grow grand in style.

When Mark Twain visited on a lecture tour in 1895, he was entranced by what he saw: 'It is a stately city architecturally as well as in magnitude. It has an elaborate system of cable-car service; it has museums, and colleges, and schools, and public gardens, and electricity, and gas, and libraries, and theatres, and mining centres and wool centres, and centres of the arts and sciences, and boards of trade, and ships, and railroads, and a harbor, and social clubs, and journalistic clubs and racing clubs, and a squatter club sumptuously housed and appointed, and as many churches and banks as can make a living. In a word, it is equipped with everything that goes to make the modern great city.'

Federation in 1901 saw Melbourne become Australia's political capital city, until Canberra was ready to assume that mantle in 1927. The Depression of the 1930s was followed by a spell of industrial growth and development, given extra impetus by post-war migration. When it hosted the 1956 Olympics, Melbourne was

Melbourne's skyline.

⊙ **Tip**

For marvellous city views and a peaceful drink in stylish surroundings right in the heart of the city, try **Transit** (www.transitrooftopbar.com.au), the rooftop cocktail bar above the Transport Hotel in Federation Square. There's live music most weekends.

more than ready to take its place on the world stage. Substantial investment in the local equivalent of François Mitterrand's *grands projets* – particularly under Liberal Premier Jeff Kennett in the 1990s – transformed the city and shifted its geographical axis.

FEDERATION SQUARE

The completion of **Federation Square** (tel: 03-9655 1900; www.fedsquare.com) in 2004 gave Melbourne its first popularly embraced public space. The ornately Victorian **Flinders Street Station** had been the city's signature building for years, and 'under the clocks' was the traditional rendezvous point for a night out, a practice immortalised in a song of that name by seminal local band Weddings Parties Anything. But station steps are not necessarily the best place to loiter. Federation Square, on the other hand, has plenty of space, places to sit, cafés and bars, and is right opposite the station.

The deconstructivist design of Federation Square has its detractors,

some of them vehement, but no one can deny its impact on the city. Built above unsightly railway yards, it serves to unite the Central Business District (CBD) with the Yarra. At its heart is a gently scalloped piazza paved with variegated sandstone, which inclines towards a small stage and a giant video screen. Concerts and public events attract large crowds and there always seems to be something going on.

The buildings behind, designed as 'shards' sticking out of the ground, look as if they have been crazy-paved in a combination of glass, stone and zinc. The riches within include a branch of the National Gallery of Victoria – **The Ian Potter Centre** (tel: 03-8620 2222; www.ngv.vic.gov.au; daily 10am–5pm), which is one of those buildings that, inside, has an air of unpredictability. Walls are coming at you from all angles and there's no clue as to what may be around the next corner. Somehow it all works; the daylight comes in where it should and the art – all Australian – is displayed sympathetically. The **Australian Centre for the Moving**

Federation Square.

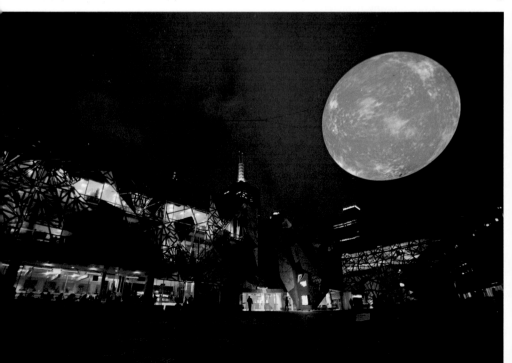

Image (tel: 03-8663 2200; www.acmi.net. au; daily 10am–5pm; cinema times as advertised; free except for some exhibitions and cinema) has screenings, exhibitions, even video games; the programming is sometimes populist and always eclectic. There is also the **Edge** performance space and a variety of bars, cafés and restaurants.

Behind Fed Square (as it's locally known) is **Birrarung Marr** (tel: 03-9658 9658; www.melbourne.vic.gov. au/parks), an area of parkland on the riverbank designed to acknowledge the original Aboriginal occupants of the land. Rock carvings and sculptural representations of shields and spears reflect the various tribes. Further on, the striking **Federation Bells** installation is worth seeing (and hearing), and the passage of a bridge through to the Melbourne Cricket Ground ensures that plenty of people get to enjoy them.

TAKING THE TRAM

Melbourne's CBD revolves around an easily navigable grid, and is very walkable. Acting as backup is the **Circle Tram**, a free service that operates in a loop round the edge of the CBD. The tram system is one of Melbourne's great resources and, if you pick your route judiciously, a great way to discover the city.

St Paul's Cathedral (tel: 03-9653 4333; www.stpaulscathedral.org.au), opposite Federation Square, was built between 1880 and 1891 to a design by William Butterfield, who never bothered to travel from England to see it. The stained glass and tiled floors are among the highlights.

On the other corner of Flinders and Swanston streets, **Young and Jackson's** pub (tel: 03-9650 3884; www.youngandjacksons.com.au) is a Melbourne institution, renowned for the 19th-century nude portrait *Chloe* on the first floor, which was considered rather racy in its day.

Continue along Swanston Street to **Melbourne Town Hall** . Typical of the grand public buildings of the gold boom, it comes into its own during the **Melbourne International Comedy Festival** (www.comedyfestival.com.au) every April, when various performance spaces are carved out of its halls and meeting rooms and it takes on a real club atmosphere.

Collins Street crosses Swanston Street at this point. If you go right, up Collins and past the magnificent **Regent Theatre** – pop into the foyer if it's open – you will come to the 'Paris end', where a bunch of exclusive boutiques and designer stores tempt wealthy tourists. To avoid that, go in the opposite direction.

SHOPPING ARCADES

Were you to continue walking a couple of blocks, you would be rewarded with the remarkable Gothic Revival facade of the **ANZ Bank Building** at the junction with Queen Street. But before that comes the **Block Arcade** (tel: 03-9654 5244; www.theblock.com.

The Windsor Hotel on Spring Street is a Victorian Heritage Hotel and dates from 1883.

Cast-iron details on Powlett Street.

The famous grounds of the MCG.

au) between Elizabeth and Swanston streets. In this Victorian marvel, check out the mosaic floors, etched glass roof, and the original shop fittings. The **Hopetoun Tearooms** (tel: 03-9650 2777; www.hopetountearooms.com.au) has been purveying refreshment to refined shoppers for generations. Wind through to Little Collins Street and cross the road to **Royal Arcade** (tel: 0425-738 042; www.royalarcade.com.au; Mon–Thu 9am-6pm, Fri 10am-8pm, Sat 9am-5pm, Sun 10am-5pm). You'll run the gamut of the slightly cartoonish statues of Gog and Magog, just behind you as you enter.

The far end opens into **Bourke Street Mall** ❻, the epicentre of old-style city shopping with the flagship department stores of the Myer and David Jones chains. At the Elizabeth Street end, the old GPO building has been successfully converted into a high-end shopping complex. The Myer store runs back across two blocks and has a bridge over to the bustling retail hub **Melbourne Central** (www.melbournecentral.com.au; daily 10am–7pm, until 9pm Thu and Fri), which completely encloses the 1890 Shot Tower.

The Swanston Street entrance to Melbourne Central faces the imposing **State Library of Victoria** ❻ (tel: 03-8664 7000; www.slv.vic.gov.au; Mon–Thu 10am-9pm, Fri-Sun 10am-6pm), which has had a rather large fortune spent on it in renovations. The **Reading Room** copies the famous one in London's British Museum. (Some temporary closures will take place during the library's 'Vision 2020' redevelopment programme – check the website.)

The **QV Centre** (www.qv.com.au; Mon–Tue 10am–7pm, Fri 10am–9pm, Sat 10am–6pm, Sun 10am–5pm), next to the library, is another shopping development, which attempts to emulate the feel of Melbourne's laneways in a more modern structure.

Following Latrobe Street beside the library and turning left on Russell Street, you'll find **Old Melbourne Gaol** ❻ (tel: 03-8663 7228; www.oldmelbournegaol.com.au; daily 9.30am–5pm). This is where Ned Kelly met his end. His death mask is on display along

⊘ SPORTS SOCIETY

If Australians are sports mad, then Melbourne must be the asylum. It's not just the obsession with the sports themselves, but the determination to make every contest an event.

The first Tuesday of November is a public holiday, because that's when the Melbourne Cup horse race is run. Each year the crowds at Flemington Racecourse seem bigger than the year before. In 2006, the record-breaking 129,000 crowd was not at Cup Day but at the previous Saturday's Derby Day.

Boxing Day cricket invariably sells out at the MCG, but in 2010, for an exciting Ashes series, the first four days of the test match sold out in advance; that's nearly 400,000 people if everyone turned up. The biggest single recorded cricket crowd, however, was in 2015, when 93,013 watched the World Cup Final between Australia and New Zealand.

The Australian Rules football Grand Final at the MCG in September is the biggest event of them all though; over 100,000 were in attendance when the West Coast Eagles beat Collingwood in 2018. When local rivals Collingwood and St Kilda drew in the 2010 final, the match had to be replayed, prolonging cup fever by another week; Collingwood eventually won by 56 points.

Aussie Rules dominates Melbourne for seven months of every year. Although this is a very Victorian sport, teams from Queensland, NSW and Western Australia have all won the premiership title.

with some of his armour. The building is grimly atmospheric as it is, but extreme thrill-seekers can join evening ghost hunts.

Return along Russell Street before turning left to go up Little Bourke Street, Melbourne's **Chinatown**, a buzzing and colourful lane with several good eateries. Turn left on Spring Street and continue to the end, where the **Carlton Gardens** across the road lead up to Australia's first World Heritage-listed structure, the **Royal Exhibition Building**. Access is normally only available for special events, but if you get a chance, nip in and have a look. It's a lovely spot.

MELBOURNE MUSEUM

On the far side, that striking modern pavilion is the **Melbourne Museum ❶** (tel: 131102 (Victoria only), 1300-130152; www.museumvictoria.com.au; daily 10am–5pm). There is masses to see in the country's largest museum, and it's all presented so alluringly that you can spend hours here without realising it.

The children's section is pitched just right, and other areas appeal to all ages, especially the Melbourne Story Gallery and the Bunjilaka Aboriginal Centre. There's an IMAX cinema too.

SPRING STREET

Return to Spring Street and the state's seat of government at **Parliament of Victoria House ❶** (tel: 03-9651 8911; www.parliament.vic.gov.au), another grandiose Victorian pile, which still awaits the dome originally designed for it. Free tours (Mon–Fri 9.30am, 10.30am, 11.30am, 1pm, 1.30pm, 2.30pm, 3.30pm, 4pm) are available unless the houses are in session, in which case try for the public gallery.

The **Princess Theatre** opposite Parliament House is typical of its era, even down to the ghost story; ask for details at the box office. Continue along Spring Street to another monolithic public building. This is the **Old Treasury** (tel: 03-9651 2233; www.oldtreasurybuilding.org.au; Sun–Fri 10am–4pm). The permanent exhibits are linked to the history of the building and its role as

Bourke Street.

The Old Melbourne Gaol also runs night tours four nights a week.

Victoria's repository of gold. **Treasury Garden**, alongside, crawls with possums after dark.

FITZROY GARDENS AND THE MCG

Walk through to **Fitzroy Gardens**, where, under towering old trees, you will find **Cooks' Cottage** (tel: 03-9658 9658; www.thatsmelbourne.com.au; daily 9am–5pm). It's not hard to discover Australia if you were brought up there, you might think. But no, the whole thing was disassembled in Yorkshire, shipped round the world and rebuilt in Melbourne, making it the only 18th-century building in town. Elsewhere, look out for the model **Tudor Village**, sent as a gift from the people of Lambeth in London, grateful for Australian food parcels during World War II; and the **Fairies Tree**, a tree trunk carved with cute little figures.

Across Wellington Parade, the Melbourne Cricket Ground, better known as the **MCG** , beckons to sports fans. Try to get in to see some kind of sporting action, but if not, there are tours

A country locale for a weekend stroll.

(Gate 3; tel: 03-9657 8888; www.mcg.org. au; daily 10am–3pm if no event) of the 100,000-seat stadium. The **National Sports Museum** (tel: 03-9657 8879; www.nsm.org.au; daily 10am–5pm; upgrade in process) is housed here and has interesting exhibits on cricket, racing, Aussie Rules and the Melbourne Olympics, all enhanced by the latest technology.

SOUTH OF THE YARRA

Return to Federation Square, turn left to cross the river, and go down St Kilda Road. Directly ahead of you is the grey stone **Shrine of Remembrance** (tel: 03-9661 8100; www.shrine.org.au; daily 10am–5pm). Built to commemorate the dead of World War I, it is aligned so that once a year at 11am on the 11 November – Remembrance Day – a beam of light shines on to the Stone of Remembrance and illuminates the word 'love'. A visitor centre nestles in the shadow of the main building.

Just across the way from the shrine is the Observatory Gate, one of the entry points to the **Royal Botanic**

Gardens (tel: 03-9252 2300; www. rbg.vic.gov.au; daily 7.30am–sunset). Enthusiasts will enjoy the specialist areas, like the cactus garden or the cycad collection, but many simply wander through the beautifully tended grounds and drink in the tranquillity of the lakeside – as recreational runners do laps of the 'Tan'. There is also an excellent children's garden.

ARTS PRECINCT

Return to St Kilda Road and cross over to the bluestone bulk of the **National Gallery of Victoria** (tel: 03-8620 2222; www.ngv.vic.gov.au; Wed–Mon 10am–5pm). This is, in fact, **NGV International**, which houses the NGV's collection of work from overseas, as opposed to the Ian Potter Centre at Federation Square, which specialises in Australian works. Stick your fingers in the water wall at the entrance, as generations have before you, and take your pick of the permanent exhibits or the visiting shows (for which a charge is usually levied). Leonard Hall's stained-glass ceiling of the **Great Hall** accounts for all the people lying on their backs within, and beyond is the doorway to the **Sculpture Garden**.

Next door, distinguished by the huge mesh spire above it, is the **Arts Centre** (tel: 03-9281 8000; www. artscentremelbourne.com.au). This cultural powerhouse has three theatres presenting **Melbourne Theatre Company** productions and visiting opera, dance and drama companies. In 2012 work finished on the renovation of **Hamer Hall**, the city's formal concert venue. If you carry on past the NGV and turn right, the striking building with the white geometric shapes all over it is the new MTC Theatre, and just beyond it, the equally new Melbourne Recital Centre.

At the river, turn left along the South Bank where the promenade provides good views over the city, but not as good as those from the top of the **Eureka Tower** and its Eureka Skydeck 88 (tel: 03-9693 8888; www. eurekaskydeck.com.au; daily 10am–10pm) which, predictably, is on the 88th floor. If you don't mind heights, try The Edge experience, during which you're pushed out the side of the building in a glass cube, 300 metres above Melbourne's streets.

You may want to cross over the river to visit the absorbing **Immigration Museum** (tel: 131102 (Victoria only), 03-9927 2700; www.immigration.museum. vic.gov.au; daily 10am–5pm), or **Melbourne Aquarium** (tel: 1800-026 576; www.melbourneaquarium.com.au; daily 9.30am–6pm, Jan 9.30am–8pm).

Crown Casino (tel: 03-9292 8888; www.crowncasino.com.au; daily, 24 hours) on your left seems to go on forever; given the turnover on the tables and through the one-arm bandits, or 'pokies' as they're known, the management probably hopes it will. Shops, restaurants, show venues and a cinema can be found inside.

⊙ Tip

A card showing membership of any National Trust organisation from around the world will secure free admission to Old Melbourne Gaol, managed by National Trust Victoria (www. nationaltrust.org.au). For those without a card, buying one in Victoria is a cost-effective way of securing reciprocal benefits elsewhere.

Melbourne Aquarium.

DOCKLANDS

There are lots of live music venues in Melbourne.

The architecturally stimulating **Melbourne Exhibition Centre**, or 'Jeff's Shed' as the locals call it, since it was one of Premier Jeff Kennett's projects, comes next. On the river bank beyond is the distinctive outline of historic ship, the *Polly Woodside*, docked in front of the new Convention Centre.

Cross the river on the serpentine **Webb Bridge** to reach **Docklands**, the latest area of Melbourne to be given an overhaul. Follow the path through a sculpture garden that eventually leads to **Victoria Harbour,** with the **Docklands Stadium ⑤** – officially rebranded Marvel Stadium (www.marvelstadium.com.au) in 2018, after the Walt Disney Company took over naming rights from **Etihad** – on your right and glistening new developments of offices, apartments and restaurants on your left. The area is slowly finding its feet but it's worth wandering down for a look if only because it's unlike anything else in Melbourne.

It's time to hop on the Circle Tram clockwise to the junction of Latrobe and Queen streets. Walk north up Queen Street until reaching the extensive sheds of **Queen Victoria Market ❼** (tel: 03-9320 5822; www.qvm.com.au; various opening hours, see website). This is a buzzing place where locals looking for fresh produce and deli specialities mix with tourists seeking souvenirs. Beside the fruit and veg, and the speciality produce stalls, there are several side markets and seasonal offerings, including String Bean Alley (Wednesday and weekends, flowers, gifts and coffee), and a Wednesday nightmarket (5–10pm until 20 March).

LITTLE ITALY

A short distance to the north, **Lygon Street** in Carlton, just 10 minutes by tram from the city centre, is sometimes known as **Little Italy**. It was this area that the waves of post-war Italian migrants adopted as their own, and at certain times of the year, such as when the Ferrari team is in town for the Grand Prix, streets are closed and the partying doesn't let up. Today Lygon Street is touristy, but a lively community of professional people and academics from adjacent Melbourne University keeps the place grounded. Coffee bars, bistros, trattorias, noisy pubs and pool rooms, as well as edgy fashion boutiques, contribute to a vibrant atmosphere.

Brunswick Street, a few blocks to the east, is hipper. In the evenings Melburnians drift here from around the city with bottles of wine tucked under their arms, looking for the latest BYO restaurant. They find cuisines from around the world, as well as Modern Australian food. Wine bars, pubs with local bands and comedy nights, designer clothes stores, tiny retro fashion shops, LGBTQ bookshops, artists' cafés of the type popular in the 1950s and 60s, full of earnest characters confused by daylight, all happily co-exist.

Melbourne Zoo in Parkville, west of Lygon Street, has been a favourite since it opened in 1862 (Elliott Avenue;

Dining in an Italian restaurant on Lygon Street.

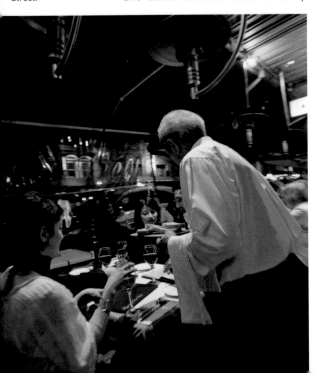

tel: 1300-966 784; www.zoo.org.au; daily 9am–5pm). It has a comprehensive collection of indigenous animals, displayed in sympathetic surroundings, as well as species from further afield. Its elephant enclosure manages to recreate an Asian setting, and the food court is themed to match.

ST KILDA

St Kilda has always been fun. Often sleazy, frequently illicit, but fun nonetheless. This bayside suburb is Melbourne's urban beach. There's no surf and few would brave a dip in the water, but the sand is clean and the beach-front on weekends is rather like Los Angeles' Venice Beach: rollerbladers and cyclists speed past, models preen themselves in the sun, and bodybuilders work out on the grass. Fight for an outside table at a beach-front restaurant, or walk along the jetty for a distant view of the city skyline (there's a café at the end).

Acland Street is famous for its cafés and cake shops. It displays the palate-delighting influences of Mittel Europe, reflecting a strong Jewish presence, but other nationalities are crowding in. At the end of the street, Luna Park's gap-toothed grin invites you to try the clattering roller coaster (tel: 03-9525 5033; www.lunapark.com.au; Sept–Apr Fri 7–11pm, Sat 11am–11pm, Sun 11am–6pm, Jan–Feb Thu 7–11pm, May–Sept Sat–Sun 11am–6pm; charge for rides).

The Upper Esplanade hosts a Sunday arts and crafts market, while in Fitzroy Street the restaurants take over the footpaths, Mediterranean-style, with their tables and umbrellas.

WILLIAMSTOWN

On the other side of the bay, over the Westgate Bridge (or take a ferry from Southgate), is Williamstown, a bayside village with plenty of cafés, restaurants and great views back to the city. On its outskirts lies one of Melbourne's best museums: Scienceworks (2 Booker Street, Spotswood; tel: 131 102; www.

scienceworks.museum.vic.gov.au; daily 10am–4.30pm), set in the grounds of an old pumping station. Its hands-on displays include House Secrets, which reveals what's really going on under the surface of a domestic environment.

PRAHRAN AND SOUTH YARRA

North of St Kilda, Prahran has one of Melbourne's best markets (163 Commercial Road; tel: 03-8290 8220; www.prahranmarket.com.au; Tue, Thu, Sat 7am–5pm, Fri 7am–6pm, Sun 10am–3pm) and, in Chapel Street, a shopping strip that runs from op-shop (charity shop) to designer chic, with prices rising as you move north into South Yarra and affluent Toorak.

Como House (corner Williams Road and Lechlade Avenue, South Yarra; tel: 03-9656 9889; www.nationaltrust.org.au; gardens and cafe Mon–Sat 9am–5pm, Sun from 10am, house tours Sat–Sun in summer at 10.30am, 12pm, 2pm, 3pm and 3.30pm) is a graceful colonial mansion built in 1847, set in grounds that demand you go equipped with a picnic.

The St Kilda Markets in front of the Palais Theatre.

VICTORIA

All the destinations in Victoria are within a day's drive of Melbourne – alpine mountains, desert plains, pristine beaches, historic wineries, gold-mining villages and quaint spa towns.

Almost 6.5 million people live in Victoria, the smallest of the mainland states, which makes it heavily populated by Australian standards. Over four million are in Melbourne though, so parts of Victoria can still feel pretty empty. Squashed down in the bottom right corner of the country, its northern border defined over hundreds of kilometres by the Murray River, Victoria is at its emptiest in the northwest, where the Mallee, a semi-arid land of open plains, is given over to farming (of sheep and grain) and national parks; and in the east, where the end of the Great Dividing Range curls round to peter out a few kilometres short of Melbourne. This high country of timber and cattle farming gets busier in winter as snow opens up the ski fields.

Victoria stuttered into life with the first permanent European settlement at Portland in 1834. Two years later pastoralists started crossing the Murray from the east and, with Melbourne growing, population increase was rapid. Aboriginal numbers, though, fell rapidly as introduced diseases and firearms took their toll.

In 1851 Victoria seceded from New South Wales. Within weeks gold was discovered and the new state's population and prosperity boomed. Indeed, the countryside is still littered with colonial mansions, and the towns with stately public buildings and hotels.

For such a small state, Victoria manages to pack in a lot of attractions. The Great Ocean Road, the Goldfields and **Wilson's Promontory** are among the best known, but there are also coastal resorts, wineries, the inland ports of the Murray and some wonderful mountain scenery to explore. With good roads and comfortable distances to cover, Victoria is an easy state to explore.

Main attractions
Geelong
Queenscliff
The Great Ocean Road
Port Fairy
The Grampians
The Murray River
The Dandenongs
Beechworth
The Mornington Peninsula

Map on page 172

Playing in the waves at Torquay.

WEST OF MELBOURNE

From Melbourne the Princes Freeway speeds through the plains along the western shore of **Port Phillip Bay**. For a glimpse of opulence, take the exit to **Werribee Park** (tel: 13 1963; www.parkweb.vic.gov.au; Oct–March daily 10am–5pm, Apr–Sept Mon–Fri 10am–4pm, Sat–Sun 10am–5pm). In a 60-room Italianate mansion built in 1877 by the pastoralist Chirnside family, visitors can sample a vivid display of flamboyant wealth. The extensive grounds are set off by a sculpture walk mostly made up of past winners of the Helen Lampriere Sculpture Prize. There are more fragrant pleasures to be found in the adjoining **Victoria State Rose Garden**.

Nearby, the **Werribee Open Range Zoo** (tel: 1300-966 784; www.zoo.org.au; daily 9am–5pm) re-creates African savannah, with safari buses driving you among the animals.

GEELONG AND THE COAST

As you drive on, the volcanic **You Yangs** (tel: 13 1963; www.parkweb.vic.gov.au) dominate the skyline. Get closer to them by detouring to **Anakie**, home of **Fairy Park** (tel: 03-5284 1262; www.fairypark.com; daily 10am–5pm), 'Australia's first and oldest theme park', where dioramas from fairy tales unfold by the winding path to the top of a granite crag. It's very low-tech by today's standards, but kids love it and there's an excellent playground, including the irresistible 'do not touch this button'.

Return to the highway and Victoria's second city. In its early days **Geelong ②** rivalled Melbourne as an outlet for Western District wool and later became an important manufacturing centre. After years of somnolence the city has shaken itself up – particularly by the waterfront, where quirky sculptures and a renovated pier are the focus.

A drive along the waterfront shows Geelong past and present – the old mansions, wool stores and piers, and the new industries, wharves and container terminal. Along the Barwon River are fine homes such as **Barwon Grange** (Fernleigh Street; tel: 03-9656 9800; www.nationaltrust.org.au; Sept–April 1st, 2nd and 3rd Sun of each month 1–4pm, May–Aug 3rd Sun of the month 1–4pm), refurnished in the style of 1855, when it was built by a merchant ship owner.

For a whiff of nostalgia, take the Bellarine Highway out of Geelong and travel to **Queenscliff ③**. This was 'Queen of the Watering Places' in the 1880s, when paddle steamers brought the fashionable to the handsome turreted hotels. There is still a haughty grandeur to the place. The **Queenscliff Fort** (King Street; tel: 03-5258 1488; www.fortqueenscliff.com.au; tours Sat–Sun and school holidays, 1pm and 3pm), with red-brick walls and cannon, was built in the 19th century to defend Melbourne against a Russian invasion.

The winding Great Ocean Road.

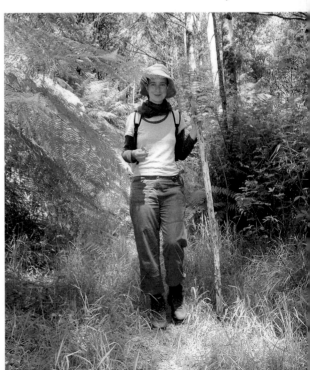

Bushwalking in Great Otway National Park.

Beach bollards decorate the sands at Geelong near the town of Port Phillip Bay.

The Great Ocean Road leads past Apollo Bay.

GREAT OCEAN ROAD

The road on to **Anglesea** meanders through seaside settlements, sleepy in winter and pulsing with life in summer. **Torquay** is the surf centre of Victoria, and **Bells Beach** is famed worldwide for its Easter surf contest. Beyond Anglesea, whose main claim to fame is the mob of kangaroos that live on the golf course, is the start of the **Great Ocean Road** (www.visitgreatoceanroad. org.au) 200km (125 miles) of the state's most spectacular coastal scenery.

A favourite weekend spot from Melbourne is **Lorne ➍**, set on a picturesque bay with a bush backdrop and several restaurants and shops. The annual Pier-to-Pub Swim in January attracts entrants from across the nation.

In the **Great Otway National Park** (www.visitotways.com) tracks wind through eucalyptus forest and fern gullies to waterfalls and lookouts. Walks vary from a gentle stroll along the St George's River to rock-hopping along to the Cora Lyn Cascades. A three-hour hike up to the **Erskine Falls** can

be strenuous, while the less energetic can drive to a lookout.

Along the coast at **Kennett River**, a 6km (3.5-mile) drive leads to the **Grey River Scenic Reserve**. It's a short walk (1.5km/1-mile round trip), one of the best in Victoria, up a fern gully amid towering blue gums.

For a panoramic view of the **Otway Ranges**, turn inland at **Skenes Creek** and drive up into the hills. After 15km (9 miles), turn left into the fern and mountain-ash forest along Turton's Track. When the country opens out again you are on a ridge. On the left, wooded spurs reach down to the sea; on the right are the volcanic lakes and plains of the Western District.

From **Apollo Bay**, with its mixed artsy and fishing vibe, the Great Ocean Road leaves the coast to wind through the forest behind Cape Otway. Find the **Otway Fly** (tel: 03-5235 9200; www. otwayfly.com; daily 9am–5pm), and enjoy a walk through the forest canopy on 600 metres/yds of steel walkway, 25 metres (82ft) above the ground. At **Cape Otway** a tour of the **Lighthouse**

(tel: 03-5237 9240; www.lightstation.com; daily 9am–5pm), which has watched over the hazardous entrance to the Bass Strait since 1848, is worthwhile. The setting is sublime.

THE TWELVE(ISH) APOSTLES

Past Princetown lies the spectacular coastline of **Port Campbell National Park ❺** (tel: 13 1963; www.parkweb. vic.gov.au), where breakers have battered the soft limestone cliffs, creating grottoes and gorges, arches and sea sculptures rising from the surf. The road gives only occasional glimpses of the drama below, which includes the stark rock stacks of **The Twelve Apostles** and the spray billowing through the fallen arch of **London Bridge**. It is an evolving landscape; as over time some of the stumps have collapsed into the sea due to erosion, most recently in 2005, leaving just eight remaining Apostles. Stop at all the vantage points, follow the various trails at **Loch Ard Gorge**, and make the most of the new visitor centre. This shoreline – between dramatic

Cape Otway and pretty Port Fairly, known as the Shipwreck Coast – is the final resting place for over 50 vessels, of which the *Loch Ard* is one.

Beyond Peterborough and the dramatic **Bay of Islands** lies **Warrnambool ❻**, once a busy port and now a holiday centre. People flock here in winter to see southern right whales, which calve off Logans Beach. Around the lighthouse is the **Flagstaff Hill Maritime Village** (tel: 03-5559 4600; www.flagstaffhill.com; daily 9am–5pm), a re-created 19th-century port complete with chandlers, shipwrights and sailmakers. The spectacular *Shipwrecked* sound-and-laser show runs nightly at dusk (see website for precise times). **Warrnambool Art Gallery** (tel: 03-5559 4949; Mon–Fri 10am–5pm, Sat–Sun noon–5pm) has a large collection of Australiana.

Beyond Warrnambool is **Tower Hill State Game Reserve**, a volcanic crater containing smaller cones where ducks nest, emus share your picnic and there's a good chance of seeing koalas. At dusk the 'roos come out as well.

An innkeeper in Flagstaff.

Coastline near Loch Ard Gorge.

PORT FAIRY

Along the coast is the fishing-village charm of **Port Fairy 7**, where brightly painted boats tie up at the jetty with their catches of crayfish and crab. Port Fairy was named by Captain James Wishart who brought his tiny cutter, the *Fairy*, into the Moyne River to find shelter during a sealing expedition in 1810 (although it was renamed Belfast for a time). Sealers and, later, whalers built stone cottages that still nestle under the tall Norfolk Island pines shading the streets. You can drink (and stay) at the **Caledonian Inn**, which opened in 1844 and has been in business ever since.

Griffiths Island, at the mouth of the river, was a whaling station, but is now a rookery for thousands of mutton birds that return in September from the north Pacific. The young hatch in January, and every evening until they leave in April, you can watch the adult birds swoop in from the sea to feed their chicks, if you can see them – it can get very dark by the time they arrive and you simply hear a low whirring as they cruise past your head.

Cattle graze in the shadow of a mountain.

Portland 8 – big wharves on a broad bay and solid 19th-century bluestone buildings – was a whaling station when Edward Henty arrived in 1834 and ploughed the first furrow in Victorian soil. Take the cliff walks at **Cape Nelson** and view the moonscape bluff of **Cape Bridgewater**, where wind and water have fashioned a petrified forest from scrub.

The coast road to South Australia skirts **Mount Richmond**, a sand-covered volcano ablaze with wild flowers in spring. It borders **Discovery Bay Coastal Park**, with its vast rolling sand dunes and stretches of unspoilt beach, and runs along the southern margin of **Lower Glenelg National Park 9**, known for its gorge and delicate cave formations. You can drive or take a boat tour from **Nelson** up the gorge to the caves. The park is rich with 700 species of native plants, but most of it can be explored only by river or on rough, sandy tracks.

THE GRAMPIANS

Pass through the wool town of **Hamilton** – spot the **Big Wool Bales**

– towards **Halls Gap**, where the ranges of the **Grampians National Park** ⑩ (www.visitvictoria.com/regions/grampians) rise abruptly to dominate the surrounding plains. These craggy mountains are a series of rocky ranges thrown up by the folding of a sandstone mass into an uncommon cuesta formation – spectacular escarpments on the east side and gentle slopes to the west. Erosion has shaped bizarre rock sculptures, and waterfalls cascade over the sheer face.

Many scenic points are accessible by car, but there is wilderness aplenty for the more adventurous and walking tracks to suit all grades of hiker. You can drive past **Lake Bellfield**, where koalas feed in the manna gums, to the highest peak in the ranges, **Mount William** (1,367 metres/3,829ft). A 1.5km (1-mile) walk takes you to the summit. Return to Halls Gap via the Silverband Road to take in some of the highlights of the **Wonderland Range**.

On Mount Victory Road, short detours lead to **Reid Lookout**, high over the Victoria Valley, and home to kangaroos and emus. A 15-minute walk along the cliff top brings you to **The Balconies**, outcrops of sandstone that hang like giant jaws over the precipice.

As the road winds through the forest, stop at the viewpoint for the **McKenzie Falls** or take the walking track to the falls along the river, before going on to **Zumstein**. Walter Zumstein, a beekeeper and bush-lover who was a pioneer in this valley in the early 20th century, befriended the kangaroos, and each afternoon their descendants still leave the forest to be fed.

THE WIMMERA

The Western Highway travels through the heart of **The Wimmera**, the granary of Victoria. This sweep of golden wheat fields in an area the size of Wales stretches west to the South Australia border and north to the sand dunes and dry lake beds of **Wyperfeld National Park** ⑪. It is dotted with small townships and soaring silos, and is populated by more sheep than people.

Horsham ⑫ is a small town, which punches above its weight with the

Climbing in Grampians National Park.

ⓞ ABORIGINAL ART

More than 40 Aboriginal art sites have been found in caves and rock shelters in the Grampians. Some of the more accessible are in the **Victoria Range**, where you can see hand stencils in red ochre in the **Cave of Hands**, and a variety of paintings including animals, human figures and a kangaroo hunt in the **Glenisla Shelter**. Many of the geographical features of the region are woven into the Dreamtime legends, including the splitting of one of the Grampian ranges by Tchingal, a giant emu, to create **Roses Gap**. You can learn more about the area's traditional inhabitants at the **Brambuk Aboriginal Cultural Centre**, a striking building 2km (1.2 miles) south of Halls Gap (tel: 03-5361 4000; www.brambuk.com.au; daily 9am–5pm).

*Carman's Tunnel
Goldmine, Maldon.*

excellent **Horsham Regional Art Gallery** (tel: 03-5362 2888; www.horshamartgallery. com.au; Tue–Fri 10am–5pm, Sat–Sun 1–4.30pm) and the **Botanic Gardens**.

Return east along the Western Highway towards **Ararat**. The town's first settler named a nearby peak Mount Ararat ('For like the Ark, we rested there'). Two French settlers, who saw that the soil and climate between Ararat and Stawell resembled that of France, planted the first vines in 1863, and wines, both red and sparkling white, have been produced at **Great Western** ever since. The road continues past forested hills to **Beaufort**, notable for its iron-lacework band rotunda topped with a clock tower.

THE EUREKA STOCKADE

Ballarat ⓭ is within an hour's drive of Melbourne, a far cry from the jolting day-long journey along potholed tracks that faced the miners bound for the gold-diggings in the 1850s.

On the southern side of the city is the **Eureka Centre** (tel: 03-5333 0333; www. ballarat.vic.gov.au; daily 10am–5pm). At the

*Sovereign Hill,
Ballarat.*

site, a diorama brings to life the day in December 1854 when the name Eureka was etched into Australian history.

The rumbustious life of those times is re-created in the mocked-up gold-mining town of **Sovereign Hill** (tel: 03-5337 1199; www.sovereignhill.com.au; daily 10am–5pm). In the main street, resembling Ballarat in the 1850s with its old-fashioned wooden shops, apothecary and confectioners, you can watch blacksmiths, tinsmiths and potters at work; sample a digger's lunch at the New York Bakery; or have a drink at the United States Hotel next to the Victoria Theatre where Lola Montez performed her famous and risqué spider dance. Take a ride on a Cobb & Co. coach and pan for gold in the creek. After a look around the Red Hill gully diggings, slake your thirst at the 'lemonade' tent – the sly-grog shop where diggers celebrated their luck or drowned their sorrows. Then walk along the underground tunnel of the Quartz Mine, typical of the company mines where, in later years, the real money was made. *The Blood on the Southern Cross*, a sound-and-light show, which has thrilled audiences for 25 years by re-creating the drama of the Eureka Stockade, finished in July 2018, to allow an A$8-million rejuvenation project to take place. A new show will launch in 2019 – check the website for details.

Ballarat was born in the boom time, and its wide streets, verandahs and iron lace, towers and colonnades give it grace and distinction. **Ballarat Fine Art Gallery** (40 Lydiard Street; tel: 03-5320 5858; https://artgalleryofballarat.com.au; daily 9am–5pm) is renowned for its Australian paintings, while the **Botanic Gardens** beside **Lake Wendouree** sport Italian statues and a blaze of begonias.

GOLD TOWNS

Other gold towns lurk to the north of Ballarat, where thousands of men dug their 12ft by 12ft (13.4sq-metre) claims with ant-like ardour. **Clunes**, the scene of the first gold strike on 1 July 1851, has an ornate town hall, and elegant banks and bluestone churches. **Daylesford** a picturesque town on Wombat Hill, is known (along with its neighbour Hepburn Springs) as the spa centre of Australia. Nowadays, it's also a thriving weekend retreat for Melburnians, including a strong LGBTQ contingent.

In **Castlemaine** the Greek temple-style market building and other fine edifices date from an era of promise never quite fulfilled. A short ride on one of the steam trains of the **Victorian Goldfields Railway** (tel: 03-5470 6658; www.vgr.com.au; mostly Wednesday and weekends, check website for monthly timetable) will take you to **Maldon**, once declared the first 'notable town in Australia' by the National Trust. Its gold-rush era streetscapes are terrific, as much for their tranquillity as their remarkable state of preservation.

In **Bendigo** , some of the richest quartz reefs in the world created a Victorian extravaganza. The scarlet **Joss House** is an interesting reminder of the thousands of Chinese who came to the 'Big Gold Mountain', bringing with them temples, teahouses and festivals. The colourful Chinese dragon, Sun Loong, is 100 metres (330ft) long and the star of the Bendigo Easter Fair. It is to be found in the **Golden Dragon Museum** (1–11 Bridge Street; www.goldendragonmuseum.org; Tue–Sun 9.30am–5pm). Elsewhere there are extravagant hotels, another good art gallery (Bendigo; 42 View Street; tel: 03-5434 6088; www.bendigoartgallery.com.au; daily 10am–5pm; donation) and the **Central Deborah Goldmine** (76 Violet Street; tel: 03-5443 8322; www.central-deborah.com; check website for tour times), where you can take an underground tour.

THE MURRAY

Echuca , 88km (55 miles) north of Bendigo, was an important port on the

Murray River and its magnificent old timber wharf is now a major draw for visitors. You need a ticket to get in (tel: 03-5481 0500; www.portofechuca.org.au; daily 9am–5pm) but it allows access to displays in two historic pubs, and can be boosted to include a cruise on one of the historic paddle steamers. A cruise is *de rigueur* and allows you to relive the days when these mighty vessels, laden with cargo and passengers, made the river a busy thoroughfare, before the railways made them obsolete. Think about renting a houseboat and making the river, lined with tall red gums, your home for a few days. Back on land, **Sharps Magic Movie House and Penny Arcade** (tel: 03-5482 2361; daily 9am–5pm), in the historic precinct behind the wharf, lets you relive the simple pleasures of pre-electronic entertainment.

The Murray Valley Highway loosely tracks the river as it heads northwest and rejoins it at **Swan Hill** where the principal pull is the **Pioneer Settlement** (tel: 03-5036 2410; www.pioneersettlement.com.au; daily 9.30am–4.30pm),

The clock tower in Bendigo peers out from what was once the post office; the building has now been renovated as a museum.

Paddle boats still ply the river.

⦿ Fact

The Murray River once supported many native fish such as the Murray cod and the silver perch. But the introduction of other species, particularly carp, destroyed aquatic plants and became a threat to the native fish, many of which have consequently become threatened species.

a collection of original historic buildings transplanted to this site to create a typical township of the 19th century. Time rushes by as you stroll in and out of shops and houses. You can cruise on a paddle steamer and, at dusk, take in a sound-and-light show.

It is another 196km (122 miles) to the city of **Mildura ⑰**. While many Australian centres claim the biggest of something, Mildura aims for the longest bar in the world – 91 metres (298ft) long, at the **Workingman's Club**; the largest fruit-juice factory; and the largest deckchair ever built (in front of a main-street motel).

Mildura is an exceptionally pleasant and friendly city, with its great climate and water pastimes of fishing, swimming and boating. The town, and the irrigation system that drew settlers to the area, were established by two American brothers, George and William Chaffey. William's imposing homestead, **Rio Vista** (199 Cureton Avenue; tel: 03-5018 8330; www.milduraartscentre.com.au; Wed–Mon 11am–4pm), can be seen at **Mildura Arts**

⦿ BLACK SATURDAY

On Saturday 7 February 2009, some of the worst bushfires on record roared through great swathes of Victoria and took the lives of 173 people. Years of drought, combined with a baking-hot summer, turned much of the country to tinder that was just waiting for the right spark.

As temperatures headed above 47°C (116°F), winds whipped up, some gusting over 120kph (75mph). Several dangerous, but to that point manageable, bushfires began to run out of control. Blazes jumped control lines and embers were blown hundreds of metres, setting off more spot fires, which soon combined to create unstoppable fire fronts roaring across thousands of hectares. Houses, farmland and forests were razed and entire settlements were destroyed.

The Kilmore fire, as it became known, devastated Kinglake, Strathewen, Flowerdale and other townships to the north of Melbourne. When it combined with the Murrindindi blaze to the east, it virtually wiped out Marysville, where 34 people perished. Further east, in Gippsland, vast areas of forest were destroyed and much of Wilson's Promontory was affected. Over 1,200 homes were lost across the state and, as well as the human toll, wildlife was decimated and millions of hectares of forest and bushland were destroyed.

Centre. His other legacy is that, in US style, Mildura has streets with numbers rather than names.

The Murray River, of course, is the dominant attraction, and you can take to it and its series of locks with two-hour trips on the steam-driven *Melbourne* and dinner cruises on the *Rothbury* or *Mundoo*. There is also a wide range of houseboats for hire. From here the Calder Highway runs back to Melbourne.

THE DANDENONGS

Approximately 50km (31 miles) east of Melbourne lie the **Dandenong Ranges ⑱** (www.visitdandenongranges.com.au). Here, the mountain bluffs are riddled with both fern gullies and art galleries, while small towns like **Belgrave** and **Olinda** make lovely destinations for day trips, offering browsing opportunities in antique shops and cafés serving cream teas.

Attractions include the **William Ricketts Sanctuary** (tel: 131 963; www.parkweb.vic.gov.au; daily 10am–4.30pm), where romantically idealised Aboriginal spirit figures have been carved from wood by an elderly white sculptor and placed in a forest setting, and **Puffing Billy**, a narrow-gauge steam train that plies a 24km (15-mile) track from Belgrave to Gembrook (tel: 03-9757 0700; www.puffingbilly.com.au; daily).

The **National Rhododendron Gardens** at Olinda (tel: 131 963; www.parkweb.vic.gov.au; daily 10am–5pm) are at their spectacular best in October and November but are well worth a visit all year.

Directly north of the Dandenongs, the **Yarra Valley ⑲** (www.visityarravalley.com.au) now claims over 55 wineries in its gently rolling countryside. Organised wine-tasting tours can be arranged or you can dip into the odd cellar door as you pass through. One to look out for is **Yering Station** (38 Melba Highway; tel: 03-9730 0100; www.yering.com; Mon–Fri 10am–5pm, Sat–Sun 10am–6pm), Victoria's first vineyard but now a sparkling modern enterprise with a dramatic architect-designed centre and stunning views. Having the sumptuous **Chateau Yering** hotel with its excellent restaurants next door only adds to its appeal.

Yarra Glen is a relaxed centre to the area and a stop at the historic **Grand Hotel** is recommended. Take the road towards Healesville and pause at the **TarraWarra Museum of Art** (tel: 03-5957 3100; www.twma.com.au; Tue–Sun 11am–5pm), which has changing exhibitions in its sleek, airy, award-winning space.

Only 61km (38 miles) from Melbourne is **Healesville** ⓴ , best known for the **Healesville Sanctuary** (tel: 1300-966 784; www.zoo.org.au; daily 9am–5pm). This renowned open-air zoo was established in 1934 to study and breed native fauna and has played a key role in helping to replenish Australia's endangered wildlife.

Travel north on the Maroondah Highway and after 24km (15 miles) turn off to **Marysville**, the base for Melbourne's closest ski field: the cross-country resort of **Lake Mountain** (www.lakemountainresort.com.au), which has emerged from the flames of the Black Saturday bushfires in 2009, and is back in business as a year-round outdoor adventure hub with cross-country skiing, mountain-biking and road cycling. A winding road through **Yarra Ranges National Park** leads to the pretty village of **Warburton**.

For downhill alpine action, return to the Maroondah Highway and work round to the northeast towards **Mansfield**, an important grazing and timber centre and the gateway to **Mount Buller** (1,808 metres/5,932ft; www.mtbuller.com.au), Victoria's largest ski and mountain biking resort. It lies just 3km (2 miles) from **Lake Eildon**, a 130-sq-km (50-sq-mile) body of water formed from the damming of five rivers to irrigate thousands of square kilometres of farmland. Today the lake is a paradise for water-skiers and fishermen angling for trout, perch and Murray cod.

KELLY COUNTRY

Take the Midland Highway north and join the Hume Highway eastward.

The Puffing Billy makes its way through the winding Dandenongs.

The wine barrels of Coldstream Hill Estate.

⊘ THE KELLY TRIAL

Glenrowan Inn, 16km (10 miles) southwest of Wangaratta, was the site of Ned Kelly's last stand. Kelly's comrades were killed in a shoot-out with police as the inn burned to the ground, and Ned himself was brought to trial in Melbourne, subsequently to be hanged in the gaol there in November 1880.

Glenrowan has rather gone to town on its role in all this. **Kellyland** features computerised mannequins judderingly re-enacting the last stand at regular intervals throughout the day. Outside, a gigantic, technicolour Ned Kelly, in full armour and clutching his gun, looms over a block of tacky shops pushing Kelly kitsch. Many heinous crimes have been linked to Australia's most infamous bushranger, and there's no sign of it ending any time soon. See www.glenrowantouristcentre.com.au for more.

This is the heart of Kelly Country, the stamping grounds of the legendary Ned Kelly. Today, travellers on the Hume Highway through **Glenrowan** ㉑ can't miss his presence.

Benalla calls itself the 'Rose City' after the thousands of bushes that bloom from October to April. These add colour to the unusual **Benalla Art Gallery** (Bridge Street; tel: 03-5760 2619; www.benallaartgallery.com.au; daily 10am–5pm) overlooking the Broken River.

Wangaratta ㉒ is a skilfully planned agricultural centre with a population of 17,000 on the Ovens River. Today it is noted for its wool mills, two interesting 19th-century churches, and the **Wangaratta Jazz Festival** (www.wangarattajazz.com), which draws crowds every spring.

All towns here have one thing in common – a history linked to gold. In 1853, when gold was discovered in the valley of the Ovens River, dozens of prosperous mining settlements sprang into life almost overnight. By 1870, most of them had folded as the precious mineral became harder to find,

but some of the towns survive as vital reminders of a thrilling history in a valley better known today for its wines.

Chiltern was originally established in the 1850s as Black Dog Creek. With its wide streets flanked by shops with Old West-style facades, the town has proved a popular film set. Today its main claim to fame is **Lake View Homestead** (tel: 03-5726 1317; www.nationaltrust.org.au; Wed 11am–2pm, Sat 10am–1pm, Sun 1–4pm), the childhood home of novelist Ethel Richardson, who, as Henry Handel Richardson, wrote some of Australia's classic works, including *The Getting of Wisdom*.

Some 16km (10 miles) northwest of Chiltern is **Rutherglen**, centre of Australia's oldest vine-growing district and still the foremost producer of fortified wines.

THE NORTHEAST BORDER

Wodonga is the Victorian half of Australia's fastest-growing inland metropolis. Its big brother, **Albury**, across the Murray River in New South Wales, gives the twin cities a combined population of more than 90,000. Hub of the Riverina district, which produces prodigious quantities of grain, fruit and livestock, Albury marks the site where the explorers Hume and Hovell discovered the Murray in 1824 after trekking south from Sydney.

The Murray Valley Highway passes through **Tallangatta**, at the eastern tip of **Lake Hume**. It is a new town, built in 1956 to replace the former community flooded by the damming of the Murray River. Traces of the old township – lines of trees, streets, even some buildings – eerily reappear at times of low water. The lake, four times the size of Sydney Harbour, is now a playground for swimmers, water-skiers, anglers and birdwatchers.

Corryong ㉓, the last town before the border with New South Wales, features the **Man From Snowy River Folk Museum** (103 Hanson Street; tel: 02-6076 2600; www.manfromsnowyrivermuseum.com; daily, Sept–May

Old Farmhouse in the Victorian Goldfields, Castlemaine.

10am–4pm, June–Aug 11am–3pm); its varied collection includes what has been enticingly described as 'the most recognised snow-ski collection in Australia'.

To the south is the village of **Nariel Creek**, where folk-music festivals are held on an old Aboriginal corroboree ground on New Year holidays and Victorian Labour Day weekend. Northwest of Corryong (access from Cudgewa) is **Burrowa Pine Mountain National Park** with rugged walks and views of the Snowy Mountains.

BEECHWORTH

Return west, where the entire township of **Yackandandah** has been classified by the National Trust. Miners who came from California and the Klondike in the 1860s helped to give the place a lingering air of the American West. Today it is the centre of Victoria's largest strawberry industry.

Nestled in the midst of rolling hill country is northeast Victoria's best-preserved gold town, **Beechworth** ㉔. No fewer than 32 of its buildings have been classified by the National Trust, including the towered **Post Office** (1867) with its Victorian stone construction, **Tanswell's Commercial Hotel** (1873) with its handsome facade and wrought-iron veranda, and the **Robert O'Hara Burke Memorial Museum** (1856; tel: 03-5728 8067; www.burkemuseum.com.au; daily 10am–5pm), part of the historic precinct on Loch Street. This museum (named after the local superintendent of police-turned explorer, Robert O'Hara Burke, who perished attempting to cross the continent in 1861) exhibits relics of the gold-rush era – when 3 million ounces of gold were garnered in just 14 years. There is even a life-sized re-creation of a section of Beechworth's former main street. During its heyday the town had 61 hotels and a theatre that hosted international acts.

MOUNT BUFFALO

South from Beechworth is a region of considerable natural beauty, the beginning of Victoria's high country. **Myrtleford** is the thriving centre of a walnut, tobacco and hop-growing region.

Watch the birdy.

A gazebo decorates the main street of Bairnsdale.

The Ned Kelly statue at Glenrowan.

Mount Buffalo National Park , a vast plateau at 1,370 metres (4,495ft), becomes a huge snowfield in winter, a carpet of wild flowers in spring, and a popular spot for bushwalking in the summer and autumn.

Bright, a town of over 2,000 famed for its autumn colours, is a short distance away. Oaks, maples and other hardwoods promote a serenity which belies its violent gold-rush days, including the notorious 1857 Buckland riots when white prospectors brutally ousted Chinese miners from their claims.

Mount Beauty is the gateway to the largest of the alpine resorts at smart Falls Creek (www.fallscreek.com.au) in Alpine National Park, where the après ski is as important as what happens on the slopes. Working south along the Great Alpine Road, Mount Hotham (www.mthotham.com.au) has downhill and cross-country runs, while Dinner Plain (www.visitdinnerplain.com.au) is an arresting 1980s resort.

Continue for 160km (100 miles) of attractive high-country motoring until the road joins the Princes Highway.

GIPPSLAND LAKES

Bairnsdale, the commercial centre of East Gippsland, lies 285km (177 miles) east of Melbourne. A sheep, dairy and timber centre, it is best known for its fine Botanic Gardens and the 'Sistine Chapel' murals in St Mary's Catholic Church. Nearby Paynesville, a boating resort, features the bizarre yet interesting Church of St Peter: a sailors' house of worship, it has a spire like a lighthouse, a pulpit shaped like the bow of a boat, and a sanctuary lighting fixture that was once a ship's riding lamp.

The Princes Highway eastwards runs all the way to Sydney but the only time it touches the coast in Victoria is at Lakes Entrance . This resort is situated at the narrow man-made inlet to the Gippsland Lakes, a long string of interconnected lagoons stretching west along the inner shore of the Bass Strait for some 80km (50 miles). They are separated from the sea only by a narrow band of dunes and hummocks called Ninety Mile Beach.

The normal population of Lakes Entrance increases by a factor of six in summer as holidaymakers pack the motels and caravan parks. Up-market accommodation is on offer at quiet Metung, a few kilometres to the west.

Fishing, boating and swimming are the main draws, while cruise boats offer regular sightseeing tours of the lakes. Sometimes called the Victorian Riviera, the area has consistent temperatures of about 20°C (68°F) in winter. The Gippsland Lakes Coastal Park, a reserve of dunes and heath along the lakes' seaward edge, and the Lakes National Park, a bird-filled woodland on a sandy peninsula between Lake Reeve and Lake Victoria, help protect natural features.

SNOWY RIVER NATIONAL PARK

Logging trucks seem to congregate at Orbost, a prosperous town of about 3,000 people near the banks of the lower Snowy River.

Snowy River National Park ㉘, in the mountains above, is popular with whitewater canoeists, who relish the challenge of riding the water through the deep gorges that contribute to the spectacular scenery of this often overlooked area. The Princes Highway then winds through its most remote stretch, 208km (129 miles) of mountains and rainforest, to reach the state border.

At Nowa Nowa, 22km (13 miles) from Lakes Entrance, a winding road will take you to **Buchan** ㉙. It hosts a rodeo over Easter, and a lumberjacks' contest in May, but its main attraction is its limestone caves, unquestionably the finest in Victoria. There are 350 here, but only three are open to the public, including the **Fairy Cave**, whose numerous honeycombed chambers are embedded with ancient marsupial bones (tel: 131 963; www.parkweb.vic.gov. au; tours daily).

THE SOUTHEAST

At the hamlet of Genoa near the NSW border, a sealed side road turns south towards **Mallacoota**. This tiny resort town, much beloved by anglers and nature-lovers, is at the end of a 24km (15-mile) journey off the Princes Highway at Victoria's southeastern-most tip. It is surrounded by **Croajingolong National Park** ㉚, 86,000 hectares (212,500 acres) of rocky cliffs and open beaches, rainforest, open woodland and heath, stretching some 100km (60 miles) from the NSW border to Sydenham Inlet. Numerous nocturnal mammals (including possums and gliders) and many snakes – some venomous – make their homes in the park; hundreds of bird species include lyrebirds, oystercatchers, sea eagles and kingfishers. The pub at the charming village at **Gipsy Point** overlooks the inlet between Mallacoota and Genoa.

It's time for the long trek back towards Melbourne. The string of small cities along the Princes Highway from **Sale** comprises the **Latrobe Valley** ㉛, whose coal produces about 90 percent of the electricity for Melbourne and Victoria. The valley sits

Speleothem formations in Royal Cave, Buchan.

⊘ PENGUINS ON PARADE

Every day at sunset at **Summerland Beach** (tel: 03-5951 2800; www.penguins. org.au; daily dusk; bookings 10am–5pm) on Phillip Island, hundreds of little penguins – we're not to call them fairy penguins any more – waddle from the waters of the Bass Strait to their protected burrows in the sand. Wings outstretched, they strut in small groups up a concrete ramp past throngs of curious human onlookers. This has developed into a serious, packaged tourist spectacle: there can be days when humans outnumber the penguins. In response to this there are now elite ticketing options, involving a 'penguin sky box' or a small-group 'more personalised intimate wildlife experience', which sees wealthier tourists led to a quiet beach by their own ranger.

Walking on the beach on the Mornington Peninsula near Sorrento.

Little penguins.

upon the world's largest deposit of brown coal, and open-cut mines and the steaming towers of power stations are everywhere.

Moe, the valley's largest and most modern city, is the site of **Old Gippstown** (tel: 03-5127 3082; www.gippslandheritage park.com.au; daily 10am–4pm), an 1850s heritage park, where industrial and agricultural structures and machinery have been transplanted to a garden setting. To see the real thing, and with a more dramatic backdrop, make your way to the tiny mountain community of **Walhalla** ㉜, where what was once Victoria's richest gold mine sits in a beautiful valley, now almost deserted.

Long Tunnel Extended Gold Mine is open for tours (tel: 03-5165 6259; daily) and there's plenty more to keep you in this lovely spot.

Mount Baw Baw ㉝ (www.mountbaw baw.com.au), the nearest downhill ski resort to Melbourne and a National Park, is a short distance to the northwest on the map, but to actually get there is a long and complicated drive down towards Moe and up again.

THE PROM

The final swathe of goodies is to be found along the coast. **Wilson's Promontory** ㉞ (tel: 131963; www. parkweb.vic.gov.au), a huge granite peninsula that represents mainland Australia's furthest thrust towards Antarctica, is the most popular national park in Victoria. The Prom, as it is affectionately called by regular visitors, features more than 80km (50 miles) of walking tracks to long sandy beaches, forested mountain slopes, and heath and marshes packed with bird, animal and plant life. An estimated 100,000 people visit the park each year; access is managed carefully, and even the hot spots of **Tidal River**, **Squeaky Beach** and **Picnic Bay** rarely feel crowded. Just don't expect to find a camping spot in peak season without booking well ahead.

The historic township of **Port Albert** to the east is worth a look for the old timber jetty – at which eager 19th-century Chinese gold miners once disembarked. The Port Albert Hotel (1842) was destroyed by fire in 2014. The **Gippsland Regional Maritime Museum** (tel: 03-5183 2520; www.victorianmuseums. com.au; Sept–May daily, June–Aug Sat–Sun, 10.30am–4pm) is housed in the old Bank of Victoria.

PENGUIN ISLAND

For many travellers, the most interesting stop on this final stretch to Melbourne is **Phillip Island** ㉟ (www. visitphillipisland.com). It is connected to the mainland fishing community of **San Remo** by a bridge under which a flock of pelicans gathers daily for a feed. In an area of about 104 sq km (40 sq miles), there is a bewildering array of tourist attractions.

Phillip Island was the site of Australia's first motor-racing circuit (1928), and it still attracts crowds today when it hosts the Australian 500cc Motorcycle Grand Prix in

October and the V8 touring car championship shortly afterwards. Among other attractions are koala and bird sanctuaries, scenic offshore rock formations, historic homesteads, pottery shops, and sports – from surfing, diving, sailing and fishing to golf, tennis, bowling and croquet. The relaxed north-coast summer resort town of **Cowes** is the tourist centre.

However, unquestionably the biggest regular attraction for Phillip Island visitors is the **Penguin Parade** (see box). About 1.5km (1 mile) off the western tip of the island are the **Seal Rocks**, the breeding ground for Australia's largest colony of fur seals. Early December – the peak of the breeding season – is the best time to watch thousands of seals through coin-operated telescopes in the kiosk on the clifftop at Point Grant.

THE MORNINGTON PENINSULA

The most popular weekend destination for Melburnians is the **Mornington Peninsula** ㊱ (www.

visitmorningtonpeninsula.org), which stretches down the eastern side of Port Phillip Bay. The Nepean Highway follows the bayside coast from St Kilda through a whole series of small resorts, all with beaches (the pick being **Brighton**, with its much-photographed beach huts, **Sandringham** and **Black Rock**) from Melbourne to the peninsula. **Sorrento**, towards the tip of the peninsula, is the most attractive settlement, and offers a bayside beach as well as the more rigorous waters of the ocean. A ferry makes the short trip across the mouth of the bay to Queenscliff.

Further up on the eastern side of the peninsula sits **French Island** ㊲ (www.frenchislandinfo.com). It used to be a prison farm and retains some of the old buildings. Most of the land is given over to a national park, with farming taking up the remainder, and it's one of the most peaceful places in the state, with hardly any cars. Visitors travel around by bike. Ferries to the island leave from Stony Point, or Cowes on Phillip Island.

◎ Tip

Just off the north coast of Phillip Island and accessed by a causeway, Churchill Island Heritage Farm has a very well-preserved homestead built in 1872 by Samuel Amess, formerly Mayor of Melbourne (tel: 03-5951 2800; www. penguins.org.au; daily 10am–5pm). A walk around the island is recommended too.

Sorrento Back Beach in Victoria.

Iconic sign on Eyre Highway, Nullarbor Plain, warning motorists to look out for camels, wombats and kangaroos.

NEXT

Pine trees at Lady Bay, just
outside Normanville.

SOUTH AUSTRALIA

South Australia is renowned for food, wine and festivals. It is also blessed with a Mediterranean-esque coastal climate, great beaches and awesome expanses of Outback.

For a state that covers the gamut of Australian landscapes and culture – from the pastures of the coast, with its easy-going capital city, to the endless vineyards of the Barossa Valley, the barren beauty of the Coorong, the harsh grandeur of **the Nullarbor Plain** and the shifting colours of the Flinders Ranges – South Australia is surprisingly neglected by many visitors, both from overseas and interstate. No other Australian state has such a high proportion of classic Outback desert and arable land. This vast hinterland has seen some strange sights, including the secretive rocket and defence system test site at Woomera.

If you love the outdoors, then getting out in the timeless landscapes of the Outback is really something special. You could find yourself enjoying a desert sunset as you bathe in the warm springs at Dalhousie in the far north, sleeping underground in subterranean Coober Pedy, or dealing with feelings of insignificance when you're the only person for kilometres on end. The vast landscapes of South Australia's Outback are steeped in Aboriginal history and culture and are pretty much untouched by the modern world. This is where you can experience the quintessential Australia that you may have seen in popular films such as *Rabbit-Proof Fence* or *The Adventures of Priscilla, Queen of the Desert*.

Glenelg pier at sunset.

ADELAIDE

Both visitors and residents often refer to **Adelaide ❶** as a big country town. Maybe it's the clean air, the friendly locals who smile at you on the street, the views of the green Adelaide Hills from the central business district (CBD), or maybe it's the space; the roads are wide, there are plenty of parks and the suburbs don't suffer from dense high-rise living. Combine this with a cheaper cost of living than the major cities on Australia's east coast, and you've got one very liveable city.

Main attractions
Adelaide
The Barossa Valley
The Flinders Ranges
Lake Eyre
Coober Pedy
The Fleurieu Peninsula
Kangaroo Island
The Yorke Peninsula
Nullarbor National Park

Maps on pages 192, 198

ⓘ Tip

The City Loop Bus (route 99A and 99C, and 98A and 98C) is a convenient way to see the sights of Adelaide's CBD, and it's free. It operates daily at regular intervals both clockwise and anticlockwise and takes in many of the city's attractions, including the Central Market and North Terrace. Visit the Adelaide Metro InfoCentre (corner of King William and Currie streets; www.adelaidemetro.com.au) for timetables.

Situated roughly one-third of the way from Sydney to Perth, this city of 1.7 million people is ideally placed to ignore the rest of the world – which, for most of its history, it did quite happily. Among Australians, Adelaide used to epitomise conservatism with a small 'c'. In the 1970s the city went through a cultural revival under the premiership of Don Dunstan, and for a while Adelaide led Australia on social and cultural reforms. While a legacy of world-class festivals and food and wine still remains, other parts of the Adelaide scene have not quite kept up.

Adelaide is a city that should be savoured slowly. It is possible to rock around the clock in Adelaide, if you know where to go, but it can be done better elsewhere (except at festival time, when no other Australian city can compare). For most of the year, to get the most out of Adelaide you should shift down a gear or two, move at a leisurely pace and meet the City of Churches on its own terms.

One's first impression of Adelaide is its sheer prettiness. This isn't an accident of nature. The city was laid out in a choice location according to the grand design of a British Army engineer, Colonel William Light, who founded the city in 1836. He came with a bevy of free settlers who had the express idea of founding a Utopia in the Antipodes. Sadly, Light – who was suffering from tuberculosis – was given a breakneck two-month deadline to choose a location and survey it. He managed the feat, choosing an inland site that was controversial at first, but his health collapsed; he had to retire, and died soon after.

The City of Light still follows the colonel's original design. From the air, the original city resembles a lopsided figure eight, with residential North Adelaide on one side of the Torrens River and the central business district on the other.

North Adelaide has some of Australia's grandest homes. It was intended as an exclusive enclave for the transplanted English gentry, who shipped out grand pianos and chandeliers from England to put in their colonial salons. Despite the prevailing local opinion that many were the 'idiot sons' for whom there was no room in the old country, the gentry more or less thrived, in spite of itself, on the mineral and agricultural wealth of South Australia.

Also on the north side of the Torrens is historic **Adelaide Oval,** arguably the most beautiful cricket ground in all of Australia, and well worth a visit during the summer cricket season. At the northern end of the Oval stands the neo-Gothic **St Peter's Cathedral**, which has an ornate rose window above the door that depicts stories from South Australia.

South of the river, the central business district was designed for walking; it measures one imperial square mile and is surrounded by extensive parklands, studded with majestic gum trees, which act as a scenic buffer between the city centre and the suburbs. This leafy moat means it is quite impossible to enter or leave the city without passing through restful greenery. The two halves are connected by King William Street, at 42 metres (138ft) wide, the broadest main street

of any Australian capital city – one reason for the lack of traffic jams.

The main intersection in Adelaide is where North Terrace crosses King William Street. Most major attractions are within a few minutes' walk of this intersection.

The **Adelaide Festival Centre Ⓐ** (tel: 08-8216 8600; www.adelaidefestivalcentre. com.au) is the oldest multi-purpose performing arts centre in Australia. Its four performance spaces host a variety of events and one-off shows including the nation's premier arts festival. The centre overlooks **Elder Park** by the River Torrens – once a rather unimpressive trickle, but dammed to form an artificial lake. Visitors can choose to take a two-person pedal boat out on the river or cruise to the zoo on board a Popeye cruise boat, an Adelaide tradition that dates back to 1935; a 40km (25-mile) cycle and walking track also runs along the river.

Back on North Terrace is the monumental **Parliament House Ⓑ**, completed in 1939, which is open to visitors (tel: 08-8237 9100; www.parliament.sa.gov.

Adelaide's Festival Centre.

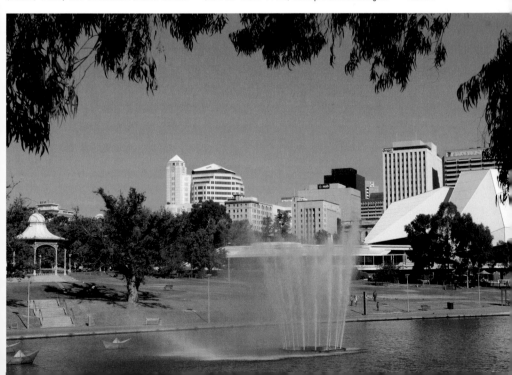

au; guided tours Mon–Fri 10am and 2pm, when parliament is not sitting). Across the road is **Government House** (closed to visitors), the official residence of the governor of South Australia.

The eastern wing of **North Terrace** is the cultural heart of Adelaide, with museums and galleries situated within easy walking distance of one another. Just behind the **State Library**, which houses a tribute to Australian cricket legend Sir Donald Bradman, the **Migration Museum** (tel: 08-8207 7580; migration.history.sa.gov.au; Mon–Fri 10am–5pm, Sat–Sun 1–5pm) is an excellent place to explore South Australia's cultural diversity.

The **University of Adelaide**, which runs along North Terrace between Kintore Avenue and Frome Road, could have been transplanted from Oxford, with its ivy-covered walls and dreaming spires. Also found along this block, the **South Australian Museum** (tel: 08-8207 7500; www.samuseum.sa.gov. au; daily 10am–5pm; general admission free, charge for some exhibitions) houses the world's largest collection of Aboriginal artefacts, as well as an extensive Pacific exhibit and a broad survey of regional natural history (the building can be identified by the huge whale skeletons displayed behind glass walls). The **Art Gallery of South Australia** (tel: 08-8207 7000; www.artgallery. sa.gov.au; daily 10am–5pm, until 9pm first Fri of the month; general admission free, charge for some exhibitions) has a renowned collection of 35,000 works. It displays a comprehensive collection of Australian art, including landscapes by Sir Hans Heysen and Aboriginal Western Desert dot paintings, along with tasteful pieces by overseas artists.

North Terrace was once lined with buildings like **Ayers House** (tel: 08-8223 1234; www.ayershousemuseum. org.au; guided tours on the hour 10am–3pm, self-guided tours Tue–Sun 10am–4pm), the home of Sir Henry Ayers, who contrived to be premier of South Australia seven times – an Australian record – and for whom Ayers Rock (Uluru) was named. The house is now a restaurant and living museum protected by the National Trust. The elegant

The Art Gallery of South Australia.

bluestone mansion contains 40 rooms dating from 1846 to the 1870s, and the hand-painted ceilings and ornate chandeliers of the dining room and ballroom are particularly remarkable.

To the north of Ayers House lie the **Botanic Gardens** ❺ (tel 08-8222 9311; www.botanicgardens.sa.gov.au; guided walks daily 10.30am), 16 hectares (40 acres) of manicured lawns, trees, shrubs and lakes, with an impressive rose garden and some exceptional botanical buildings as well, from the old Palm House brought from Germany in 1875 to the extraordinary Bicentennial Conservatory of 1988.

South of Ayers House, in Grenfell Street, is the **Tandanya National Aboriginal Cultural Institute** ❻ (tel: 08-8224 3200; www.tarnanthi.com.au; Tue–Fri 11am–4pm, Sat noon–4pm), the city's venue for theatre, dance, talks, demonstrations and constantly changing exhibitions of arts and crafts, representing all aspects of contemporary Aboriginal culture. The Institute has a shop selling native arts and crafts, and a café where visitors can try bush tucker.

The lively, busker-filled **Rundle Mall** ❼ was the country's first traffic-free shopping mall, an idea of former state premier Don Dunstan, who in the 1960s turned Adelaide from a musty provincial centre into 'the Athens of the South'. He also instigated the Festival Centre and introduced some of the most progressive state laws in Australia – laws to recognise Aboriginal land rights, decriminalise homosexuality and guarantee equal opportunity. Dunstan shocked staid old Adelaide, and much of Australia besides (on one occasion, he caused a media frenzy when he wore what were described as 'pink hot-pants' to parliament).

In the centre of the city's square mile, King William Street opens out into **Victoria Square** ❶, which is where you can catch the tram to the beachside suburb of Glenelg. Just to the west

is Adelaide's **Central Market** ❿ (tel: 08-8203 7494; www.adelaidecentralmarket.com.au; Tue 7am–5.30pm, Wed–Thu 9am–5.30pm, Fri 7am–9pm, Sat 7am–3pm) – easily one of the most colourful in Australia. A giant covered area packed with more than 200 shops and stalls, it sells cheap fruit, vegetables, cheeses, meats, spices and a variety of esoteric imported foods. But the main attraction is the wealth of local produce that South Australia is famed for, from Maggie Beer's pâtés and Adelaide Hills' cheeses, to gourmet delights from the Barossa Valley and fresh local fish such as the delicately sweet King George whiting. There are plenty of tastings to be had as well. It's no wonder this is one of Adelaide's most popular attractions for both locals and visitors. There are also stalls selling books, crafts, jewellery and clothing, alongside cafés and inexpensive eateries.

The market encompasses Adelaide's **Chinatown,** which spills out into Gouger Street, one of the city's main restaurant strips. The others include O'Connell Street (North Adelaide),

Fresh blooms at the Adelaide Botanic Gardens.

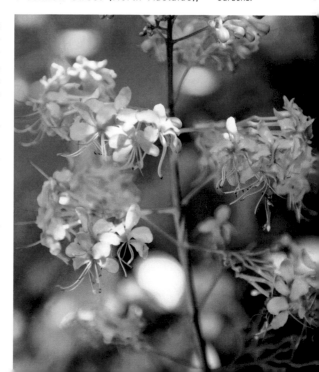

FESTIVAL FRENZY

Sydney, Melbourne and Perth all have their arts festivals, but none compares in size, prestige or sheer excitement to Adelaide's.

The Adelaide Festival (www.adelaidefestival.com.au) is held every March and trades on the city's natural advantages. Few places in the world have such an extraordinary range of performance spaces, from the gleaming Festival Centre to the many outdoor amphitheatres and numerous intimate loft spaces. The weather is nigh perfect, with dry, hot days and clear, star-studded nights – and you can walk to every venue within about 15 minutes.

The festival operates on several levels. The official festival lures the high-profile international acts, and kicks off with free weekend concerts in Rundle Park, followed by firework displays. Tickets to the official shows are very reasonable compared with the prices charged in Sydney and Melbourne, and there is usually a string of free events.

At the same time, the **Adelaide Fringe** (www.adelaidefringe.com.au) is for lesser-known (or more leftfield) performers and artists. It is second in size only to Edinburgh's annual shindig: literally thousands of acts arrive from all over Australia, Europe and North America. Its popularity has seen it become an annual event. The chaotic, organic nature of the Fringe is what

Adelaide Fringe Festival.

gives Adelaide its buzz. The focus tends to be around the bars and restaurants of Rundle Street East, where the festivities continue until dawn at the Fringe Club, while buskers and performers spread throughout the city. With nearly 500 events in the programme, every spare corner of indoor space is devoted to some art exhibition, and every stretch outdoors to a site-specific installation. By any standards, it's a remarkable event.

Happening at the same time, **Adelaide's Writers' Week** lures the literary elite from around the globe. It is entirely free, with readings by famous authors and book launches held in the Pioneer Women's Memorial Gardens on King William Street, across from the Festival Centre.

Although nothing quite matches the festival for action, things are not too quiet in South Australia for the rest of the time. Also in March, Adelaide hosts an enormous world music festival, **Womadelaide** (www.womadelaide.com.au), in Botanical Park. Tasting Australia (www.tastingaustralia.com.au) is a huge food and wine festival held in the city and surrounds in April.

The **Adelaide Festival of Ideas** (www.adelaidefestivalofideas.com.au) is a recent addition, but it attracts some of the world's leading writers and thinkers such as ex-prime ministers, journalists, political commentators and university professors. A typical festival could touch on such varied topics as the Middle East, globalisation, cloning, theology or even the existence of extraterrestrials.

The Barossa Valley hosts myriad musical and epicurean events throughout the year, ranging from comedy and classical music recitals (often held in Lutheran churches) to beer versus wine degustation experiences – see www.barossa.com for more. One not to miss if you're here at the right time is the **Barossa Vintage Festival** (www.barossavintagefestival.com.au), a thanksgiving celebration for the region's grape harvest. The seven-day event, based in Tanunda, includes lavish tastings, grape picking and treading contests, and a vintage fair.

Between May and October most wine-producing areas hold food, wine and music festivals, the most notable being the **Clare Valley Gourmet Weekend** (www.clarevalley.com.au) in May; McLaren Vale holds several too, including the **Sea and Vines festival** (www.seaandvines.com.au) in June.

Rundle Street (East End) and Hindley Street (West End). Between them, they provide a fine choice of Chinese, Indian, Turkish, Italian, Malaysian, Japanese, Greek, African, Vietnamese, Russian, Lebanese, Thai and Australian eateries. Adelaide reputedly has more restaurants per capita than any other Australian city; it would be a shame not to visit as many as possible during your trip.

HILLS AND BEACHES

Cosmopolitan though it can be, Adelaide has never lost that country-town feeling. You can drive across the city in half an hour, and you can be in beautiful countryside in a fraction of the time it takes to leave the other major cities in Australia. Take any one of a dozen roads up into the **Adelaide Hills** and you can happily get lost in leafy, winding laneways. The hills are littered with small commuter suburbs such as **Blackwood, Aldgate** and **Crafers**, some of which are strikingly pretty. There are pubs with hilltop views and restaurants like Windy Point, where you can dine overlooking the expanse of the city's twinkling lights.

Adelaide Hills offers something for most tastes, with bushwalks, markets, wineries, award-winning restaurants, wildlife parks and Birdwood's **National Motor Museum** (tel: 08-8568 4000; https://motor.history.sa.gov.au; daily 10am–5pm), which is the largest of its kind in Australia. You can easily spend a day lapping up the pretty German town of **Hahndorf** (www.hahndorfsa.org.au) and its surroundings, a favourite weekend excursion for Adelaideans.

Another Adelaide ritual is to take the Glenelg tram from the city centre to the beach. The ride takes about 20 minutes and, while **Glenelg** (www.glenelgsa.com.au) has seen better times and now suffers from overdevelopment, the beach is wide, the sand is white and the site is wonderful.

If Glenelg is too crowded for your liking, Adelaide is blessed with a coastline fringed by spacious, clean beaches that stretch for many kilometres. **Henley Beach** is a popular, more low-key option, and after a dip or a walk you can dine on some fish and chips at the grassy, beachside square.

If you like to feel the warm sun all over your skin, drive down Main South Road (A13) for 20km (12 miles) until you see the turn-off on the right to **Maslin Beach**. It's an official nudist beach and its backdrop of sandstone cliffs makes it one of the most beautiful seaside settings in the state. Maslin is friendly and family-oriented, but be warned: the gulf waters are fed by the Southern Ocean and the water can be brisk.

THE BAROSSA VALLEY

Adelaide sits amid the country's greatest wine regions, of which the **Barossa Valley** ❷ (www.barossa.com) is easily the most famous. It was named in 1837 by Colonel William Light, Adelaide's far-sighted planner, because it reminded him of the countryside in Spain where he fought against Napoleon's army in the Battle of Barrosa (note the different

The covered market in Adelaide is great for shopping regardless of the weather.

South Australia

```
0          200 km
0                    200 miles
```

spelling, which came from a clerical error and stuck). The valley was settled in the 1840s by Germans seeking freedom to worship in the Lutheran Church. They brought the first vine cuttings with them, and, more than 150 years later, wine drinkers worldwide thank them for their forethought.

The Barossa is accessible either via the direct route from Adelaide through Gawler, or you can choose the scenic route via the Adelaide Hills, which takes you through Cudlee Creek, onto Williamstown and then **Lyndoch**, which is the first major town in the valley. The enjoyable drive takes you past some of the city's reservoirs. Just beyond Williamstown, stop at the **Whispering Wall**, which is not only an engineering feat but an acoustic phenomenon. The wall is curved in such a way that whisperings at one end can be clearly heard at the other, which is 140 metres (460ft) away.

From Lyndoch in its forest setting, the Barossa Way continues on to **Tanunda**, the most distinctly German town in the region, which is renowned for its fine butchers and bakeries. Following the road to Nuriootpa, you can take a detour to the left down Samuel Road to visit **Maggie Beer's Farm Shop** (tel: 08-8562 4477; www.maggiebeer.com.au; daily 10.30am–5pm). Maggie is one of Australia's leading celebrity cooks and a Barossa icon – at her farm shop you can catch a daily cooking demonstration at 2pm or pick up some picnic supplies.

Back on the road it's not far to **Nuriootpa**, the commercial centre of the Barossa Valley. Keep following the road to Angaston, where the popular Barossa Farmers' Market takes place each Saturday morning.

CLARE

Although the Barossa is the best-known wine-producing area in Australia, it is only one of five major wine regions within easy driving distance of Adelaide. **Clare** ❸ is the centre of the wine area of the Clare Valley/

Watervale region about 130km (80 miles) north of Adelaide. Jesuit priests fleeing persecution in Silesia settled in the **Clare Valley** (www.clarevalley.com.au) in 1848 and began making sacramental wines at Sevenhill Cellars. Today there are more than 20 wineries and 40 cellar doors in a 25km (15-mile) strip. The region is famed for its rieslings, but you will also find some fine shiraz and cabernet sauvignon. Many are boutique wineries whose labels are taking their place on some of the world's finest wine lists.

Some of the more renowned names in the business include Neil Paulett, Jeffrey Grosset, David O'Leary, Neil Pike and Mount Horrocks.

More than 60 cellar doors are dotted throughout **McLaren Vale** ❹ (www.mclarenvale.info), 42km (26 miles) south of Adelaide. Cartographers battle to fit all the vineyards on the map; they read like a wine-lover's roll of honour: Geoff Merrill, Hardy's Tintara and Wirra Wirra. This region is renowned for its reds, although there is plenty on offer

The wet weather of 2011 caused problems with the harvest.

The Barossa Valley wine region.

to please lovers of white wine, including some fine sauvignon blanc and viognier.

In the southeast of the state, on the way between Adelaide and Melbourne, the vineyards of the **Coonawarra** ❺ (www.coonawarra.org) area are justly famed for their reds. Vineyards at **Keppoch** and **Padthaway** are becoming equally well known. **Padthaway Estate Homestead**, now an exclusive hotel, is an imposing stone mansion in an oasis of green English-style gardens. The property was taken up as a sheep run in 1847, and the homestead was built in 1882. Today a number of vineyards spread over the acres where sheep once grazed.

The orchards of the **Riverland**, on the Murray River, produce nearly half of the state's wine grapes. The specialities of the region are brandies and fortified dessert wines. **Berri Estates** is the largest winery in the country, while smaller wineries include Bonneyview Wines at Barmera.

The most famous is **Banrock Station** near Kingston-on-Murray, which is well worth a visit. Their eco-friendly philosophy is reflected in the design of the visitor centre, which has information on how the winery helps to fund environmental programmes. The winery overlooks restored wetlands.

NORTH FROM ADELAIDE

If you're not too keen on driving the vast distances of the Outback on your own, then you could choose to watch the scenery glide past you from the comfort of the **Ghan** (www.greatsouthernrail.com.au), one of the world's great rail journeys. It links Adelaide to the Red Centre, before continuing on to the tropical Top End. The Ghan gets its name from the Af*ghan* camel traders who pioneered travel from Adelaide to the Red Centre.

THE FLINDERS RANGES

The **Flinders Ranges** (www.frc.sa.gov.au/tourism) extend from near Port Pirie, where Mount Remarkable (975 metres/3,150ft) is the first major peak, to past Mount Painter in the desert and salt lakes to the north. At the top of the **Spencer Gulf**, the road turns away from the ocean and heads into the arid heart of the continent. Here lies **Port Augusta**, which, with Port Pirie and Whyalla, forms the basis of South Australia's industrial heart, known as the Iron Triangle. From Port Augusta, the road runs northeast through **Quorn**, then on to **Hawker**, the nearest township to the northern Flinders Ranges. You can travel between Port Augusta and Quorn on the steam locomotive of the historic **Pichi Richi Railway** (www.pichirichirailway.org.au), which operates on the oldest section of the Ghan track.

By a fortunate coincidence, the most spectacular feature of the Flinders Ranges is also the most accessible. **Wilpena Pound** at the southern end of the **Flinders Ranges National Park** ❻ is a raised valley surrounded by quartzite hills. St Mary's Peak is the highest point in the ranges at 1,165 metres (3,758ft).

⊘ VALE OF CHEERS

It takes just over an hour to drive to the Barossa Valley, which lies 60km (35 miles) northeast of Adelaide. Along the way you will pass the actual Jacob's Creek, where the famous winery gets its name from, and then row after row of vines belonging to one of the more than 60 local wineries which produce more top-of-the-range wines than anywhere else in Australia, and include some of the most famous names in the business – **Peter Lehmann**, **Yalumba**, **Grant Burge**, **Penfolds** and **Wolf Blass**.

Alongside these giants can be found numerous boutique producers who grow, not for quantity, but to make the highest-quality wine possible from their venerable vines. Nearly all the wineries have tasting and sale rooms, and many have barbecue and picnic areas as well as restaurants and cafés. Like a well-stocked cellar built up over many years, the wineries are spread the length of the Barossa Valley Way, which links most of the main towns in the region. Many Barossa wineries not only produce excellent vintages but also have magnificent grounds and buildings, like the palm groves at **Seppeltsfield**, picturesque **Chateau Yaldara**, and the two-storey historic blue-marble buildings at **Yalumba**. **Bethany Winery** has panoramic views of the valley, while **Rockford Wines** is one of the last bastions of traditional basket-press wine-making.

The only way into Wilpena Pound is on foot: there are a number of hikes that begin at the visitor centre. By comparison with the thin, rocky soil and arid landscape outside, the pound floor is richly vegetated. In fact, Wilpena Pound attracts considerably more rainfall than neighbouring regions. Although the exterior walls of the pound are steep, the inside slopes are relatively gentle. The six-hour return hike up St Mary's Peak rewards you with breathtaking views. Although Wilpena Pound looks like a crater, it is the result of folding rocks, not the impact of a celestial object.

If Wilpena is your only destination in the Flinders, it is worth your while taking the time to detour north past the natural rock feature known as the Great Wall of China, then through **Parachilna Pass** to join the main Leigh Creek Road before heading south. Coming out of the pass, you emerge onto plains that typify central Australia; from here, as you look back, the open lip of Wilpena Pound clearly shows its strikingly symmetrical form.

The northern end of the Flinders Ranges more closely resembles the other mountains of central Australia than any other features in the south. The base for exploring the **Vulkathunha-Gammon Ranges National Park ❼** (tel: 08-8648 4829 / 0408 378 284; www.parks.sa.gov.au) is **Arkaroola**, a small settlement geared to the needs of tourists. Gorges and valleys filled with wild flowers and endless variations on the recurrent themes of rock, eucalyptus and folded hills prevail.

DESERT TRACKS

The rugged wilderness and abundant wildlife of the northern Flinders can be easily explored by either foot or four-wheel-drive vehicle. There are several good vantage points where you can see the Flinders Ranges stretching south for many kilometres.

The roads north into the Outback – the **Birdsville Track ❽** or the **Strzelecki Track ❾** – are rough adventures, aiming towards the distant Queensland border. Not everyone likes the desert, but those who do will find the continual but

> **◉ Fact**
>
> In Aboriginal Dreamtime (mythology) the encircling walls of Wilpena Pound (Ikara) were created by two snakes who came to rest here after eating so many participants at an initiation ceremony that they couldn't move. St Mary's Peak is seen as the head of one of them, and the local Aboriginal people prefer visitors not to climb it.

Chateau Tanunda.

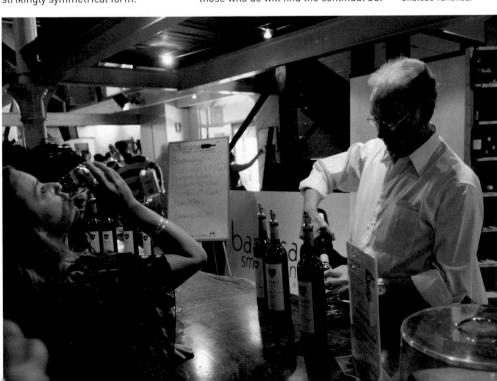

Australia produces 97 percent of the world's opal, from the common, milky opal to the rare and valuable black opal.

almost imperceptible changes in scenery endlessly fascinating (see box about driving in the Outback).

Along the Strzelecki Track, the last stop in South Australia is **Innamincka** , a settlement with a population of fewer than 200 people where the only two buildings of note are the general store and the pub. Locals will be able to direct you to the Dig Tree, a few kilometres to the east on the border with Queensland, which marks the spot where a supply of food was left for starving members of the ill-fated transcontinental expedition led by Burke and Wills. Camping by Coopers Creek after a few beers at the pub is now the embodiment of the Outback.

The Birdsville Track is deeply entrenched in the Australian psyche. It was developed as a route for driving cattle from western Queensland to Marree, SA, where they could be loaded onto railcars heading south. **Marree** ⓫ itself was a trading depot for the Afghan camel drivers who opened up much of central Australia.

The Oodnadatta Track northwest from Marree follows part of the original route that these Afghan traders took. The track skirts around the southern end of **Lake Eyre**, which is Australia's largest lake when there is water in it – a relatively rare event, although it has happened several times in recent years, inclusing 2009–11, 2014 and 2015. At 15 metres (50ft) below sea level, Lake Eyre is the lowest part of the continent, a bowl that collects the monsoon rains of northern Australia. The lake can be accessed at William Creek, where the pub bursts with character.

Dalhousie Springs is an Outback oasis and is worth a 180km (112-mile) detour (one-way) off the track north of Oodnadatta.

Driving this far north into the Outback of South Australia you will eventually cross the **Dingo Fence**, which was completed in 1885 to keep dingoes to the north and out of the fertile sheep country of southeast Australia. It is the world's longest fence, stretching 5,320km (3,300 miles) from the Great Australian Bight in South Australia to southeast Queensland. It's questionable whether it has been successful – dingoes can still be found in the southern states – while it is thought feral animal populations in the south are booming due to lack of competition from native predators.

On the sealed Stuart Highway, which stretches 1,370km (850 miles) from Port Augusta to Alice Springs, the tiny settlement of **Pimba** marks the turnoff to **Woomera** ⓬, the rocket and research base that was only opened to the public in 1982. Around 10km (6miles) off the Stuart Highway, a visitor centre (tel: 1300-761 620; daily, Mar–Nov 9am–5pm, Dec–Feb 10am–2pm) has displays detailing the early days of rocketry. (Woomera is the Aboriginal term for spear launcher.) The Woomera Prohibited Area is adjacent to the town and spans 127,000 sq km

(49,000 sq miles) – about the size of England. British nuclear tests took place at Maralinga, at the western reaches of the area, during the 1950s.

COOBER PEDY

Coober Pedy ⑬, halfway to Northern Territory on the Stuart Highway, is the best-known town in Outback South Australia. This is the world's largest opal field (for white opals), where the relentlessly hot climate (sometimes soaring to 50°C/122°F or more) has forced the inhabitants to live underground in dugouts. The 2006 film *Opal Dreams* offers an entertaining insight to the area and lifestyle of its inhabitants.

At first glance, the town looks like a hard-hit battlefield. The almost treeless terrain consists of hundreds of mounds of upturned earth and abandoned mines, where noodlers or fossickers have rummaged through the landscape in search of precious gems. If you should arrive during one of the area's regular dust storms, you could be excused for believing the apocalypse was nigh. But beneath the surface there are homes, shops, restaurants and even churches. There is an underground hotel, too, though suitable only for non-claustrophobics. Visitors should note the beautiful natural patterns in the bare clay walls (and the lack of windows, compensated for by good air conditioning).

Unfortunately, the rapid increase in traffic aiming for the centre has rubbed off some of Coober Pedy's rough edges. For a more unique experience of an Outback opal town, venture off the beaten track to **Andamooka** ⑭, due north from Woomera, where fewer than 500 people dwell, but be aware that any rainfall can quickly leave you stranded. The striking ochre-coloured hills of the **Breakaways** lie 33km (20 miles) north of Coober Pedy. This arid landscape was an inland sea 70 million years ago.

COORONG AND BEYOND

To the southeast of Adelaide, around the mouth of the Murray River, lies an indefinable maze of sandbanks and estuaries. This is the **Coorong National Park** ⑮ (tel: 08-8575 1200; www.parks.sa.gov.au), a haven for numerous species of waterfowl. The main features are the sand dunes of the **Younghusband Peninsula**, which separates the shallow waters of the **Coorong** from the Southern Ocean, and the Coorong itself (*karangh* or '*narrow neck*' to the Aborigines), a long, thin neck of water stretching 120km (75 miles) from Lake Alexandrina and Lake Albert at the mouth of the Murray River to the saltpans and marshy ponds at the southern end.

If you lack a four-wheel-drive vehicle, it's a half-hour walk across the dunes to the ocean beach, an endless area of golden sand left mostly to the seagulls, oystercatchers, pelicans and only the occasional angler. A great number and variety of waterfowl feed on the water plants in the lagoons and drink at the freshwater soaks. For thousands of years Ngarrindjeri

⊘ **Tip**

You should not attempt the Strzelecki, Oodnadatta or Birdsville tracks without extensive Outback driving experience, a four-wheel-drive vehicle and a lot of preparation. The Strzelecki Track has no petrol, water or supply station for 500km (300 miles) between Lyndhurst and Innamincka. All the tracks are likely to close after heavy rain.

An opal miner's dugout home at Coober Pedy.

> **Tip**

If you decide to explore the Outback, make sure you are thoroughly prepared and do your research, because once out there you are quite often on your own. Permits are required to visit most desert national parks; you can purchase these at major Outback towns.

Aboriginal people lived here, netting fish in the lagoons, collecting cockles on the beach and fashioning reeds into rafts and baskets. You may come across their ancient shell middens in the sand dunes – you should not interfere with them in any way, out of respect for the Aboriginal culture.

To explore the Coorong fully, you need time, preferably a boat and, in the heat of summer near the drying salt flats, a strong nose. The spirit of the Coorong was well captured in the 1976 film *Storm Boy*.

South of the Coorong is a series of seaside holiday resorts, with this part of the coast renowned for its shellfish. At **Kingston** you can buy delicious fresh lobster at the jetty. In **Robe**, once an important port and retaining much of its early character, the Caledonian Inn, licensed in 1858, still caters to weary travellers.

A stone near the harbour commemorates the thousands of Chinese who disembarked here in the 1850s and tramped hundreds of kilometres through the bush to the Victorian gold diggings, to avoid the £10 arrival tax imposed at Victorian ports. Robe tends to be full in school holidays and overflows at Christmas and on New Year's Eve, but is a lovely, peaceful spot for the rest of the year.

Mount Gambier ⓰ (www.mountgambierpoint.com.au/attractions) nestles on the side of a 5,000-year-old extinct volcano. Within its rim lie three craters, four lakes, the largest being the enigmatic **Blue Lake**, which mysteriously turns from winter grey to brilliant azure from November through to March. Outside the city are the Tantanoola limestone caves.

Further north, the **Naracoorte Caves** (tel: 08-8760 1210; www.naracoortecaves.sa.gov.au; various tours daily between 9am and 5pm) contain not only beautiful limestone formations but also a fossil cave where the traces of many extinct animals are being unearthed. They include giant kangaroos, a wombat the size of a hippopotamus and a marsupial lion.

THE RIVERLAND

Renmark ⓱, northeast of Adelaide near the Victorian border, was the birthplace of the Murray River irrigation area in 1887. The drive along the **Sturt Highway** roughly follows the river through extensive orchards and vineyards supported by the Murray's waters. Half of South Australia's grapes and 90 percent of the state's stone fruit and citrus are grown in the **Riverland** (www.destinationriverland.org.au). River transport is prominent here, too, with the paddleboat days remembered in the old steamer moored as a floating museum.

Barmera and nearby **Lake Bonney** are the recreational heart of the Riverland. Lake Bonney attracts a wide variety of watercraft: mainly windsurfers and sailing boats. In 1964, the pace increased considerably when Sir Donald Campbell used the lake for an (unsuccessful) attempt on the world water-speed record.

Kangaroo Island is full of playful creatures, large and small.

The air currents from the plains around **Waikerie** have made it one of the world's leading soaring centres. In summer, when sun-heated air rises in powerful thermals, gliders can be seen throughout the region. For flights, check with the Waikerie International Soaring Centre (tel: 0429-413 570; www. waikerieglidingclub.com.au). Waikerie's Aboriginal name means *many wings*, after the giant moth *wei kari*. It could easily refer to the abundant birdlife in the nearby Hart Lagoon.

KANGAROO ISLAND

The deeply indented coastline of South Australia has made a set of natural divisions, each with its own appeal. The **Fleurieu Peninsula** (www.fleurieupenin sula.com.au), south of Adelaide beyond McLaren Vale, is a popular holiday area for South Australians. **Victor Harbour** is the main resort – its hotels, motels and guesthouses are often full during school holidays. Among Victor's attractions are the little penguin colony on **Granite Island** (connected to the mainland by a causeway with a horse-drawn tram), an adventure park and winter whale-watching trips.

Cape Jervis, at the end of the peninsula, is the stepping-off point for **Kangaroo Island** ⑱. Until the end of the last ice age, 9,000 years ago, the island (Australia's third largest, after Tasmania and Melville) wasn't separated from the mainland. Even now, the finger of the Dudley Peninsula on the island appears to be reaching towards Cape Jervis. The island's main towns are **Kingscote, American River** and **Penneshaw**. Fishing, exploring the scenery and observing wildlife are the main activities for visitors. Seals, sea lions, penguins, echidnas, kangaroos, emus and koalas all live here in abundance. Nightly processions of penguins can be seen on the beaches around Kingscote and Penneshaw, and you can walk among one of Australia's largest colonies of sea lions at Seal Bay. At the large **Flinders Chase National Park** (tel: 08-8553 4470; www. parks.sa.gov.au), the only enclosures are to keep the persistent wildlife away from picnickers.

From the gentle sandy beaches of the **Dudley Peninsula** to the pounding surf on the headland of **Cape du Couedic, Kangaroo Island** has a wide range of terrains. The lighthouse at the cape was built in 1906 as an essential navigation aid for coastal shipping. Near it lie two unusual features: **Remarkable Rocks**, a collection of granite boulders worn by the sea into fantastical shapes, some resembling animals and birds, others akin to Henry Moore sculptures; and **Admirals Arch**, a 20-metre (64ft) maw rimmed with fang-like blackened stalactites, framing a maelstrom of surging waves. These are primeval sites at odds with the placid nature of other parts of the island.

YORKE PENINSULA

A loop of picturesque towns, **Yorke Peninsula** ⑲ (www.visityorkepeninsula.

> ◉ **Tip**
>
> There are several paddlewheel vessels (the *Proud Mary, Murray Princess* and *Murray River Queen*) running five- and six-day cruises along the Murray River. Houseboats can be hired at Renmark, Loxton, Berri and Waikerie – you just have to be over 18 and hold a driver's licence. More details: www.murrayriver.com.au.

The Remarkable Rocks are a granite formation in Flinders Chase National Park.

Limestone bunda cliffs, Nullarbor National Park.

com.au) takes in the east-coast port of **Ardrossan** with its attractive water access and, down the coast, **Edithburgh** with its splendid clifftop views and its famous old pub, the Troubridge Hotel. The town's cemetery includes the graves of the 34 victims of the 1909 wreck of the *Clan Ranald*. The scenic route south to Yorketown is a magical drive offering great coastal views of offshore reefs popular with local scuba divers. **Yorketown** is a small farming town surrounded by a series of salt lakes.

Towards the southwestern extremity of the peninsula is the great horseshoe-shaped sweep of **Pondalowie Bay**. Located in a national park, the bay is a fishing, diving and surfing paradise made even more appealing by its remoteness. A full seven hours' drive from Adelaide, it is a great place to camp and enjoy the beauty of the Southern Ocean coastline.

The ports of the Yorke Peninsula's west coast indicate its importance as a grain-growing area. It was from places such as **Port Victoria** that great windjammers left to race back to Britain and Europe with their cargoes of grain. Farming and fishing still play important parts in the peninsula's modest economy, but mineral wealth contributed a colourful chapter to the area's history. The discovery of copper at **Kadina** and **Moonta** led to the mass migration of Cornish miners and their families from southwest England. Along with the port town of **Wallaroo**, the two hamlets grew as solid Cornish communities with strong Methodist influences, catering to about 30,000 people. The boom period has long passed, but the contribution of the Cornish Cousin Jacks and Cousin Jills, as they were known, remains an indelible part of the peninsula's heritage.

THE LONG ROAD WEST

Of all the great Australian highway routes, the 2,000km (1,240-mile)-plus stretch from Adelaide to Perth is the one most frequently flaunted, with 'We crossed the Nullarbor' stickers displayed on car and van windows. However, the road itself is no longer the challenge – rather it's the cost of fuel to propel a vehicle across several thousand kilometres of nothingness.

On the drive west towards Perth, the **Eyre Peninsula** ㉒ (www.eyrepeninsula. com) and the attractive township of Port Lincoln exert strong pressure to detour. Explorer John Eyre ploughed through the area in 1841 and, although burnt almost to a frazzle by the harshness of the hinterland, he was impressed by the spectacular coastline. The peninsula has its own historical charm in places like **Coffin Bay**, famous for its delicious oysters, and **Anxious Bay. Port Lincoln** itself has a large tuna-fishing fleet, cruises, and great white shark diving tours. Some of the shark scenes from the film *Jaws* were filmed here.

At **Point Labatt**, on the Flinders Highway, is the only seal colony on mainland Australia. If you would like to get a little closer, dolphin and sea-lion swimming tours depart from Baird Bay in the warmer months.

Ceduna ㉑ is the centre of a large pastoral industry, but surfers from both east and west coasts know it as a favoured stopping-off place in their pursuit of waves. It's blessed with golden beaches; Cactus is the break surfers speak of with the greatest reverence. But be warned, great white sharks prowl this coastline and attacks have occurred.

The navigator Matthew Flinders named nearby **Denial Bay** when he realised it was not the access to the elusive inland sea that was rumoured to exist in central Australia.

Inland from Ceduna is the 106,000-hectare (262,000-acre) tract of **Yumbarra Conservation Park.** Its sandy ridges and granite outcrops appear inhospitable, but the local wildlife (particularly emus and kangaroos) find it ideal. In winter the top of the bight is also a favourite spot for whale watching. Head of the Bight whale-watching centre (tel: 08-8625 6201; www.headofbight.com.au; whale season June–Oct daily 8am–5pm), 25km (15 miles) east of Nullarbor, offers a great opportunity to get out of the car and stretch your legs. Southern right whales are regularly seen from the spectacular cliffs here during the winter.

Ceduna is South Australia's most westerly town. From here to Norseman in Western Australia it is 1,232km (765 miles), and any other point shown on a map along the way is nothing more than a water storage base or a fuel station. That's what makes crossing the Nullarbor Plain such an intimidating prospect. There are no trees on the plain (nullarbor is Latin for *no tree*), as the limestone is unable to hold rainwater.

THE NULLARBOR PLAIN

The **Eyre Highway** hugs the coastline on its long route to Western Australia, passing through **Nullarbor National Park ㉒** (tel: 08-8625 3144; www.parks.sa.gov.au) during the last stretch of South Australia. For the earlier pioneers, the coastal route was much harsher than the alternative of the interior. While vast stretches of the coastline are devoid of fresh water, limestone sinkholes in the plain might have provided ready supplies.

The desert is also traversed by the Trans-Australian railway, one of the world's great rail journeys, with one straight section that stretches 479km (298 miles), making it the world's longest. It is part of the Indian–Pacific passenger rail service (www.greatsouthernrail.com.au) that links Sydney to Perth.

A lasting impression of the coastline of the **Great Australian Bight** is the sheer cliff formations that make the coastal strip near the Western Australian border so spectacular.

> **Tip**
>
> Overtaking a road train requires strong nerves, and you shouldn't even try on dirt roads. Courteous truckers will blink their right-turn indicator to show that the road ahead is clear.

Playful seals on the beach.

Aerial view of Hardy Reef.

Mossman Gorge.

QUEENSLAND

This is Australia's holiday state and the most visited destination after Sydney. Its major attractions include magnificent beaches, the Great Barrier Reef and unique rainforest.

Queensland represents a sizeable chunk of Australia. At more than 2,000km (1,240 miles) from top to bottom and 1,450km (900 miles) at its widest point, its 1.73 million sq km (667,000 sq mile) area could happily contain an assortment of European countries or a few hefty American states. It is unsurprising then that within its confines can be found such a range of terrain: unsullied tropical rainforest, broad expanses of dusty cattle-grazing country – indistinguishable from desert at times – the ragged peaks of the Great Dividing Range, rolling hills and, to cap it all, some great beaches. Plus, tethered along the eastern shoreline, just beyond a scattering of achingly beautiful desert islands, is one of the world's natural wonders, the Great Barrier Reef.

INWARD MIGRATION

Queensland's proud claim to be the Sunshine State has been readily accepted, not just by overseas visitors but also by other Australians, who have been flocking to the state for their holidays for years. When winter arrives many dwellers in the cooler southern states hanker for a spot on one of the endless golden beaches on Queensland's vast coastline. And once they've tasted paradise it's a short

step to opt for the sea change – the exchange of the perceived drab urban existence for the joys of perpetual summer. Some move at once, others wait for retirement. Either way, a pattern of migration has been established, with Queensland's population rising by 24,000 purely from interstate immigration in 2017–18.

Incomers can be found all along the coast, but the clearest concrete (in every sense of the word) evidence is to be found in the developments to the north and south of Brisbane, on

Main attractions
Brisbane
Sunshine Coast
Fraser Island
Carnarvon Gorge
Cairns
The Atherton Tableland
Cape York Peninsula
Lawn Hill Gorge
Mount Isa
Longreach

Maps on pages
212, 214

The Eternal Flame of Remembrance burns for all fallen ANZAC soldiers.

Queensland

0   200 km
0   200 miles

N

Badu I. Moa I.
Thursday I. 23 Horn I. Torres Strait
Prince of Wales I. Cape York
Bamaga 23
Jardine River N.P.

Cape Grenville

Weipa Iron Range N.P.

Coral Sea

Cape

Coen Princess
Charlotte
Bay Cape Melville

Gulf of
Carpentaria

York

Kowanyama Lakefield
National Park

Peninsula 22 21 Cooktown
Quinkan Laura Helenvale
Reserve PACIFIC
Lakeland Downs Cape Tribulation 20
Daintree N.P. Mossman
Mornington I. Port Douglas 19
Wellesley Is 24 Mareeba 18 Cairns
Bentinck I. Chillagoe Atherton OCEAN
Burketown Atherton Innisfail
Karumba Tableland
Normanton Mt Ravenshoe Tully
Boodjamulla 26 Surprise Mission Beach 17
N.P. Croydon 25 Undara Hinchinbrook I.
Lawn Hill Georgetown Lava Tubes Ingham
Gorge Undara Greenvale
27 Volcanic Paluma Range N.P.
Riversleigh Norman N.P.
Camooweal Magnetic I. 16
Townsville
Lake Charters Ayr
Moondarra Towers Bowen
2 Flinders Hwy 6 Airlie Beach 15
Mount Isa 29 Cloncurry Porcupine Whitsunday Group
28 Julia Creek Gorge N.P. Proserpine
McKinlay Richmond Hughenden
Dajarra Kynuna Mackay 14
Matilda Hwy Sarina
Middleton Broad
Boulia Winton Muttaburra Sound
Tropic of Capricorn Clermont Yeppoon
Lark Quarry 30 Great Keppel I.
Dinosaur Barcaldine 32 Emerald Rock- 13 Heron I.
Trackways Longreach 31 Capricorn Hwy hampton
Bedourie Blackall Dingo 4
Gladstone
Barcoo Biloela 1770
Carnarvon Agnes Water
National Bundaberg 11
Windorah Yaraka Park 12 Childers Hervey Gt Sandy NP
Birdsville Queensland Carnarvon Bay
35 Gorge Augathella Taroom 9 Fraser I. 10
Maryborough
Clifton Hills Charleville 33 Mitchell Roma 34 Murgon Gympie 8
South Warrego Miles Nanango Noosa Heads
Innamincka The Dig Tree Hwy Maroochydore
Australia Sturt Darling Dalby Caloundra
Desert Downs Australia Zoo 7 Sunshine Coast
Thargomindah Moonie Caboolture
Cunnamulla St George Toowoomba 5 Moreton I.
Grey Geondiwindi 3 Brisbane 1
Hungerford Bollon Warwick Ipswich Surfers 2
Sturt N.P. Wompah Dirranbandi 4 15 Paradise
Marree Wanaaring Barringun Stanthorpe Gold Coast
Gammon Milparinka 6 Lamington N.P. Murwillumbah
Lyndhurst Ranges Goodooga Gwydir Hwy Lismore
N.P. New South Moree Ballina
Leigh Lake Packsaddle Bourke 39
Creek Frome Wales Brewarrina Tenterfield
Lake Walgett 76 Glen Innes
Torrens Mutawintji N.P. 71 55 Narrabri 15
Flinders Euriowie Coolabah Coonamble New England Range Grafton
Ranges N.P. Broken Wilcannia Cobar Nyngan Tamworth Coffs Harbour
Hawker Hill 32 Barrier Hwy 32 Gilgandra
Cockburn Menindee

the Sunshine and Gold coasts. Queenslanders tend to take a laconic approach to the arrival of so many incomers from the southern states, seeing it as an affirmation of what they've always known about the superiority of life in the tropics.

Queensland is a gorgeous place, but sometimes great beauty comes with a price. Much of the state was inundated with floodwaters at the beginning of 2011, and the area around Townsville was badly hit by huge floods again in early 2019. The tough Queenslander spirit has enabled people to bounce back, though. Recovery has been swift for the most part, but it's wise to double-check conditions when planning adventure, particularly if you're travelling to the tropical north of the state.

BRISBANE

The state capital, **Brisbane ❶** (or *Brissie* as it's known to the locals), is Australia's third-largest city and has been transformed over the past few years. Close to half of the state's 4.5 million people are to be found within its ambit, scattered over a series of low hills with the Brisbane River at its heart. Until quite recently there was much in the claim that it was 'the world's biggest country town', but visitors today will find an urbane and cosmopolitan city, where café culture has colonised the once musty streets.

Like Sydney and Hobart, this easygoing city emerged from nightmarish beginnings. A convict settlement was established at nearby Moreton Bay in September 1824, when the first party of prisoners – the hardest cases, convicted of further crimes since arriving in Australia – arrived from Sydney. Many of the convicts died, victims of the tyrannies of the guards, hunger, tropical disease and an indifference towards prolonging their own miserable lives.

The first convict establishment was at Redcliffe, but due to a shortage of water the penal settlement moved upriver to the site of today's city centre. It was named after Sir Thomas Brisbane (then Governor of New South Wales). The present government and shopping precincts overlie the original settlement.

Today's central business district (CBD), in an area cupped by the river, is a mixture of stately colonial buildings and eye-catching modern architecture, with greenery provided by the City Botanic Gardens at one end and Roma Street Parkland at the other.

The visitor information centre (Queen Street Mall between Albert and Edward streets; tel: 07-3006 6290; www.visitbrisbane.com.au; Mon–Thu 9am–5.30pm, Fri 9am–7pm, Sat 9am–5pm, Sun 10am–5pm) can help with the usual brochures.

One of the city's more prominent landmarks, **Brisbane City Hall ❹** makes a good starting point. It's an overbearing structure on King George Square with layered stone and concrete, broken up by entranceways to the transport hub underneath, which

The Brisbane Botanic Gardens lie at the foot of Mount Coot-tha.

Brisbane City Hall.

has struggled to become the great civic space its architects intended. The **Brisbane Museum** (tel: 07-3339 0800; www. museumofbrisbane.com.au; daily 10am–5pm, Fri until 7pm), hosts short-term, locally themed exhibitions and work by contemporary artists.

THE HISTORIC CENTRE

Anzac Square ⑧ further up Ann Street is a place for reflection. A perpetual flame commemorating the city's war dead is aligned directly between the clock tower of the Central Railway Station and the **General Post Office (GPO)**. The latter, with its Corinthian colonnades, can be accessed through tranquil Post Office Square. Follow the narrow lane flanking the building to Elizabeth Street and **St Stephen's Cathedral ⑥**. Within this precinct you will find the gracefully weathered Pugin's Chapel, also known as old St Stephen's Church, completed in 1850 to a design by celebrated Victorian (the era, not the state) Gothic architect Augustus Welby Pugin. Beside it reposes the more substantial cathedral

that replaced it as Brisbane's seat of Catholicism in 1874.

Returning to the GPO and heading west, the shopping hub of **Queen Street Mall** stretches towards the river. The foyer of the former Regent Theatre is an unmissable paean to kitsch medievalism, which has survived virtually unchanged since 1929, although for now it is only visible through glass doors at the back of a café occupying the old ticket office. Another slice of history remains in the refined Edwardian-style **Brisbane Arcade**, built in 1924 and now the city's oldest surviving shopping arcade.

Architectural historians acclaim the **Treasury Building ⑩** as the finest example of Italian renaissance style in the country. Walk south along George Street to **The Mansions**, a group of 1890 terraced houses with handsome red-brick facades and pale sandstone arcading, now occupied by classy shops and restaurants.

Further down George Street is Queensland's **Parliament House ⑨** (tel: 1800-197 809; www.parliament.qld.

Brisbane

0 — 500 m
0 — 500 yds

gov.au; Mon–Fri 9am–4.15pm), begun in 1865. To the frustration of the architect, Charles Tiffin, who won a nation-wide contest with his design on French renaissance lines, it took 24 years to see the work completed. There are guided tours, or, when Parliament is sitting (usually May–Oct), a gallery pass enables you to sit in on debates which, given the abrasive nature of the state's politics, can be riveting. Another Tiffin design, **Old Government House**, is now part of Queensland University of Technology and can be found down the road.

Dropping away to the left is the inviting green expanse of the **City Botanic Gardens ❺**. Originally a vegetable garden for the penal settlement, its 20 hectares (50 acres) of formal lawns and flora now provides respite from the city's bustle for hordes of office workers, students and tourists. Highlights include an avenue of weeping willows planted over 150 years ago, and a boardwalk through mangroves growing on the riverbank.

THE BRISBANE RIVER

Leaving the gardens at the northeastern corner, pass the Former Naval Offices, follow the riverside pathway and take in the views. Eagle Street Pier is the starting point for various waterborne sightseeing cruises. Then comes the acclaimed modernist construction that is Harry Seidler's **Riverside Centre ❻** (www.riversidecentre.com.au), which houses some fine eateries. A short distance further on lies the **Customs House** – now a function centre – opened in 1889 and crowned by a distinctive copper dome.

Looming ahead is Brisbane's most distinctive structure, the **Story Bridge ❼** joining Kangaroo Point with the CBD. Tram tracks were removed in 1959 but otherwise it stands unchanged since its opening on 6 July 1940. At the time, it symbolised progress in an era of political and economic uncertainty,

and even now it radiates pride and permanence. Test its sturdiness and your fortitude by booking a bridge climb (tel: 07-3514 6900; www.storybridgeadventureclimb.com.au).

A walk across the bridge is rewarded with fine views back across the city, but the easier way to **Kangaroo Point** is to hop on to one of the buzzing water ferries, the River Cats. Once across, there are plenty of adventures on offer at **Riverlife** (www.riverlife.com.au), an activity centre based in the old Naval Stores, or you can just enjoy a pleasant stroll through the parkland, where sculptures of varying degrees of accomplishment are lurking. Climb up the cliff steps for spectacular views and a glimpse of the historic **St Mary's Anglican Church**.

City-centre completists, however, will defer such delights and follow the road north behind the Riverside Centre, turn left up Wharf Street, and investigate **St John's Cathedral ❶** in Ann Street. This probably qualifies as Australia's newest Gothic cathedral; although work started in 1901, the final

The George Street mansions.

Brisbane's Treasure Casino.

touches to the facade were only completed in 2009.

Just down Ann Street, **All Saints Church** (1862) is the oldest Anglican church in Brisbane. Cross into Wickham Terrace, nod in a knowing manner at Wickham Terrace Car Park, which won architect James Birrell awards for his innovative use of concrete, and amble along to the **Old Windmill ⊙**. Built in 1829 and one of only two convict buildings surviving from the first wave of construction, it is small and unprepossessing. A design flaw meant it never worked as a windmill, so to grind corn for the settlement, convicts were put to work turning a treadmill. It soon earned a soubriquet as the 'tower of torture'.

Continue along Wickham Terrace for 300 metres/yds or so and take a path into **Roma Street Parkland ⊙**. Here the Roma Street railway shunting yards have been converted into a splendidly diverse area of waterfalls, lakes, misty crannies of tropical vegetation, and cultivated floral displays that attract their own ecosystem of insects and birds.

⊙ FORTITUDE VALLEY

Many of Brisbane's suburbs will clamour for your attention, but none more brazenly than Fortitude Valley to the north of the CBD. Once Brisbane's premier commercial and retail hub – with some grand old buildings to match – it has been reborn as a cosmopolitan precinct of cool bars, funky eateries, pounding clubs, sweaty music venues and residential apartments. Street action radiates around the pavement cafés in **Brunswick Street Mall**, though new bars have begun surfacing in some of the surrounding blocks. Either way, the precinct pumps at weekends when the bohemian and fashionable let their hair down.

Family (MacLachlan Street; www.thefamily.com.au) claims a 33,000-watt sound system and runs at weekends; the **Press Club** (Brunswick Street; www.pressclub.net.au) sees itself as cooler; while **The Zoo** (Ann Street; www.thezoo.com.au) is the live band venue; and the **Wickham Hotel** (www.thewickham.com.au) is the gay HQ.

Chinatown Mall in Duncan Street provides a range of Asian gastronomical possibilities including Thai, Malaysian, Korean and Japanese... but not so much Chinese. Excellent Chinese restaurants do operate within Chinatown but, in general, Chinese restaurateurs and shopkeepers have gravitated to Sunnybank, a well-to-do fringe suburb with a large expatriate Chinese community.

The nearby old residential area of **Spring Hill** is an attractive maze of early houses, some of them old Queenslanders – distinctive, shady, wooden homes built on stilts to maximise the circulation of cooling air. Worth seeking out are the Spring Hill Baths in Torrington Street, the first public baths in the state and sufficiently atmospheric to feature heavily in the film *Swimming Upstream*.

SOUTH BANK

Across the river to the west of the CBD is one of Brisbane's most vibrant areas, the rapidly evolving South Bank, with its impressive complex, the **Queensland Cultural Centre,** and the sprawling pleasure gardens of South Bank Parklands. Cross over from the CBD by the Victoria Bridge and on the right can be found four key attractions. The **Queensland Museum ⊙** (tel: 07-3840 7555; www. qm.qld.gov.au; daily 9.30am–5pm) has several million items including everything from Muttaburrasaurus, the most complete dinosaur skeleton found in Australia, to the tiny aeroplane Bert Hinkler flew from England to Australia in 1928. The museum also contains the **Dandiiri Maiwar Centre** devoted to Aboriginal and Torres Strait Islander cultures.

At the **Queensland Art Gallery ⊙** (tel: 07-3840 7303; www.qagoma.qld.gov. au; daily 10am–5pm; main gallery free, charge for some visiting exhibitions and touring art shows). A second gallery, the **Queensland Gallery of Modern Art ⊙** (hours and details as above), or GoMA as it is known, has an impressive presence with exhibitions of modern contemporary works in a sparkling, purpose-built structure. Just behind it, a dramatic new footbridge links the precinct with the CBD. This is one of two new river crossings in the city, the other being the new Go Between Bridge upstream, named, following a public vote, after Brisbane's quirkily perfect rock band, the Go-Betweens. (Somewhere in the process the bridge lost the hyphen.)

The **State Library** holds important historical archives. To the left after crossing Victoria Bridge is the fine Queensland Performing Arts Centre (QPAC; www.qpac.com.au) and behind it the Convention and Exhibition Centre. On the riverbank is the **Wheel of Brisbane** (tel: 07-3844 3464; www.thewheelofbrisbane.com.au; Sun–Thu 10am–10pm, Fri–Sat until 11pm), a giant Ferris wheel offering superb views over the surrounding country.

SOUTH BANK PARKLANDS

The site of the 1988 World Expo, **South Bank Parklands** 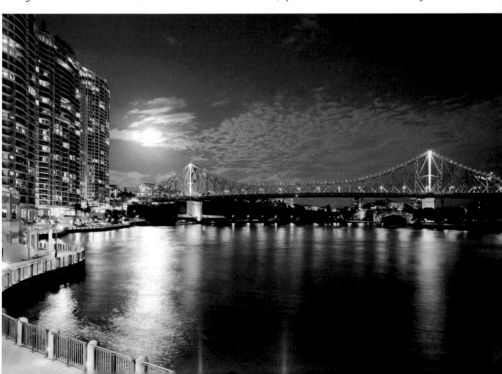, has put many of the former Expo pavilions to innovative use. Attractions in the 16 hectares (40 acres) of riverside parkland include a diverse array of restaurants that take maximum advantage of the city's weather. Brisbane, once a culinary desert, now enjoys a reputation for chefs who take advantage of the state's natural resources: giant mud crabs, macadamia nuts, coral trout, oysters, mangoes and other delicacies.

South Bank even has a large swimming lagoon at Streets Beach, complete with imported sand.

Stick with the promenade by the river and at the end of the striking Goodwill Bridge, which takes pedestrian traffic across to the CBD, you will find the **Queensland Maritime Museum** (tel: 07-3844 5361; www.maritimemuseum.com.au; daily 9.30am–4.30pm) with its collection of all things nautical, including a handful of vessels moored by the bank.

OUTSIDE BRISBANE

Urban Brisbane gives way quickly to rural. Just 8km (5 miles) west of the centre, the **Mount Coot-tha Botanic Gardens** consist of over 57 hectares (141 acres) of ponds and parkland, where thousands of plant species thrive. Further west, rainforest-cloaked mountains shelter the city and offer a generous choice of picnic spots, bush walks and wilderness areas, all within half an hour's drive of the city centre.

To the east, downstream along the Brisbane River, you can reach the

The storied Story Bridge.

⊙ Tip

Descendants of the Kombumerri people, who once inhabited the area around Burleigh Heads, run various guided tours that explain the significance of rock formations and middens (ancient feasting grounds, not rubbish tips). Contact **Jellurgal Cultural Centre** (tel: 07-5525 5955; www.jellurgal.com.au).

Enjoying the sun on the Gold Coast.

various beaches of **Moreton Bay** and the islands (some unpopulated) that make this a vast fishing and sailing paradise. **Moreton Island** (www.visitmoretonisland. com) is home to Mount Tempest, at 285 metres (935ft) the world's highest stabilised coastal dune.

THE GOLD COAST

South of Brisbane, the 32km (20-mile) stretch of coast from South Beach, just above Surfers Paradise, down to Coolangatta – which was pure bushland just two generations ago – is the fastest-growing tourist and residential area in Australia. On the Gold Coast (www. destinationgoldcoast.com), the beaches, particularly **Burleigh Heads** set in a national park, are strikingly gorgeous, and from a heady apartment or hotel room on the umpteenth floor of a high-rise at **Surfers Paradise** ❷ the sight of sands stretching away to the north and south can be breathtaking. Down below, though, it's somewhat different. On the beach you can feel crowded in by towers thrown up with little evident architectural merit; height is the only yardstick,

and the current leader is the Q1 building, which offers visitors the chance to scare themselves silly by climbing around the building's exterior on the SkyPoint Climb (tel: 07-5680-7700; www.skypoint.com.au). Its claim to capture 'the aura of modernity evident in world-famous buildings by architects such as Renzo Piano and Frank Lloyd Wright' seems to be the height of folly. Which, incidentally, is 323 metres (1,060ft).

Comparisons between Surfers Paradise and Ipanema, Miami and Cannes also seem wide of the mark. There's little sense of the style or class that such parallels might suggest. Stores are functional at best, tacky souvenir shops abound and patches of ground are purloined for haphazard collections of glorified fairground attractions, such as the Vomatron or the Sling Shot, both to be found on the corner of Gold Coast Highway and Cypress Avenue.

Night time is when the place really comes alive, possibly because you can't see it so well. Party people take over the streets, casinos and restaurants and the clubs start buzzing. Unsurprisingly,

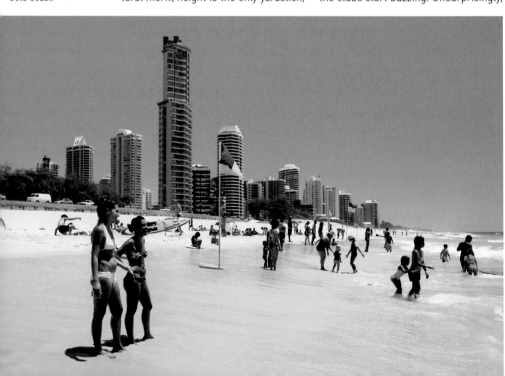

the beaches can be pretty quiet in the morning; that's when families are out in force. If raucous young crowds are likely to bother you, avoid the 'Schoolies' season (late November–early December), when large groups of post-exam school leavers arrive en masse.

Away from Surfers, the super-rich are indulged at **South Beach** in the six-star (sic) resort, Palazzo Versace. Further south, numbers of international visitors diminish and domestic tourists and hard-core surfies dominate.

THEME PARKS

The Gold Coast scores strong popularity points among the locals with its family-oriented theme parks. Performing dolphins (which have attracted protests in recent years) and a dynamic water-ski show are the main pulls at **Sea World** (tel: 07-5519 6200; www.seaworld.com.au; daily 10am–5.30pm); **Dreamworld** (tel: 07-5588 2222; www.dreamworld.com.au; daily 10am–5pm), a large amusement park with a reassuringly Australian atmosphere, combines laid-back fun with adrenaline-pumping rides as well as a section devoted completely to the Wiggles; while **Wet 'n' Wild** (www.wetnwild.com.au; daily May–Aug 10am–4pm, Sept–Apr 10am–5pm) is a huge aquatic park with a mind-boggling variety of rides and adventures.

Surpassing them all as a tourist attraction is **Warner Brothers' Movie World** (www.movieworld.com.au; daily 10am–5.30pm), where startling rides such as Superman Adventure and the Wild West Falls Adventure are augmented by stunt shows and special-effects displays. **Whitewaterworld** (tel: 07-5588 1111; www.whitewaterworld.com.au; daily 10am–4pm), the latest addition to the list, is a sister operation to Dreamworld and will make you soggy in ever-more imaginative ways. Unfortunately none of these theme parks is cheap, but you can easily spend a day in each of them. The best plan is to arrive early and get the best value for your money.

Finally, the **Australian Outback Spectacular** packages up 'a genuine Aussie Outback experience', which is, of course, nothing of the kind (tel: 133 386; www.outbackspectacular.com.au; Tue–Sun 7.30pm).

For an antidote to excess, the **Currumbin Wildlife Sanctuary** (28 Tomewin Street, Currumbin; tel: 07-5534 1266; www.currumbinsanctuary.com.au; daily 8am–5pm) offers every variety of indigenous fauna, as well as the chance to act as a perch for flocks of lorikeets at feeding time.

THE DARLING DOWNS

Inland from Brisbane, the countryside is almost entirely ignored by tourists. Here, the tablelands give way to the Darling Downs, a vast area of beautiful, rolling plains and rich soil. **Ipswich ❸**, now an easy commute from Brisbane, is an old railway town whose history is well displayed at the Workshops Rail Museum (North Street; tel: 07-3432 5100; www.theworkshops.qm.qld.gov.au; daily 9.30am–4pm), but there are plenty of other interesting features on its heritage trail.

The wheel of Brisbane.

The pleasant city of **Warwick** ❹ serves as a livestock industry hub. The second-oldest town in Queensland retains a good deal of historical character, much of it linked to prosperity deriving from the discovery of gold nearby. There are some beautiful buildings, but its most famous feature is the month-long Rose and Rodeo Festival, which attracts the country's best cowboys every October.

Hilly **Toowoomba** ❺ is not just Queensland's largest inland conurbation but also a garden city of some note. Situated on the rim of the Great Dividing Range, with the Darling Downs laid out before it, Toowoomba is colourful all year but sensational when spring flowers bloom.

Lamington National Park ❻ (parks. des.qld.gov.au), in the McPherson Ranges directly behind the Gold Coast, is vast and offers some fabulous bushwalking through dramatic rainforest. Occupying part of the rim of an ancient volcano, Lamington has a wide range of ferns and hundreds of species of orchid.

The Glasshouse Mountains.

THE GLASS HOUSE MOUNTAINS

North of Brisbane there are more of the contrasts between the sublime and the kitsch that characterise the Gold Coast, but with the Sunshine Coast the balance is very different. The beaches are just as glorious, but the resorts are less brash.

Follow the Bruce Highway out of Brisbane, and as the suburbs are left behind look out for the unique geological formations of the **Glass House Mountains** looming up on your left, which dominate the landscape for several kilometres. Walks up them or drives between them are recommended. And it's the Glass House Mountains Road you'll want anyway for the **Australia Zoo** ❼ (tel: 07-5436 2000; www.australiazoo.com; daily 9am–5pm), near Beerwah. The organisation has adjusted to life after 'crocodile hunter' Steve Irwin – who was killed by a stingray barb in 2006 – by shifting the focus to his children Bindi and Robert, but otherwise continues virtually unchanged as both a tribute to Irwin and as a focus for the environmental work that he so assiduously promoted.

Back on the highway, a cartoon Aussie boozer, the **Ettamogah Pub**, reacquaints us with the trashy, while **Aussie World** (tel: 07-5494 5444; www. aussieworld.com.au; daily 9am–5pm), next door, is really a glorified fairground. Stay inland and take the Nambour Tourist Drive. Six kilometres (4 miles) south of Nambour, marvel at an enormous fibreglass fruit: The Big Pineapple. Buy local fruit, tour a pineapple farm, and learn about the pineapple industry in a theatrette inside the structure. This is but one of dozens of 'Big Things' that litter eastern Australia, and, in its attention to detail, it's one of the less tacky. Really.

THE SUNSHINE COAST

All this can distract visitors from what is one of the most gorgeous stretches

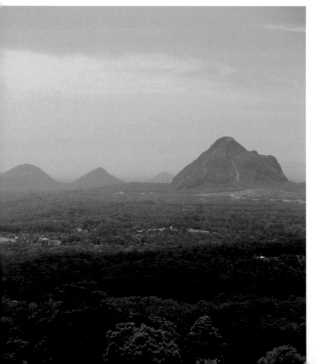

of Queensland's coastline. The action begins at **Caloundra**, where Bribie Island lies just across the Pumicestone Channel, but, more importantly, where the serious surf beaches begin. Caloundra is now a blossoming family resort. Further up, Mooloolaba is also seeing a spate of high-rise development. Beaches all along this stretch are gems. Try seeking out the unspoilt Marcoola Beach at Coolum, a relaxed and up-market settlement.

Many visitors stick with the Sunshine Highway all the way to **Noosa Heads ❽**. Noosa has been called the Cannes of Australia, a heady blend of beauty, sophistication and wealth. Nestling beside the tranquil waters of Laguna Bay, it comes close to distilling the essence of the Australian Dream. Today Noosa is a collection of townships strung along the coast. The perfect waves that wrap around the points of Noosa's National Park rank among the world's finest, and surfers were the first to populate the area.

Publicity soon lured a different clique – the wealthy early retirees of Sydney, Melbourne and Adelaide. From the moment they saw Noosa Heads, these refugees from colder climes began buying up large tracts of the best land. Today, the village of Noosa is lined with glitzy restaurants and boutiques, although it can't seem to entirely shake off the raffish charm of old. Only a few metres from Hastings Street, Noosa's main business thoroughfare, swimmers still float lazily in a sea so clear you can see whiting and flathead scud across the bottom. Sheltering Noosa from the prevailing southeasterly winds is the headland, gateway to the 334-hectare (825-acre) Noosa National Park, an area of woodland and marshes on the south bank of the Noosa River.

TRAVELLING NORTH ON HIGHWAY 1

Highway 1, the main coastal route from Brisbane to Cairns, stretches for 1,703km (1,058 miles), and, although it is being continually improved, don't think of it as a highway in the American or European sense; much of it is just a good-quality undivided two-lane road.

⊘ Tip

The sleek new Noosa Visitor Information Centre (Hastings Street, Noosa Heads; tel: 1300-066 672; www.visitnoosa.com.au) provides information about accommodation as well as events like the Noosa Long Weekend in June, the Celebration of Food and Wine in May and Noosa Jazz Festival in September.

Feeding the birds at Currumbin Wildlife Sanctuary.

Distances between coastal centres can be vast and, by comparison with more populated areas in the south of Australia, rural Queensland remains something of a diamond in the rough. Still, small diversions from the route north will reveal magnificent and uncrowded beaches, pristine rainforests, tropical islands, authentic country pubs, splendid fishing and diving, and the most mouth-watering local tucker.

Highway 1 runs through Gympie, a one-time gold-mining town which hosts a week-long Gold Rush Festival (www.rushfestival.com.au) every October, then to atmospheric **Maryborough ⑨** which has a railway museum and some fine old Victorian buildings. From nearby Hervey Bay, a barge will carry you and your vehicle over to **Fraser Island ⑩** (www.fraserisland.net; see box).

Childers, on the highway to the north, is a National Trust–listed town surrounded by rolling hills covered in sugar cane. The town encapsulates the region's early architecture. A turn-off to Woodgate Beach and Woodgate

The Ettamogah Pub tilts in all directions.

National Park, about 40km (25 miles) down the side road, pays dividends.

The next major town north is **Bundaberg ⑪** on the coast, 45km (28 miles) from Highway 1. For millions of Australians, Bundy is synonymous with rum. Here, in the heart of sugar country, is the distillery that put the town on the map. An inexpensive tour provides an insight into the production process, a visit to a museum and a taste of the product (Whittred Street; tel: 07-4131 2999; www.bundabergrum.com.au; tours run on the hour Mon–Fri 10am–5pm, Sat–Sun 10am–4pm). There is much else to see around town, including a selection of museums and a turtle hatchery. From Bundaberg, cruises and flights operate to **Lady Elliot Island** (www.ladyelliot.com. au), 85km (53 miles) away, at the southern end of the Great Barrier Reef (GBR).

The twin coastal resorts of **Agnes Water** and **1770** (a town, visited by Captain Cook in 1770) have become popular fishing and boating centres as well as being the departure point for visits to Eurimbula and Deepwater national parks, with their pristine coastal landscapes.

The surprisingly attractive industrial centre of **Gladstone** is next, home to the world's largest aluminium plant (A$355 million to construct) and departure point for the fortunate heading out by ferry or helicopter to the reef-ringed eco-resort of **Heron Island** (www.heron-island.com).

CARNARVON GORGE

The Dawson Highway, heading west from Gladstone, is the route to one of Queensland's most outstanding national parks at **Carnarvon Gorge ⑫**. This 30km (16-mile) sandstone gorge has a profusion of palm trees, cycads, ferns and mosses as well as fine examples of Aboriginal rock paintings.

ROCKHAMPTON

Back on Highway 1, and north of the Tropic of Capricorn (marked by a

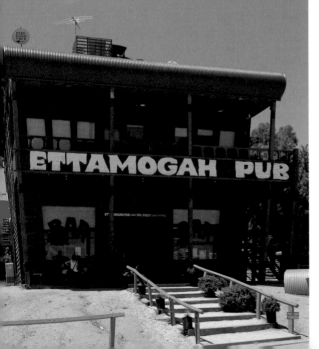

roadside spire), **Rockhampton** ⑬ made headlines around the world when it was the first city hit by the massive floods that inundated Queensland in January 2011. Normally it hums quietly as the commercial heart of central Queensland. A colourful former mayor, Rex Pilbeam, had a Brahman bull cast in concrete and erected at the northern entrance to the city (the Brahman is the breed favoured by cattlemen to the north), and a similar sculpture of a Hereford (the breed favoured in the south) at the southern end. When the beasts were made, Pilbeam – anticipating playfulness by locals – had several spare sets of testicles placed in storage. Hooligans struck the Brahman almost immediately. They were dumbfounded when workmen bolted on a replacement appendage the same day.

Rockhampton has a population of about 80,000, with modern pubs and office blocks interspersed among older buildings – and what buildings! Most of Quay Street is heritage listed, and superb colonial homes are found in Agnes Street. Look out for the excellent collection of Australian art at **Rockhampton Art Gallery** (62 Victoria Parade; tel: 07-4936 8248; www.rockhamptonartgallery.com.au; daily 10am–4pm), and the outstanding Botanic Gardens. Pick up a heritage guide from the visitor information centre in the old Customs House on Quay Street.

The starting point for **Mackay** ⑭ (www.mackayregion.com), 333km (207 miles) to the north, is the large tourist information centre set in a replica of the Richmond Sugar Mill, the first in the area. Fanned by tropical breezes and surrounded by a rustling sea of sugar cane, Mackay is a pleasant city of wide streets and elegant old hotels. A stroll through the centre reveals an assortment of Victorian buildings interspersed with several displaying the sleek lines of 1930s Art Deco. North of the centre there are fine beaches and the new Marina Village.

Airlie Beach ⑮ and neighbouring **Shute Harbour**, 135km (84 miles) to the north, act as the gateway to the Whitsunday Islands, see page 241 (www.tourismwhitsundays.com.au). There

Waiting for the lunch boat to arrive.

⊘ THE GEM FIELDS

Fortune hunters should head 270km (170 miles) inland from the town of Rockhampton to **Emerald**, a centre for the farming of cotton, citrus fruits, grapes and fodder crops. It is also a gateway to the famous central Queensland gem fields, where scores of latter-day pioneers fossick for precious stones. There's nothing fancy about the gem fields; in tents, caravans and tumble-down tin shacks the miners have traded traditional comforts for the freedom and excitement of their own frontier, their rewards being sapphire, topaz, amethyst and jasper. These are the largest sapphire-producing fields in the world, and some fossickers have struck it rich in their first week, but most haven't. Various fossicking parks give visitors a chance to try their hand.

FRASER ISLAND

Fraser is the world's largest sand island and its ecology is unlike any other – a fact that put it on the UN's World Heritage list in 1992.

Instead of barren desert, which you might expect from a sand island, the entire interior is covered with a rich patchwork of forests, whose muscular vegetation manages to survive on the nutrients in only the top 15cm (6ins) of soil.

The island's landscape changes every few hundred metres, from classic Aussie scrub and reed-filled swamps surrounded by 60-metre (200ft) satinay trees, to expanses of lush rainforest, with plants so dense that they almost block out the sunlight. Amid the forests are some 40 freshwater lakes, including both perched (above sea level) and window lakes (at or below sea level). Some of them have water the colour of tea, while others are perfect blue with blinding white sands – **Lake Mackenzie**, for example, could be in the Caribbean.

This magnificent island has been reshaping itself over thousands of years. Enormous sand dunes creep like silent yellow glaciers, consuming entire forests

The beaches of Fraser Island are made up of sand that has been accumulating for 750,000 years.

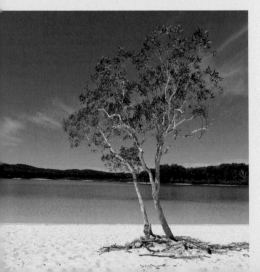

then leaving them behind, petrified and ghostly. But plant life always revives; there are more independent dune systems on Fraser, showing sand and vegetation in different stages of interaction, than anywhere else on earth. The island entered the history books in the 1830s, when a British ship was wrecked here. The lone survivor, Eliza Fraser, spent many months living with the local people before being 'rescued' by an escaped convict. British settlers then used the island as a sort of natural prison camp for Aborigines. When fine wood was discovered soon after, the British herded the Aborigines off, killing many, it is said, by driving them into the sea.

There are arguments about how to manage the booming number of annual visitors – from 10,000 in the early 1970s to 350,000 today. There can be few other World Heritage sites so readily available to the public, and the island's four ranger stations are kept busy managing the place in such a way that visitor pressures don't cause more damage.

Anglers head for **Waddy Point**, while nature-lovers seek out the soft sands of the deserted beaches (swimwear optional). The **Great Sandy National Park**, covering 840 sq km (325 sq miles), is a jigsaw of lakes, dunes, forest and beach.

For a small fee, anyone can bring a four-wheel-drive vehicle from the mainland, bounce along the island's trails, rip up and down **Seventy-Five Mile Beach** on the east coast and camp in designated areas. (Note that a four-wheel-drive is essential; tyre pressure should be reduced for beach travel, which should be attempted only at low tide. Count on getting bogged at least once during your visit.) There are plenty of organised tours for those daunted by off-road driving.

Non-tented sleeping options include Kingfisher Bay Resort, shrewdly conceived to repose so lightly amid scrub and natural lagoons as to be barely noticeable from the beach or from passing yachts. Even with 1,000 guests, it maintains an uncrowded sense of serenity and is the accommodation of choice for affluent guests.

The island is also famous for its dingoes – lovely looking, but potentially dangerous wild dogs. It's great to see these native animals, but there have been attacks (some fatal), so exercise caution and never approach or feed them, and keep children close.

are fine eateries and accommodation from backpackers' hostels to four-star resorts. This is the place to find a berth on one of the many island-hopping yachts.

TOWNSVILLE

Eyebrows used to be raised at the idea of visiting **Townsville** ⑯ (www.townsvillenorthqueensland.com.au), but these days the state's second-biggest city is a relaxed and graceful place with plenty to attract the casual visitor. This is due in part to two destructive cyclones that ripped the foreshore apart in 1997 and 1998, prompting a A$29-million restoration along The Strand. The resultant 2.2km (1.5-mile) stretch of white sand, swaying palms, water parks, play areas and casual restaurants redefined Townsville as a tropical resort city of considerable appeal. Townsville's residents congregate here to sunbathe, barbecue, browse and birdwatch.

Flinders Street, the main thoroughfare, has notable late 19th-century architecture, including many of the city's 58 National Trust-listed buildings.

At its northern end the **Museum of Tropical Queensland** (tel: 07-4726 0600; www.mtq.qm.qld.gov.au; daily 9.30am–5pm), its atrium dominated by a huge cross-section of an 18th-century naval frigate, provides a good child-friendly introduction to the history, peoples and geology of the area.

Next door, **Reef HQ** (tel: 07-4750 0800; www.reefhq.com.au; daily 9.30am–5pm) has a huge coral-reef aquarium as its centrepiece.

Overlooking everything is the craggy Castle Hill. In a typical display of civic pride, an early resident worked out that if Castle Hill were just a few metres higher, it could officially be called a mountain. He began carting soil up the hill and dumping it on top. The town never got its mountain, but the project became a kind of monument to obscure endeavour everywhere. Climb, or more likely drive, to the top for a different perspective of the city and look out to sea, where **Magnetic Island** can be seen offshore.

It's only a 20-minute ferry ride from Townsville, but Magnetic Island (www.visitmagneticisland.com.au) feels worlds

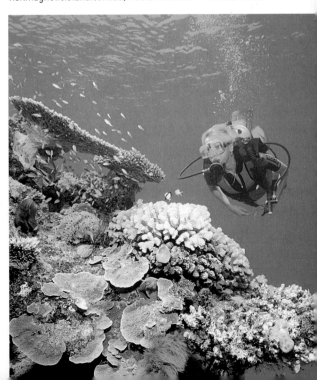

Diving at the Great Barrier Reef.

⊙ GOLD TOWNS

Head west from Townsville to gold country, and the vistas along the Flinders Highway rapidly turn from lush green to the parched semi-arid savannah of Australian myth. **Charters Towers**, 135km (84 miles) inland, owes its heyday to an Aboriginal boy who found gold in 1872 while on an expedition with prospector Hugh Mossman. A tiny town suddenly boomed. Of the splendid architecture that resulted, the restored Stock Exchange in the historic Royal Arcade is one of the city's 19th-century highlights. Gold is still produced locally, with companies reworking old sites. One is in **Ravenswood**, 38km (24 miles) south of the Flinders Highway, where among deserted shacks and derelict equipment two ancient pubs still function and there's a small museum.

All kinds of boards are welcome on the beach.

away. Hire a Mini Moke and hop from one bay to another, follow one of the many trails into the forest, or maybe stumble over an old wartime lookout post. There are plenty of places to stay at all budgets.

Townsville's relatively green hinterland strip is bordered by rocky mountain ranges that eventually give way to the inland savannah. About 10km (6 miles) north of Ingham, as you reach the top of a steep hill, you are suddenly treated to one of the most breathtaking sights of the whole coastal trip. Be ready to stop and admire the view of **Hinchinbrook Island** across the narrow mangrove-lined channel.

MISSION BEACH AND INNISFAIL

From Cardwell northward the highway sticks pretty close to the coast, offering plenty of diversions to peaceful little spots for picnics, fishing and water sports. A trip up **Tully Gorge** offers dramatic scenery and the opportunity to take in some whitewater rafting.

Mission Beach ⑰, an 18km (11-mile) detour off the highway, is a relaxed, low-rise destination. The beach is perfect, the restaurants are good and there's always the option of a quick trip across to Dunk Island if you crave a spell on a westward-facing strand for a change.

This stretch of coastline bore the brunt of Cyclone Yasi in February 2011. Rebuilding was swift and even devastated Dunk and Bedarra islands reopened within the year. Yasi followed Cyclone Larry of 2006, when the brunt of the damage was inflicted on **Innisfail**, 49km (30 miles) to the north. Even before that, locals' claims that this would be the next happening place in the region aroused some scepticism, but it's a nice enough town and its Art Deco architecture and Chinese temple are worth a look.

CAIRNS

And so on to **Cairns ⑱** (www.cairnsvisitorcentre.com) pulsating visitor centre of tropical north Queensland. Until the 1980s, this was a sleepy provincial backwater wallowing in a swamp. Not terribly much had changed since it was founded just over a century before, on some not very picturesque mangrove flats, to service the gold and tin fields further inland. Then the tourism boom hit. There's still a core of old-style tropical charm in the languid pubs and distinctively Queensland-style porches, but today Cairns, with a population of 164,000, has a modern international airport, bustling shopping malls and a vast variety of restaurants. Almost any sporting activity – diving trips to the Reef, bungy jumping, whitewater rafting, tandem parachuting, hiking the Atherton Tableland – can be arranged.

The focus of Cairns remains the **Esplanade**. The waterfront is lined by high-rise hotels and backpacker accommodation, and there's always an array of picnicking locals beneath the Moreton Bay figs and palms. Its centrepiece is a huge landscaped swimming lagoon, classic red-and-yellow-garbed lifeguards in attendance, its lawns carpeted with minimally clad sunbathers. A leisure and shopping centre, the Pier is still struggling to impose itself, but weekend markets, and a marina for the region's marlin fishing fleet and pleasure boats, give verve to the waterfront.

The **Cairns Historical Museum** (corner Lake and Shields streets; tel: 07-4051 5582; www.cairnsmuseum.org.au; Mon–Sat 10am–4pm) has exhibits on the more rough-and-ready past of the area, while the elegant **Regional Art Gallery** (corner Abbot and Shields streets; tel: 07-4046 4800; www.cairnsregionalgallery.com.au; Mon–Fri 9am–5pm, Sat 10am–5pm, Sun 10am–2pm) has local artists' work on display as well as visiting exhibitions.

But the real attractions of Cairns lie beyond the town limits; either out to sea for the **Great Barrier Reef** (www.greatbarrierreef.org) or inland where the lush, cool plateau of the **Atherton Tableland** (www.athertontablelands.com.au) deserves extensive exploration. Like the rest of the region, it was opened up by prospectors in the 1870s. It is now a major dairy farm area, with a range of B&Bs and farm-stay accommodation with faintly chi-chi names.

However, for many tourists there is only time for a day-trip package. This means taking the pleasant 64km (44-mile) return trip from Cairns to the village of **Kuranda**; one way by train, with vintage coaches climbing tortuously through spectacular scenery, tunnels and past impressive waterfalls; the other half of the journey by Skyrail, a cable car that almost brushes the rainforest tree tops. Kuranda is one big shopping opportunity, with a daily craft market, galleries, didgeridoo outlets and a host of restaurants and cafés. Beyond that, the station is charming and there's a butterfly sanctuary and aviary.

THE FAR NORTH

North of Cairns, the Cook Highway runs through one of the most classically gorgeous parts of Australia. Strings of uncrowded, palm-fringed beaches (including those of the beachside

Palm Cove has been designed around the 500-year-old Melaleuca trees that dot the town and beaches.

⊘ THE ATHERTON TABLELAND

The hill country inland from Cairns offers respite from the tropical heat of the coast; with its sprinkling of attractive townships, inviting lakes, picturesque waterfalls and towering forests, it is deserving of proper investigation over a few days. With its elevation and associated rainfall, this fertile plateau at the northern end of the Great Dividing Range is prime dairy country. In the early days of colonial settlement, great areas of forest were cleared of valuable timber, leaving today's rolling pastureland.

It was the Chinese, originally drawn by tin and gold mining in the region, who led the way in agriculture, and evidence of their presence is manifest in **Atherton**, the main town in the area. The 1903 Hou Wang Temple (Herberton Road; www.nationaltrust.org.au; Wed–Fri 9am–4pm, Sat 10am–2pm) was the focal point of Chinatown.

Yungaburra, a few kilometres to the east, is dotted with heritage buildings and has a famed 500-year-old curtain fig tree, as well as being a good spot to see platypus – by the bridge. **Malanda** is worth a look, and **Millaa Millaa** is a pretty place to join a waterfalls circuit taking in four examples, with Millaa Millaa Falls being the highlight.

Millstream Falls are the widest in the country and can be found outside **Ravenshoe**, if you're not detained by the town's steam train.

⊙ Tip

Drop in at the century-old Cairns Yacht Club to meet barnacled locals while washing down prawns with beer. Hemmed in on all sides by high-rises, the club has been assured that its two-storey weatherboard headquarters will remain unmolested by developers – for now. Its veranda is a fine place to sit and sip.

A well-lit walkway along the water in Cairns.

suburbs of Trinity, Kewarra and exclusive Palm Cove) look out across the reef-calmed Coral Sea. Construction is moving apace, however, and for Palm Cove in particular it's worth checking in advance on the likely impact that the latest building works may have on your holiday haven.

The Great Barrier Reef comes within 15km (9 miles) of the shoreline, and from various ports diving boats head out to the sand cays and coral reefs. One of the most popular starting points lies some 80km (50 miles) north of Cairns. **Port Douglas** ⓳, like most of the coastal settlements, was founded after a gold rush in the 1870s, when the Gugu-Yalangi people were forced from their land. For a time it was more important than Cairns, but its popularity faded when the gold ran out. For the next century, Port Douglas boasted little more than two pubs and a pie shop. Today, the pubs and pie shop are still there, but they've been joined by glitzy new resorts like the Sheraton Grand Mirage, which continues to attract world leaders and household names

from the entertainment industry. There are also some fine restaurants and chic boutiques on Macrossan Street, and you can find nightly cane-toad races in one of the bars; the palm-fringed village atmosphere that could still be enjoyed in the 1990s has long gone.

However, Four Mile Beach is among the region's most beautiful, while every morning dozens of boats head out from the marina for day trips on the Reef. Just offshore are the immensely popular Low Isles, and a string of excellent snorkelling spots is only an hour away. Passages are available on everything from tiny yachts catering for only a dozen passengers right up to the massive Quicksilver catamarans that can shuttle hundreds of people at a time.

CAPE TRIBULATION RAINFOREST

Returning to the highway, just north of the Port Douglas turn-off, is Mossman and the road to **Mossman Gorge**. The brand-new $20 million Mossman Gorge Centre (tel: 07-4099 7000; www.mossmangorge.com.au; daily 8am–6pm)

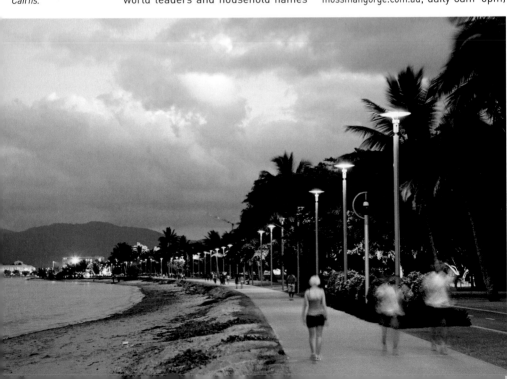

is the starting point for self-guided walks or insightful Dreamtime walks, led by the gorge's traditional owners, the Kuku Yalanji. Slightly further north, past rich sugar-cane country, the village of **Daintree** is the starting point for river trips. Just after dawn, the birdlife is extraordinary (parrots, ospreys, great white herons). Later in the day, you'll see saltwater crocodiles lounging in sunny bliss.

Cross the Daintree River by ferry (6am–midnight) and drive for 36km (23 miles) to **Cape Tribulation ⑳** (www.cape-trib.com). It's an incongruous name for one of Australia's most serene corners, but then Captain Cook was in a poor mood after his ship, the Endeavour, ran onto a reef in 1770. 'This was where our troubles began,' he noted in his log, and his subsequent naming of Mount Misery, Cape Sorrow and the like indicate a man who hadn't perked up.

Troubles returned in the early 1980s, when the Queensland government decided to push a road through the rainforest to improve access for tourists and remote Aboriginal communities. Hundreds of eco-activists descended on Cape Trib to throw themselves in front of the bulldozers. Ironically, this focused so much attention on the area that Cape Trib became a household name in Australia, and is now firmly on the tourist map. The road was eventually completed, but the outcry prompted a United Nations World Heritage listing for the Daintree area, which is now part of a national park.

Today, the isolated, otherworldly atmosphere of Cape Trib appears to have barely changed. There is a scattered community with a few grocery stores and, except for a couple of hours in the middle of the day, when tour buses arrive from Cairns, there are usually few people on the beaches. Meanwhile, a cluster of new high-quality eco-lodges nestles in rainforest-covered hills. There are also coral reefs quite close to the shore, a very unusual phenomenon.

The contentious coastal road to Cooktown is now a reality – although barely. You need a four-wheel-drive vehicle to bounce through tunnels of virgin forest, plough across shallow rivers and up 45-degree inclines along sections of the Bloomfield Track beyond Cape Tribulation. Although you glimpse the sea rarely, the views and sense of isolation are worth it. The road is open all year (except after heavy rain, always check before leaving) with extreme caution – watch the tide at Bloomfield River unless you'd like to contribute to the crocodiles' diet. Otherwise, in a conventional vehicle, you can make the journey from Cairns on the inland Cape York Development Road, which was only fully sealed in 2006. Call in at the Lion's Den pub, just off the highway at Helenvale – it's one of the oldest in north Queensland, with the original wooden bar, piano and a vast array of pickled snakes.

Quay Street is noted for its history and most of the buildings in it are beautiful examples of Australia's early architecture.

THE WORLD'S OLDEST RAINFOREST

The rainforest here is at least 100 million years old (compared with the Amazon's 10 million) and is a vital component of Queensland.

All the Earth's rainforests are thought to have begun around present-day Melbourne some 120 million years ago, when Australia was a part of the great continent of Gondwanaland. When Oceania broke away, 50 million years ago, the drier land began to replace tropical conditions. The rainforests that once covered Australia retreated to less than 1 percent of the continent; logging has reduced that by more than half.

North Queensland's rainforest – now protected as part of the Wet Tropics World Heritage area and a patchwork of national parks – has the highest diversity of local endemic species in the world. Fully one-fifth of Australia's bird species, a quarter of its reptiles, a third of its marsupials, a third of its frogs and two-fifths of its plants are here in a tiny fraction of the Australian landmass.

Conservationists waged battles with the timber industry and the Queensland government throughout the 1980s. Ultimately, the eco-activists triumphed over the bulldozers; today most North Queenslanders

Be careful not to venture off the path when visiting the rainforests of Queensland.

accept the importance of the wet zones. With its capacity to attract visitors, it doesn't do the local economy any harm either.

As for the seething tangle of vines and ferns itself, the rainforest has always deployed a wide array of defences against intruders. First off, there's the taipan snake, whose bite is 300 times more toxic than a cobra's. Some other native snakes are nearly as dangerous. However, death by snakebite is rarer than death by lightning strike.

The local (non-venomous) python is hardly worth a mention, although the largest recorded scrub python, found in the Tully area, measured 8.5 metres (28ft) long. The saltwater crocodiles that lurk in the remoter rivers here only grow up to about 6 metres (20ft) – but that's still enough to grab the unwary by the legs and spoil their day with the death-roll they use to disable and eventually kill their victims.

If you see a tree goanna – a giant speckled lizard with enormous claws – don't startle it: it may confuse you with a tree, climb up your leg and disembowel you. (Why it would attack a tree in the first place isn't entirely clear.) A kick from a frightened cassowary – a 2-metre (6ft) -tall flightless bird with a bony crown – can tear open your ribcage so, if you meet one in the bush, give it plenty of room.

The barking or bird-eating spider, with a leg span up to 15cm (6 inches), may be found in areas bordering on rainforest and can deal you a nasty bite.

Even some plants are armed and dangerous. The heart-shaped leaves of the stinging tree (Gympie vine), for example, inject silica spines into any skin unlucky enough to brush it. It's 'like a blow-torch being applied to your flesh', apparently.

The chances of encountering any of these horrors are minimal – but do take notice of signs, especially around waterways. If in any doubt, err on the side of caution when it comes to swimming.

You can take it a step further by visiting the excellent **Daintree Discovery Centre** (Tulip Oak Road, Turn off Cape Tribulation Road, Cow Bay; tel: 07-4098-9171; www.discoverthedaintree.com; daily 8.30am-5pm), where the whole rainforest experience is packed into a fenced compound and enjoyed from either the raised boardwalk on the forest floor or an aerial walkway.

COOKTOWN

At the end of the line is **Cooktown** ㉑, a place that has always had a Wild West reputation as an isolated tropical refuge which you could escape to when nowhere else would have you. It is located on the mangrove estuary where Captain Cook spent seven weeks repairing the *Endeavour*. The local Gugu-Yalangi people were friendly, and it was the most significant contact between Aborigines and Europeans to that date. The time ashore gave Sir Joseph Banks the opportunity to make more detailed studies of local wildlife than he had been allowed at Botany Bay.

When an Irish prospector struck gold at Palmer River in 1873, Cooktown became one of Australia's busiest ports, with 94 pubs (many little more than shacks) and 35,000 miners working on the claims. There's a mural in the Middle Pub depicting those days, when miners blew thousands of pounds' worth of gold dust in a single night, chased women such as the legendary Palmer Kate, passed out on drugged whisky and then woke up penniless in the swamps.

Cooktown still thrives on those memories, and it has maintained a languid charm. Poking between palm trees on the wide main street are many late 19th-century buildings, including the three surviving watering holes (colloquially known as the Top, Middle and Bottom pubs).

The **James Cook Historical Museum** (corner of Helen and Furneaux streets; tel: 07-4069 5386; www.nationaltrust.org.au; daily 9.30am–4pm) is one of the best in Australia and is located in the former convent of St Mary; exhibits include the original anchor of the *Endeavour*, retrieved from the Reef. A major upgrade is planned to commemorate the 250th anniversary of Cook arriving on this coastline in 2020. The Cooktown cemetery, just north of town, is full of its own stories of the old pioneers.

THE CAPE YORKE PENINSULA

Beyond Cooktown sprawls the **Cape York Peninsula**, a popular destination for four-wheel-drive expeditions in the dry season. The red-dust road runs from one lonely bush pub to the next, past anthills, forests full of screaming cockatoos, and vast sandstone bluffs rich in Aboriginal rock art. It can take several days to get to Australia's northernmost point, the tip of Cape York, and it's essential that you travel with someone who has serious off-roading experience. It's best to go in convoy with at least one other vehicle.

The tiny township of **Laura** ㉒ at the southern tip of the Lakefield National Park (an expanse of marshland, lagoons, mangrove swamps and rainforest that is rich in flora and fauna) is one of the last accessible spots without a four-wheel-drive vehicle as long as you stay outside the park. It's worth the trip to see some fabulous Aboriginal rock art. Split Rock can be explored on your own, while other sites can be enjoyed in the company of Aboriginal guides booked through the Quinkan

⊙ Tip

Lizard Island (www.lizardisland.com.au) 27km (19 miles) off the coast and about 100km (60 miles) north of Cooktown, is a dry, rocky, mountainous island with superb beaches for swimming and pristine reef which makes for great snorkelling and diving. Charter flights operate from Cairns and Cooktown.

Zip-lining above the trees.

Balancing Rock is not a trick of the eye, but rather a matter of physics.

Signpost at Mount Isa City lookout.

Regional Cultural Centre (tel: 07-4060 3457; www.quinkancc.com.au).

Heading north, the journey passes the bauxite-mining town of **Weipa** and the Jardine River Crossing (which has a ferry). Torres Strait is the end of the line, where there are campgrounds; 6km (4 miles) to the northeast, at Punsand Bay, is the closest population to the continent's northernmost tip.

Boats run from Red Island Point (**Bamaga**) to Thursday Island, the administrative centre of the Torres Strait Islands, many of which were named by Captain Bligh when he passed through on an open longboat after the 1789 mutiny on the *Bounty*. From June to September, the ferry also operates from Punsand Bay. **Thursday Island ㉓** (pop. 2,600) was once one of the world's great pearling stations. Although there are no tourist traps or beaches of note, it's a pleasant enough place to lay up after the rigours of the road. The cosmopolitan mix of inhabitants is a carefree and friendly crowd who like to party. There are four old pubs, the more modern

Jardine Motel, and a Japanese cemetery from pearling days.

A special way to take a close look at the far north Queensland coastline and the Torres Strait is a five-day return voyage from Cairns on the MV *Trinity Bay*, a working cargo ship supplying the remote Cape York communities all the way up to Thursday Island. It's air-conditioned and comfortable, and dress and conversation are informal. (Tel: 07-4035 1234; www.seaswift.com.au).

THE QUEENSLAND OUTBACK

Most of Queensland's key destinations (and by far the majority of the population) are on the coast, and yet much that is most fascinating about the place is to be found inland. It's impossible to get a real handle on the state until you've headed off into the Outback. There are countless ways to do it, but with the idea of describing a circuit (which needs a good parcel of time) let's look at a journey moving inland from Cairns. This is the starting point of the Savannah Way (www.savannahway.com.au), which eventually winds up in Broome in northern

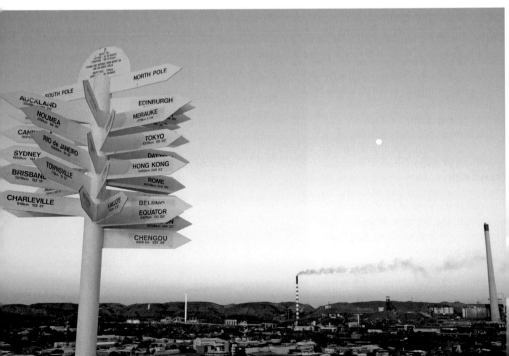

Western Australia. The land is vast and there may be hundreds of kilometres between destinations, so keep a keen eye on the fuel gauge and keep a can of spare fuel in the trunk, along with spare wheels and parts. Let people know your plans, and if you do break down, stay with your vehicle. It's a good idea to travel with another vehicle.

Chillagoe ㉔, 215km (134 miles) west of Cairns, is not actually on the Savannah Way but is worth a visit. It's a mining town with plenty of detritus from the industry to provide character. Limestone bluffs around the town add drama to the harsh terrain, while spectacular caves in the **Chillagoe-Mungana National Park** can be explored on your own or with guided tours. Book at the Hub (21–3 Queen Street; tel: 07-4094 7111; www.nprsr.qld.gov.au).

More subterranean wonders are to be found at the **Undara Lava Tubes** ㉕ a few kilometres south of the Savannah Way, one of the best examples of lava-tube formation anywhere on the planet. These are created when lava follows the line of riverbeds, the lava surface cools but the molten material within flows out, leaving a tube behind. Some of the tubes are 15–20 metres (50–65ft) in diameter. Full resort accommodation is offered in beautifully restored vintage rail carriages relocated there for the purpose. (tel: 07-4097 1900; www.undara.com.au; various times). It's also a Savannah Guide Station.

The Savannah Way continues on through **Georgetown,** where there are a few significant buildings and the **Terrestrial Centre** (Low Street; tel: 07-4062 1485; www.etheridge.qld.gov.au/terrestrial-information-centre; Apr–Sept daily 8am–5pm, Oct–Mar Mon–Fri 8.30am–4.30pm), which highlights the importance of minerals to the area. It's another 148km (92 miles) to **Croydon** ㉖, a friendly township with a well-preserved timber pub and an interesting historic precinct. From here there's an old railway service, the **Gulflander** (www.

gulflander.com.au), which runs through to **Normanton**, just a short distance from the **Gulf of Carpentaria.**

Towards the border with the Northern Territory, where the terrain becomes drier and less hospitable, **Lawn Hill Gorge** ㉗ provides a green oasis and stakes a claim to be one of the most spectacularly beautiful locations in the state. Not many people get out this far, but, for those who do, there are kayaks to paddle down between sheer red sandstone cliffs, and easy hikes through the surrounding **Boodjamulla National Park**. A half-hour drive away is the World Heritage-listed **Riversleigh** fossils site.

MINING TOWNS

Head south down dirt roads to **Mount Isa** ㉘ and discover the full significance of the finds at the **Riversleigh Fossil Display & Interpretive Centre** attached to the Outback at Isa complex (tel: 07-4749 1555; www.outbackatisa.com.au). Mount Isa is a mining city truly in the middle of nowhere. A rich lode of lead, silver, copper and zinc was discovered

⊙ Tip

For a scenic overview of Mount Isa, head for the **City Lookout** (a short drive off Hilary Street), preferably at dusk when the mine lights up. You can see the whole city sprawled out across a flat valley, backed by low hills, and all dominated by the mine.

Road train on a dirt road to Chillagoe.

here in 1923, and a tiny tent settlement rapidly developed into Australia's largest company town, dominated by the looming presence of the mine and its tailings. Working mine tours are no longer available, but you can take a two-hour underground tour of the ersatz Hard Times Mine, through the Outback at Isa operation.

The municipal boundaries of the Isa extend for 41,000 sq km (15,830 sq miles) – an area the size of Switzerland. Away from the mines, people relax at the artificial Lake Moondarra or socialise in any of the numerous licensed clubs, which welcome visitors. In August, Mount Isa hosts a three-day rodeo, the largest and richest in Australia.

The **School of the Air** (Abel Smith Parade; tours Mon–Fri 9am and 10am in term time; tel: 07-4743 2788; www.mtisasde.eq.edu.au), first established in Cloncurry, now operates from here, providing children on remote properties with direct radio and internet contact with a teacher. Its premises adjoin the Kalkadoon High School on Abel Smith Parade, and it's possible to visit.

The Big Red.

Cloncurry ㉙ is also a mining town, but in this case the main employer, the vast open-cut **Ernest Henry Mine,** is a bus ride away from the centre. Conducted tours are comprehensive and informative (tel: 07-4769 4500). Among the attractions in town, John Flynn Place (corner Daintree and King streets; tel: 07-4742 4100; www.johnflynnplace.com.au; Mon–Fri 8.30am–4.30pm all year, May–Sept Sat–Sun 9am–3pm also) contains a museum devoted to the Royal Flying Doctor Service and its founder.

THE MATILDA HIGHWAY

The Matilda Highway heads southeast through **McKinlay**, home of the pub used in the Crocodile Dundee films and now called the Walkabout Creek Hotel.

Some 241km (150 miles) further on sits **Winton ㉚**, a town full of character and home to the Waltzing Matilda Centre (tel: 07-4657 1466; www.matildacentre.com.au; 50 Elderslie Street; Nov–Mar, Mon–Fri 9am–5pm, Sat–Sun 9am–3pm, Apr–Oct daily 9am–5pm), which celebrates the song, its composer Banjo Paterson and all aspects of Outback life. This is also dinosaur country.

From Winton, the Matilda Highway continues to **Longreach ㉛**, where two major attractions await. A local manufacturer helped develop the **Australian Stockman's Hall of Fame** (Landsborough Highway; tel: 07-4658 2166; www.outbackheritage.com.au; daily 9am–4pm) as a fascinating tribute to the cattle drovers, shearers, jackaroos and entrepreneurs who opened up Australia to settlement.

Longreach was where Qantas set up its first operational base in 1922, and its original hangar, with the old sign still on it, has become part of the multimillion-dollar **Qantas Founders Outback Museum** (Landsborough Highway; tel: 07-4658 3737; www.qfom.com.au; daily 9am–4pm), which displays a retired Qantas Boeing 747 jumbo jet (still in flying condition), replicas of its early fleet of biplanes, and a comprehensive record of the national airline's growth.

Barcaldine ㉜, to the east, is notable for a collection of vintage hotels and pubs, and as home to the Workers' Heritage Centre (Ash Street; tel: 07-4651 2422; www.australianworkersheritagecentre.com.au; Mon–Sat 9am–5pm, Sun 10am–4pm), where a collection of historic structures house displays commemorating the role played by workers in the development of Australia.

The Matilda Highway continues south all the way to **Charleville** ㉝. The usual assortment of historic buildings is worth a look, but the points of difference are the **Cosmos Centre** (Qantas Drive; tel: 07-4654 7771; www.cosmoscentre.com; Apr–Oct daily 10am–4pm, Nov–March closed Sun, evening sessions available), an observatory and museum which host astral viewing sessions; and the **Steiger Gun**, a bizarre device designed in 1902 to fire hot air into the sky in order to create rain.

Heading east through **Roma** and then **Miles** ㉞, with its charming **Historical Village** (Murilla Street; tel:

07-4627 1492; www.mhv.org.au; daily 8am–5pm), would eventually lead back to the east coast.

QUEENSLAND'S FAR WEST

But that would be to ignore two of Queensland's iconic sites. **The Dig Tree**, on the border with South Australia, is where the famous base camp of the Burke and Wills expedition just missed a rendezvous with the men who could have rescued them from starvation and death.

Finally, there is **Birdsville** ㉟. This isolated far western settlement has a population of 120, but each September it grows by five or six thousand for the Birdsville Races (www.birdsvilleraces.com), an utterly unique Outback horse-racing event where 300 light aircraft cram the airport, with their pilots camped under the wings. The 1884 Birdsville Hotel is a legendary watering hole. West of here are only the sand dunes of the Simpson Desert. A huge sandhill called **Big Red**, 36km (22 miles) to the west, marks the beginning of the famous Birdsville Track and is a popular spot for sunset parties.

Café proprietor in Wyandra, 100km (60 miles) south of Charleville.

The Ernest Henry Mine.

⊘ DINOSAUR DISTRICT

Detour south from Winton to **Lark Quarry Dinosaur Trackways** (tel: 07-4657 1466; www.dinosaurtrackways.com.au; daily 1st Apr–31st Oct, Mon–Sat 1st Nov–31st Mar 8.30am–5pm, regular tours), where petrified footprints denote a dinosaur encounter millions of years ago. The theme is maintained in two towns to the north: **Richmond** has Kronosaurus Korner (91–93 Goldring Street; tel: 07-4741 3429; www.kronosauruskorner.com.au; daily 8.30am–4pm), a marine fossil museum, while **Hughenden** (www.visithughenden.com.au) is home to the Flinders Discovery Centre (37 Gray Street; tel: 07-4741 2970; daily 9am–5pm), with a replica of a dinosaur skeleton found locally. A concrete dinosaur in the middle of town presses the point home. Nearby is the majestic **Porcupine Gorge** with its 120-metre (400ft) -high walls.

◉ THE RAINFOREST

Tropical or temperate, Queensland's
rainforests are among the state's
defining characteristics, and
a major tourist attraction.

High rainfall – at least 2 metres (6.5ft) – is a pre-
requisite for rainforest, and then it's generally a
matter of latitude and proximity to the ocean that
defines it as either tropical or temperate. The Australian state of Queensland is big enough to meet
both of these requirements.

Rainforests are nature in *extremis*. Two-thirds
of all the Earth's plant and animal species can be
found within them, and in north Queensland the
highest diversity of local endemic species in the
world is present. It is the last bastion for many of
these animals, while others are still being discovered, particularly in the upper regions under the
canopy, an area only recently appreciated for the
richness of its various flora and fauna.

It is estimated that the tropical rainforest
stretching from just north of Cairns to Cape Tribulation and on to Cooktown is in the region of 110
million years old, and constitutes the last remnant
of the forest that used to cover all of Australia and,
before that, Gondwanaland. Now protected as an
element of the Wet Tropics World Heritage Area,
it is a key attraction for tourists. The economic
rationale that has seen the destruction of forests
elsewhere in Australia and round the world will
probably now protect it.

*The orange-thighed frog (Litoria xanthomera) is a tree frog
native to a small area in tropical northern Queensland. The
call of the frog is a long 'aaa-rk', followed by a soft trill. The
call after heavy monsoon rain, and often congregate aroun
ponds, or at the edge of any standing body of water.*

*When the platypus was first discovered in Australia, ma
European naturalists were convinced it must be an
elaborate hoax. It is the only living member of its family
(Ornithorhynchidae) and genus (Ornithorhynchus), and i
one of the few monotremes.*

*There are more than 520 species of lizards found in
Australia. The five main families of lizards are geckos,
legless lizards, dragon lizards, monitor lizards (or
Goannas), and skinks.*

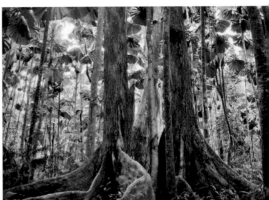

Gigantic trees in Daintree National Park.

The Daintree

Some of the most easily accessible rainforest, and therefore most visited, is in the Daintree National Park. There's a well-worn route from Cairns or Port Douglas up to Cape Tribulation, and every tour bus or expedition will stop at least once for a walk in the woods. In several places there are short boardwalk circuits from handy parking spots, and the way is marked by a series of interpretive boards. This makes it easy for the visitor to explore, and also helps in managing the forest by keeping tourists away from more pristine areas.

The complete packaged rainforest experience can be enjoyed at the Daintree Discovery Centre (tel: 07-4098 9171; www.discoverthedaintree.com; daily 8.30am–5pm), a short distance north of the Daintree ferry. Boardwalks wend along the forest floor, and a steel walkway through the canopy allows an entirely different perspective on life as the birds see it. Audio guides are available and there are more of the ubiquitous interpretive boards. The cassowaries here seem used to visitors.

To see the rainforest from a different perspective, take a zip-line tour that stops at several platforms perched among the tree tops.

The red-necked pademelon (Thylogale thetis) is a small, forest-dwelling marsupial. The animal is very shy, and typically hides in the forest during the day, only emerging to look for food at night. The pademelon was nearly hunted to extinction by imported foxes on the mainland, but can be found throughout Tasmania.

e cassowary (Casuarius suarius) is the third-largest ightless bird, after the ostrich d the emu. Its claws are rticularly sharp, and ssowaries have been known strike out at humans, hough the legend that a man can be disembowelled th a single kick by the ssowary's strong legs has ver been proven.

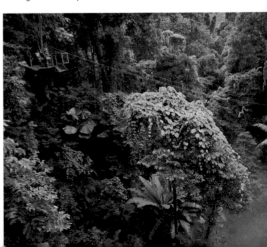

THE GREAT BARRIER REEF AND THE ISLANDS

The Great Barrier Reef is not only Queensland's major attraction, it is one of the natural wonders of the world. It's both the largest coral reef on Earth and one of the most accessible, and has a selection of stunning islands.

◉ Main attractions
Lady Elliot Island
Heron Island
Great Keppel Island
Magnetic Island
Agincourt Reef
Osprey Reef
Wolf Rock

📍
Map on page 240

The world's largest coral reef consists of more than 2,500 separate, interconnected reefs, stretching more than 2,300km (1,430 miles) from just above the tip of the Cape York Peninsula in the north to just north of Bundaberg in the south.

The reef won its World Heritage status in 1981, when the nomination noted that it supported 'the most diverse ecosystem known to man'. At the heart of that ecosystem is the polyp, a tiny animal consisting of little more than a mouth and surrounding tentacles to feed it – plus a limestone carapace into which it withdraws during the day. It is the skeletal remains of these creatures that form the basis of the reef. Individual polyps are linked by body tissue, thereby sharing the colony's food, but the main nutrient for a photosynthetic coral's food is algae cells within its tissue called zooxanthellae, which convert the sun's energy into nutrients.

In 2017, Deloittes calculated that the Great Barrier Reef is worth A\$56 billion. It contributes A\$6.4 billion to Australia's economy and supports 64,000 jobs. Queenslanders are extremely proud of this natural treasure, yet at times it has been treated with appalling carelessness by the national government.

THE FRAGILE CORAL
Over millions of years the reef has grown into the largest living entity in the world. This structure is fragile, however, and it only takes small environmental changes to disrupt its delicate balance. Coral bleaching is the major threat. If the water temperature rises by just a degree or two over a sustained period, the corals expel their zooxanthellae, lose their capacity for photosynthesis and become colourless. If the water does not cool quickly, the coral becomes permanently lifeless.

The Great Barrier Reef.

Severe damage was caused by extended hot spells in 1997–8 and again in 2002. Australia finally signed the Kyoto Protocol in December 2007 after the long-serving climate-change-sceptical coalition government of John Howard was defeated at the ballot box. In December 2015, at a UN conference in Paris, over 190 countries signed an agreement to limit global warming. However, a report published in *Nature* in 2018 shocked the world by revealing that 30 percent of the Great Barrier Reef had been killed by a 9-month heatwave in 2016. It's now beyond debate that global warming exists, and marine reefs worldwide are both indicators of this, and the first casualties. Co-author of the report, Professor Terry Hughes, says if the Paris agreement's targets are met, the reef will survive in some form, although 'biodiversity will likely be less, coral cover will likely be less'. If warming continues apace, Hughes warns, 'then it's game over'. In response, in July 2018 the Australian and Queensland governments hastily revised their Reef 2050 plan (which details how they intend protecting and managing the Reef until 2050).

There are other dangers, too. In December 2013, the Australian government under then-Prime Minister Tony Abbott controversially gave the go ahead for increased industrial activity around the reef, permitting dredging and dumping to occur within the World Heritage–listed area in order for big tankers to pass through – a decision that horrified the public and Unesco, especially since it came just a few years after a Chinese tanker ran aground on the reef, tearing a huge gash in the coral and haemorrhaging thousands of litres of oil into the fragile eco system.

Even small-scale human traffic can cause significant damage to coral, through chains and anchors from boats, and snorkellers and divers who brush against polyps and damage or kill them. The reef is also under pressure from the effects of poor water quality, which is often caused by soil and fertiliser runoff from the shore,

Exploring the reef.

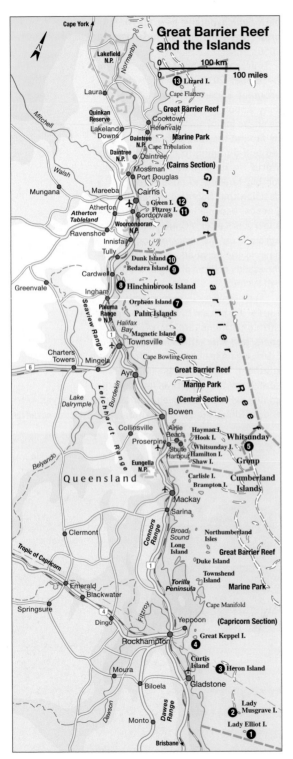

Great Barrier Reef and the Islands

0   100 km

0   100 miles

Great Barrier Reef Marine Park
(Cairns Section)

Great Barrier Reef Marine Park
(Central Section)

Great Barrier Reef Marine Park
(Capricorn Section)

and it takes a pounding from cyclones (also worsened by climate change). The Great Barrier Reef Marine Park (www.gbrmpa.gov.au) was established in the 1970s to protect this magnificent resource, and the associated authority monitors the effects of tourism and fishing. In 2014, Google teamed up with Catlin Seaview Survey to create Street-View style 3D mapping of the Great Barrier Reef, which helps scientists monitor developments, and allows people to take virtual tours of the reef without getting wet.

THE ISLANDS

While only a few are literally coral islands, the 20 odd resort islands inside the Great Barrier Reef Marine Park offer many attractions. Lodging varies from five-star resorts to backpacker hostels and campsites. Some islands are dry, barren and windy; others are lush and rainforest covered.

THE SOUTH

Lady Elliot Island ❶ (www.ladyelliot.com. au): dubbed an 'Eco Island', this is a quiet and beautiful 42-hectare (103-acre) coral cay, with bungalow accommodation and some permanent tents. It is 80km (50 miles) from Bundaberg and reached by air. Its coral setting ensures easy access to good diving and snorkelling.

Lady Musgrave Island ❷ (www. ladymusgraveexperience.com.au): a tiny uninhabited cay, visited only by daytrippers or campers (with a National Parks permit). Access is by boat from Bundaberg. It offers diving and snorkelling within a brilliant blue lagoon.

Heron Island ❸ (www.heronisland. com): only 1km (0.5 miles) long, this is the reef's most famous coral cay and is number one for diving (along with Lizard at the northern fringe of the Reef). The reef is certainly at its most accessible: where the beach ends, the coral begins, with its abundant marine life.

Great Keppel Island ❹ (www.great keppelislandhideaway.com.au): there are excellent white sandy beaches, long hiking trails, views of the mainland, and plenty of social activities. Great Keppel is not directly on the reef; short cruises run out for divers. Access is by air from Rockhampton or by sea from Rosslyn Bay.

THE WHITSUNDAYS

At the southern end of **The Whitsundays ⑤** archipelago, **Lindeman Island** was once home to Australia's first Club Med. That closed in 2012, but a new three-resort development is expected to open by 2021 (check www.lindeman. net.au for details). The island boasts 20km (12 miles) of bushwalking trails through 500 hectares (1,230 acres) of national park. Access is from Mackay, Hamilton Island and Proserpine.

Various resorts have co-existed on **Long Island,** which is only a short boat trip from Shute Harbour. The most enduring, Peppers Palm Bay (www. palmbayresort.com.au), is ideal for a back-to-nature holiday with lovely beaches, clear water and coral, and solitude.

With a pseudo-South Seas main street once described as 'Daiquiri Disneyland', **Hamilton Island** (www.hamiltonisland.com.au) is not the place for a quiet island sojourn, although it does have a wide range of great accommodation options, including the utterly stunning five-star qualia resort (www. qualia.com.au) – arguably the reef's most luxurious hideaway.

The largest of the group, **Whitsunday Island** covers 109 sq km (42 sq miles) and has no resort, but does offer the fabulous Whitehaven Beach – a great option for campers (with permits – see www.whitsundaycamping.com.au).

Once home to a popular resort, **South Molle Island** was battered by Cyclone Debbie in 2017 and remains closed at the time of writing. **Daydream Island** (www.daydreamisland. com), however, remains a popular family resort with all the necessities for a good time at a reasonable all-inclusive

tariff. Great beaches and a wide range of activities are just 15 minutes from Shute Harbour or Hamilton Island.

The second-largest island in the Whitsundays, **Hook Island** has Aboriginal cave paintings at Nara Inlet. The budget resort that once operated here has fallen into disrepair, as has the underwater observatory, which is no longer open, however you can still camp on several beaches (see parks. des.qld.gov.au for more).

Hayman Island (www.hayman.com.au) is an exclusive five-star resort set in a coral-trimmed lagoon, close to the outer Reef and a favourite with honeymooners. Access is from Hamilton Island, Proserpine, Shute Harbour and Townsville.

THE CENTRE TO THE NORTH

Magnetic Island ⑥ (www.visit magneticisland.com.au) is a large (5,000-hectare/12,400-acre) island and a national park; this pleasant, populated (2,300) haven is almost an outer suburb of mainland Townsville. There are plenty of walks in the rainforest,

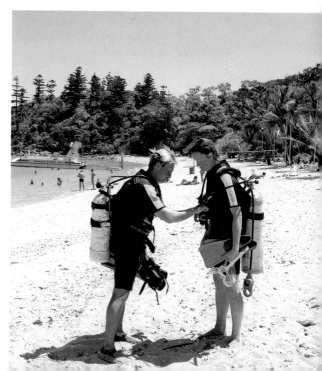

Diving and snorkelling are the islands' principal businesses.

VISITING THE REEF

Every morning, dozens of boats head out from Cairns and Port Douglas to various pre-selected sites, some reaching gorgeous coral within an hour.

The easiest way to visit the Reef is to take a day trip. You can also take trips from Cape Tribulation and some of the island resorts and coastal towns further south.

Because the water is so shallow, snorkelling is perfectly satisfactory for seeing the marine life (in fact, many people prefer it to scuba diving; even so, most boats offer tanks for experienced divers and resort dives for people who have never dived before). Above the waves, the turquoise void might be broken only by a sand cay crowded with sea birds, but as soon as you poke your mask underwater, the world erupts. It's almost sensory overload: there are vast forests of staghorn coral, whose tips glow purple like electric Christmas-tree lights; brilliant blue clumps of mushroom coral; layers of pink plate coral; bulbous green brain coral.

Tropical fish with exotic names slip about as if showing off their fluorescent patterns: painted flutemouth, long-finned batfish, crimson

An aerial view of Green Island, where a luxury resort will cater to your every need.

squirrelfish, hump-headed Maori wrasse, cornflower sergeant major. Thrown into the mix are scarlet starfish and black sea cucumbers. You definitely don't pick up the sleek conus textile shells – they shoot darts into anything that touches them, each with enough venom to kill 300 people. There are 21 darts in each shell and so, as one captain notes, 'if they don't get you the first time, they'll get another try'.

Almost all Reef trips follow a similar format. There's a morning dive or snorkel, followed by a buffet lunch; then, assuming you haven't eaten too much or availed of the free beer, an afternoon dive. There should be a marine biologist on board to explain the reef's ecology. Before you book, ask how many passengers the boat takes: they vary from several hundred on the Quicksilver fleet of catamarans to fewer than a dozen on smaller craft.

The reef is at its best from late April through to October, the clear skies and moderate breezes offering perfect conditions for coral viewing, diving, swimming, fishing and sunning. In November the first signs of the approaching 'Wet' appear: variable winds, increasing cloud and showers. By January it rains at least once most days. And when the winds are up and the waters are stirred, visibility under the water diminishes. Furthermore, in rough seas excursion boats have fewer places to anchor and may be restricted to areas which have been over-visited and where, consequently, the coral has been damaged. Pick the time of your visit carefully.

In general, the further out the boat heads, the more pristine the diving (the Low Isles, for example, near Port Douglas, have suffered). The much-touted 'Outer Reef' on the edge of the continental shelf, sometimes called the 'real' reef, requires a much longer trip and such sites are typically visited by more expensive 'live-aboard' dive boats. Here you get to enjoy superb coral with just a handful of other divers, and stand a good chance of spotting various oceanic and pelagic species, including sharks.

Even in the winter months, the water around the reef is never cold, but it's worth paying extra to hire a wetsuit; most people find it hard not to continue snorkelling for hours on end in this extraordinary environment.

or up to the 500-metre (1,640ft) Mount Cook. Horseshoe Bay has a koala and wildlife park. Bikes, scooters and Mini Mokes can be rented.

Orpheus Island (www.orpheus. com.au) is in the Palm group northeast of Townsville and is very close to the outer Reef. An exclusive resort hidden among the trees has good accommodation and entertainment. Seaplane access from Townsville.

Hinchinbrook Island (www.parks. des.qld.gov.au) is accessible from Cardwell by boat. The jagged peaks, golden beaches and luxuriant rainforests of Hinchinbrook National Park can be explored by experienced hikers. The island's signature east-coast track, the 32km (20-mile) Thorsborne Trail, has limits on walker numbers, though, so book in advance.

A small fragment of the Family Islands, **Bedarra Island** (www. bedarra.com.au) has an exclusive resort set in rich rainforest with pure beaches and tranquil coves. Go via **Dunk Island** (www.dunk-island.com), where the recluse E.J. Banfield lived for 26 years at the turn of the 20th century, writing his *Confessions of a Beachcomber*. The island is a rainforested national park. The resort remains closed after damage sustained during cyclone Yasi, but day visits and camping are possible. Access is from Townsville, Cairns and Mission Beach.

Surrounded by coral reef, **Fitzroy Island** (www.fitzroyisland.com) is a great place for diving and fishing. **Green Island** (www.greenisland. au) is a tiny coral cay just off Cairns with a good underwater observatory, but it's mostly for day-trippers. The most northerly island, **Lizard Island** (www.lizardisland.com.au) is home to the marlin boats. Lizard allows access directly from the beach to the reef and has stunning diving. Fly from Cairns.

THE DIVING

With more than 2,000km (1,240 miles) of reef to choose from and numerous departure points, it is useful to have a grasp of the diving that awaits you.

Cod Hole, just off Lizard Island, is one of the best-known dive

Electric buggies are the popular way for tourists to get around Hamilton Island.

Lizard Island.

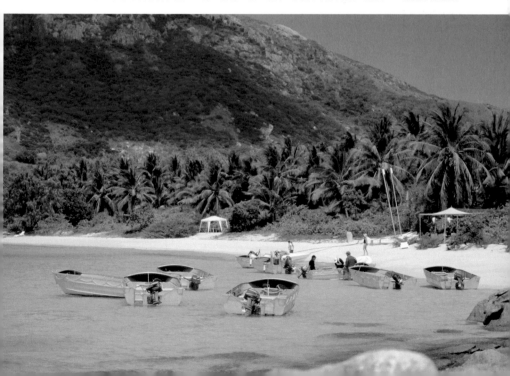

Moore Reef.

destinations because this one isn't just about coral gardens. You also get the chance to encounter potato cod, giant (up to 100kg/220lbs) man-sized fish that will nuzzle up to you in the hope of the food that most expeditions take along.

The SS *Yongala* passenger ship sank in 1911, but the wreck was only discovered 100km (60 miles) east of Townsville in 1958. The remains of the 110-metre (360ft) -long vessel are still intact and attract thousands of divers every year. Expeditions run from Townsville. **Wheeler Reef** is also accessed from Townsville and has a reputation for being one of the finest night dive sites, although, with its range of coral, eels, sharks and countless other fish, it's good at any time of day.

Lady Elliot Island has several outstanding dive sites, including the **Blow Hole**, a cave dive accessible via two openings 25 metres (82ft) down on the eastern side of the Island. Lion fish and gnome fish are among the company likely to greet you. The **Anchor Bommies** nearby also has rays and the added interest of two coral-encrusted naval anchors sitting on the sea bed.

Agincourt Reef is the destination of the substantial Quicksilver operation. You can't miss their massive silver catamarans, which transport visitors in their hundreds from pick-up points in Cairns, Palm Cove and Port Douglas out to their two-storey floating pontoon on the outer reef. Despite the numbers, the reef is well stocked with coral and associated marine life and ideal for beginners wanting a trial dive.

Heron Island has numerous attractions, including the Heron **Bommie**, one of the most famous dive sites on the reef. It is a nesting ground for green turtles between October and March. **Osprey Reef** is spectacular for its colony of white-tip reef sharks and some of the finest coral to be seen anywhere. Grey reef sharks, potato cod and dogtooth tuna are amongst the other inhabitants. Cairns and Port Douglas are the departure points.

Bait Reef is in the Whitsundays so boats run out of Airlie Beach to this wonderland of tropical marine life. Much of what interests is close to the surface, so snorkellers are well catered for, along with novice divers who are comfortable up to 10 metres (32ft) down. **Hardy Reef**, also in the Whitsundays, is notable for a 70-metre (230ft) reef wall where numerous species of fish drift around both hard and soft coral.

Wolf Rock's four submerged volcanic peaks have swim-throughs and ledges along with a rich selection of subaquatic life. It's to be found on the Sunshine Coast off Double Island Point.

Ex-HMAS *Brisbane*, a former Royal Australian Navy destroyer, was scuttled off Mooloolaba on the Sunshine Coast as a wreck site. It's now 28 metres (92ft) down and experienced divers can look around parts of the ship's interior, helped by access holes.

Ex-HMAS Brisbane.

📷 PROTECTING THE GREAT BARRIER REEF

The world's largest living entity is top of the list on many tourist itineraries, but its fragility means it's important to minimise visitor impact.

The Great Barrier Reef may be the largest collection of living organisms on Earth, but it is also extremely fragile. Rising sea temperatures have added to the already considerable risk posed by tourism, pollution and natural enemies such as the crown-of-thorns starfish. Protecting the reef from its natural and mad-made enemies has become more important than ever, as we learn about the biodiversity under the waves. The reef's astonishingly complex and diverse ecosystem will disappear forever if precautions aren't taken immediately.

The appeal of the Great Barrier Reef to visitors is undeniable, and tourism is big business. But should you decide to visit the park, there are a number of things you can do to limit your environmental impact. Scuba diving is one of the main tourist draws to the reef, but it can take an average of 25 years for coral to recover from an accidental knock and scrape from an inexperienced diver. The main way to avoid causing damage to the reef is to take scuba lessons before you travel, and then to make sure you choose a recognised dive operator to take you to the site. Smaller groups of divers are also preferable as they are less likely to cause disturbance to the coral and its inhabitants.

If you fish, make sure you use the Marine Park Authority's zoning maps, which will let you know of any restrictions in the area. Be sure to return any unwanted or undersized fish to the water as quickly as possible. Use official campsites and take all litter, including fishing lines, with you when you leave.

Clownfish live at the bottom of the sea in sheltered reef or in shallow lagoons, usually in pairs. In the wild, they live in a symbiotic relationship with the sea anemone.

A diver contemplates a sea fan, or gorgonian. A colony can be several metres high and across but only a few centimetres thick. There are more than 500 species of gorgonians in the ocean.

A giant potato cod.

yellow crinoid (phylum Echinodermata) waves in
e waters of the Great Barrier Reef. The name
rinoid comes from the Greek word for lily,
though this is an animal, not a plant.

sea slug.

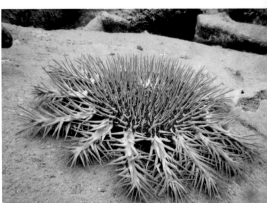

A crown-of-thorns starfish.

The Reef's greatest enemy?

For years, the worst threat to the Reef was thought to be the crown-of-thorns starfish, an ugly creature that clamps on to coral and effectively spits its stomach out. Its digestive juices dissolve the polyps and leave great expanses of coral bleached and dead. The crown-of-thorns is poisonous to other fish and is almost indestructible: it can regenerate to full size from only a single leg and small piece of intestine.

With only a few around, it was easy to ignore its depredations on the Reef, but in the early 1960s the pattern changed. Instead of a few crown-of-thorns starfish, suddenly there were millions. Green Island was the first to see the plague in 1962. From there it spread southwards, reaching the reefs around Bowen by 1988. Surveys between 1985 and 1988 established that about 31 percent of the reefs examined had been affected. Even after millions of dollars' worth of research, no one knows what caused the proliferation of the starfish. Furthermore, no economic way to get rid of the pest has presented itself.

The latest concentrated outbreak of crown-of-thorns starfish occurred at the southern end of the reef, on Swain Reefs off Yeppoon, in 2018. The reef has survived previous attacks on this scale, however, and the biggest existential danger remains rising sea temperatures and coral bleaching.

Six species of sea
turtle call the Great
Barrier Reef home,
while there are two
distinct genetic
groups of the green
sea turtle: one at the
north end of the reef,
and one at the south.

Uluru at sunset.

Simpson's Gap, near Alice Springs.

NORTHERN TERRITORY

Fewer than one in 100 Australians live in the vast Northern Territory, an untamed region with a climate, a landscape and a history all of its own.

The Northern Territory, or just 'NT', is Australia in epic mode. Things here are larger than life – the sky, the distances, people's dreams and visions, the Earth itself. An area of 1.35 million sq km (521,240 sq miles) – more than double the size of France, yet inhabited by just 244,000 people – provides plenty of room to move.

The locals are a breed apart: tough, laconic, beholden to no one. Like the inhabitants of any inhospitable environment, they possess friendliness by the bucketful, a truly egalitarian spirit, and a wicked sense of humour.

Many urban Australians visiting NT's Outback feel as though they have entered a foreign land. They find a kind of detachment, a floating feeling of insubstantiality inspired by the uncomfortable knowledge that nothing human beings do here can ever touch the soul or the brute power of this ancient land.

LONG DISTANCES

Despite its size, the Northern Territory fits neatly into a travel itinerary. There is the Red Centre (Alice Springs and the stunning hinterland in the Territory's south); various points along 'The Track' (the Stuart Highway) heading north; and the Top End (Darwin, Kakadu and surroundings).

The distance between points of interest can be intimidating – roughly 1,600km (1,000 miles) from Alice to Darwin – but only by driving through NT do you get a true sense of its grand and ancient terrain.

Apart from the Top End, which is swamped by tropical monsoons from February to March each year, most of the Territory is an arid zone. Rainfall is minimal, averaging about 250mm (9.8ins) a year. But, when rain does come, it comes Outback-style: no half measures.

☑ **Main attractions**
Alice Springs
Uluru and Kata Tjuta
Tennant Creek
Kakadu National Park
Darwin
Tiwi Islands

◉ **Maps on pages 252, 263**

The Rim Walk in Kings Canyon.

Northern Territory

0   200 km
0   200 miles

Timor Sea

Cobourg Peninsula

Arafura Sea

Melville I.

Wessel Islands

Bathurst I. **21** **22**

Garig Gunak Barlu N.P. **20**

Van Diemen Gulf

Nguiu
Beagle Gulf Clarence Strait

Nhulunbuy
Cape Arnhem

Darwin **18**
Territory Wildlife Park★

Arnhem Hwy

Kakadu National Park

★Cahills Crossing

Gove Peninsula

Litchfield National Park **19**

Adelaide River

Hayes Creek

Jabiru
★Nourlangie Rock

Cooinda **17**

Gunlom Falls

Arnhem Land

Pine Creek

Bulman

Groote Eylandt

Daly River

Daly

Nitmiluk National Park **16**

Wadeye

Katherine
Katherine Gorge **15**

Numbulwar

Gulf of Carpentaria

Joseph Bonaparte Gulf

Mataranka
Elsey N.P. **14**

Roper Bar
Roper

Wyndham

Keep River National Park (Proposed)
Timber Creek

Larrimah

Limmen Nation Park (Proposed)

Sir Edward Pellew Group

Lake Argyle

Keep River National Park

Gregory

Victoria River Downs

Victoria Hwy

Daly Waters **13**

Borroloola

Mornington Island

Lake Argyle

National

Park

Top Springs

Carpentaria Hwy

Purnululu National Park (Bungle Bungle)

Newcastle Waters

Hwy

Buchanan
Kalkarindji

Elliot

Sturt Plain

Burketown

Nicholson

Tarrabool Lake

Renner Springs

Lake Sylvester

Barkly Tableland

Boodjamulla N.P.

Northern Territory

Stuart Hwy

Tablelands Hwy

Tanami Desert

Tennant Creek **12**

Tablelands (Barkly Homestead Wayside Inn)

Barkly

Camooweal
HWY

Western Australia

Tanami Track

10

Davenport Ranges N.P. (Proposed)

Karlu Karlu/ Devils Marbles **11**

Mount Isa

Lake MacKay

Barrow Creek

Ti-Tree

Sandover Hwy

Urandangi

Dajarra

Yuendumu

MacDonnell Ranges

Plenty Hwy

Queensland

Tropic of Capricorn

Papunya

Haasts Bluff

West MacDonnell National Park **2**

Hermannsburg

Trephina George

Arltunga

Ross River
N'dhala Gorge

Great Artesian

Watarrka National Park **4**

Finke Gorge National Park **3**

Kings Canyon

Alice Springs **1**

Emily & Jesse Gaps N.P.

L. Neale

L. Amadeus

Henbury Meteorite Craters **7**

Rainbow Valley **5**

Henbury

Titjikala

Basin

Bedourie

Uluru-KataTjuta National Park
Yulara

Curtin Springs

Chambers Pillar **6**

Kata Tjuta (The Olgas) **9**

867
Uluru (Ayers Rock) **8**

Mt Ebenezer

Erldunda

Finke

Simpson Desert

Kulgera

Birdsville

Great Victoria Desert

Mt Woodroffe
▲ 1440
Musgrave Ranges

Agnes Creek

South Australia

Clifton Hills

THE RED CENTRE

Australia's Red Centre is the heart of the country in more ways than one. For many visitors, Australia is primarily a nature trip, and it is here in central Australia that the continent's greatest natural feature stands – **Uluru**, or **Ayers Rock**. But just as two-thirds of the Rock's awesome mass lies hidden beneath the ground, so Uluru and the other main tourist sights represent the mere tip of the great iceberg that is the Outback.

Incidentally, the Red Centre isn't just a cute name. The sand and rock around here are red because of iron oxides found in the sandstone. The sun is red when it drops, and red scars mark the flow of mineral-rich, ultra-healthy water. Even some of the kangaroos are red.

ALICE SPRINGS

Alice Springs ❶ – or the Alice – is the natural base for exploring the Red Centre. It is a grid-pattern, sun-scorched town of squat, mostly modern buildings, which crouches in one of many gaps (or Outback oases) in the rugged **MacDonnell Ranges**. These hills – which turn an intense blue at sunset, as if lit internally – act like a wagon train, a protective ring that might just keep the expanse of the Outback at bay.

Alice has enjoyed a tourist boom, based on Uluru and Aboriginal art and culture. Its present population of over 25,000, one-tenth of which is Aboriginal, represents the greatest demographic concentration for 1,500km (900 miles) in any direction.

By no means a picture-postcard town, Alice has strange powers of attraction: visitors find themselves drawn again and again to this incongruous outpost, and many who come here for short-term work wake up 10 years later and wonder what happened. It's not necessarily easy to meet someone who was actually born in Alice.

Settlement began here in 1871 in the form of a repeater station on the Overland Telegraph Line, constructed beside the permanent freshwater springs. Lying 4km (2.5 miles) north of the present township, the **Telegraph Station** (tel: 08-8952 3993; www.alicespringstelegraphstation.com.au; Mon–Fri 8.30am–5pm; Sat–Sun 8am–5pm) and **Springs** form a popular tourist site. Then, as now, water dictated all human movement and settlement, and the line, running from Adelaide through Alice and up to Darwin, followed virtually the same route as The Track does now. The line linked the cities of Australia's south and southeast with the rest of the world, as it continued from Darwin through Indonesia to Singapore, Burma, British India and across Asia and Europe to colonial headquarters in London. Keeping the line open was a full-time job, and it is still possible to see some of the original telegraph posts, now disused, rising from the hard earth.

Alice developed slowly; in 1925, it had just 200 residents. Four years later, the coming of the Ghan train – which at that time ran from Adelaide via Oodnadatta to Alice and is named after Afghan camel drivers who pioneered

⊙ ABORIGINAL FESTIVALS

Many tourists want to experience life in remote Aboriginal communities. This is not always possible with the permit system for travel into the communities, but there are a number of annual festivals at which visitors are welcome. If you want to enjoy one of these opportunities you will need to rough it a little: camping is usually the only accommodation option.

The **Barunga Festival** (www.barungafestival.com.au), held on the Queen's Birthday weekend in early June, is a celebration of sports and culture. More than 20 communities come together at the festival, a four-hour drive from Darwin. The program includes a battle of the bands and the sports programme, and there are performances of traditional dance, arts and crafts. Note that this is a strictly drug- and alcohol-free event.

Beswick Falls (djilpinarts.org.au), south of Katherine, hosts the Walking with Spirits festival every July. In a spectacular lakeside setting, guests can enjoy not just traditional corroboree, but also songs and stories told in dance, music, puppetry, fire and film.

August brings the **Garma Festival** (www.garma.com.au), a huge, vibrant annual celebration of 40,000-year-old Yolngu (Aboriginal people of north-east Arnhem Land) culture, that takes place near Nhulunbuy in north-east Arnhem Land, where around 2,000 indigenous and non-indigenous Australians, plus international visitors, gather for the annual festival.

The Royal Flying Doctor service operates more than 50 aircraft and has around 500 full-time staff. It can make over 160 landings and deal with more than 600 patients each day, nearly 100 of whom will need an aerial evacuation.

View towards the West MacDonnell Ranges, Alice Springs.

transport in these parts – saw things pick up, but the trip was fraught with hazards. In the mistaken belief that the Outback never flooded, the track was routed across low-lying terrain; consequently, the train was often stranded, with additional supplies having to be parachuted in to the hapless passengers. A new, flood-proof route was completed in 1980, and the Ghan remains one of Australia's great rail journeys. In February 2004 Alice Springs ceased to be the end of the line, when the Alice–Darwin 1,420km (880-mile) extension was completed. The event fulfilled a century-old promise of a key economic and tourism link.

THE FLYING DOCTOR

In Alice, spend your first sunset on **Anzac Hill** to get the lie of the land. One of the town's most popular attractions is the **Royal Flying Doctor Service Visitors' Centre** (8–10 Stuart Terrace; tel: 08-8958 8411; www.rfdsal icesprings.com.au; Mon–Sat 9am–5pm, Sun 1pm–5pm, tours every half hour to 4pm). The service, established in 1928 by the Rev. John Flynn – who you can meet in hologram form at the centre, and who graces the A$20 bill – provides essential medical treatment to many isolated communities and cattle stations the length and breadth of the Outback. Flynn's grave is 7km (4 miles) west of Alice on Larapinta Drive – he is pinned down in perpetuity by one of the Devil's Marbles, poor chap.

Another popular spot is the **Alice Springs School of the Air** (80 Head Street; tel: 08-8951 6834; www.assoa. nt.edu.au; Mon–Sat 8.30am–4.30pm, Sun 1.30pm–4.30pm), which services the educational needs of far-flung children. The school, unique in the world, conducts primary-level classes via radio, and the most notable of its 26 bases across the Outback is in Alice, covering an area of 1.3 million sq km (500,000 sq miles). It is the world's biggest classroom, and visitors can listen to lessons being taught there.

The **Alice Springs Desert Park** (871 Larapinta Drive; tel: 08-8951 8788; www.alicespringsdesertpark.com.au; daily 7.30am–6pm), situated just outside Alice at the base of the MacDonnell Ranges, is a must-see primer for anyone about to explore the desert. Its 35 hectares (86 acres) contain 320 arid-zone plant species and more than 400 desert-dwelling animals. The birds of prey nature theatre, where wild birds interact with park rangers in an astonishing way, is unforgettable.

The **Araluen Cultural Precinct** (tel: 08-8951 1122; www.araluenartscentre. nt.gov.au; daily 10am–4pm) on Larapinta Drive contains the Strehlow Research Centre, the Museum of Central Australia, the Memorial Cemetery, the Central Australian Aviation Museum and the Araluen Centre, including the Namatjira Gallery.

The **Strehlow Research Centre** (Alice Springs Cultural Precinct, Larapinta Drive; tel: 08-89511111; Mon–Fri 9am–4pm) chronicles the life and work of Ted Strehlow, who was born at Hermannsburg, the Lutheran mission established in 1877. He became a patrol officer and researcher among the Arrernte people, winning their trust, and artefacts from his comprehensively documented collection that are not culturally sensitive are on display at the centre.

The **Central Australian Aviation Museum** (6 Memorial Avenue; tel: 08-8953 8554; www.centralaustralianaviationmuseum.org.au; Mon–Fri 10am–4pm Sat–Sun 11am–4pm) features various flying machines that opened up the Red Centre. The nearby cemetery is arguably more interesting, because the famous Aboriginal landscape painter Albert Namatjira and the legendary gold seeker Harold Lasseter (whose lives form a pretty comprehensive recent history of the region) are buried there, as are a number of Afghans, in a separate section at the back, facing Mecca.

If you find yourself in Alice in August, don't miss the **Henley-on-Todd Regatta** (www.henleyontodd.com.au). This grandly named event is a boat race unlike any other. The 'boats' are bottomless wraparounds, and teams of about eight runners inside each one race along the dry bed of the Todd River. Much merriment is had by all.

AROUND ALICE

Alice's immediate surroundings offer numerous attractions. To the east, in the **Eastern MacDonnell Ranges**, **Emily Gap, Jesse Gap, Trephina Gorge, N'dhala Gorge** and the old gold town of **Arltunga** are interesting excursions.

Stretching west from Alice is the **West MacDonnell National Park** ❷ (www.nt.gov.au/leisure/parks-reserves), incorporating many of the gaps in the ranges. These include **Simpson's Gap** (tel: 08-8955 0310), accessible via an excellent cycle path from Alice; **Standley Chasm**, whose steep walls become alive with colour an hour either side of midday; **Serpentine Gorge**; the **Ochre Pits**, used by Aborigines for centuries; **Ormiston Gorge and Pound** (tel: 08-8956 7799), with some fine walking trails; **Glen Helen Gorge**, with a comfortable lodge nearby; and **Redbank Gorge**. A 223km (138-mile) walking track, the

Alice Springs at night.

The view from an aircraft provides a unique perspective on the arid land around Alice Springs.

Larapinta Trail (www.larapintatrail.com.au), constructed by local prisoners, connects many of the attractions of the MacDonnells. Guided treks along the whole track can be arranged in Alice.

To the south is **Finke Gorge National Park ❸** (tel: 08-8956 7401; www.nt.gov.au/leisure/parks-reserves), featuring the picturesque Palm Valley, with its distinctive red cabbage palms, and the Finke River, whose watercourse is one of the oldest in the world at 350 million years in some areas. This park is accessed via Hermannsburg, by four-wheel-drive only.

Due west of here is one of Central Australia's star attractions – spectacular **Kings Canyon** and **Watarrka National Park ❹** (tel: 08-8956 7460; www.nt.gov.au/leisure/parks-reserves). The 350-million-year-old canyon shelters a permanent rock pool, aptly named the Garden of Eden and visited during the magnificent four-hour **Canyon Rim Walk**. The nearby Kings Canyon Resort offers a range of accommodation. There is also accommodation 36km (22 miles) from the Canyon Rim Walk

at Kings Creek Station, which offers basic cabins and a camping ground.

The **Mereenie Loop Road** is a dirt road that connects Watarrka National Park with Namatjira Drive and attractions like Glen Helen Gorge. The track skirts the desert's eastern edge and should not be tackled by a conventional vehicle without local advice. Beware of crossing camels. The road crosses Aboriginal land so you will need a permit; these are issued by the Northern Land Council (www.nlc.org.au) and can be obtained at tourist centres in the area (check up-to-date details during planning).

ROCK FORMATIONS SOUTH OF ALICE

South of Alice lies **Pine Gap**, off-limits to visitors but notable as the largest US communications and surveillance base in the Asia-Pacific region. Most of the 400-odd Americans employed here live in Alice; they hold weekend barbecues and baseball games in town parks.

The Aboriginal rock carvings at **Ewaninga**, of undetermined age, remain cryptic and alluring. Kaleidoscopic **Rainbow Valley ❺** is a stunning rock formation (with primitive camping conditions), as is **Chambers Pillar ❻**, a solitary upstanding red ochre outcrop inscribed with the names and dates of early explorers, who used it as a convenient landmark.

The **Henbury Meteorite Craters ❼**, just off the highway, consist of 12 indentations, about 5,000 years old, the biggest of which (180 metres/590ft wide by 15 metres/49ft deep) was caused by four meteors, each the size of a 200-litre (44-gallon) drum. The craters have become occasional pools, sprouting plants and attracting a variety of animal life.

En route to Uluru is **Curtin Springs** (tel: 08-8956 2906; www.curtinsprings.com) a sprawling cattle station established in 1930 to breed horses for the British Indian Army. It offers accommodation (rooms and camping), food

A painting on display at the Northern Territory Aviation Museum.

and the roadside pub is a bit of a showroom for weird and wonderful tourist paraphernalia.

Dominating the horizon is **Mount Conner**, a table-top monolith that many people initially mistake for Uluru (some locals call it 'Fool-uru'). Conner, at 700 million years old, is 150 million years older than Uluru and Kata Tjuta and just 4 metres (13ft) lower than Uluru. It's on private land, but you can visit Mount Conner with SEIT Outback Australia (tel: 08-8956 3156; www.sei toutbackaustralia.com.au), with pick-ups from Curtin Springs.

ULURU AND KATA TJUTA

From here, the road leads to Australia's great Outback icon, **Uluru** ❽ (Ayers Rock; tel: 08-8956 1128; www. parksaustralia.gov.au/uluru; charge for a three-day pass). The surrounding Uluru-Kata Tjuta National Park was World Heritage-listed for its natural significance in 1987, and for its cultural significance in 1994. It was first sighted by a European in 1872 when explorer Ernest Giles noted a prominent hill in the distance. The following year, William Gosse discovered that the hill was in fact 'one immense rock rising abruptly from the plain'. After climbing it barefoot and soaking up its mystical aura, he enthused: 'This rock appears more wonderful every time I look at it.'

Uluru means 'meeting place', and many Aboriginal Dreaming tracks or songlines intersect here. Spirituality is often grounded in common sense, and Uluru, with its permanent waterhole, abundant animal life, shelter and firewood, has been saving lives for millennia. The rock is sacred to the local Anangu people, who resumed ownership of the lands inside the national park in 1985, in a historic handover ceremony. The Anangu have a controlling interest on the park's board of management; the chairperson is Anangu, and the meetings are bilingual (Pitjantjatjara and English). No park policy or development occurs without consultation. The Anangu receive more than A\$2 million in revenue under the terms of the hand-back, but there was a caveat: tourists were allowed to climb the rock on a defined path until 2019, when it was finally stopped. Various other Anangu sacred places are also out of bounds.

Climbing Uluru was a major attraction for many visitors, but it was always considered by resident park rangers and rescue teams to be dangerous, and by many people as disrespectful to the Anangu. Over a dozen climbers have been killed, and many more have had to be rescued. Until 2019, the Anangu (who feel culturally responsible for guest's safety while on their land) permitted the activity, but strongly requested visitors choose not to climb the rock, which has been soiled and scarred by decades of white people clambering up it. (In one local language, the word for the ubiquitous tiny black ant is *minga* – it is also the word for tourist.) In 2019, however, climbing was stopped altogether.

The Henley-on-Todd Regatta.

Uluru is the world's largest monolith. It stands 348 metres (1,142ft) tall and its circumference at the base is almost 9km (5.5 miles). Its elevation is 867m (2,844ft) above sea level.

Walking around the rim of Kings Canyon.

Recognising that the climb couldn't be closed until more alternative activities were in place, the board of management opened an excellent cultural centre in 1995 to mark the 10th anniversary of hand-back. A really good alternative to climbing is the 9.4km (5.8-mile) 'base walk' around the rock, which is well marked and much more interesting than the summit (which only offers a view of a vast amount of nothing, with the rock itself being the main local feature). A self-guiding brochure is available from the cultural centre and numerous interpretive signs are displayed.

There are other walks in the rock's vicinity, but **Kata Tjuta ❾** (The Olgas) in particular offers a number of excellent trails, including the three-hour 'Valley of the Winds' circuit. No climbing of Kata Tjuta (which means 'many heads', referring to the 36 domes) is permitted and, just in case you get the urge to take home any souvenir rocks or sand, bear in mind that it is disrespectful to Aboriginal sentiments and that park authorities receive, on average, two letters a week from visitors returning rocks they had taken, claiming that their luck has been bad ever since their stay in Uluru.

Hundreds of thousands of visitors annually flock to Uluru-Kata Tjuta National Park. They are all serviced by the award-winning **Ayers Rock Resort** (tel: 02-8296 8010; www.ayersrockresort. com.au), which offers a complete range of accommodation from camping (tel: 08-8957 7001) to hotels and cabins, through to ultra-luxe tented accommodation on the edge of the park at **Longitude 131°** (www.longitude131.com. au), where the tents are all air conditioned and boast views of the rock from the enormous beds.

A wide range of tours and activities are available, and the sight of a sunset traffic jam has to be seen to be believed. Uluru, like the entire Red Centre, will humble you with its scale and overwhelm you with its beauty.

THE TRACK TO TENNANT CREEK

Anyone seeking the old-style Outback experience of endless long, hot, dirt roads may like to leave the highway 21km (13 miles) north of Alice Springs and head northwest along the **Tanami Track ❿** to rejoin civilisation 1,050km (660 miles) away at Halls Creek in the Kimberley. But, for most tastes, the 1,500km (930-mile) route along a good paved road to Darwin will suffice.

Heading north from Alice, one passes through the tiny community of **Barrow Creek**, before reaching the **Karlu Karlu / Devil's Marbles Conservation Reserve ⓫** (403km/250 miles from Alice; tel: 08-8962 4599; www. nt.gov.au/leisure/parks-reserves), a series of granite boulders that lie either side of the highway for several kilometres. Some of the larger ones stand precariously balanced on tiny bases. It's thought they were once part of one solid block, broken and gradually rounded by wind and water erosion.

The local Aboriginal people (Kaytete, Warumungu, Warlpiri and Alyawarra) believe them to be the eggs of the rainbow serpent. Climbing is not allowed. There are facilities, including a basic camping area.

Tennant Creek ⑫ (504km/313 miles from Alice) is a gold town, although only one major mine is still in production. Gold was discovered in 1932 but the rush was short-lived, and the place seemed destined to become a ghost town until the discovery of copper in the 1950s brought new prosperity. The town is 12km (7 miles) from the creek; the story goes that a cart carrying timber to build the first pub for the miners became bogged here. It was too much trouble to continue, so the hotel was erected on the spot. With a tree-lined double highway and a population of over 3,500, the town bears few signs of such a haphazard beginning.

To explore the remote **Barkly Tableland**, take the Barkly Highway east for 185km (115 miles) to the Barkly Homestead Wayside Inn, then turn left (north) onto the Tablelands Highway and towards the remote township of **Borroloola** (pop. 900), just inland from the Gulf of Carpentaria and famous for its barramundi fishing. Like any journey that involves driving into the true Outback, this route requires ample preparation, including fuel, emergency rations and water. The last leg to Borroloola is on the Carpentaria Highway, an excellent sealed road.

INTO THE TOP END

North of Tennant Creek, the tiny township of **Renner Springs** marks a geographical and climatic end to the long, dry journey through the Red Centre: this is the southern extremity of the monsoon-affected plains of the Top End. But the changes between the desert and the plans are slow and subtle. Termite mounds are fascinating features of this scrubby country. They are usually about 3 metres (11ft) high and point

north–south, a position that allows termites the maximum benefit of both heat and shade. This orientation inevitably led to them being called 'magnetic anthills'; at first glance it does look as if they are built on compass bearings.

At **Elliott**, golfers can enjoy the far-out experience of playing nine holes on a desert course with well-kept greens.

Newcastle Waters is an historic stock-route junction town established as a telegraph station. In 1872 at **Frew's Ironside Ponds**, some 50km (31 miles) north of Newcastle Waters, the respective ends of the telegraph wire were joined to establish the overland communication link.

The **Daly Waters Pub ⑬** (tel: 08-8975 9927; www.dalywaterspub.com) is worth a pause for a drink and rest (accommodation available). Built in the 1930s as a staging post for Qantas crew and passengers on multi-hop international flights, it is full of related memorabilia. **Mataranka ⑭** is a small town that was really put on the map only when an earlier rail track from Darwin was laid in 1928. Before that,

The Yulara Resort has seven different tiers of accommodation, ranging from a camping ground to a luxury resort. Its water supply is drawn from underground rivers.

Walking around Uluru.

it was part of the huge Elsey farming property (in 1916 Mataranka Station was established as an experimental sheep run, a project doomed to failure in this classic cattle country). Today, the surprise attraction is the **Mataranka Homestead Tourist Resort** (tel: 08-8975 4544; www.matarankahomestead.com.au), a 4-hectare (10-acre) section of tropical forest, including palms and paperbark trees adjoining the **Elsey National Park**. The nearby sparkling **Mataranka Thermal Pool**, with a water temperature of 34°C (93°F), is a real oasis amid the north's arid surrounds. Also adjacent to the tourist park is a replica of the Elsey Station homestead, made for the 1981 film *We of the Never Never*.

Katherine, 103km (63 miles) to the north, is the Top End's second most important town after Darwin. It has a population of 10,500 and a well-developed infrastructure of shops, camping grounds, hotels and motels. Since colonial days, Katherine has been an important telegraph station and cattle centre.

KATHERINE GORGE

To the east of the township, **Katherine Gorge** ⑮ is one of the best-known features of the Territory. It's a massive stretch of sandstone cliffs rising to more than 100 metres (330ft) above the Katherine River, with 13 main canyons. The gorge is best explored by water. Tour boats operate mostly on the lower two canyons, but the more inquisitive traveller can explore the other 11 gorges upstream – you can canoe to the fourth, sixth and ninth gorges, and even camp overnight; book ahead with **Nitmiluk Tours** (tel: 08-8972 1253; www.nitmiluktours.com.au). The small crocodiles looking on are freshwater and don't attack humans, although they can be unnerving. In recent years 'saltie' crocs have been found; this has led to a ban on swimming. Check current recommendations before getting into the water.

The gorge system is part of the 1,800-sq-km (695-sq-mile) **Nitmiluk National Park** ⑯ (tel: 08-8973 8821; www.nt.gov.au/leisure/parks-reserves), which deserves at least a couple of days. There are also several walking trails in the park that follow the top of the escarpment, looking down into the gorge. Katherine is also home to a Savannah Guide Station. These eco-accredited specialist guides focus on heritage, culture, and the preservation of the natural environment.

From Katherine, the Victoria Highway strikes west towards the Kimberley region of Western Australia. Just before the WA border, there is a turn-off to **Keep River National Park** (tel: 08-9167 8827; www.nt.gov.au/leisure/parks-reserves). Like the better-known formations across the border in the Purnululu National Park, Keep River features a series of fascinating banded sandstone towers that shelter a wide range of vegetation and animal life.

THE RICHNESS OF KAKADU

One of the brightest jewels in the whole array of Australian wilderness lies to

Kata Tjuta.

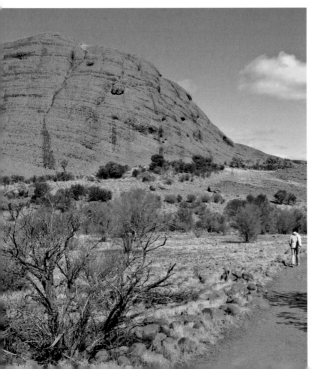

the north of Katherine, at **Kakadu National Park** ⑰ (tel: 08 8938 1120; www.parksaustralia.gov.au/kakadu). The park's prime accommodation and commercial centre is Jabiru, 250km (155 miles) southeast of Darwin. The richness of Kakadu defies description. Here, where the Arnhem Land escarpment meets the coastal floodplains, scenic splendour, ancient Aboriginal culture and paintings and an incredible array of flora and fauna come together in a brilliant, coherent whole.

The statistics of Kakadu – which is now on the World Heritage list – give some indication of what this area has to offer. The park covers 19,804 sq km (7,200 sq miles), with further extension likely. It is home to a quarter of all Australian freshwater fish, more than 1,000 plant species, 300 types of birds, 75 species of reptiles, many mammals and innumerable insects. Its world-famous galleries of Aboriginal art – particularly at Nourlangie and Ubirr rocks – give a significant insight into early man more than 20,000 years ago. In Kakadu the oldest evidence for the technology of edge-ground stone axes has been found.

Coming into Kakadu from the south, via the road from **Pine Creek**, one should detour into **Gunlom**, with its magical combination of waterfall and plunge pool. This oasis featured in the 1986 film *Crocodile Dundee* and is even more beautiful than its celluloid image.

Most visitors approach Kakadu along the sealed **Arnhem Highway** from Darwin. This road terminates at **Jabiru**, a service town for the Ranger Uranium Mine; the mine operates in an enclave surrounded by the national park and near to **Arnhem Land**, a great expanse of Aboriginal land that is closed to tourists. The juxtaposition of national park and uranium mine has provided ongoing controversy in Australian politics for years.

A good introduction to Kakadu is a boat tour on **Yellow Water**, at Cooinda, which offers the finest natural wildlife viewing anywhere in Australia. Yellow Water boat cruises (tel: 08-8979 1500) operate throughout the year. You are likely to see saltwater crocodiles, Jabiru storks, brolga cranes and a host of water birds, resident and migratory – but only during the dry season (May–Sept). During The Wet, when water is plentiful, the animals disperse across the region, and successful viewing is more haphazard.

Other easily accessible sights within the park are the paintings of **Ubirr Rock** and the towering faces of **Nourlangie Rock**. The splendid **Bowali Visitor Centre** (tel: 08-8938 1120) has a permanent display setting out the features of the park. The **Marrawuddi Gallery** (tel: 08-8979 2777; www.marrawuddi.com.au; daily 9am–4pm) features displays of Aboriginal art, books and gifts.

To see what makes Kakadu special, however, head out to one or more of the waterholes nestled at the base of the escarpment.

The most popular conjunction of swimming hole and waterfall is **Jim Jim Falls**. The deep, cool pool and the

A boat trip through the Katherine Gorge.

Kakadu National Park.

nearby sandy beach are remarkably attractive and have the distinct benefit of being easy to visit, at least when the access road is open (June–Nov). Effort is well rewarded for those who decide to walk into nearby **Twin Falls**, where the two strands of water drop right onto the end of a palm-shaded beach. However, don't swim there because large and possibly hungry crocodiles have been known to move in. Both Jim Jim and Twin Falls turn into seething maelstroms during wet-season flooding, at which time they are inaccessible to anyone without a helicopter. In the dry season, they are tranquil places of exquisite beauty. You can join a tour or self-drive (but you will need a four-wheel-drive vehicle).

THE ADELAIDE RIVER

On the Arnhem Highway to Darwin you cross the **Adelaide River**, and at that point you'll find the *Adelaide River Queen* (tel: 08-8988 8144; www.jumpingcrocodilecruises.com.au), which can take you on a short (90-minute) river cruise to see the 'jumping crocodiles', which leap almost clear of the water when offered a slice of steak, just as they do when catching birds and bats in midair. There are more croc cruises just down the river.

DARWIN

Darwin ⑱, capital of the Northern Territory, was founded in 1869, after more than four decades of failed settlements in the north – abandoned one after another because of malaria outbreaks, cyclones, and supply failure due to the sheer distance from the other settlements. Named after the naturalist Charles Darwin, one of whose shipmates on the *Beagle* discovered the bay in 1839, it drifted on in a tropical stupor for decades, punctuated only by the discovery of gold at Pine Creek in 1870 and a minor revolution in 1919. Some 243 people were killed and another 300 injured in the first savage surprise Japanese bombing attack in February 1942, and Darwin suffered repeated raids over the following 18 months.

Today's Darwin has a pace that might – almost – be described as brisk, at least by Northern Territory standards. Once the neurotic front line of colonial Australia, the city's populace now reflects its proximity to Asia: the mix of some 50 cultures and people – including Aborigines, Vietnamese, Filipinos, Malays, New Guineans, Pacific Islanders, Japanese and Indonesians, Greeks and other Europeans – provides a strong cosmopolitan flavour.

Discoveries of oil and gas in the Timor Sea have led to an influx of mining engineers, refinery workers and skilled tradesmen, feeding an economic boom. In turn, this has led to a housing boom, with apartment blocks proliferating and real estate prices rocketing. Many locals have cashed in on the housing boom, while doomsayers predict that the levels of economic and housing activity are not sustainable in the long term, and that the downturn will surely come. Meanwhile, the defence forces give another boost to the economy, with army, navy and air force personnel spending at least two years in Darwin as part of their service.

Everywhere there is a spirit of optimism, although population mobility remains an important factor. Many people leave the Territory on retirement to head south, where health and aged care facilities are better.

DARWIN SIGHTS

The focal point of the city's defence was the **Old Navy Headquarters Ⓐ**. This simple stone building, dating from 1884, was a police station and courthouse. It and other historical buildings, such as **Fannie Bay Gaol** (1883) and **Brown's Mart** (built in 1885, and the oldest in the city centre), contrast with Darwin's new cyclone-proof architecture, represented by the city's high-rise hotels, **Sky City Casino** and **Parliament House**.

Despite the changes, it is Darwin's natural charm and the relaxed Top End lifestyle that give the new city its appeal. The town is flanked by great expanses of golden beaches and in the dry season – April to October – the vision of sand, clear blue skies and tropical flora makes Darwin immensely attractive.

For six months of the year **Darwin Harbour Ⓑ** becomes the playground of the area's boating populace. Huge saltwater crocodiles are regularly seen here, and on other city beaches such as **Vestey's** (named after the cattle company that once employed most Darwinians), and jellyfish and sharks are also present, so swimming is strongly discouraged. **Mindil Beach** is the scene of a popular sunset market every Thursday (5pm–10pm) and Sunday (4pm–9pm) April to October only (www.mindil.com.au). The Asian food stalls are marvellous.

Other markets are in **Parap** on Saturday morning (8am–2pm; www.parapvillagemarkets.com.au), in **Rapid Creek** on Saturday and Sunday (7–2pm; www.rapidcreekmarkets.com.au) and in **Nightcliff** on Sundays (8am–2pm).

When the tides are right in July/early August at **Fannie Bay**, about 4km (2.5 miles) from the city centre, Darwin

Rock paintings in Kakadu National Park.

Ⓞ CYCLONE TRACY

In four furious hours on Christmas Eve 1974, Cyclone Tracy swept in from the north and flattened the city of Darwin. With gusts up to 280kph (175mph), the hurricane destroyed more than 5,000 homes – 80 percent of the city. The dead and missing totalled 66 in one of the most dramatic natural disasters in Australian history. With massive government funding, the city was rebuilt in the knowledge that the character and ambience of the old Darwin had been blown away forever.

Most of the old-style Darwin was levelled, to be replaced by a modern, more commercialised city. But of the over 30,000 residents evacuated in the nation's fastest-ever mass population shift, the majority returned. Today the city has 140,000 inhabitants.

☉ Tip

However tempting the water might seem, it is unwise to swim off the coast of the Northern Territory between October and May, when box jellyfish (whose sting can be fatal), are usually present in significant numbers. At other times, saltwater (estuarine) crocs are always a serious danger. Always observe the warning signs and see www. becrocwise.nt.gov.au for more information.

conducts its famous **Beer Can Regatta** (www.beercanregatta.org.au). Thousands of beer cans are used to build a fleet of wildly imaginative, semi-seaworthy craft. The whole city turns out to watch them race or wallow in the bay. This event is in keeping with Darwin's reputation as the world's beer-drinking capital.

In 1981 the excellent **Museum and Art Gallery of the Northern Territory** ❸ (Bullocky Point, 19 Conacher Street; tel: 08-8999 8264; www.magnt.net.au; daily 10am–5pm) was opened. Its five galleries include one of the world's best collections of Aboriginal art and cultural artefacts, and archaeological finds from the Pacific region. Don't miss the fine collection of Aboriginal contemporary art, the Tiwi Pukumani burial poles and 'Sweetheart', a stuffed saltwater crocodile 5 metres (17ft) long.

The **Fannie Bay Gaol Museum** ❹ (tel: 08-8999 8264; www.magnt.net.au/fannie-bay-gaol; daily 10am–3pm) displays old cells and gallows from the prison's grim past.

Darwin's tropical nature makes a visit to the 34-hectare (84-acre)

Botanic Gardens ❺ worthwhile, and fish-feeding at the **Aquascene** (tel: 08-8981 7837; http://aquascene.com.au) in Doctor's Gully Road, near the corner of Daly Street and the Esplanade, is lots of fun, especially with children. Fish can be hand-fed at high tide every day; check website for times.

Finally, the **Wharf Precinct** ❻ (www.waterfront.nt.gov.au) has undergone a major renovation: on any balmy afternoon, head out to the end of the pier, where dozens of restaurants have set up outdoor tables. It's the perfect place to drink in the tropical air, or drop a line to catch a passing Spanish mackerel. The waterfront boasts swimming lagoons, including a wave pool where you can bodyboard without worrying about crocs.

EXPLORING THE TOP END

About 60km (40 miles) south of Darwin on the Cox Peninsula Road, the **Territory Wildlife Park** (tel: 08-8988 7200; www.territorywildlifepark.com.au; daily 8.30–6pm) provides a potted display of the Top End's varied bird, marine, and bush

Children of the Tiwi Islands.

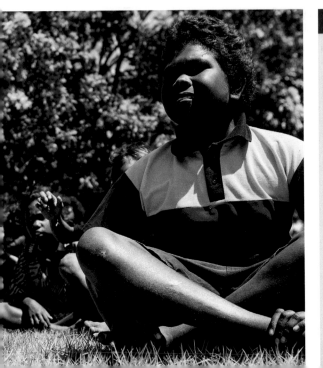

☉ VISITING THE ISLANDS

The best time to visit the Tiwi Islands is in late March or early April, during the Aussie Rules Tiwi Islands Football League Grand Final. This is the only day you can visit most of the islands by yourself without a permit. On the same Sunday there is also the Tiwi Islands Annual Art Sale, where local jewellery, paintings and crafts are sold.

A SeaLink (www.sealinknt.com.au/tiwi-islands) ferry service runs from Darwin to Wurrumiyanga on Bathurst Island. Permits are required to go beyond Wurrumiyanga – contact the Tiwi Land Council for more info (www.tiwiislands.org.au), or join an organised tour with a company such as AAT Kings (www.aatkings.com). For more information and tours visit the Tourism Australia website (www.australia.com).

wildlife, and an aquarium representing an entire Top End river system, viewed from a shuttle train that potters around the 400-hectare (988-acre) property.

A two-hour drive to the southwest of Darwin is **Litchfield National Park** ⑲ (tel: 08-8976 0282; www.nt.gov.au/leisure/parks-reserves), 153 sq km (59 sq miles) of sandstone plateau with pockets of rainforest. It is one of the best areas in the Top End for bushwalking, but is even more popular for its waterfalls and clear pools, which provide excellent swimming (check with park authorities before entering the water).

Darwin is the ideal base for exploring the remote, mangrove-filled north. **Cobourg Peninsula** ⑳ and **Garig Gunak Barlu National Park** (www.nt.gov.au/leisure/parks-reserves) are easily reached by light plane (or road if you have a 4WD and experience of driving remote unsealed roads – be aware of tide times at Cahills Crossing on the East Alligator River, which is every bit as full of crocs as the name suggests). Because it is on Aboriginal land, permission is required before visiting, but that can be arranged by tour operators. Cobourg was the site of one of the earliest attempts to establish a British base in northern Australia. Through a series of misadventures and bungles, Port Essington failed, but the bay in which it was built is a place of extravagant beauty in one of the most remote corners of the continent. **Seven Spirit Bay** (tel: 1800 688 222; www.sevenspirit bay.com.au) is perhaps the most out-of-the-way five-star resort in the world.

THE TIWI ISLANDS

Splaying out to the north of Darwin like a giant ink blot, the twin Tiwi Islands – **Bathurst** ㉑ and **Melville** ㉒ – are among Australia's most isolated outposts. Although the mainland is only 80km (50 miles) away, dugout canoes rarely survived the journey, so the Tiwi culture and language developed separately from that of other Aboriginal

groups. Early Dutch explorers met with hostility. When the British set up an outpost on Melville in 1824 it lasted less than five years, owing to Tiwi sieges and tropical disease. As a result, the Tiwis largely escaped the scorched-earth period of Australia's colonisation.

Control of their own affairs was returned to the Tiwis in the 1970s; most crucially, since they have never been moved, their land rights have never been disputed. This confident sense of possession may be why they are so outgoing; despite their once-fearsome reputation, they now bill their lands as the 'Isles of Smiles'.

Unless you're there for the Grand Final (see box), to explore the Tiwi Islands any further than Wurrumiyanga requires a permit, organised by the Tiwi Land Council (tel: 08-8970 9500; www.tiwiislands.org.au/the-region/tiwi-land-council). It's worth the journey: this remote coastline alternates between croc-infested mangrove swamps and blinding-white beaches where you can walk for many kilometres without seeing another person.

⊙ Tip

As an alternative to walking, take the Darwin Hop-on Hop-off Bus Tour (tel: 0416 140 903; www.bigbustours.com/en/darwin), which allows you to get on and off anywhere on its circular route. It can often be unbearably hot in the middle of the day. If exploring the city on foot, take your tour in the early morning or late afternoon.

Termite mounds in the Northern Territory.

📷 ULURU AND KATA TJUTA

Held sacred and owned by the Anangu Aboriginal people, natural rock formations Uluru and Kata Tjuta are two of the Northern Territory's largest and most iconic sites.

In the southern part of the Northern Territory stands the colossal Uluru, a giant, sandstone rock which rises up 348 metres (1,160ft) above sea level from the flat desert floor. Also known by its colonial name, Ayers Rock, the title changed to Uluru when ownership was transferred back to the Anangu (the indigenous traditional owners) in 1985.

Uluru measures 5km (3.25 miles) in length and 9.4km (5.75 miles) around. The rock changes colour depending on the light and atmospheric conditions, and never remains the same hue. For the best experience, visit at sunrise and watch from the new viewing area, Talinguru Nyakunytjaku (which means 'look from the sand dunes'). Uluru is a sacred site for the Anangu. From a distance, the rock looks smooth and featureless, but up close its face is weather-beaten, pitted with holes and gashes, ribs, valleys and caves. In the 'Tjukurpa' or Creation Time (the traditional Anangu law that explains how the world was created) these features are related to the journeys and actions of ancestral beings across the landscape. It is hard to come away from Uluru without feeling enriched by its calm spirituality.

Climbing Uluru has always been a controversial activity (it is a sacred site), but from 2019 it is being banned altogether. Instead, visitors are encouraged to explore the excellent 10km (6-mile) walking route around the base of the rock, which is far more rewarding and interesting than the climb anyway.

The area that would later become the Uluru–Kata Tjuta National Park was separated from the Petermann Reserve in 1958; it was placed under the management of the Northern Territory Reserves Board and originally named the Ayers Rock–Mount Olga National Park.

Aboriginal pictograms, or rock art, can be seen in several caves near Uluru; these typically represent Dreamtime stories.

When visiting Uluru, be mindful of the fact that the site is sacred.

A view of Kata Tjuta.

Kata Tjuta

Kata Tjuta, also known as Mount Olga (or colloquially as The Olgas), means 'many heads' and is a group of more than 30 rounded red rock domes rising from the desert floor. The product of 550 million years of pressure from water and wind erosion, the natural phenomenon is under the protection of its Aboriginal owners in the Uluru-Katja Tjuta National Park and is inscribed on the World Heritage List.

Thirty kilometres (19 miles) west of Uluru, Kata Tjuta is a sacred Aboriginal men's place relating to knowledge that is considered powerful and dangerous. Most of this sacred knowledge has never been revealed to outsiders.

There are three walking trails: the Walpa Gorge, The Valley of the Winds and the Kata Tjuta dune viewing area. As you walk these peaceful trails, you may hear the sounds of birds such as Port Lincoln parrots and grey-headed honey-eaters piercing the silence.

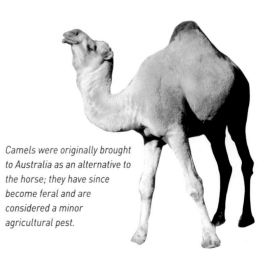

e first dirt roads to the area now recognised as the ıru-Kata Tjuta National Park were developed in 1948. e first tourists arrived by bus in the 1950s, but it wasn't til the early 1970s that the decision was made to nove all tourist accommodation to an area outside the rk. By the year 2000 there were more than 400,000 ıual visitors to the park, which is now jointly managed the local Pitjantjatjara Aborigines and the National rks and Wildlife Agency.

Camels were originally brought to Australia as an alternative to the horse; they have since become feral and are considered a minor agricultural pest.

The Perth skyline.

Karijini National Park.

WESTERN AUSTRALIA

Three-quarters of the population of WA live in its attractive capital, Perth; the vast emptiness beyond includes barren desert, lush forests, rugged canyons and gold-mining towns.

Western Australia is, quite simply, enormous. Covering more than 2.5 million sq km (960,000 sq miles), it is much larger than the states of Alaska and Texas combined. In fact, if WA were a separate country, it would be the ninth largest in the world – and the emptiest. India is about the same size, with a population of over 1.3 billion, whereas the whole vast, dry expanse of Western Australia is inhabited by just 2.7 million people, about 75 per cent of whom live in Perth.

Being so far from the main Australian population centres on the east coast, WA conveys a feeling of utter isolation. **Perth** is one of the world's remotest cities, closer to Singapore and Jakarta than it is to Sydney. Most of the state is parched and barren, but the north is lushly tropical and the southwest is temperate. In springtime, between September and November, many visitors travel from the eastern states just to see the profusion of wild flowers that turn the south into a riot of colour. Western Australia's vastness, small population and rugged scenery give this state a strong sense of being a new frontier.

When planning a trip in WA, it's a good idea to keep an eye on the map scale and distances. It's all too easy to outline a weekend tour through an apparently tiny proportion of the state – only to add up the distances and find

this would mean driving some 1,600km (1,000 miles). If you are based in Perth, with limited time to spare, consider joining an organised tour group or excursion. Several Perth tour operators run day, overnight and longer tours to WA's scenic highlights, such as the Margaret River region, Albany, Kalbarri National Park and the Pinnacles.

THE FIRST ARRIVALS

Western Australia was inhabited by the first Australians. It is thought that, more than 50,000 years ago, the forebears of

⊙ **Main attractions**
Perth City
Swan River
His Majesty's Theatre
Rottnest Island
The Pinnacles
Monkey Mia

⦿ **Maps on pages**
272, 276

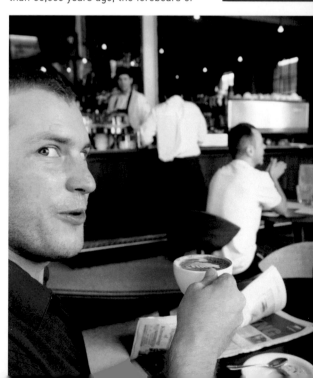

Enjoying a coffee.

today's Australian Aborigines crossed from New Guinea by foot on land bridges exposed by lower sea levels caused by the last ice age. From the north, they gradually spread west and south, ultimately occupying the whole continent.

The first recorded European visit to the Western Australian coast occurred in 1616, when Dirk Hartog, a Dutch captain, sailed the *Eendracht* into Shark Bay and left a tin plate nailed to a tree as proof. Dirk Hartog Island near Carnarvon is named after him. The first English explorer known to have visited Australia was the one-time pirate William Dampier in 1688, who repaired his ship in Cygnet Bay (named after his ship) in the Kimberley. He was unimpressed, dismissing the land as useless and the Aborigines the 'miserablest people in the world'.

In 1827, amid fears that the French might seize the coast, Captain James Stirling was despatched from Sydney to find a potential site for a western settlement. In 1829 the first colonists arrived to set up shop on a site he had spotted 16km (10 miles) upstream on the Swan River. Surrounded by black swans, a village of some 300 residents was founded and named Perth.

Inducing other colonists to head west was no easy matter. An acute labour shortage led to convicts being imported in 1850; by 1858, the population of Perth was still barely 3,000. But gold changed all that.

When news of the great finds of the 1890s in fields at Kalgoorlie, located to the east, reached the outside world, Perth became the leaping-off point for one of the last great gold rushes. Still, many parts of the northeast of the region were among the last to be settled in Australia, when some of the world's largest cattle stations were opened in the Kimberley. Throughout the 20th century, the discovery of mineral deposits throughout the state provided the main basis of its wealth – from uranium to gas and oil on the northwest shelf.

PERTH

As in the gold-rush days, almost all visits to the wild west start in **Perth ❶**, whose population now stands at about

2.3 million. Set on the west coast, a high-tech counterweight to the older, heavily populated eastern cities, the city has become a symbol of Australian confidence.

Perth experienced a massive resource-driven boom in the first decade of the 21st century, similar to one that took place during the roaring 1980s, when it was the base of a posse of high-profile multimillionaires, exemplified by Alan Bond, who worked so closely with the Labor politicians of the time that the state was referred to as 'WA Inc'. But the powerful alliance collapsed in the wake of the 1987 Wall Street crash, when one tycoon after another was implicated in corrupt dealings, charged and jailed. The recent boom has slowed down, but Perth has been transformed in recent years and is arguably Australia's most modern city.

The city takes full advantage of its setting on the serpentine Swan River. The dominant view is over **Perth City**, where the **Swan River** widens into a broad bay about 1km (0.5 miles) across. On the edge of the business district, set high on an escarpment, is **Kings Park Ⓐ** (www.bgpa.wa.gov.au), a 400-hectare (988-acre) reserve of botanical gardens and bushland offering panoramic views over the city and the river.

Opened in 2016, and still evolving, a new development called **Elizabeth Quay** (www.mra.wa.gov.au) has completely transformed the CBD side of the riverfront. Esplanade Reserve has been flooded by an artificial inlet with jetties and an island, linked to Riverside Drive to the west by a stunning bridge for pedestrians and cyclists. The quay is surrounded by ultra-modern hotels, recreation, retail and living space, and prominent public art including *Spanda* (9-metre concentric-hoops created by Australian artist Christian de Vietri) and *First Contact* (a 5-metre aluminium artwork by indigenous artist Laurel Nannup, depicting the arrival of European settlers).

Still standing nearby are the sail-shaped copper wings of the tower containing the **Swan Bells** (Barrack Square Riverside Drive; tel: 08-6210 0444; www.thebelltower.com.au; daily from 10am), a gift from the church of St Martin-in-the-Fields, Trafalgar Square, London, to mark Australia's bicentenary in 1988. Next to it is the new **Signature Ring** installation by local artists Simon Gauntlett and Matthew Ngui. Resembling giant headphones, it's threaded with fibre optics that illuminate movement on interactive panels and is symbolic of the passage of time. It also features hundreds of thousands of school students' signatures etched in copper plates, collected in 1999 as part of millennium celebrations.

PERTH'S EARLY BUILDINGS

Successive mining booms since the 1970s have led large multinational and West Australia-based companies to build high-rise office blocks in Perth. Their presence has dramatically changed the city skyline, but the odd architectural gem can

Perth's riverfront along Kings Park.

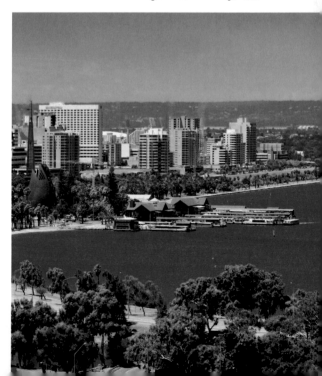

still be found. Tucked into the back of **Stirling Gardens** is the **Old Court House** Ⓑ (1837), Perth's first brick building, which has a modest facade of Doric columns. Buildings predating the state's 1890s gold rush are rare, but **Government House** Ⓒ (Stirling Gardens; www.govhouse.wa.gov.au), constructed in the 1860s by convict labour, stands as a true reflection of the beginning of the state.

Other early buildings include the **Deanery** Ⓓ, on the corner of Pier Street, opposite Stirling Gardens, built by paroled convicts in 1859, and the Elizabethan-style **Cloisters** building Ⓔ, at the western end of St George's Terrace, established in 1858 as the first public school for boys. The old **Town Hall** Ⓕ (Hay Street Mall) was the last building in Perth to be built by convict labour (commenced in 1867). It was a rallying point for conscription during both World Wars.

The city architecture of the 1890s gold rush includes **His Majesty's Theatre** Ⓖ (www.ptt.wa.gov.au), also known as His Maj, at the west end of Hay Street.

To discover more about the gold rush and its pivotal role in the city's development, visit the 1899 **Perth Mint** (310 Hay St; tel: 08-9421 7428; www.perthmint.com; daily 9am–5pm), among the world's oldest operating mints. Try picking up a block of gold worth A\$250,000, minting your own medallion, or watch gold being smelted.

Two sections of town with contrasting histories are **London Court** (www.londoncourt.com.au) and **East Murray Street Precinct**. London Court dates back to 1937, a monument to mock-Tudor kitsch, whose curiosities include a clock tower at each end: one a replica of London's Big Ben, the other of the Gros Horloge in Rouen, France. East Murray Street is the genuine colonial item. It appears on the original town plans of 1838 and now stands lined by early 20th-century buildings.

CULTURAL CENTRE

Perth's Cultural Centre – and bohemian Northbridge beyond – are no longer separated from the CBD by the Fremantle railway line and Wellington Street Bus Station, which have been sent underground by the Perth City Link project, with new **Yagan Square** (www.mra.wa.gov.au), named after a Noongar warrior who resisted British settlement, built over the freshly healed scar.

Just across the lovely **Horseshoe Bridge**, lies the **Perth Cultural Centre** Ⓗ (www.perthculturalcentre.com.au), comprising the **Art Gallery of Western Australia** (www.artgallery.wa.gov.au; Wed–Mon 10am–5pm; free entrance and guided tours) and the Western Australian Museum. The art gallery displays more than 1,000 works of art, including one of the continent's best collections of Aboriginal art. One painting that is almost always included in a guided tour is *The Foundation of Perth* by George Pitt, depicting the wife of an early dignitary ceremoniously felling a tree to mark the city's founding.

'The Caller', a sculpture by Gerhard Marks outside the Art Gallery of Western Australia.

The **Western Australian Museum** (www.museum.wa.gov.au; daily 9.30am–5pm; donations) traces the history of the state from the formation of the Australian continent 120 million years ago to the present day. Don't miss the fascinating natural history section or the illuminating Katta Dijinoong Gallery, devoted to Aboriginal history and culture. In the museum's beautifully preserved **Old Gaol** (1856), life in the early days of the colony has been recreated in a collection of period interiors, including a 1917 pharmacy and an original court room. There is also a good little courtyard café here.

Perth's creative arts scene revolves around the Northbridge end of the Cultural Centre, location of the **Perth Institute of Contemporary Art** (PICA; James Street, Northbridge; www.pica.org.au; Mon–Fri 10am–6pm, gallery Tue–Sun 11am–6pm), the **Blue Room Theatre** (53 James Street, Northbridge; www.blueroom.org.au), and the **State Theatre Centre** (174–176 William Street; www.ptt.wa.gov.au), home to the Heath Ledger Theatre, named in honour of the late Perth-born actor. The cultural centre stands on the doorstep of **Northbridge ❶**, where Perth's ethnic diversity is displayed on a plate. You can walk past tanks of live mud crabs and crayfish, smell the sharp tang of lemongrass, chew on chickens' feet or dim sum at eight in the morning, or have a beer on the balcony of a pub, watching all the action on the streets below. Northbridge also has nightclubs and discos as lively as any in Sydney.

Another fruitful neighbourhood for restaurants and bars is **Subiaco**, a fashionable suburb on the western side of town (direct access on the Perth–Fremantle railway). Come here for brunch on Friday or Saturday, perhaps after a walk in nearby Kings Park.

FREMANTLE

Fremantle ❷, just 19km (12 miles) from Perth's city centre but deemed a city in its own right, was brushed up for the America's Cup race in 1987 and has since become one of Western Australia's most popular attractions. Unlike glittering Perth, the old port's colonial charms remain intact, including the **Round House** (www.fremantleroundhouse.com.au), which actually has 12 sides; WA's oldest public building (1830); and its first jail, built where Captain Fremantle landed to claim Western Australia for the Crown.

If you arrive by ferry, you will disembark at Victoria Quay, at the far end of which you will notice the sail-like roof of the excellent **Maritime Museum** (Slip Street; tel: 08-9431 8334; www.museum.wa.gov.au/maritime; daily 9.30am–5pm), exploring all aspects of Fremantle's seafaring heritage from whaling and pearling to its role in World War II and as the place of disembarkation for thousands of post-war immigrants. The **Shipwreck Galleries** (same hours as the Maritime Museum, but free) on Cliff Street, is devoted to marine archaeology. It has relics from some of the many ships wrecked off WA's coast

Leafy, laid-back Northbridge.

Perth's Town Hall is the only convict-built Town Hall in Australia.

Western Australia

0   400 km

0   400 miles

N

Timor Sea

Admiralty Gulf

Cape Londonderry

Wadaye

Kalumburu

Joseph Bonaparte Gulf

Bonaparte Archipelago

Drysdale River N.P.

Kimberley

Wyndham

Mt Hann 779 ▲

Plateau

33

Kununurra

Buccaneer Archipelago

27

Gibb River

Lake Argyle

Cape Leveque

Lombadina

Beagle Bay

King Sound

Gibb River Road

King Leopold Ranges

Mt Bedford 914 ▲

Purnululu National Park (Bungle Bungle)

Darwin

I N D I A N

Dampier Peninsula

Windjana Gorge N.P.

32

Derby

25

26

Tunnel Creek N.P.

28

29

Geikie Gorge N.P.

30

Nicholson

O C E A N

Broome

Fitzroy

Fitzroy Crossing

Halls Creek

Lagrange

Great Northern Hwy

Eighty Mile Reach

1

Great Sandy

31

Wolfe Creek Meteorite Crater

Desert

Dampier Archipelago

Port Hedland

24

Goldsworthy

W e s t e r n

Montebello Is.

Barrow I.

Karratha

Cossack

Roebourne

Marble Bar

Nullagine

A u s t r a l i a

Lake MacKay

Dampier

North West Cape

Onslow

Exmouth

1

Millstream Chichester N.P.

Fortescue

Hamersley

Wittenoom

Roy Hill

Rudall River N.P.

22 **Cape Range N.P.**

Tom Price

Mt Bruce 1235 ▲

Range

Tropic of Capricorn

Ningaloo Marine Park

Coral Bay

Paraburdoo

23 **Karijini N.P.**

Newman

Little Sandy Desert

Lake Disappointment

Gibson

Desert

Bernier I.

Carnarvon

21

Dorre I.

Monkey Mia

Collier Range N.P.

1105 Mt Augustus

Robinson Ranges

95

Ashburton

Great Northern Hwy

Canning Stock Route

Carnegie

Gunbarrel Highway

Warburton

20

Shark Bay

Denham

Dairy Creek

Lake Carnegie

Dirk Hartog I.

Meekatharra

Wiluna

Mt Maiden 590 ▲

Warburton Road

Murchison

Lake Austin

Agnew

Leinster

Laverton

Great

Kalbarri

19

Kalbarri N.P.

Northampton

Sandstone

Mt Magnet

Leonora

Victoria

Anne Beadell Hwy

Houtman

Mullewa

Yalgoo

Leonora

Lake Carey

Desert

Abrolhos Islands

18 Geraldton

Morawa

Mongers Lake

Lake Barlee

Paynes Find

Menzies

Forrest

Indian Pacific Railroad

Port Denison

Three Springs

Eneabba

Kanowna

Kalgoorlie

Boulder

Nullarbor Plain

Adelaide

Jurien

17 **Nambung N.P.**

Moora

Wubin

Kambalda

Cocklebiddy

Madura

Eucla

Cervantes

Pinnacles Desert

New Norcia

Coolgardie

13

Lancelin

94

Southern Cross

Merredin

Johnston Lake

Lake Cowan

Eyre Hwy

Eyre

1

Yanchep N.P.

3 Rottnest I.

4 Northam

Guildford

Kellerberrin

Norseman

Balladonia

Great Australian

2 Fremantle

1

Perth

15 **Wave Rock**

Brookton

Hyden

Lake Dundas

Bight

Rockingham

Mandurah

30

Harvey

Narrogin

Lake King

I N D I A N

Yalgorup N.P.

5 Bunbury

Donnybrook

Wagin

Ravensthorpe

Esperance

Cape Le Grand N.P.

Cape Arid N.P.

Israelite Bay

6 Busselton

1

Jerramungup

11 Hopetoun

12

O C E A N

Cape Naturaliste

7 Margaret River

Nannup

Manjimup

9

1

Fitzgerald River National Park

Archipelago of the Recherche

8 Cape Leeuwin

Pemberton

Mt Barker

Stirling Range N.P.

D'Entrecasteaux N.P.

Walpole

Denmark

Albany

10

over the centuries, including original timber (partially reconstructed) and treasures from the Dutch ship *Batavia*.

Fremantle Prison (1 The Terrace; tel: 08-9336 9200; www.fremantleprison. com.au; daily 9am–5pm), a maximum security prison until 1991, offers a variety of tours including a torchlight tour. Ghost sightings are not guaranteed, but the tours include the gallows yard and hellish cell blocks built by convict labour in 1855.

One pleasure of Fremantle is to wander at random, soaking up the laid-back atmosphere and admiring the frilly ironwork of the gold-rush architecture. It has no shortage of restaurants and coffee shops (explore South Terrace, aka Cappuccino Strip), and plenty of interesting shops. Dip into the splendidly restored **Fremantle Markets** (corner of South Terrace and Henderson Street; www.fremantlemarkets.com. au; Fri 9am–8pm, Sat–Sun 9am–6pm) for interesting crafts and souvenirs.

PERTH'S BEACHES

From Fremantle a string of soft, sandy beaches stretches all the way to Hillary's Boat Harbour, 50km (30 miles) north. Development, though continuous, is almost without exception low-rise and low-key, set well back from the shore. Each of the beaches has its fans. For surfing, head for **Scarborough** or **Trigg**; for a lively après-beach scene, choose **Indiana Cottesloe Beach**, which offers good food, cocktails and fabulous sunset views.

For family-friendly attractions, head for **Hillary's Boat Harbour**, where the AQWA (Aquarium of Western Australia; www.aqwa.com.au; daily 10am–5pm) re-creates WA's five coastal environments. The highlight is the walk-through aquarium, representing the shipwreck coast where sharks, loggerhead turtles and stingrays glide smoothly overhead within centimetres of upturned faces. Other highlights include a touch pool, saltwater

crocodiles of the far north coast and tropical fish of the coral coast.

ROTTNEST ISLAND

Hillary's Boat Harbour is, along with Barrack Street Jetty in Perth and Fremantle, one of the springboards for **Rottnest Island ❸** (www.rottnestisland. com), an idyllic getaway just 19km (13 miles) offshore. First settled as a natural prison for West Australian Aborigines, Rotto (as it is known locally) is now a favourite holiday spot. Private motor vehicles aren't allowed on the island, so visitors tend to wobble along on bicycles, which can be rented on the island, along with snorkelling equipment.

Visitors can spend their time swimming, snorkelling or just lazing on a quiet beach. Divers come here to explore the world's southernmost coral reef. The island's pub, the Hotel Rottnest, originally served as the official residence of the Australian state governor; it now has live music on summer evenings. Facilities have recently been upgraded with a A$6.5 million makeover. Various accommodation

⊙ Tip

Fremantle is a 30-minute train ride from Perth railway station, and Transperth buses to Fremantle leave from St George's Terrace. But try to arrive by boat along the Swan if you can. The ferry from Barrack Street Jetty takes about an hour.

A perfect white-sand beach.

The Round House.

options are available, in rented bungalows, rooms at historical Hotel Rottnest, dorm bunks at Kingstown Barracks or a pitch at the campsite (book in advance for summer months).

THE SWAN VALLEY

If you have limited time during your stay in Perth, and can manage only one out-of-town trip, it is worth venturing into the **Swan Valley**. A major wine-producing area, it offers vineyard tours and elegant towns such as **Guildford ④**, one of the earliest settlements in Western Australia, and is only 30 minutes by train or road from Perth's CBD. To follow the Swan Valley food and wine trail, a 32km (20-mile) loop linking some of the best vineyards and microbreweries, as well as the Margaret River Chocolate Company, leave the town via the West Swan Road and return by the Great Northern Highway. Also along the route is **Caversham Wildlife Park** (www.cavershamwildlife.com.au), the best place in the region for kangaroo-spotting for visitors too short of time to go into the bush. Caversham

Goode Beach, near Albany.

forms part of Whiteman Park, packed with family attractions, including an excellent **Motor Museum** (www.motormuseumofwa.asn.au; daily 10am–4pm).

DOWN THE COAST FROM PERTH

Head south of Perth for the region's top wineries and dense karri and jarrah forests, but be careful not to miss things along the way. The Perth-to-Bunbury Highway is a direct and efficient way to get to Bunbury and Margaret River, but you'll have to take the old coast road if you don't want to miss the bits in between.

Immediately south of Fremantle the landscape is fairly industrial apart from **Rockingham** (47km/30 miles south of Perth), a springboard for Penguin Island (www.penguinisland.com.au), named after its colony of 1,100 penguins, and **Mandurah** (74km/40 miles from Perth), a fast-growing but nonetheless delightful town on the Peel Estuary. In high season the towns and campsites around Mandurah are busy with holidaymakers, but

---

⊘ GETTING TO ROTTNEST

Rottnest's proximity to the mainland makes it an easy day trip by ferry from Perth. Rottnest Express (tel: 1300-467 688; www.rottnestexpress.com.au) operates from Rous Head Harbour in Northport, the B Shed at Fremantle, and from the Barrack Street Jetty in Perth (the last option includes a Swan River cruise with commentary). **Rottnest Fast Ferries** (tel: 08-9246 1039; www.rottnestfastferries.com.au) operates from Hillary's Boat Harbour.

It takes approximately 25 minutes to get to the island from Fremantle, around 45 minutes from Hillary's and 90 minutes from Perth. The cost of the ferry crossing includes the entrance charge to the island. The ferry crossing to Rottnest can get choppy. If you're prone to seasickness, or have children with you, take tablets beforehand.

for the rest of the year they can be enjoyed in relative peace.

Further down the coast (140km/75 miles from Perth) is the dairy town of **Harvey**, dating back to 1890. The nearby **Yalgorup National Park** can be reached by the old coast road. It is a sanctuary for water birds and wildlife, though it is the colony of living, rock-like creatures known as thrombolites (the earliest-known life on Earth and very rare) that makes it special. The only access point is via the coast road, 25km (15 miles) south of Mandurah, indicated by a large brown sign for the Lake Clifton platform, an observation walkway built across the shallows containing the thrombolites.

The city of **Bunbury** ❺ (180km/110 miles south of Perth) is a busy port that owes its existence to Lt Henry St Pierre Bunbury, who travelled overland to the coast from Pinjarra in 1836. At **Koombana Beach**, just north of town, visitors can feed a community of bottlenose dolphins that visit the beach daily at the Dolphin Discovery Centre (www.dolphindiscovery.com.au; daily 9am–2pm in winter, 8am–4pm in summer).

FORESTS AND VINEYARDS

It was logging of the nearby forests that brought prosperity to the region; jarrah and blackbutt hardwoods abound here, and can be seen in much of the early architecture. Bunbury sits at the northern end of **Geographe Bay**, a large, sheltered waterway that has **Cape Naturaliste** as its northern spur. From here the Cape-to-Cape hiking trail (www. capetocapetrack.com.au) leads south to Cape Leeuwin, 135km (84 miles) away.

On the southern coast of the bay, the resort town of **Busselton** ❻ has a fine setting on the Vasse River. Its 2km (1.2-mile) jetty, the longest in the southern hemisphere, has an interpretive centre and a multimillion-dollar underwater observatory (www.busseltonjetty.com.au; daily Sept–Apr 8.30am–6pm, May–Aug 9am–5pm) that takes visitors 8 metres

(26ft) below sea level for amazing views of fish and coral.

Margaret River ❼ (www.margaretriver. com), 280km (173 miles) from Perth, is internationally famous for estate-grown and bottled wines. Names like Leeuwin, Xanadu, Moss Wood, Devil's Lair, Howard Park and dozens more rival the world's best. This is crafted wine and a far cry from the mass production of Australia's eastern states. Margaret River's success sparked a Western Australian wine revolution that has encouraged quality production from Swan Valley down to the Great Southern region. Not only do many of these vineyards offer fantastic wine, but their restaurants represent better value for money than most establishments in Perth.

Surfing the big waves and swimming are two popular reasons locals visit the region. Yallingup, Injidup, Smiths Beach, Bunker Bay and Three Bears (only accessible by 4WD) are among the many surf breaks, but if you plan to tan, they are equally as inviting to lie on the sand and have a quick dip when the time comes to cool off.

The busy port of Bunbury.

Margaret River is also renowned for its cheese (www.mrdc.com.au), chocolate (www.chocolatefactory.com.au) and local microbrews. Check out the Duckstein (www.duckstein.com.au) for a refreshing ale.

Visits to spectacular caves such as **Mammoth**, **Lake** and **Jewel**, and browsing in arts and crafts shops, are alternatives to wine (and beer) sampling.

Cape Leeuwin ❽ marks the southwest extremity of Australia and the junction of the Indian and Southern oceans. This point marked the start of Matthew Flinders' odyssey when he set out to circumnavigate and chart the Australian coastline in 1790.

Inland lies **Pemberton**, surrounded by three national parks – a region of giant karri and jarrah trees. Some of the trees are over 50 metres (160ft) tall – the world's tallest hardwoods. The adventurous can climb the **Gloucester Tree** to the fire tower, 60 metres (190ft) above the ground.

THE SOUTH COAST

Travelling east along the coast road towards Denmark and Albany, stop at **Walpole** to explore the Valley of the Giants (www.valleyofthegiants.com.au) and experience the Treetop Walk (daily 9am–5pm; wheelchair access), a lofty ramp looping over the forest.

Further east is the **Stirling Range National Park ❾**, its conical hills and jagged peaks rising to 1,000 metres (3,300ft), presenting challenging walks. A seasonal centre for wild flowers, including native orchids, it receives Western Australia's only snowfall.

To the south, **Albany ❿** is where European settlement was first established in the western half of Australia. On Christmas Day 1826, Major Lockyer arrived from Sydney in the brig *Amity*, attracted by the splendid expanses of **King George Sound**, an enclosed waterway twice as large as Sydney Harbour. Today tourists flock here from July to November to spot whales – an ironic attraction for a town that (until 1978) was the last operating whaling station in the southern hemisphere. A **museum** (www.discoverybay.com.au/historic-whaling-station; daily 9am–5pm; guided tours every hour from 10am to 3pm) tells the story.

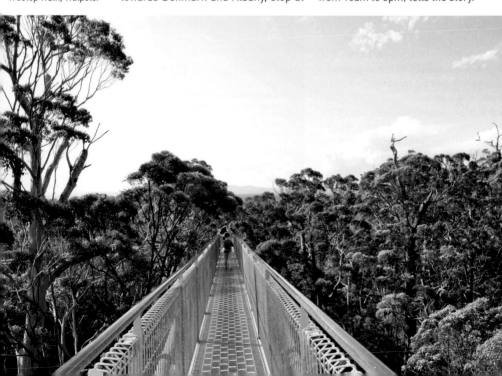

Albany is also one of Australia's most picturesque towns, with a wonderful bay-side location and well-preserved 19th-century streetscapes. At nearby **Strawberry Hill** stands the state's oldest house, built in 1836 for the first government resident, Sir Richard Spencer. There is plenty of exploring to be done here. The post office, with its shingled tower, is the oldest in Western Australia, and the **Church of St John the Evangelist**, built in 1848, is the earliest house of worship in the state. Overlooking King George Sound is a memorial to the **Australian Light Horse** that served in Egypt and Gallipoli in World War I. It was moved here from Port Said, Egypt, after the 1956 Suez War. Nearby Mount Adelaide, a military history precinct, looks down on the waters where the ANZAC Dardanelles invasion fleet assembled in 1914.

Perhaps the most spectacular park in the region is **Fitzgerald River National Park ⓫**, 185km (115 miles) northeast of Albany. It includes an impressive stretch of coastal landscape and also contains a group of mountains known as the **Barren Range**, with dramatic views of the Southern Ocean.

The easternmost town of **Esperance ⓬** is 750km (465 miles) from Perth. Local attractions include the salt-rich **Pink Lake** and the grave of Tommy Windich, an Aboriginal guide who accompanied explorer John Forrest on his two overland treks to Adelaide in 1870 and 1874.

Cape Le Grand and **Cape Arid** national parks offer superb beaches, an abundance of birdlife and some terrific campsites. Offshore lies a maze of beautiful islands called the **Recherche Archipelago**. On the road from Albany to the capes, opportunities for camping, fishing and surfing present themselves at almost every turn.

THE GOLDFIELDS

Around 200km (125 miles) north of Esperance is the crossroads town of Norseman, from where the Eyre Highway heads east across the vast Nullarbor Plain to eastern Australia, crossing the border into South Australia after 725km (450 miles). Alternatively, the route north heads to Kalgoorlie and the goldfields.

The birthplace of the West Australian goldfields was **Coolgardie ⓭**, 190km (118 miles) north of Norseman. In September 1892 it was the site of Australia's richest strike – producing 85kg (200lbs) of gold in a single month. By 1900, it was a town of 15,000 people with a score of hotels, half a dozen banks, three breweries, two stock exchanges and seven newspapers. By 1905, however, the lode was running out. Today Coolgardie is an attractive, historic township with elegant buildings.

Kalgoorlie ⓮, 40km (25 miles) away, started off as Coolgardie's twin city, but it has survived as a thriving mining town of over 30,000, the hub in a region full of boom and bust. When Irishman Paddy Hannan discovered gold here in 1893, it was soon realised that the wealth of the Kalgoorlie find far exceeded anything else ever found in Australia.

The Super Pit at Kalgoorlie.

Kalgoorlie's Golden Mile became the richest piece of real estate in the world.

However, water in the area was in short supply, so the celebrated Irish engineer C.Y. O'Connor built a pipeline from Mundaring Weir near Perth, more than 500km (300 miles) away. Today, the area continues to yield 241 million grams (850,000oz) of gold per year.

Kalgoorlie's architecture retains much of its early charm, with the **Palace Hotel** (www.palacehotel.com.au) being a fabulous example of Edwardian excess. The business district of Kalgoorlie is a leafy refuge from the moonscape of the mines; the continuing trade in beer, prostitution and minerals still reflects much of the town's earlier freebooting ways. For miners who gamble on the Earth's riches every day, other (less legitimate) forms of gambling thrive – especially 'two-up', a uniquely Australian game based on the toss of two pennies. When the Burswood Casino was about to open in Perth, the manager visited Kalgoorlie to see how Australia's most famous two-up school operated.

Emus are a fairly common sight in the road-side bush.

The main reason for visiting Kalgoorlie is to see the **Super Pit** (www.superpit.com.au). This enormous open-cut gold mine can be viewed from the Super Pit lookout (daily 7am–9pm), just off the Goldfields Highway. Night viewing is recommended, with the pit illuminated by high-voltage lights. Kalgoorlie Tours and Charters (tel: 08-9021 2211, www.kalgoorlietours.com) run regular tours (charge) of the pit and the goldfields, and KCGM facilitate free tours on the third Sunday of every month as part of the Kalgoorlie-Boulder Market Day. The one-hour tours depart 9am, 10am and 11am; places available from the Eastern Goldfields Historical Society, Hamilton Street, from 8.30am – first come, first served.

Many towns haven't fared as well as Kalgoorlie. Ghost towns such as **Gwalia** and **Kanowna** dot the area, while many outposts have seen their populations dwindle so much that they, too, will soon be deserted. In many of these centres stand the imposing relics of Australia's Wild West era.

WAVE ROCK

The most famous inland attraction in the southwest is **Wave Rock** ⑮ (4km/2.5½ miles east of Hyden; tel: 08-9880 5052; www.waverock.com.au). Around 15-metres (50ft) high and 110-metres (340-feet) long, this unique formation resembles the perfect ocean wave, ripe for surfing, but frozen in time. In a dreaming-trail recounted by generations of Ballardong people, it was made by the Rainbow Serpent as she dragged her swollen body along, having consumed all the water in the land. A more prosaic explanation claims it's one wall of a huge granite dome, underscored by erosion.

Due west of the goldfields, farmers harvest the state's other golden bounty: wheat. **Merredin** is a busy town at the heart of one of the world's great grain belts. It was founded in 1891 around a water hole on the way to the goldfields, and has since become a research centre for improving the wheat yield of the area. Merredin's annual agricultural show is one of the most prestigious in the state. The town's tree-lined main street is best in November, when the jacarandas bloom.

Situated on the Avon River, **Northam** is the central hub of the western wheat fields, and also the scene of a hell-for-leather river race each August, when hundreds of canoeists and powerboaters dash madly downstream in the Avon River Descent.

It wasn't until Robert Dale led an expedition over the Darling Range and into this 150km (90-mile) stretch of fertile valley that the early settlers could be certain that the west held land capable of sustaining livestock and crops. The valley's towns were settled soon after Perth. For an insight into the pioneering history, **York**, with its extravagantly designed town hall, **Toodyay** and **Mahogany Creek** are well worth exploring.

NORTH OF PERTH

The Perth to Darwin route is a desolate 4,027km (2,502-mile) trek. A major attraction of taking the Great Northern Highway inland route rather than the coastal Brand Highway is **New Norcia** ⑯, 130km (80 miles) from Perth. The settlement was established by Benedictine monks in 1846 as an Aboriginal mission. The monastery is still operating, although many of the town's more impressive buildings are closed to the public. However, the Spanish architectural influence is interesting and the museum and art gallery (www.newnorcia. wa.edu.au; daily 9am–4.30pm) provide fascinating insights into pioneer life. Guided tours of the settlement are available, or visitors can take a self-guided 2km (1.2-mile) walk linking the major sites, including the Abbey Church. This is decorated with locally inspired sgraffito and an image of Our Lady of Good Counsel, said to have been held up to repel a bushfire in 1847. Be sure to

come away with some of the delectable treats, such as New Norcia nut cake and Dom Salvado Pan Chocolatti, produced by the monastery's bakery.

Heading up the coastal Brand Highway, the tiny town of **Gingin** – 82km (51 miles) north of Perth – is a good first stop. There are excellent fishing grounds off the coast, 48km (30 miles) to the west: estuaries such as the mouth of the Moore River at **Guilderton** are ideal for casting a line. Just to the south of Guilderton is the **Yanchep National Park** (vehicle charge), offering wetlands, woodlands, bushwalks, caves and an Aboriginal heritage trail.

Further north along the coast road is **Lancelin**, 127km (79 miles) north of Perth, protected by two large rock islands and surrounded by towering sand dunes. Gutsy winds off the Indian Ocean make it ideal for windsurfing and surfing. It attracts top international surfers, but also caters to novices keen to learn.

THE PINNACLES

Proceeding north from Lancelin you can either go inland and take the Brand

The Exchange Hotel, a pub in Kalgoorlie.

> **Tip**
>
> The best time to view Wave Rock is Aug–Dec when wild flowers are in bloom. Other interesting rock formations in the immediate area are Hippo's Yawn, a 20-minute walk away, and the Humps and the Breakers. For details on how to get to these rocks, check with the tourist office at the Wave Rock Wild Flower Shop and Visitor Centre (tel: 08-9880 5182).

⊙ Tip

To discover more about Western Australia's history and heritage, visit the Greenough Historical Hamlet (daily 9am–5pm) on Brand Highway, a 20-minute drive south of Geraldton. Its collection of 19th-century colonial buildings, restored by the National Trust, includes a church and a schoolhouse.

Highway, or hug the coast to Cervantes along the newer Indian Ocean Drive.

Nambung National Park ⑰, 29km (18 miles) south of the coastal town of Cervantes and 245km (153 miles) from Perth, shouldn't be missed. The **Pinnacles Desert** within the park is a bizarre sight: a world of limestone spires all rising from smooth sand dunes. When Dutch explorers first saw the Pinnacles from their vessels, they thought they had found the ruins of a long-deserted city. In fact, they are entirely natural. A circular track leads around the spires (vehicle charge).

A short distance up the coast is **Jurien**, a lobster-fishing centre set on the shores of an attractive sheltered bay, framed by spectacular sand dunes. **Port Denison** (now referred to as Dongara-Denison), 170km (105 miles) further up the coast, has Australia's biggest rock lobster grounds; more than 400 fishing boats work the area.

MARITIME GERALDTON

From the Pinnacles, continue north towards Geraldton. About 25km (13 miles) south of the city, look out for **Greenough Historical Hamlet** (www.nationaltrust.org.au; daily 9am–5pm), a collection of 19th-century colonial buildings, restored by the National Trust, that presents a vivid picture of life for the early settlers.

Geraldton ⑱, 425km (265 miles) north of Perth, supports a population of about 35,000 and is the administrative centre for West Australia's mid-coast region. It has a near-perfect climate, superb fishing conditions and fine sandy beaches that stretch north and south of Champion Bay. This stretch of coast saw many shipwrecks when early Dutch mariners heading for the East Indies were swept too far south.

The **Abrolhos Islands**, 64km (40 miles) offshore, have claimed many ships over the years, including the Dutch East Indiaman *Batavia*, which ran aground in 1629. Survivors waited behind while the captain and a few crew headed off for Java in an open boat. While the survivors were awaiting rescue, a mutiny broke out, driving loyal crewmen to a separate island. When the captain finally returned

The Pinnacles.

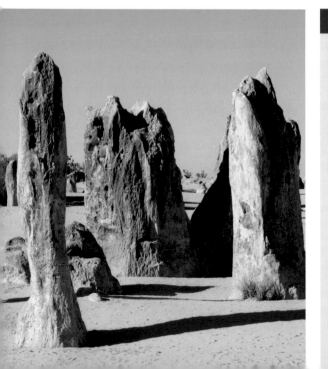

⊙ THE PINNACLES

Most organised tours north of Perth include a stop at the Pinnacles in Nambung National Park. These strange limestone formations are believed to have been shaped around 30,000 years ago by winter rain leaching into the sand dunes and turning the lower levels of the lime-rich sand into a soft limestone. Plants then grew upon the surface of the dunes, accelerating the leaching process and causing a hard cap to form around the roots of the plants. Wind erosion eventually removed the surrounding sand, leaving the hard rock exposed and moulding it into weird and wonderful shapes. The process continues to this day: submerged sections of the Pinnacles are thought to be as least as deep as the exposed sections are high.

from his epic journey, many of the mutineers were hanged; two others were cast ashore to fend for themselves.

The Abrolhos sit on one of the finest reefs on the west coast, and divers can visit various wrecks. Many relics rescued from the deep are on view in the **Western Australian Museum** (http://museum.wa.gov.au; daily 9.30am–4pm; donation) in Geraldton and at Fremantle's Shipwreck Gallery, where the hull of the *Batavia* is on display.

For panoramic views of the area surrounding Geraldton, head for **Waverley Heights**. **Ellendale Bluffs** are notable for their sheer cliffs, at the base of which is a permanent water hole. Locals will advise you to visit **Chapman Valley**, at its most spectacular in spring (Sept–Nov) when the wild flowers are in bloom.

A century ago, **Northampton**, 48km (30 miles) north of Geraldton, was an important rural outpost. Recently it has been spruced up by residents to create an unusually pretty Outback town. Buildings such as **Chiverton House Museum** (Fri–Mon, Wed 10am–noon, 2–4pm) were built by convict labour; the cemetery in the grounds of Gwalia Church records the passing of the convicts and free settlers who first came to the area.

About 20km (12 miles) away is **Horrock Beach**, with fine sand expanses and bays. When there is water in it, don't be surprised to see **Lake Hutt**, near Port Gregory, turn pink in the midday sun – a bizarre phenomenon caused by light refraction and naturally occurring beta carotene in the water.

KALBARRI NATIONAL PARK

Comprising 186,000 hectares (460,000 acres), **Kalbarri National Park** ⑲ (tel: 08-9937 1140) features a combination of stunning river gorges and towering sea cliffs. The park is set around the lower reaches of the Murchison River, which weaves its way to the Indian Ocean past the multi-hued sandstone formations of Red Bluff.

South of Carnarvon is the great system of peninsulas and inlets of **Hamelin Pool** and **Denham Sound**. These two huge expanses of water are protected in the northwest by **Dirk Hartog Island**. A pewter plate, nailed in 1616 to a post on Cape Inscription by the Dutch explorer Hartog, marked the first known landing of Europeans on Australia's west coast. A replica of this plate is in the **Shark Bay Shire Office** (the original is in Amsterdam).

SHARK BAY

Despite its name, **Shark Bay** (www.sharkbay.org) is one place where every visitor ventures into the water, at least up to their knees. That's because this is the site of **Monkey Mia** ⑳, perhaps one of Australia's most delightful tourist attractions. In the small bay near Denham township, wild dolphins come to shore to be fed and mingle with visitors. This came about when local fishermen started tossing fish scraps overboard to following dolphins – by 1964, they were coming in to be hand-fed. This unique

New Norcia's St Gertrude's College.

⊘ Tip

Virgin and Qantas fly to Geraldton daily, departing from Perth domestic terminal. In Geraldton, hire a car from Avis, Budget or Hertz, which all have offices at the airport, and drive to Greenough and surrounding areas.

interaction between humans and dolphins is still very delicate, so follow the rangers' instructions.

Monkey Mia is only the best-known corner of Shark Bay, which was declared a World Heritage area in 1991. Covering 2.3 million hectares (5.7 million acres), it comprises a series of cliff-lined peninsulas and islands with some 145 species of plants (28 endemic to the region, having developed in isolation). The extraordinary salinity of the southern parts of Shark Bay has allowed the growth of stromatolites at Hamelin Pool – giant masses of algae that are considered the oldest form of life on Earth (they probably first formed 3 billion years ago). Somewhat more exciting to observe are the many dugongs, humpback whales and green and loggerhead turtles that roam the splendid arc-shaped bays.

On Shark Bay's slender land prongs, scientists are reintroducing furry marsupials with quaint names like burrowing bettongs and western barred bandicoots. These native species, almost eaten to extinction by introduced foxes and cats, now live behind predator-proof fences.

THE TROPICAL NORTH

Carnarvon ㉑ is 1,000km (600 miles) north of Perth on the beautiful **Gascoyne River**. Sitting just below the Tropic of Capricorn, Carnarvon has warm winters and tropical summers that encourage vibrant tropical wildlife, and yield a huge banana crop and boatloads of prawns. The town was established in 1883, though Dutch explorer Willem de Vlamingh first landed nearby in 1697. Picturesque **Pelican Point** is good for swimming. **Miaboolya Beach** is worth a look, as is the **Bibbawarra artesian bore**, where water surface temperatures are 70°C (158°F).

Further north, a spectacular coastline unfolds, with blowholes, sheltered beaches and wild seascapes. The landlocked **Lake MacLeod** is famous for salt production. Inland, southwest of **Exmouth** is the **Cape Range National Park ㉒**, based along a rugged, dry limestone ridge. Boat trips through

Feeding a dolphin at Monkey Mia.

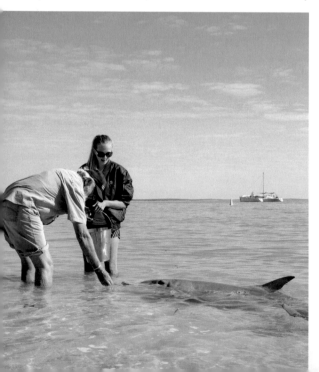

Yardie Creek Gorge are good, with predictable sightings of rock wallabies.

Offshore, **Ningaloo Reef** (www.visitningaloo.com.au) in its protected marine park stretches 260km (160 miles) from Amherst Point around North West Cape into the Exmouth Gulf. Western Australia's largest coral reef, with 250 species of coral and more than 500 fish types, Ningaloo is an unspoilt delight for divers. Coral outcrops can be reached just 20 metres (65ft) from the beach, though they extend 7km (12 miles) into the ocean. Dolphins, dugongs, manta rays, giant cod and sharks abound. Whale sharks visit the reef from March to June, and swimming with these gentle giants (the biggest fish on the planet) is a major attraction.

Coral Bay, 1,132km (703 miles) from Perth, is renowned for fishing and diving. Snorkelling tours go out from here or Exmouth.

THE PILBARA

To the east of Exmouth lies the region called **The Pilbara**, focal point of the state's mineral wealth and one of the world's richest series of holes in the ground. Here, iron ore is king, and company towns seem to appear overnight amid the spinifex. Ore mined at such places as Tom Price and Mount Newman is freighted by rail systems to the coastline, where it is shipped off for national or overseas processing.

The northwest was first explored by the English pirate and explorer William Dampier in 1688 and 1699, so names based on *Buccaneer*, *Cygnet* and *Roebuck* (his vessels) litter the coast. The **Dampier Archipelago** includes **Barrow Island**, the centre for the North West Shelf oil and gas fields. Far from being an environmentally threatened area, it is classified as a wildlife sanctuary and has some unusual animal, bird and plant life.

Roebourne is the oldest town in the northwest, but in recent years its importance has waned because of the clout of the newly established mining towns. The ghost town of **Cossack** is a reminder of the one-time might of the local pearling industry (before it moved

The Kalbarri Wild Flower Centre provides a nature trail or a guided walk through Kalbarri's Native Botanic Garden.

Driving through the Outback in Pilbara.

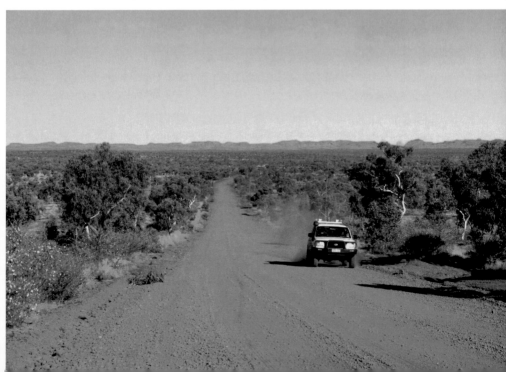

north to Broome and beyond), while a jaunt up the **Fortescue River** reveals the lush area around the Millstream, a bountiful supply of fresh water for many Pilbara towns. The **Millstream-Chichester National Park** is a fine outing for naturalists or hikers.

The magnificent **Karijini National Park ㉓** (previously Hamersley Range National Park), with spectacular gorges and bluffs, can be reached from **Tom Price**. Karijini's visitor centre (tel: 08-9189 8121; parks.dpaw. wa.gov.au; daily 9am–4pm; closed late Dec–late Feb) is worth a look. Designed to withstand bushfires, the centre is shaped like a goanna (an animal sacred to the local Banyjima Aboriginal people) and contains information on the natural and cultural history of the area. Karratha, 40km (25 miles) from the port of Dampier, has been developed as the work base for the mighty Hamersley Iron concern.

For an indication of just how much ore might be coming out of the ground, take a look at the loading facilities at

Port Hedland ㉔. This seaside town, which copes with more tonnage than any other port in Australia, is almost exclusively geared to handle the iron ore from the huge open-cut and strip mining centres of the Pilbara. Port Hedland is built on an island linked to the mainland by three long causeways. Visitors can view the loading from the wharves, where some of the world's largest ore carriers dock. The Port Hedland visitor centre offers daily tours of the BHP-Billiton Nelson Point and Port Authority workings, and half-day tours of Dampier Salt and BHP's Boodarie Iron.

Port Hedland has no shortage of drawbacks. Its tropical setting makes it prone to cyclones; its seas are considered unsafe for swimming, thanks to sharks and stonefish; and its industrial and mineral landscape might not be to everyone's liking. But the local fishing is excellent, there are nearby Aboriginal carvings, bird life is abundant, and you can cool off in the town swimming pool or at Pretty Pool inlet.

To sample a real Western Australian Outback town, detour 193km (120 miles) southeast to **Marble Bar**. With a population of less than 400, it owes its existence to the discovery of gold in 1891 and 1931. The disused **Comet Gold Mine**, 10km (6 miles) south of town, has a museum and visitor centre.

☉ THE DAMPIER PENINSULA

For those with a sense of adventure, a road trip from Broome to Cape Leveque traverses the whole Dampier Peninsula. Most people drive or fly straight through to Kooljaman Resort (www.kooljaman.com. au). But there are several Aboriginal communities who welcome visitors and offer accommodation and tours, and who are happy to share their traditional knowledge. Parts of the Cape Leveque Road are still unsealed, very sandy, and can be badly corrugated, so it is a good idea to hire a 4WD; the journey takes about two-and-a-half hours. Destinations include **Beagle Bay**. There is no accommodation but check out the famous Sacred Heart Church and its beautiful altar decorated with mother-of-pearl shell. **Middle Lagoon** (www. middlelagoon.com.au) offers great fishing, a lagoon safe for swimming, camping, beach shelters and self-contained log cabins. **Lombadina** (tel: 08-9192 4936; www.lombadina.com) is another Aboriginal community offering accommodation and tours from a stunning beach. One Arm Point (aka Ardyaloon; tel: 08-9192 4932) is another welcoming community where you can visit an aquaculture hatchery breeding juvenile trochus shells. When travelling across Aboriginal land, respect for the culture, privacy and people is paramount, so if you see a sign that says 'no entry', abide by it.

BROOME

Coming from the south, along the vast monotony of the road between Port Hedland and Broome, the highway describes a gentle arc along a stretch of coastline known aptly as the **Eighty Mile Reach**.

During the 1920s, **Broome ㉕** was the capital of the world's pearling industry, with more than 300 luggers (pearling vessels) competing for finds off the northwest coast of Australia. For the mostly Japanese divers, the real wealth lay in the mother-of-pearl shell, which was used in jewellery and for buttons; a pearl was an unexpected bonus. But it was a dangerous job, as the Japanese Cemetery testifies. Broome went into the doldrums when plastic buttons flooded the market after World War II. The recent development of cultured pearls has revitalised the industry (although the harvesting now occurs in remote aquatic farms), and several Broome jewellery shops, including one owned by the dominant pearling operator, Paspaley Pearls, sell fine pearls in a variety of settings. A stroll through the timber dwellings of Chinatown, with its multilingual street signs, provides an insight into what the town was like in the pearling days.

With a large Asian population, Broome has retained enough character to be one of Australia's most fascinating communities. Aboriginal culture thrives here, with an Aboriginal radio and TV station (Goolari, known as GTV), which broadcasts partly in local dialect. The town comes alive each August when fishermen, farmers, miners, drovers and tourists swell the population tenfold for the Shinju Matsuri – Festival of the Pearl (www. shinjumatsuri.com.au).

Residents will point out such exotic attractions as the 'Staircase to the Moon', an optical illusion created when light from the full moon reflects on the ocean bed at low-water spring tides. At **Gantheaume Point**, when the tide is low, giant dinosaur tracks thought to be 130 million years old can be viewed.

The 22km (14-mile) **Cable Beach** was named after the underwater communication link between Broome and Java (and on to London), which was established in the 19th century. Today it is the core of Broome's tourist industry, with an up-market resort and crocodile farm complementing the glorious ocean beach. A ride on a camel train along the beach at sunset is a great experience.

THE KIMBERLEY

For Australians, the **Kimberley** region is the final frontier. About half the size of Texas but with only 26,000 inhabitants, encompassing 0.5-million-hectare (1.2-million-acre) cattle ranches and enormous Aboriginal tribal lands, it was first explored in the 1890s but has opened to travellers only over the past 20 years. The landscapes here are awe-inspiring, even by Australia's high standards. The blood-red desert is sliced by lush, forest-filled gorges, where freshwater crocodiles and stingrays swim; the coastline is torn by tropical fjords with tidal waterfalls that flow horizontally. Everything is on a gargantuan scale: vast meteor craters, petrified coral reefs and desert rivers that swell from 100 metres (330ft) wide in the dry season to 13km (8 miles) wide in the wet.

Generations of isolation have left the Kimberley region the most Aboriginal part of Australia, with some immense tracts of tribal land. Remote communities have their own language,

Karajini National Park.

Snorkelling from a catamaran.

newspapers and radio stations; Aboriginal guides work at the national parks and conduct tours of ancient cave paintings; and it has one of Australia's few Aboriginal-owned resorts (at Cape Leveque).

This independence was hard-won. White ranchers arrived here in the 1890s after the world's longest – and most gruelling – cattle drive across central Australia. Soon the Kimberley was the scene of a little-known Aboriginal uprising and of several massacres of indigenous peoples by settlers. Aboriginal bushrangers roamed the Kimberley, easily evading mounted police in the rugged terrain.

Derby ㉖, 216km (134 miles) along the highway northeast from Broome, is the administrative centre for the huge cattle-producing region of West Kimberley. Unlike bustling Broome, with a population of 10,000, Derby is a sleepy town where little seems to have changed over the decades. From here, sightseeing is mostly done by light plane: taking a flight from Derby over **King Sound** and the **Buccaneer**

Archipelago ㉗ beyond will unfold one of the world's most spectacularly beautiful coastlines, a maze of islands, red cliffs and white beaches – uninhabited except for the mining communities of **Cockatoo Island** and **Koolan Islands**.

From Derby, you can either follow the main all-weather **Great Northern Highway** or turn off onto the 'Beef Road', which cuts through the heart of the Kimberley. Some 7km (4.5 miles) outside Derby is a huge boab tree that is reputed to have been used as an overnight prison when transporting prisoners in colonial times. The boab (a close relation of the southern African baobab tree) is often known as the 'bottle tree' and can have a circumference greater than its height – the girth frequently exceeds 10 metres (33ft).

Windjana Gorge National Park ㉘ (tel: 08-9195 5500), 145km (90 miles), to the east, is worth a visit for its eerie Windjana figures in Aboriginal rock paintings, and its huge flocks of spooky, screeching white cockatoos. **Tunnel Creek National Park** ㉙, 35km (22 miles) further on, allows you to walk through an underground stream course populated by bats. Only recently has this part of the Kimberley become accessible to people other than the toughest pioneers, cattlemen or prospectors. The roads are constantly being improved.

East of Derby, on the Fitzroy River near the township of Fitzroy Crossing, is **Geikie Gorge** ㉚, 14km (9 miles) long, with limestone cliffs up to 30 metres (100ft) high. This is one of the most spectacular gorges in the northwest and a pleasant camping spot. Interesting tours conducted by Aboriginal rangers can be taken along the river, where freshwater crocodiles sunbake at the water's edge; down below, you can see sawfish and stingrays that have adapted to life in fresh water. On the eastern side lies **Fossil Downs**, a huge private cattle station (over 405,000 hectares/1 million acres), founded in 1886. It is the only Kimberley cattle station still owned by descendants of the original pioneers, the MacDonalds.

EAST KIMBERLEY AND THE BUNGLE BUNGLES

The Great Northern Highway cuts along the southern perimeter of the Kimberley before entering the new township of **Halls Creek**, which, with its comfortable hotels and air-conditioned supermarkets, serves as a base for the regional pastoral industry. At Old Halls Creek, remnants of the 1884 gold rush can be seen. The rush made a few prospectors rich, but the harsh environment and shortage of water ruined a good many more.

South of Halls Creek, 130km (80 miles) away, is the meteorite crater at **Wolfe Creek** ③ , the second largest in the world – although it really comes into perspective when seen from the air.

The turn-off 110km (68 miles) north of Halls Creek leads to a 4WD track to one of the most astonishing natural features in the world: the **Bungle Bungle Range**. The Bungles cover some 640 sq km (247 sq miles) of the Ord River Valley with a labyrinth of orange and black (caused by the black lichen and orange silica) horizontally tiger-striped, domed mountains. Within the canyons and gorges of the **Purnululu National Park** ㉜ are palm-filled grottoes, enormous caves and white-sand beaches. The rough track from the highway deters many, so a thriving industry has arisen in **Kununurra** to fly tourists over (and, more recently, into) the Bungle Bungles.

A true gem of the Kimberley lies to the north of Purnululu: **Argyle Diamond Mine** is the world's largest, extracting some 1,000kg (6.5 tons) of diamonds each year. The Argyle Diamond Pipe was discovered in 1979 and remains the only source of deep-pink diamonds. Air tours to the mine are available from Kununurra.

Wyndham ㉝ is the most northerly port in Western Australia, a small scattered community that has changed little since the days of the gold rush. You can see large crocodiles lying on the mudflats below the Wyndham wharf. Cattle that miss their footing when being loaded onto ships provide an occasional meal.

The Ord River was dammed in 1971 to harness the monsoon runoff for irrigation; in recent years, this has opened up the East Kimberley to the cultivation of tropical crops. To the south, Lake Argyle in the **Carr Boyd Range** is the main reservoir (boat tours are available). The damming of the Ord River would have submerged **Argyle Downs Homestead**, home of one of the northwest's great pioneering families, the Duracks, so it was moved to a new location to escape the rising waters. It is now a museum about life for the early settlers of the Kimberley, with changing artworks from all around Australia.

Sunset at Cape Leveque.

A dry river bed in Bungle Bungle National Park.

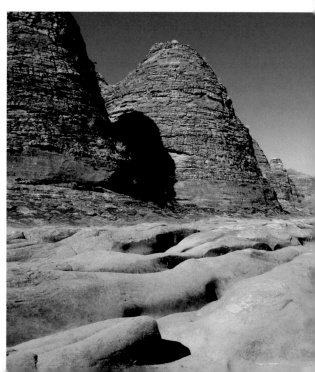

📷 THE WILDFLOWERS OF WESTERN AUSTRALIA

In spring, the Western Australian bush is set ablaze with wild flowers, from bold and brilliant banksias to delicate ice daisies.

Western Australia is known for its beautiful wild flowers. People travel from all around the country – and the world – to view the impressive display. The flowering is most spectacular during spring (August through to November), though at almost any time of year you will find some flowers brightening the olive- and sage-greens of the bush. Banksias, for example, often bloom in autumn or winter.

It might seem strange that such a dry landscape should produce so many wild flowers; there are various reasons for this success. For millions of years Western Australia has avoided the sort of landmass upheaval that has caused species in other parts of the continent to die out. The flowers have also benefited from the lack of shade-casting trees and have enjoyed the protection of less engulfing plants and shrubs.

The state has some 10,000 species of wild flowers, 6,000 of which are native. Some areas are particularly well endowed: Kalbarri National Park, the karri forests around Pemberton, and the Stirling Ranges north of Albany. The southwest is known for its delicate flowers such as orchid, kangaroo paw and mountain bell.

Closer to Perth, John Forrest National Park is another rich area, or you could simply visit Kings Park Botanic Garden. We recommend you pack a picnic and a camera and take your time enjoying the rich palette of the blooms. The Western Australian Visitor Centre in Perth has maps to ensure you make the most of the wild-flower season.

A display of spring wildflowers. If you have a special interest in wild flowers it is worth taking an escorted wi flower tour, an option offered by most of the day-tour operators in Perth.

Albany bottlebrush. Bottlebrush is more commonly associated with the eastern states (it was one of the plants the naturalist Joseph Banks collected on Cook voyage of 1770), but you will also find it in WA, especially in damp habitats.

In spring, daisies of many types and colours carpet forest clearings, heathlands and fields.

Grass tree (Xanthorrhoea), with its distinctive fire-blackened trunk surmounted by a mop of spiky grass and spear-like flower shaft.

Grass trees

Even if you are not in Western Australia during the wildflower season, the bush is a fascinating landscape with a rich biodiversity that is at last being championed by conservationists after well over a century of indiscriminate land clearance for agriculture.

Among the many types of eucalyptus (gumtrees), paper bark and banksias, the tree that perhaps stands out above all others is the grass tree *(Xanthorrhoea)*, with its distinctive fire-blackened trunk surmounted by a mop of spiky grass and spear-like flower shaft.

Grass trees are very slow-growing (about 1 metre/3ft every 100 years) but can live for hundreds of years, and their ability to survive in tough conditions has made them a symbol of the Australian Outback. Like many other bush plants, they have evolved to withstand bushfires; germination is actually assisted by fire. The distinctive flower shaft will often shoot up in the year following a bushfire, providing valuable food for wildlife in an otherwise charred, barren landscape. In contrast to the slow-growing trunk, the flowering stalk grows rapidly after germination, at a rate of 2–3cm (1in) a day.

Succulents, such as these in a forest near Karridale, also flourish in the south. Succulents survive in hot, arid areas. Their characteristic fleshy leaves, stems and roots store water and their compact shape reduces dehydration. The best-known type of succulent is the cactus, but there are many other forms.

The grass trees are known as balga (black boys) to the Aborigines, who traditionally used a waterproof resin produced from the base of the plant to make glue. The shafts could also be used as spearheads, and the dried flower shafts could be rubbed together to create fire. The tender shoots could be eaten, and the nectar from the flowers of the plant was used to make a sweet drink. Today the grass trees are prized by horticulturalists – plants saved from the developers' bulldozers can, with great skill and care, be transplanted and coaxed into life.

nksias have large cone-shaped wers comprising hundreds of tiny dividual flowers. The temperate uthwest corner of WA supports ne 60 different species, many of ich flower in winter. Banksias are ned after Joseph Banks, Captain ok's botanist, and were celebrated the Snugglepot and Cuddlepie ok and bushbaby drawings of the ldren's author and illustrator May bs (1877–1969).

The distinctive flower shaft of the grass tree will often shoot up in the year following a bushfire, providing valuable food for wildlife in an otherwise charred, barren landscape. In contrast to the slow-growing trunk, the flowering stalk grows rapidly after germination, at a rate of 2–3cm (1 inch) a day.

Cradle Mountain and Lake St Clair National Park.

The bridge at Richmond.

TASMANIA

Australia's smallest and remotest state is also the most temperate. It has no arid Outback, but there's an abundance of cool forests, rugged mountains, highland lakes, lush pasture and fruitful orchards.

'How beautiful is the whole region, for form, and grouping, and opulence, and freshness of foliage, and variety of color, and grace and shapeliness of the hills, the capes, the promontories; and then, the splendor of the sunlight, the dim rich distances, the charm of the water-glimpses!' Such was the view of inveterate traveller Mark Twain, commenting on his voyage to Tasmania in the 1890s.

However, he then went on to point out the irony behind this observation: 'And it was in this paradise that the yellow-liveried convicts were landed, and the Corps-bandits quartered, and the wanton slaughter of the kangaroo-chasing black innocents consummated on that autumn day in May, in the brutish old time. It was all out of keeping with the place, a sort of bringing of heaven and hell together.'

This is the paradox of Tasmania, nowhere more so than at the Port Arthur Penal Settlement, the most popular of the state's myriad tourist attractions. It sits in a jaw-droppingly gorgeous setting: an amphitheatre of rolling green meadow leading down to the tranquil blue waters of Mason Cove, dotted with picturesque sandstone ruins glowing golden yellow in the watery sunlight. Even without the sun, there is something magisterial and uplifting about the setting. Yet this

must be reconciled with its original role as a setting for a prison regime, which was considered by many to be the harshest in the British Empire.

VAN DIEMEN'S LAND

That was in the days when the island was called Van Diemen's Land (after being so named by Abel Tasman in 1642) and when British colonists were establishing their second toehold on the Australian continent. It was a struggle to tame the inhospitable land and establish viable agriculture. Still today,

Main attractions
Hobart
Richmond
Port Arthur
Freycinet National Park
Bay of Fires
Cradle Mountain

Maps on pages
298, 304

Hobart and Mount Wellington.

The Salamanca Market is the perfect place to browse for used books.

vast stretches of Tasmania are accessible only by tough walking tracks. Even in populated regions, there is a sense of space. It's to be expected in an island the size of Ireland but with a tenth of the latter's 6.5 million people.

Tasmania's appeal resides in the range and beauty of its landscapes and natural features, from the lakes and mountains of the central highlands (culminating in Cradle Mountain), to the deserted beaches of the east coast, where the aquamarine of the sea is offset by the vibrant orange lichen on the rocks. And if this isn't enough, try the islands in the Bass Strait, where – such is the sparseness of the population – every motorist acknowledges every other.

Few venture to such far-flung outposts on their first visit, though. There are no international flights to Tasmania and just the odd cruise ship, so most visitors come via the mainland (or 'the big island' as Tasmanians call it), either on the *Spirit of Tasmania* ferries from Melbourne to Devonport or by air into Hobart or Launceston.

HOBART

If you follow Twain's lead and make **Hobart ❶** your first port of call, you'll find a small, distinguished city nestling between the waters of the Derwent Estuary and the brooding bulk of Mount Wellington. These features have prevented the urban sprawl that affects many mainland cities, while a spell in the economic doldrums in the 1960s and 1970s meant that much of the old colonial architecture was spared from development. Today there are numerous well-preserved Georgian and Victorian buildings to give character and a nod back to old England.

Hobart's waterfront is a magnet, thanks to the classic backdrop views to Mount Wellington and the atmospheric and still-active 19th-century port. At **Victoria Dock Ⓐ**, the beautifully restored **IXL Jam Factory** is on the site of the first wharf and now contains the remarkable, award-winning **Henry Jones Art Hotel** (www.thehenryjones. com), and the University of Tasmania's **Centre for the Arts** (www.utas.edu.au/ creative-arts/art).

Visit both, then wander across to the adjoining **Constitution Dock**. Consider fish and chips from one of the floating stalls, then head to **Salamanca Place Ⓑ** (www.about-salamanca.com.au). This is the site of a pulsating weekend **market** (www.salamancamarket.com. au; Sat 8.30am–3pm), but even without that, the old stone warehouses are atmospheric and appealing. They house a lively arts centre as well as the usual selection of galleries, bars and cafés. Behind them is the pedestrianised **Salamanca Square**, a modern development that successfully latches on to the original buildings.

East along Salamanca Place, turn up Kelly's Steps to the eyrie of **Battery Point Ⓒ**, where a pristine collection of the city's earliest dwellings is to be found. At its centre is Arthur's Circus, doing a fine impression of a village green, while Hampden Road's range of eateries includes the peerless **Jackman & McRoss** bakery/café. The **Narryna Heritage Museum** (tel: 03-6165 7000; www.tmag.tas.gov.au; 26 Dec–31 Mar daily 10am–4pm, 1 Apr–24 Dec Tue–Sun) preserves a merchant's house in Victorian splendour.

Westwards along Salamanca Place brings you to the administrative centre of the state. The discreet sandstone-clad modernism of the Supreme Court on the left is balanced by the more conventional Victorian bulk of **Parliament House** on the right (tel: 03-6233 2200; www.parliament.tas.gov.au; Mon–Fri or daily 10am and 2pm; tours when houses not sitting).

MACQUARIE STREET

A block further back, Macquarie Street has **St David's Cathedral** ⓓ – the Georgian-style seat of the local Anglican bishop; the **Treasury Building** facing onto the formal gardens of Franklin Square; the **General Post Office**, built with the grandeur that characterises these buildings; the **Town Hall** ⓔ; the Art Deco sleekness of the **Mercury**

Newspaper Building; and the **Tasmanian Museum and Art Gallery** ⓕ (tel: 03-6165 7000; www.tmag.tas.gov.au; 26 Dec–31 Mar daily 10am–4pm, 1 Apr–24 Dec Tue–Sun). The museum is a repository for colonial and contemporary art, local fauna, a collection of Chinese antiquities, and material illustrating early polar exploration.

The **Maritime Museum of Tasmania** (tel: 03-6234 1427; www.maritimetas.org; daily 9am–5pm) is small but worthwhile for its collection of photos, models, navigational instruments and relics exploring Tasmania's link with the sea.

An exhibit at the Maritime Museum of Tasmania.

Another block back from the water, the main downtown shopping area centres on **Elizabeth Street Mall** ⓖ.

North, beyond the mass of the Royal Hobart Hospital, the old **Theatre Royal** ⓗ (www.theatreroyal.com.au) on Campbell Street is undergoing an exciting redevelopment that will see it reopen in 2019 as part of the new **Hedberg** performing arts centre, along with the University of Tasmania Conservatorium of Music.

Hobart harbour.

An African figure made from beads at the Museum of Antiquities, part of Moorilla Estate Winery.

Sir John Franklin's statue in Franklin Square.

A few blocks up Campbell Street the **Penitentiary Chapel and Criminal Courts** ❶ (tel: 03-6231 0911; www. nationaltrust.org.au; access by Guided Experience only: Tue–Sun 10am, noon, 2pm, Ghost Tours Thu–Sat 8.30pm) are all that remain of the original vast Hobart Gaol. The site has recently been transformed by the National Trust and guests now watch a multi-sensory film experience entitled *Pandemonium*, intended to convey a sense of convict life, then visit underground tunnels, a chapel, solitary cells and the gallows.

THE QUEENS DOMAIN

If you head northeast and manage to cross some busy highways, **Queens Domain** has, since the early days, been a place of recreation, remembrance and, for the occupant of Government House, residence. The **Cenotaph** ❿ is flanked by a couple of interesting modern glass and stone pyramids that incorporate audio tributes to those lost in combat. The **Royal Botanical Gardens** ⓚ were established in 1828 and

are faithful to the early vision of the founders by collecting every conceivable variety of flora.

OUTER HOBART

North Hobart has a plethora of cosmopolitan bars, restaurants and entertainment venues. Further north still, **Runnymede** in New Town is an early 1830s homestead maintained by the National Trust (61 Bay Road, New Town; tel: 03-6278 1269; www. nationaltrust.org.au; Tue–Fri 10am–4pm, Sun noon–4pm) and worth a stop on the way to the **Moorilla Estate** (www. moorilla.com.au). This winery not only claims one of Tasmania's leading restaurants but also houses arguably the most significant addition to Tasmania's cultural infrastructure in years: the **Museum of Old and New Art**. MONA (Main Road, Berriedale; tel: 03-6277 9900; www.mona.net.au; Wed–Mon 10am–6pm) was built from scratch by entrepreneur David Walsh to house a wide-ranging and esoteric collection ranging from historical artefacts from the great civilisations through to challenging modern work, all loosely linked by the concept of sex and death as the driving forces of creativity. Its dramatic galleries opened at the beginning of 2011.

West of the city centre, Mount Wellington provides superb views of the city; make sure that you visit the **Cascade Brewery** (Cascade Road, South Hobart; tel: 03-6224 1117; www. cascadebreweryco.com.au; daily, tours between 10am and 5pm; booking recommended). Relish the picturesque setting, a choice of tours, and the opportunity to drink your way through the sampling room (over 18s only; all-ages heritage tours also take place). The brewery is also the starting point for *Louisa's Walk*, a promenade through the **Female Factory** (www.femalefactory. org.au) in which professional actors enact a gripping chapter in history (tel: 03-6233 6656; www.livehistoryhobart.com. au; daily 1–2pm; booking essential). You can visit the site on your own, too.

On the other side of the Derwent, the suburb of **Bellerive** fans out from **Kangaroo Bluff Battery**, an emplacement designed to guard the city from attack. The **Tasmanian Cricket Museum** (tel: 03-6282 0433; Tue–Thu 10am–3pm, Fri 10am–noon) is located at **Blundstone Arena**, where state and international cricket is played in a village-green atmosphere.

Leaving Hobart via the **Tasman Bridge** is the first step towards the Tasman Peninsula, where so much colonial history was forged.

RICHMOND

The direct route goes across Sorell Causeway, but that would be to neglect the wonderful colonial township of **Richmond ❷**. It sits in the Coal River Valley, its convict-built stone bridge offset by the English village-style church on the hill beyond. This is the kind of setting that led Mark Twain to observe: 'Wherever the exiled Englishman can find in his new

home resemblances to his old one, he is touched to the marrow of his being; the love that is in his heart inspires his imagination, and these allied forces transfigure those resemblances into authentic duplicates of the revered originals.' Most of the town was built between 1824 and 1840, and it is the consistency in style that gives Richmond its charm. There's the obligatory jail for this staging post on the Hobart to Port Arthur road, as well as a couple of churches. More recent attractions include a maze and the **Old Hobart Town Model Village** (21 Bridge Street; tel: 03-6260 2502; www. oldhobarttown.com; daily 9am–5pm).

Pass through Sorell and continue to **Eaglehawk Neck**. This isthmus to the Tasman Peninsula is where the infamous Dog Line was set. A team of ferocious fidos was chained to a row of posts so that no convict could cross without coming into range of at least one of them. See the fearsome statue.

There are gentler attractions nearby. The **Tesselated Pavement** suggests that nature has tiled the shoreline,

⊘ Tip

A booklet, *Great Short Walks*, which outlines 60 treks in some of the most beautiful areas in the state, is available from Parks and Wildlife visitor centres (www. parks.tas.gov.au) and most Tasmania Information Centres, and can be downloaded free from the iTunes Store. There are information boards at the start of each route co-ordinated with the design of the booklet.

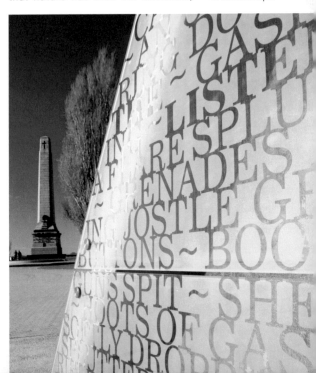

Old and new structures at the Cenotaph.

Fishermen can often be seen unloading their catches at harbours all along the east coast.

while across the isthmus the **Tasman Arch** and **Devil's Kitchen** are popular stops on the bus tours to Port Arthur.

The **Tasmanian Devil Park** (tel: 1800-641 641; www.tasmaniandevilpark. com; daily 9am–5pm, later in summer) at Taranna is an interesting stop, and your chance to see a rare animal facing extinction from a disease epidemic, as well as myriad other native species (including quolls and pademelons) before the main attraction: the **Port Arthur Penal Settlement ❸** (tel: 1800-659 101; www.portarthur.org.au; daily 9am–dusk). See page 306.

Don't miss the **Coal Mines Historic Site**. Convicts provided the labour, and the ruins reveal grim evidence of their travails (daily 24 hours).

THE EAST COAST

The Tasman Highway runs up the east coast, arriving first at the sleepy resort of **Orford**. Continue to Triabunna, where ferries operated by Encounter Maria Island (tel: 03-6256 4772; www.encountermaria.com.au) depart for **Maria Island ❹** (www.parks.tas.gov.

au). Originally a penal settlement, the island is now a national park and a haven for wildlife and walkers. No traffic is permitted unless you take a bicycle; the only accommodation is in unpowered bunkhouses in the settlement at **Darlington**. Natural wonders abound – **Fossil Cliffs** and the **Painted Cliffs** among them. Up the coast the old **Spiky Bridge** and pristine **Spiky Beach** are untrumpeted gems.

Swansea is a low-key resort with lovely views across Great Oyster Bay to the pink granite peaks of the Hazards on the **Freycinet Peninsula**, another of Tasmania's sparkling jewels. It's quite a long drive to get there, but the rewards are worth it. First stop is **Coles Bay ❺**, the service and accommodation centre that happens to have some rather fabulous beaches. However, the main attraction is **Freycinet National Park ❻** (tel: 03-6256 7000; www.parks. tas.gov.au) and the headline act, **Wineglass Bay**, a much-photographed goblet-shaped arc of golden sand regularly topped up with a translucent tipple of Tasman Bay blue juice.

View of the Freycinet peninsula.

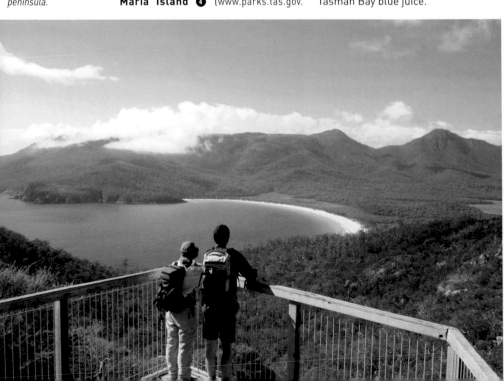

Bicheno, to the north, is a family resort with a pretty fishing boat shelter, the Gulch, and a big blowhole. The **Douglas-Apsley National Park** has a natural water hole and is a popular picnic spot.

THE NORTHEAST

After a handful of other beach resorts, you wind round into **St Helens** on sheltered George's Bay. With a population around the 2,000 mark, it is the largest town on the east coast and a nice enough place, but follow the road out to **Binalong Bay** at the southern end of one of the world's great coastal stretches, the **Bay of Fires ❼**. It consists of 30km (19 miles) of some of the finest beach in the world and much of it is inaccessible by road. There are four-day guided walks, which include a couple of nights at a stunning modern lodge, but otherwise you have to fend for yourself. Northern access is via the **Mount William National Park**, where the lighthouse at **Eddystone Point** marks the top of the bay.

The road inland from St Helens climbs steeply into tin country. A turn off to **Pyengana** reveals a cheese factory; the **Pub in the Paddock** (www. pubinthepaddocktas.com.au) home to Priscilla the beer-drinking pig; and the less contrived appeal of **St Columba's Falls**. Further inland, the tin-mining town of **Derby** provides a glimpse back to the days when the area's prosperity lay beneath the ground.

The road north runs to **Bridport ❽** with its mix of holiday shacks and a tired resort playing host to fans of fishing and beaches. The acclaimed **Barnbougle Dunes Golf Links** is a short distance out of town and appeals to a different breed of pleasure seekers.

Purple-loving people head to **Bridestowe Estate Lavender Farm** (tel: 03-6352 8182; www.bridestowelavender.com.au; daily May–Aug 10am–4pm, Sept–Apr 9am–5pm), a blanket of colour in December and January just before the crop is harvested. **Lilydale**, on the road winding down towards Launceston, has an attractive main street notable for historic **Bardenhagen's General Store**, and the imaginative paint jobs that have been applied to the town's power poles.

LAUNCESTON

Tasmania's second city has undergone a revival in recent years due, to some extent, to the advent of cheaper airfares from the mainland, and also to some shrewd investments in tourist infrastructure. Of particular note has been the development of the old railway workshops at Inveresk, especially the new site operated by the **Queen Victoria Museum and Art Gallery** (tel: 03-6323 3777; www. qvmag.tas.gov.au; daily 10am–4pm). This impressive complex combines art galleries with museum space marking the industrial history of the area. The Blacksmith Shop, complete with deafening soundscape, gives an impression of the labours of the past.

Victorian facades, Lauceston.

Artist at work in the Blacksmith Shop of the Queen Victoria Museum and Art Gallery.

Launceston has more than its share of distinguished Victorian architecture on its undulating streets, and much pleasure comes from simply walking around the city centre. Indeed, Cameron Street, with its red-brick terraces replete with filigree ironwork, must be one of the best-preserved streets of the era in Australia. It leads off **Civic Square**, which gathers up the grandiose **Town Hall**, the **Library** and the simple **Macquarie House**, a stone warehouse from 1830.

The main shopping area radiates out from **Brisbane Street Mall** and includes graceful **Quadrant Mall** and hapless modern construct, **Yorktown Square**. The **Old Umbrella Shop** (Mon–Fri 9am–5pm, Sat 9am–noon) in George Street has remained unchanged for the best part of a century and is now run by the National Trust.

To the east of the centre **City Park** is laid out Victorian style with original fountains, rotundas and a conservatory. A monkey enclosure contains macaques that have been exciting local children for years. Other highlights around the city include the original **Queen Victoria Museum** (tel: 03-6323 3777; www.qvmag.tas.gov.au; daily 10am–4pm), the **Design Centre of Tasmania** (tel: 03-6331 5506; www.designtasmania. com.au; Mon–Fri 9.30am–5.30pm, Sat–Sun 10am–4pm, to 3pm in winter), the **National Automobile Museum of Tasmania** (tel: 03-6334 8888; www.namt. com.au; daily Sept–May 9am–5pm, June–Aug 10am–4pm) and **Boag's Brewery** (tel: 03-6332 6300; www.james boag.com.au; Mon–Fri 8.45am–4.30pm; tour times vary), where enthusiasts can take a tour and drink beer.

The riverfront has enjoyed a revival with **Seaport**'s hotel, restaurants and bars making the most of the setting, and a boardwalk eastwards runs past **Ritchies Mill**, home to **Stillwater**, one of several outstanding city eateries.

Few cities have such a remarkable phenomenon as **Cataract Gorge** within walking distance of the centre. Paths run along its steep walls – the southern one tough, the northern one easy. If walking is out, then pleasure boats sail part of the way up the South Esk River.

Walkers can go all the way to the **Cliff Grounds** area, where the gorge opens out into a basin, with gardens and a rotunda on one side, and grassy banks and an open-air swimming pool on the other. A chairlift and suspension bridge link the two sides.

THE TAMAR VALLEY

Launceston's playground lies to the north in the **Tamar Valley** (www.tamarvalley.com.au) an area best known for its vineyards. Although there is an officially sanctioned **Tamar Valley Wine Route**, with special signage (blue grapes on yellow), just as much fun can be had by following your nose.

Make a stop in **George Town ⑩**, where the first settlers on the Tamar pitched up. The **Watch House Museum** (Macquarie Street; Nov–Apr Mon–Fri 10am–4pm, Sat–Sun noon–2pm; May–Oct Mon–Fri 10am–3pm, Sat–Sun noon–2pm) tells the story.

Low Head at the mouth of the Tamar has the atmospheric **Pilot Station** where whitewashed houses, some for rent, are dotted around a green. There's a **Maritime Museum** (tel: 03-6382 1143; http://museum.lowhead.com; daily 10am–4pm) and the chance to watch a pilot boat at work guiding vessels up the tricky river.

Batman Bridge is the only fixed crossing above Launceston. Turn right for **Beaconsfield ⑪**, a town which gained global notoriety when two miners were trapped in its gold mine in 2006 (they were saved after a nail-biting two-week rescue operation). The impressive **Beaconsfield Mine and Heritage Centre** (tel: 03-6383 1473; www.beaconsfieldheritage.com.au; daily 9.30am–4.30pm) is housed in old mine buildings.

Beauty Point's attractions are on its wharf. **Seahorse World** (tel: 03-6383 4111; www.seahorseworld.com.au; daily Sept–Apr 9.30am–3.30pm, May–Aug 10am–3pm; tours every half-hour) has seahorses, funnily enough, and other

sea creatures. You can guess the main attraction at the neighbouring **Platypus House** (tel: 03-6383 4884; www.platypushouse.com.au; daily 9.30am–3.30pm, Nov–Apr until 4.30pm).

Detours from the road back to Launceston may include **Grindelwald**, a resort hotel for those yearning for a faux Swiss village, and **Tamar Island**, just north of the city, a wetlands reserve with an easily accessible boardwalk.

THE MIDLAND HIGHWAY

The Midland Highway runs down to Hobart and takes in some of the best of the colonial villages. **Longford** has numerous listed buildings, especially along Wellington Street, and **Brown's Big Store** has grand Victorian style. Close by are two country estates, both open to the public. **Woolmers Estate** (tel: 03-6391 2230; www.woolmers.com.au; daily 10am–4pm; regular guided tours of the house) has an exuberant mansion and extensive grounds containing a coach house, stables, cottages, and a working

Cataract Gorge is one of Tasmania's premier attractions.

⊘ FREYCINET NATIONAL PARK

There are few places in the world where the elements of landscape combine so winningly as at Freycinet National Park. The mix of mountains, forest, beaches and achingly blue sea, not to mention the abundant wildlife, is hard to match and impossible to beat. It's best just to surrender to it and allow as much time as possible to take it all in. And the best way to see it is to get out there and walk.

The most popular trek is the fairly stiff climb up to the saddle between two of the Hazards: Mount Amos and Mount Mayson. This houses the **Wineglass Bay** lookout. Even for regulars, the view down can take you by surprise; there's the faultless symmetry of the curve that gives the bay its name and, if you're lucky and the sun's out, the searing azure of the sea. For the first-time visitor, it is just breathtaking. It is not unusual to find groups of people settled on the benches or clumped on nearby rocks, gazing down in silence, lost in contemplation. (Or getting their breath back.) Some turn back now, while others scramble down to the beach, perhaps as part of a longer hike which could take in **Mount Graham** or **Mount Freycinet**, or to return via **Hazards Beach**. There are several shorter walks too, at **Cape Tourville**, **Sleepy Bay** or **Little Gravelly Beach**, for instance. Pick up a map at the visitor centre just inside the park.

THE GULAG PENINSULA

As the most fearsome prison of the Antipodes, Port Arthur's natural isolation made it the perfect site for the worst criminals.

Port Arthur was designed to be the ultimate prison. Establishments in Hobart, Sarah Island and Maria Island predate it, but all had their problems. The new place had to be secure and remote enough to make escape difficult, if not impossible, but it was also to employ the 'enlightened' punishment regime favoured at the time.

In this setting, 110km (68 miles) from Hobart, security was not a problem; if the convicts escaped, the dog line at Eaglehawk Neck would stop them. The rumour that sharks patrolled the sea didn't exactly encourage a swim to freedom either.

With a population of prisoners, soldiers and settlers many kilometres from anywhere, this was not just a prison but a penal settlement, one built on an industrial scale. Convicts were employed in shipbuilding, timber felling, agriculture and animal husbandry. The population needed to be self-sufficient, and a thriving village grew up around the prison, with farms, shops and Australia's first railway system (pulled by convicts instead of mules).

Many of the buildings were destroyed by bushfires which ravaged Port Arthur in 1897.

Today, tourists are efficiently managed through the site. On buying your ticket you are allocated a time for a boat cruise and another for the guided tour, ensuring that the constant flow of visitors is fed through as comfortably as possible. The quieter times are first thing in the morning before the bus tours arrive from Hobart, and mid-afternoon onwards when most of them have departed.

You are also given a playing card to use in the Lottery of Life exhibition that leads out to the main site. Each card corresponds to an inmate whose history you follow through the display. You may have been transported for stealing bread but worked your way through the system to win the prized ticket of leave. Or you may be a recidivist who meets a sticky end.

After this and the guided tour you can start exploring. The best-known building in Port Arthur is the long, squat sandstone **Penitentiary**, a former flour mill converted in 1848 into a 136-cell prison for the worst offenders, although they were allowed out during the day to work. Two bushfires in the late 1890s gutted this and other edifices.

Take a stroll up the path to the left to the **Commandant's House**, with an extraordinary view over the bay and the site. It was one of the few wooden houses to survive the flames.

The path from the bay runs past the ruined hospital to the **Separate Prison** – built in the 1850s on a radical concept of punishment being developed in Britain. Instead of physical pain, prisoners were subjected to total sensory deprivation: kept in tiny cells for 23 hours a day, they were not allowed to talk or interact with others. Not surprisingly, the treatment led to more derangement than rehabilitation; Port Arthur was used as a mental asylum in later years.

Harbour cruises run out around the **Isle of the Dead** and **Point Puer Boys' Prison**, and twice a day you can land on the former, which became the cemetery for the prison colony. A lone convict once lived on the island to dig the graves.

On the way back to the visitor centre, the shell of the Broad Arrow Café is part of a **Memorial Garden** to the victims of a gunman who massacred 35 people in and around the site in April 1996. Visitors should not broach the subject with staff.

woolshed. Also at Woolmers is the **National Rose Garden**, which will eventually feature over 500 varieties. **Brickendon Estate**'s **Historic Farming Village** (tel: 03-6391 1383; www.brickendon.com.au; Tue–Sun 9.30am–5pm) has great character.

Evandale ⑫, to the east of the highway, makes much of hosting the National Penny Farthing Championships each February, but there are numerous other pretexts for a visit: the two churches to St Andrew – one Anglican, the other a more extravagant Uniting Church; the interior to **Brown's Village Store**; and the **Clarendon Arms**.

For a break from historic villages, follow the steep, winding C401 from Evandale up towards **Ben Lomond National Park** ⑬ (www.parks.tas.gov.au). Once you've negotiated the tortuous Jacob's Ladder, you arrive at the **Alpine Village**. In winter this is one of two snowfields in the state (the other is at Mount Field), and during the rest of the year there are some lovely Alpine walks.

Return to the Midland Highway for **Campbell Town**, from where the transit of Venus was observed by the US Navy in 1874. Elsewhere the theme is bricks: millions of them in the convict-built **Red Bridge**, and a few thousand set into the pavements on both sides of the highway as part of a project that will eventually see one brick for each of the 68,000 people transported to Van Diemen's Land.

Ross ⑭ is arguably the most unspoilt of all the historic towns. **Church Street** is unsurpassed in its Georgian structures and includes **Ross Village Bakery**, where you can relax with a sticky cake. Continue down to the stone **bridge** and follow the path behind the Uniting Church to the remains of the **Female Factory**.

Ross benefits from being bypassed by the highway, as does **Oatlands** ⑮, which has dozens of old sandstone buildings and the towering **Callington Mill** (tel: 03-6254 1212; daily 9am–4pm; tours available), but, lacking the shady elms that contribute so winningly to Ross's ambience, it attracts

Time stands still at the Grove in George Town for a home maid.

The bridge at Ross was constructed in 1836.

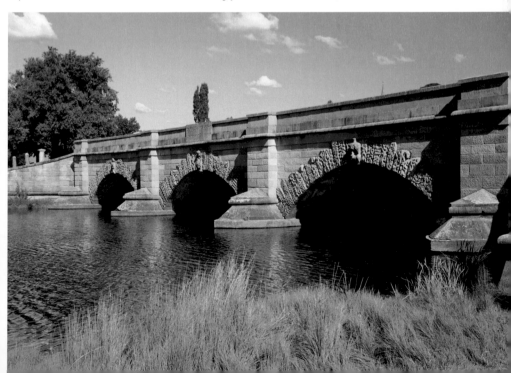

⊙ Tip

Day entry to national parks in Tasmania costs A$24 per vehicle (except for Cradle Mountain – A$16.50 per adult) and can be purchased online, at national park visitor centres and at some state visitor information centres. For multiple visits a two-month pass costs A$60. See www.parks.tas.gov.au for more information.

The beach on the Neck has protected areas for penguins and mutton birds.

fewer visitors. Make the most of this and follow the town's walking trail in peace.

Kempton is the last town worth exploring, and then it's a straight run into Hobart, unless the Romanesque church of St Mark in **Pontville** interests you.

THE HUON VALLEY

South from Hobart, the **Huon Valley** is an area that people don't necessarily see on their first visit to the island, but its gentle pleasures reward those who make the effort. For long draped with the orchards that gave the Apple Isle its name, the area is as likely to reveal vineyards or berries in its rolling meadows these days. In fact its providores and gourmet restaurants have made it something of a foodie's haunt.

Sticking to the coast road, check out the **Shot Tower** (tel: 03-6227 8885; taroona.tas.au/shot-tower; daily 9am–5pm) at **Taroona**; perhaps the exhibition in the foyer of the **Australian Antarctic Division HQ** (tel: 03-6232 3209; Mon–Fri 9am–5pm) outside

Kingston; and the novel snorkel trail at **Tinderbox**, where you swim out and read a series of information boards on plates on the sea bed.

Kettering has a sparkling cove, but most people are there for the ferry to **Bruny Island** ⑯ (www.brunyisland.org.au). It could be viewed as two islands joined by a narrow isthmus (The Neck) and locals refer to North Bruny and South Bruny. Either way, it's a lengthy 63km (39 miles) from top to bottom. **Adventure Bay** on the more rugged South Bruny is the main holiday centre, if you can call it that. Most activity involves walking or fishing, and maybe visiting **Cape Bruny Lighthouse** or **Fluted Cape**. A boat excursion will reveal seals, dolphins and any other aquatic life that turns up. **The Neck** has a penguin viewing point and a lookout reached by a steep flight of steps.

On the mainland, make your way to **Huonville**, the area's commercial centre, where visitor interest focuses on the river. There are easy walks or rigorous tests of your capacity to withstand

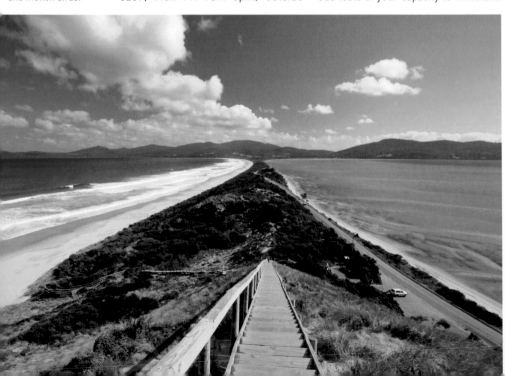

intense G-forces on the **Huon Jet** boat (www.huonjet.com).

Continuing south, **Franklin** is but a street along the riverbank. However, the **Wooden Boat Centre** (tel: 03-6266 3586; www.woodenboatcentre.com; Mon–Fri 10.30am–4.30pm, weekends to 4pm) is an interesting stop. For a small fee, you can follow the progress of students on an 18-month boat-building course. At the end of their studies they will have jointly built a complete vessel.

FORESTS OF THE SOUTH

Geeveston ⓱ is a timber town. The clues are easy to spot: the two huge trunks either side of the road as you drive in, the life-size carved wooden figures placed along the streets, and the **Forest and Heritage Centre** that doubles as the visitor centre in the middle of town. Geeveston is on the edge of a huge area of managed forest, and beyond that there's only the uninhabited wilderness of **Southwest National Park** (www.parks.tas.gov.au), a World Heritage Area.

The spectacular **Tahune Forest Air Walk** ⓲ (tel: 1300-720 507; www.tahuneadventures.com.au; daily Oct–Mar 9am–5pm, Apr–Sept 10am–4pm), a 28km (17-mile) drive west, is a 600-metre (1,970ft) steel walkway high in the canopy, which gives a new perspective on life in the forest. Part of it is cantilevered out over the banks of the Huon River. Quieter, and just as alluring, is the **Hartz Mountains National Park**, where trails take a few minutes or several hours.

Pass through somnolent **Dover** and then turn inland to the **Hastings Caves and Thermal Springs** (tel: 1300-827 727; www.parks.tas.gov.au; daily Dec–Jan 9am–5pm, Feb–mid-Apr 10am–4pm, mid-Apr–Sept 10.30am–3.30pm). Bask in one and enjoy a guided tour of the other.

A dirt road leads to **Cockle Creek** ⓳, the most southerly point you can drive

to in Australia. Consecutive settlements failed at whaling, logging and mining; now it just attracts tourists. Walkers can take on the multi-day **South Coast Track**. Many just walk the two hours each way to **South Cape Bay** and back. And everyone else does the stroll to the bronze whale by the bay.

THE GORDON RIVER ROAD

Visitors can penetrate furthest into the World Heritage Area along the Gordon River Road to Strathgordon.

Follow the course of the Derwent north from Hobart and dawdle for a while in **New Norfolk**, a town with a lumpen paper mill but also scenic stretches of hop gardens and their associated oast houses. Look out for a pair of sturdy old inns and, in **St Matthews**, traces of the oldest church in the state, buried beneath all the subsequent renovations.

It's just a few kilometres to the blissful tranquillity of the **Salmon Ponds Heritage Hatchery and Garden** (tel: 03-6261 5663; www.salmonponds.com.au; daily 9am–4pm). Its history as a

A carved statue in Geeveston, where the principal industry is timber.

The Tahune Forest Airwalk.

The playground in Mount Field National Park has a wooden wombat.

Hiking the Overland Track.

breeding ground of early introduced species is interesting, but the main pleasure is in just strolling in the glorious gardens.

Not far along the Gordon River Road, **Mount Field National Park** (www. parks.tas.gov.au) ⑳ can get busy with day-trippers from Hobart, so be prepared to share the boardwalks to the most accessible sights including **Russell Falls** and, above it, **Horseshoe Falls**. The **Tall Trees** trail provides a first taste of the giants of the forest, and another hour's walk brings **Lady Barron Falls** into range. Go deeper into the park for Alpine uplands and the snow fields.

Junee Cave, in Maydena, is the entrance to an extensive karst system. Just beyond the village, after a bridge, take a track on the right which winds round to the **Styx Valley** ㉑. At **Big Tree Reserve**, a boardwalk loop skirts through some of the highest trees in the country, all *Eucalyptus regnans* or swamp gum. There have been long battles by conservationists to save these and others like them from the loggers;

the evidence is in scrawled rebuttals to the propaganda on the information boards erected by Forestry Tasmania.

Enjoy the long drive through wild mountain scenery to **Strathgordon**, perched at the end of **Lake Pedder**, and on for a final few kilometres to the engineering marvel of the **Gordon Dam** in all its grey concrete glory.

THE LYELL HIGHWAY

As the Lyell Highway from New Norfolk climbs up to the Central Plateau, look for hydroelectric activity, with power stations and old workers' camps at **Tarraleah** and **Bronte Park**. Fishing fans should turn right down the Marlborough Highway for **Great Lake**. It has amazing trout and a remarkable collection of shack communities. Otherwise continue to **Derwent Bridge** ㉒.

This is where hikers finish the 80km (50-mile) Overland Track at the visitor centre at the end of **Lake St Clair**. Casual visitors can embark on shorter walks, take a cruise up the lake, or combine the two by chugging to the far end and walking back. Make time

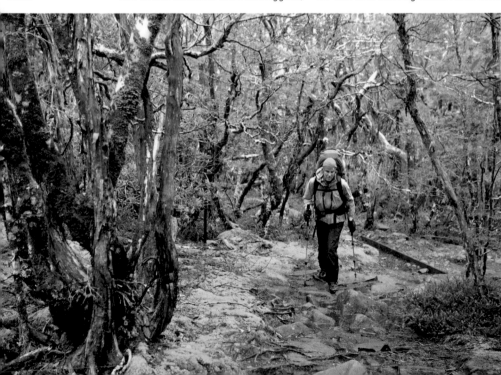

to inspect **The Wall**, a long-term project by sculptor Greg Duncan to carve a 100-metre (330ft) -long relief depicting the life and history of the Central Highlands (tel: 03-6289 1134; daily Sept–Apr 9am–5pm, May–Aug 9am–4pm).

The drive continues past access points to the **Franklin River** for kayakers and whitewater rafters, until the landscape changes from lush green hills to bleak brown and grey. Gold, and then copper, was discovered here in the late 1800s. Trees were lopped to fuel the smelters, and sulphurous outpourings put paid to any remaining vegetation. The land is now entirely denuded. It's bleak but also strangely compelling.

In the midst of all this sits **Queenstown ㉓**, a rough-and-ready mining town, which now receives a daily influx of tourists who arrive on the steam-drawn (at least for the last few kilometres) **West Coast Wilderness Railway** from Strahan on the west coast. They may take in the old-fashioned **Galley Museum** (1 Driffield Street; tel: 03-6471 1483; Oct–Apr Mon–Fri 9.30am–5.30pm, Sat–Sun 12.30–4.30pm, May–Sept Mon–Fri 9.30am–4.30pm, Sat–Sun 12.30–4.30pm) and the **Miners Siding** public sculpture, or maybe just have a drink in the historic **Empire Hotel**.

MACQUARIE HARBOUR

Strahan ㉔ (pronounced *strawn*) began life as a timber town, thrived on the copper that passed through and always supported a small fishing fleet. Now, however, it's driven by tourism; this is down to its position on **Macquarie Harbour.**

It's almost obligatory for visitors to take a cruise (World Heritage Cruises daily 9am; tel: 03-6471 7174; www.world heritagecruises.com.au; or Gordon River Cruises, daily 8.30am; tel: 03-6471 4300; www.gordonrivercruises.com.au), which includes a swing through **Hell's Gates** at the mouth of the harbour, a look at a fish farm and then a tramp around the ruins on **Sarah Island**.

Probably the toughest penal establishment in the colony, Sarah Island was for the worst recidivists. From

The Miners Siding, a sculpture in Queenstown.

The West Coast Wilderness Railway.

1822 they were put to work fashioning ships from the local Huon pine and had to suffer appalling living conditions for the 11 years the establishment existed before all convicts were transferred to Port Arthur.

The cruise continues on to the **Gordon River** and a stop for a walk through the rainforest. Back at Strahan look into the visitor centre, where, in a small theatre, the play *The Ship That Never Was* tells the story of Sarah Island (tel: 03-6471 7700; daily Sept–May 5.30pm).

The road north from Strahan passes the extensive **Henty Dunes**, which stretch for many kilometres behind Ocean Beach, and then turns inland to more mining towns. **Zeehan** is the most significant, having boomed in the 1900s on the back of silver. In those days the magnificent **Gaiety Theatre**, looking beautiful after an extensive restoration, could fill its 1,000 seats nightly with the biggest names of the era. The stimulating **West Coast Pioneers Museum** (Main Street; tel: 03-6471 6225; daily 9am–5pm) has extensive displays on mining, minerals and local history.

Walls of Jerusalem National Park.

CRADLE MOUNTAIN AND MOLE CREEK

Continue through Rosebery and Tullah before making for Cradle Valley. The first sighting of **Cradle Mountain** looming up across Dove Lake must rate alongside the first view of the Opera House in Sydney in the chart of magical travel moments; you've got a pretty good idea what it should look like but are still blown away by the real thing. Drink it in, then it's a matter of picking your walk. Most choose the **Dove Lake** circuit, which takes up to two hours, but there are plenty of other options, all outlined on the maps available at the visitor centre. Hardy hikers will tackle the 80km (50-mile) **Overland Track**.

If the weather closes in – and it often does – look around Waldheim, the lodge occupied by Gustav Weindorfer, who first campaigned to designate the area a national park.

Continuing eastwards along the edge of the Great Western Tiers, there is hiking to be done in the vehicle-free **Walls of Jerusalem National Park**, but it is not to be undertaken lightly.

Detour north for **Sheffield**, which has put itself on the tourist map by commissioning murals to cover every available wall; and maybe have a look at the wilfully eccentric **Tazmazia** and the associated **Village of Lower Crackpot** (500 Staverton Road; tel: 03-6491 1934; www.tasmazia.com.au; daily Nov–Apr 9am–5pm, May–Oct 10am–4pm), with its comical model houses.

Mole Creek Karst National Park is abundant with caves. Tours go into **Marakoopa Cave** (tel: 03-6363 5182; www.parks.tas.gov.au; daily 10am–4pm; call for tour times), which contains glow-worms, underground rivers and the superb Great Cathedral; and the smaller **King Solomon's Cave** (same details).

Chudleigh has an acclaimed honey farm, and once you've stopped for your sweet tooth you'll be in to **Deloraine** ㉖.

It's a pretty town on the banks of the Meander River, and a rewarding way of exploring it is to follow the trail of sculptures that winds along the main street and down by the riverbanks.

THE NORTH

The Bass Highway snakes its way north, but detour to **Latrobe** for its Victorian high street. **Devonport** ⓦ is the home port for the *Spirit of Tasmania* ferries that traverse the Bass Strait. The centre need not detain you, but the recently upgraded **Bass Strait Maritime Centre** (tel: 03-6424 7100; Tue–Sun 10am–4pm), formerly the Devonport Maritime Museum, is worth a visit.

The Bass Highway continues along the north coast to **Ulverstone**, a comfortable family destination with nice parks, and a smattering of Victoriana.

Industry hits you with a thud at **Burnie**, where the shell of a massive paper mill and the state's biggest container port dominate. The **Burnie Regional Museum**, formerly the Pioneer Village Museum (tel: 03-6430 5746; Mon–Fri 10am–3pm), with its reconstituted 1900 street scene, is impressive, as are some of the works in the **Burnie Regional Art Gallery** (tel: 03-6430 5875; www.burniearts. net; Mon–Fri 10am–4.30pm, Sat–Sun 1.30–4.30pm). And a short ride inland to **Fern Glade** provides a good chance of spotting platypus in the wild.

Wynyard has discreet appeal and **Table Cape** demands a visit in spring, when the tulip farm is in full flower, but the lighthouse and the views from it are worth a look at any time.

Possibly the finest bay is at **Boat Harbour Beach**, and its lovely relaxed atmosphere has remained despite the arrival of more and more beach houses and summer visitors.

Visitor favourite **Stanley** ㉘ is dominated by the Nut, a huge plug of volcanic rock at the end of a spit. You can walk or take the chairlift to the top if you don't mind the wind. Down below, Alexander Terrace has well-kept cottages, one of which was the original home of Joe Lyons, the first Tasmanian prime minister.

Cradle Mountain Lodge offers luxury accommodation on the edge of the national park.

Village of Lower Crackpot.

The Van Diemen's Land Company (VDL) was crucial to Stanley. The old company store can be found near the wharf, while the clifftop-situated **Highfield** (tel: 03-6458 1100; www.historic-highfield.com.au; daily 9.30am–4.30pm) was company HQ.

An incarnation of VDL still manages the **Woolnorth** estate that covers the state's northwestern tip. The only way to visit is on a tour (tel: 03-6452 1493; www.woolnorthtours.com.au; daily if enough interest; booking essential), taking in a wind farm placed to take full advantage of the Roaring Forties, and dramatic **Cape Grim**.

THE BASS STRAIT ISLANDS

King Island (www.kingisland.org.au) is best known for the cheese produced by **King Island Dairy**; there's a shop to visit but no tours, so try **Currie**, the main town (if a handful of streets warrants the term), with its quaint harbour where giant crabs and crayfish are landed. There's a small museum, too, just below the

lighthouse (Lighthouse Street; tel: 03-6462 1512; daily 2–4pm).

Ships have often come to grief here, but **Cape Wickham Lighthouse**, on the northern tip, has played its part in keeping the numbers down. At **Yellow Rock Beach**, wreckage from a paddle steamer can still be seen in the surf.

In the south there's the intriguing **Calcified Forest**, while the **Kelp Industries Centre** explains why tons of the stuff is hanging out to dry.

King Island is relatively flat and windswept, whereas **Flinders Island** (www.visitflindersisland.com.au) has some serious hills, culminating in **Mount Strzelecki**. The southern corner also has the immaculate sands of **Trousers Point** and **Fotheringate Beach**. The main town is **Whitemark**, but the important **Furneaux Museum** (Sat–Sun spring 1–5pm, winter 1–4pm; tel: 03-6359 8434 to confirm opening hours) is up at **Emita**. Many of the exhibits stem from the time of the forced exile of Tasmania's Aboriginal population in 1838, and the chapel at nearby **Wybalenna** is on the site of their settlement.

Strahan harbour with one of the Gordon River excursion boats.

THE OVERLAND TRACK

Tasmania's most famous hiking trail threads its way through the fabulous landscapes between Cradle Mountain and Lake St. Clair.

First blazed in the 1830s by surveyors, gold prospectors and fur-trappers, the Overland Track is Australia's most famous walk – a six-day traverse of Tasmania's central plateau through an ancient glacial landscape. About 9,000 hikers undertake the 65km (40-mile) journey from Cradle Mountain to Lake St Clair each year, carrying all their equipment and supplies both in and out.

The hike is not easy, but the rewards are spectacular and accessible to anybody reasonably fit and well prepared. For most local bushwalkers (and an increasing number are travelling here from overseas) completing the track is a rite of passage, an unforgettable expedition among stunted buttongrass moorlands, craggy snow-capped peaks, myrtle and sassafras forests, and crystalline cold-water tarns. Such is its popularity that a new online booking system and a A$200 high-season (Oct–May) charge on top of park entry fees, restricted numbers to 60 hikers per day. All hikers are required to start at Cradle Valley in the National Park's north, and finish at Cynthia Bay on Lake St Clair. This one-way traffic eases the congestion on the route and ensures that every hiker experiences the best of the Overland Track.

LODGINGS AND EQUIPMENT

Huts line the trail – seven on the main track; distances between each vary from 6.5km (4 miles) to 11km (7 miles) – although carrying a tent is essential in this World Heritage Area, with exposed escarpments subject to bitter weather. Hikers need equipment for all four seasons, regardless of when they are travelling – from sunglasses, sunblock and shirt collars, to thermals, waterproofs and a woollen beanie. Warm socks, gaiters and a good sleeping bag are also must-haves. A hiking fuel stove, medical kit and 1:100,000 map are essential. Thongs (flip-flops) are suggested for foot relief around the huts after a long day in heavy boots.

What to carry is a delicate balance between distance, time and weight. Most walkers spend five nights on the trail. It's essential to pack light, to pick each item of clothing carefully and take only what's necessary. Be sure to carry enough food and water for an extra day in case of unexpected delays. A tip for hiking dinners is to add fresh ingredients to basic carbohydrate (pasta, rice or couscous) dishes, such as a squeeze of lemon juice. Salt, pepper, curry powders and chilli are ideal – experienced trekkers often say that food cannot be flavoured spicy enough after a long walk through a cold and unforgiving climate.

One of the walk's highlights (apart from a side-trip up Mount Ossa, at 1,617 metres/5,305ft the island's highest peak) is the camaraderie to be found around the huts each night. Everybody on the walk is considered equal – regardless of age, nationality or occupation – since all share in the rigours and delights of the hike. It's an experience so detached from the daily trivialities of the world outside.

For bookings, see www.overlandtrack.com.au or www.parks.tas.gov.au, tel: 1300-827 727 or visit the Cradle Mountain and Lake St Clair National Park visitor centres. The website also gives details on accommodation, transport and park entry fees. Contact Tasmanian Travel Centres for information on tour operators that offer private guided trips.

View of Barn Bluff from the Overland Track.

📷 FREYCINET NATIONAL PARK

Wineglass Bay is the headline attraction, but there is plenty more to see; keen walkers could easily spend a few days here.

The Freycinet Peninsula is one of the most beautiful places in the world. The combination of mountains, forest, beaches and blisteringly blue sea, not to mention the abundant wildlife, is hard to match and impossible to beat. It's best to surrender to it and allow as much time as possible to take it all in. Pitch a tent just back from the beach and get close to nature (but not too close; secure food from inquisitive wallabies and wombats). Alternatively, follow the path to luxury and book into the Freycinet Lodge (tel: 03-6256 7222; www.freycinetlodge.com.au), inside the park boundary, for a couple of nights of hedonism. Settle on the balcony of your cabin and watch the scurrying animals in the undergrowth below.

In the warmer months the wild swimming is sensational, or you could take a sea-kayaking tour with Freycinet Adventures (tel: 03-6257 0500; www.freycinetadventures.com.au). Above all, though, this is a place for exploring on foot. The Wineglass Bay Track is a must, whether it's just a climb up to the saddle for the view, or perhaps as part of a longer trek, which could take in Mount Graham or Mount Freycinet. People with mobility problems or young children can still take on the shorter walks, some with views of Wineglass Bay, and trail runners will be in heaven. Another option is to join one of the boat trips around the peninsula, which embark from Coles Bay.

The bright orange deposits on boulders along the shoreline in Freycinet and all along the east coast are in fact a type of rock lichen. They are a complex mixture of fungi and algae which extract nutrients from the rocks they're attached to.

The waters around the Freycinet Peninsula are rich in marine life, as well as being incredibly beautiful.

The Cape Tourville walk, which affords partial views of Wineglass Bay, is an easy 20-minute stroll around the lighthouse. While you walk, keep your eyes and ears open for unusual birds. Freycinet's avian visitors include yellow-tailed black cockatoos, and the rare white-bellied sea eagle.

Sunset at Coles Bay.

Visitor facilities

The **Visitor Centre** (tel: 03-6256 7004; www.parks.tas.gov.au) is just a few hundred metres inside the park on the right-hand side. This is where park permits can be purchased and maps and guides picked up. Even those who have already paid their park fees will find a stop rewarding, as there are displays about many aspects of the park's history and geology, as well as useful pointers towards the weather and the state of the various walks.

One of the walks starts immediately behind the visitor centre: the Great Oyster Bay walk is a 5-minute amble down to Richardson's Beach, where the cormorants play and the Hazards loom above.

The centre is also the place to register for the campsites, which need to be booked by ringing in advance. Indeed some, such as those at Honeymoon Bay (open only at Easter and in the summer), are so popular that a ballot system is used to allocate spaces. There are powered sites for caravans and RVs, and unpowered ones for tents. Electric barbecue facilities are provided at various points as all campfires are banned, although portable fuel stoves are allowed.

...thing beats that first view of Wineglass Bay which ...mes as a generous reward for the steep climb up to the ...ddle between Mount Amos and Mount Mason.

...can take 20 minutes to walk to the end of Wineglass ...y, and then the choice must be made whether to return ... the saddle or Hazards Beach.

The 30km (19-mile) Freycinet Peninsula Circuit takes at least two days to complete.

Beachside pool at Bondi.

AUSTRALIA

TRAVEL TIPS

TRANSPORT

Getting there **320**
  By air **320**
Getting around **320**
  By air **320**
  From the airport **321**
  By bus **321**
  By train................................. **322**
  By sea................................... **323**
  Taxis **323**
  Motorcycles and bicycles...... **324**
  By car **325**

A – Z

Accommodation **326**
Admission charges **326**
Budgeting for your trip **326**
Climate..................................... **327**
Crime and safety...................... **327**
Customs regulations................. **328**
Disabled travellers................... **328**
Electricity **328**
Embassies and consulates **328**
Emergencies **329**
Health and medical care.......... **329**
Internet **329**
LGBTQ travellers...................... **330**

Maps.. **330**
Media....................................... **330**
Money...................................... **330**
Opening hours.......................... **331**
Postal services......................... **331**
Public holidays......................... **331**
Religion **331**
Student travellers **331**
Telephones............................... **331**
Time zones............................... **332**
Toilets...................................... **332**
Tourist information **332**
Useful addresses **332**
Visas and passports................. **333**
Weights and measures **333**
What to wear **333**
Women travellers...................... **333**

FURTHER READING

General..................................... **334**
History...................................... **334**
Natural history.......................... **334**
Travel....................................... **334**
Aboriginal Australia **335**
Australian language.................. **335**
Fiction **335**
Children's books **336**
Other Insight Guides **336**

TRANSPORT

By air

Almost all foreign visitors travel to Australia by air. Brisbane, Cairns, Melbourne and Sydney are the major tourism gateways, with daily flights arriving from Asia, Europe and North America. Less frequent flights also arrive directly in Adelaide, Darwin, Cairns and Perth. More than 40 international airlines currently fly to and from Australia (see Major airlines list).

Getting to Australia can be expensive. Fares vary widely, so seek advice from a knowledgeable travel agent before buying a ticket. A departure tax is included in the cost of your international ticket, so it no longer has to be paid at the airport when you leave.

There may be price advantages in pre-booking your domestic travel along with your flight to Australia, and since the launch of budget carriers Virgin Australia, Jetstar and Tigerair (see Domestic flights), competition has lowered domestic fares considerably. The early birds often secure the best deals. Special pre-booked packages tend to incorporate inexpensive hotel and car rental rates.

Qantas (www.qantas.com) offers a good service to Australia (it also operates Qantas Vacations: www. qantasvacations.com). Tickets can be booked by calling 1800-227 4500 (in the US and Canada), 0800 964 432 (in the UK), or 0800 808 767 in New Zealand.

Major international airlines flying to Australia

Air Canada
www.aircanada.com
Air China
www.airchina.com.au
Air New Zealand
www.airnewzealand.com.au
British Airways
www.britishairways.com
Cathay Pacific Airways
www.cathaypacific.com
Emirates Airlines
www.emirates.com
Etihad
www.etihad.com
Gulf Air
www.gulfair.com
Japan Airlines
www.jal.co.jp/en
Malaysia Airlines
www.malaysiaairlines.com
Qantas
www.qantas.com.au
Singapore Airlines
www.singaporeair.com
South African Airways
www.flysaa.com
Thai Airways International
www.thaiairways.com.au
United Airlines
www.united.com
Virgin Atlantic
www.virginatlantic.com

By air

Australia's national domestic airline is **Qantas** (www.qantas.com.au), with competition, on most routes, from **Virgin Australia** (tel: 136 789; www. virginaustralia.com). Qantas operate a budget regional airline, **Jetstar** (www.jetstar.com), and other options include **TigerAir** (www.tigerair. au), which is now owned by Virgin, and Regional Express (Rex; www.rex. com.au), which serves smaller airports in many areas. Each of these airlines operates regular scheduled flights between all capital cities and regional centres throughout Australia. Both Jetstar and Virgin

Australia operate from Australian cities to a number of Asian and Pacific destinations. **Qantas** also operates regular scheduled flights between all capital cities and regional centres throughout Australia.

Although many domestic flights are often fully booked, cheap flights are regularly to be found by booking in advance. All the airlines offer cheaper deals for the first few seats with the rate increasing as the aircraft fills up. Conditions can be onerous, however, with checked baggage bringing additional fees on some ticket bands, strict adherence to weight limits with hefty penalty rates for transgressors, and reduced flexibility to change flights with the lower fare bands. Some of the best deals are to be had if you are prepared to fly at off-peak times or book via the internet. Some airlines add a fee for payment by credit cards. If you catch a budget flight, make sure it is travelling to the airport you want to go to – Melbourne has two airports, the main one at Tullamarine and Avalon Airport, which is closer to Geelong.

Some of the best deals include both air travel and accommodation outside the main holiday seasons – check with airlines for special offers.

Each state is serviced by regional airlines such as QantasLink and

⊙ Flying times

Sydney–Melbourne, 1 hr 20 mins
Sydney–Perth, 4 hrs 50 mins
Melbourne–Adelaide, 1 hr 20 mins
Melbourne–Canberra, 1 hr
Brisbane–Sydney, 1 hr 25 mins
Brisbane–Melbourne, 2 hrs 20 mins
Adelaide–Alice Springs, 2 hrs
Perth–Adelaide, 3 hrs
Canberra–Sydney, 50 mins

Rex, providing access to remote destinations.

From the airport

Sydney

Situated approximately 8km (5 miles) from the Central Business District (CBD), Sydney Airport (www.sydneyairport.com.au) is best reached by car (approx 20 minutes), taxi (roughly A$45–55 one way) or train. Taking just 10 minutes to the domestic terminals and 12 minutes to the international, trains run from Central Station up to eight times an hour on weekdays, and four times an hour on weekends; for exact times and information visit www.airportlink.com.au, or tel: 02-8337 8417. Bus (approx 40 minutes) Route 400 runs between Bondi Junction and Eastgardens via Sydney Airport, and Route 420 runs between Eastgardens and Burwood via Sydney Airport.

Canberra

Canberra airport (www.canberraairport.com.au) is 7km (4 miles) from the city centre. An Airport Express bus charges A$12 each way; other bus companies run regular services into town too. The taxi fare is about A$25.

Melbourne

Melbourne's Tullamarine airport (www.melbourneairport.com.au) is 22km (14 miles) from the city centre. A taxi costs about A$50–60; for about half that price, the Skybus departs every half-hour (you can pre-book tickets at www.skybus.com.au). Avalon Airport (www.avalonairport.com.au) is 55km (34 miles) from the city on the road to Geelong. Bus transfers are available to/from Southern Cross Station in the city.

Adelaide

The dual international/domestic airport (www.adelaideairport.com.au), 8km (5 miles) from the city centre, has a Skylink shuttle bus, which runs about every 30 minutes, stopping at major hotels (tel: 1300-311 108; www.skylink.com). Adelaide Metro runs buses through the city to the airport seven days a week from 4.50am to midnight. A taxi into the city centre costs about A$25.

Brisbane

The domestic and international airport terminals (www.bne.com.au) lie 16km (10 miles) from the city centre. Passengers can expect to pay $45–55

(one way) for a trip to/from the airport from/to Brisbane City in a taxi. Con-x-ion (www.con-x-ion.com) provide a shuttle bus transfer service. At any time when flights are arriving or departing a combination of bus and fast rail transport options provides easy connections between Brisbane Airport, Brisbane city and the Gold Coast. The hub is the city coach/rail terminus, and the 'TransLink' service (tel: 131 230) or the information desks at the airport will help you identify the easiest and most convenient way to get from A to B.

Darwin

Darwin airport (www.darwinairport.com.au) is 12km (7.5 miles) from the CBD, and a taxi costs around A$25–$30 (plus A$4 exit when leaving). Darwin City Airport Shuttle Service (www.darwincityairportshuttleservice.com.au) operates shuttle bus transfers to and from the Darwin International Airport from city hotels and accommodation 24 hours 7 days per week.

Perth

Taxis from the domestic and international airports (www.perthairport.com.au) to Perth city cost around A$45 and A$35 respectively and to Fremantle A$75. TransPerth (tel: 13 62 13) operates bus Route 380 (named after the Airbus A380 and complete with dedicated luggage rucks) daily between the Elizabeth Quay Bus Station in Perth city centre and T1 and T2. Bus Route 40 operates 7 days a week between Elizabeth Quay Bus Station and T3/T4 via Great Eastern Highway, offering the most direct route between Perth Airport and Perth City.

Hobart

A taxi fare to the city from Hobart International Airport (www.hobartairport.com.au) should cost approximately A$45–50. SkyBus (www.skybus.com.au) provides fast, frequent and low cost airport transfers to Hobart.

By bus

Long-distance buses

Competition between the major bus companies means many bargains are available when travelling by bus. The biggest company, with the most services, is **Greyhound Australia** (tel: 1300-473 946; www.greyhound.com.au).

The standard of buses is high, with most having reclining seats,

⊘ Bargains by bus

If you plan extensive bus travel in Australia, several discount plans offer unlimited travel within various time frames. There are also set-duration and set-distance fares.

seats for the disabled, videos, washrooms and air conditioning. Smoking is prohibited on all buses. Bus terminals are well equipped with toilets, showers and shops, and are generally very clean. However, you should be aware that distances are enormous in Australia, so think twice before hopping, say, onto the Brisbane–Cairns leg, because it takes more than 24 hours.

Greyhound has various money-saving passes, including ones that are based on kilometres travelled.

There are many other bus companies in Australia, offering a variety of transport/hotel packages departing regularly from capital cities. Prices are per day inclusive of bus travel, accommodation and various day tours or driver commentary. Some of the more adventurous routes are taken by deluxe four-wheel-drive vehicles, incorporating camping, and are accompanied by a cook.

Sydney

Sydney has an extensive bus service with main termini at Circular Quay, Wynyard and Central Station. For all route information visit the Transport Infoline website: www.transportnsw.info, or tel: 131 500. At Circular Quay there is an information kiosk at the centre of the row of bus stops, on the opposite side of the street (Alfred Street) from the ferry wharfs. Be aware that during peak hours, many buses only accept pre-paid tickets.

City Sightseeing operates two buses along the main tourist routes: the Sydney Explorer, which covers the city, and the Bondi Explorer, which takes in the eastern suburbs. More information is available at www.city-sightseeing.com.

Canberra

In Canberra, Action bus services are adequate and modern. Plan your journey online using the trip planner at www.transport.act.gov.au or call 131 710. It is possible to purchase daily and off-peak daily bus passes that allow unlimited rides on the buses.

⊙ Sydney transport and passes

The State Transit Authority operates the buses in Sydney, and **CityRail** the trains. Ferries are run by **Sydney Ferries**. For information on buses, trains and ferries from 6am–10pm daily, tel: 131 500, or check www.transportnsw. info. The front of the White Pages phone book also has information on Sydney's transport.

Whether you want to see the sights of Sydney or explore the Blue Mountains, Southern Highlands or Newcastle, it is easy on public transport. To travel on trains, buses, ferries and light rail, all you need is an **Opal card** (www. opal.com.au). You can also buy a My Multi Day Pass in three section-based fare bands. Buy these passes from locations and stores displaying the transport symbol.

Melbourne

Public Transport Victoria or the PTV, Melbourne's public transport system is one of Australia's best. Trams form the basis of the system. There are about 750 trams venturing as far as 20km (12 miles) out of the city. Buses are the secondary form of public transport, often taking over when trams are out of service. Trains connect an underground city loop to the outer suburbs.

The Public Transport Victoria hub at Southern Cross Station can supply all the information you need about public transport. You can also buy a myki smart travel card or myki visitor pack here, and pick up timetables and maps. A Free Tram Zone was recently introduced in Melbourne CBD. It includes the area from the iconic Queen Victoria Market, across to Victoria Harbour in Docklands, up to Spring Street and over to Flinders Street Station and Federation Square. The City Circle Tram runs approximately every 12 minutes (Thu–Sat 10am–9pm, Sun–Wed 10am–6pm).

Adelaide

A free City Connector is an easy way to get around the city. The Connector buses travel in both directions within Adelaide City and North Adelaide, and you can hop on and off at various stops. It operates on two loops, an inner city loop and an extended North Adelaide loop. Routes 98A and 98C link the city and North Adelaide and routes 99A and 99C connect the city's main destinations, both run every 30 minutes daily.

All information regarding the Adelaide transport system is available from the Adelaide Metro InfoCentre on the corner of King William and Currie streets, tel: 08-8210 1000 or 1300-311 108; www. adelaidemetro.com.au.

Brisbane

For information on city buses in Brisbane, go to the Translink office in the Brisbane Visitor Information Centre, on Queen Street Mall or visit www.translink.com.au. The prepaid Go Card can be used on buses, trains, CityCats and ferries, and is available from the Translink office. Apart from the regular city buses, there are **Cityxpress** buses, which connect certain suburbs to the city, and **Rockets**, which are peak-hour commuter services. A free City Loop bus connects many of the key sites around the city centre.

Darwin and Alice Springs

Both Darwin and Alice Springs have town bus services that connect accommodation precincts with the CBD. **Darwinbus** (tel: 08-8924 7666) has Flextrip card for $20 for 10 trips, and weekly cards also for $20. In Alice Springs, there are no bus services on Sundays and public holidays. The Alice Springs Bus Guide is available from Railway Terrace, near the Coles supermarket. Comfortable, frequent and fast buses connect the three central attractions – Darwin, Alice Springs and Uluru.

Greyhound Australia (tel: 1300-3868 0998; www.greyhound.com.au) runs daily between Alice Springs and Yulara (Ayers Rock). It is 460km (286 miles) each way.

Perth

The Free Transit Zone operating in the Perth city area allows free travel on any bus – look for the red FTZ logo at bus stops to identify the travel boundaries. Free CAT (Central Area Transit) buses also operate in Perth, Fremantle and Joondalup city centres. The 'Perth Tram' (actually a bus) operates a circuit of tourist attractions. For maps and on-the-spot information about all forms of public transport, a Transperth office is in the Plaza Arcade (off the Hay Street Mall), tel: 136 213; www. transperth.wa.gov.au.

High-speed ferries travel from Perth, Fremantle and Hillarys to Rottnest Island.

Tasmania

Metro Tasmania (www.metrotas.com.au) runs an extensive network of bus services in Hobart, and they are an easy way to reach sights that are more than a casual stroll from the town centre, such as Hobart's beaches, the Taroona Shot Tower, the Cadbury Factory and Cascade Brewery. Buses run Monday–Thursday 6.30am to 10.30pm and until midnight on Friday and Saturday. There is a limited service on Sunday and holidays.

By train

A wide network of modern railways operates from coast to coast. The principal lines follow the east and south coasts, linking the cities of Cairns, Brisbane, Sydney, Melbourne, Adelaide and Alice Springs. The most comprehensive service is operated by **Countrylink**: reservations are required; tel: 132 232; www.countrylink.info.

The line between Sydney and Perth via Adelaide is the famous **Indian-Pacific** run (linking the Indian Ocean to the Pacific Ocean). On its 4,352km (2,700-mile) journey, taking 65 hours (three nights), the train crosses the treeless Nullarbor Plain, with the longest stretch of straight track in the world. Comforts include an observation lounge and bar. If money is no object you can travel in the historic Prince of Wales carriage, complete with wood panelling and cathedral glass doors.

Other popular scenic rail journeys run by Great Southern Railway (tel: 1800-703 357; www.greatsouthernrail.com.au) include the **Overland**, an overnight journey between Melbourne and Adelaide; the **Ghan**,

⊙ Melbourne transport

For information on all public transport in Melbourne visit the Public Transport Victoria hub centrally located at Southern Cross Station (open Mon–Fri 7am–7pm, Sat–Sun 9am–6pm; www.ptv.vic.gov.au).

⏀ Brisbane ferries

Brisbane ferries – City Cats – provide river crossings to Kangaroo Point, South Bank Parklands and along the river to other locations.

They depart from Eagle Street Pier and Edward Street on the corner of the Botanic Gardens. They are fast, efficient and inexpensive.

which runs straight through the middle of the country, from Adelaide in South Australia through Alice Springs and on to Darwin (the two-night, 3,000km/1,864-mile trip can be broken in Katherine for short sightseeing tours by boat or helicopter, and Alice Springs for longer stopovers); and launching in December 2019, the **Great Southern** between Adelaide and Brisbane via the Grampians, Canberra and the NSW coast.

For travel in Western Australia it is possible to take a bus or train to the southern and southwest regions in the area bounded by Kalbarri, Meekathara, Kalgoorlie, Esperance, Albany and Augusta. For more details contact **Transwa**, tel: 08-9326 2600 or 1300-662 205, or visit www.transwa.wa.gov.au.

Tickets

The classes available are first, holiday and economy. First-class passengers have sleeping berths with showers in their cabin, a first-class restaurant and lounge. Other classes get aeroplane-style reclining seats and a buffet car.

For train-travel enthusiasts, an Australian rail pass (www.australiarail-pass.com) is a good option for covering massive distances cheaply while travelling throughout Australia. The best value Australian rail passes are the Discovery Pass, the Queensland Coastal Pass and the Queensland Explorer Pass.

Sydney

Trains are the most time-efficient way to navigate Sydney. With a fairly frequent service, most of Sydney's main areas are covered, including the central 'City Circle' stations – Central, Town Hall, Wynyard, Circular Quay, St James and Museum. Most do not run between midnight and 4.30am, when a **Nightrider** bus service takes over.

The **Airport link** trains run about every 10 minutes between the city and the domestic and international terminals, and the journey to Sydney's Central Station takes about 15 minutes.

Canberra

Aside from the new Great Southern (see above), there are no train services in Canberra.

Melbourne

The city has an extensive train service, with all lines radiating out from the central Flinders Street Station. The public transport information centre (PTV), Southern Cross Station (tel: 1800-800 007) provides timetables and maps and sells tickets (also valid on city buses and trams). Apart from the underground city loop, stations are above ground. Train services on most lines depart every 15 or 20 minutes on weekdays, and every 20 to 30 minutes on weekends.

Adelaide

Train services are limited and are mostly used by locals to get out to far-flung suburbs. Generally speaking, you will need to rely on other forms of transport in Adelaide. One exception is the tram route linking Victoria Square in the city to the popular beach-side suburb of Glenelg, which tends to get quite busy in the summer months.

Brisbane

The Queensland Rail City (formerly **Citytrain**) services are very efficient. They all pass through the city stations of Roma Street, Central and Brunswick on their way out to the suburbs. The Translink information on railway services is available at the Visitor Information Centre at the former Regent Cinema in the Queen Street Mall (or call 13 12 30). There are tickets that enable unlimited travel in one day.

Darwin

Aside from the Ghan, there are no city trains serving Darwin.

Perth

Five train lines service the Perth area. Wellington Street is Perth's central station, with an underground terminal for the nearby Mandurah line.

Hobart

Regular passenger rail services ceased in Tasmania in the 1980s,

but there are a few tourist/heritage railways operating in the state. Visit www.discovertasmania.com.au and www.donriverrailway.com.au for more information.

By sea

After arriving in Australia, a number of the international cruise lines continue around the coastline at a leisurely pace.

Day-trips and cruises operate between the mainland and the Great Barrier Reef. Six-day cruises run from Cairns to Cape York. The coral-fringed Whitsunday Islands are one of the best cruising and yachting locations in Australia (rent yachts from operators at Airlie Beach – the motto is, if you can drive a car, you can sail a yacht). River cruises and houseboat rentals are available on major rivers such as the Murray, or the Myall Lakes and the Murray River.

The only regular maritime services are the passenger and car ferries called *Spirit of Tasmania I* and *II*, operating between Melbourne and Devonport. The trip from Victoria can be rough and takes about 11 hours. Tel: 1800-634 906 (in Australia) or see www.spiritoftasmania.com.au.

Taxis

In several states, including NSW and Victoria, it is compulsory to prepay taxi fares between 10pm and 5am. 'Silver' taxis, and other premier services are more expensive than standard taxis.

Sydney

All taxis are metered, so do not ride unless the meter is on. There is an initial hiring charge (called 'flag fall'), then a set rate per kilometre thereafter. Between 10pm and 6am, this rate increases by 20 percent. A phone booking costs extra. There may be additional charges for road, bridge, ferry, tunnel and airport tolls. For information on taxis in NSW see the Taxi Council of NSW website, www.nswtaxi.org.au.
Premier Cabs: tel: 1300 795 608; www.premiercabs.com.au
Taxis Combined: tel: 133 300
Legion Cabs: tel: 131 451; www.legioncabs.com.au
RSL Cabs: tel: 02-9581 1111; www.rslcabs.com.au
Silver Service: tel: 133 100; www.silverservice.com.au

◉ Sydney ferries and cruises

Weather permitting, which it usually is, ferries are by far the most picturesque way of travelling around Sydney. Departing from the wharfs at Circular Quay, all tickets and timetables can be found at the Sydney ferries office.

The trip to Manly is the longest ferry run, covering 11km (7 miles) in 30 minutes. The alternative **Jetcat** service offers the same trip in half the time for slightly more money. There are currently temporary timetables in place for both services while the east side of Manly Wharf is redeveloped. Visit www.transportnsw.info for exact times.

Ferries are a great way of getting to Taronga Zoo, Kirribilli and Watsons Bay, not to mention a good opportunity to see the harbour, bridge and Opera House from all angles.

The **Rivercat**, a high-speed catamaran, cruises all the way up the Parramatta River.

Harbour cruises are a great way to relax while seeing Sydney off dry land. Daily cruises start at 10.30am and depart from Wharf Four. With comfy seating and unlimited tea and biscuits, these STA cruises are less expensive than private options and the commentary provides an interesting addition to the scenic backdrop.

In addition, there are companies that operate water taxis on the harbour. The price depends on the distance and time of day. **Water Taxis Combined:** tel: 02-9555 8888; www.watertaxis.com.au; **Yellow Water Taxis:** tel: 1300-138 840, www.yellowwatertaxis.com.au.

Canberra

All taxis in Canberra are metered. Between 9pm and 6am, the rate goes up. For more information, contact **ACT Cabs** (tel: 02-6280 0077; www.actcabs.com.au) or try **Canberra Elite Taxis** (tel: 132 227; www.canberraelite.com.au).

Melbourne

Melbourne's transport system tends to curl up and go to sleep around midnight, after which taxis are the only form of transport available. Try **13 Cabs**, tel: 132 227; www.13cabs.com.au; or **Silver Top Taxis**, tel: 131 008; www.silvertop.com.au.

Adelaide

There are a number of taxi services available. **Adelaide Independent Taxi Service**, tel: 132 211; www.aitaxis.com.au; **Suburban Taxi**, tel: 131 008; www.suburbantaxis.com.au; **Yellow Cabs**, tel: 132 227; www.yellowcab.com.au.

Brisbane

The city's officially recognised services are **Yellow Cabs** (tel: 131 924; www.yellowcab.com.au) and **Black and White Cabs** (tel: 133 222; www.blackandwhitecabs.com.au). Both charge a booking fee, with a standard fixed flag fall weekdays 7am–7pm, and a standard rate per km. After-hours flag fall is higher.

Darwin

Darwin has a couple of taxi companies: **Darwin Radio Taxi** (tel: 131 008; www.131008.com) and **Blue Taxi Company** (tel: 138 294; www.bluetaxi.com.au).

Perth

Hail taxis on the street, find them at a rank, or phone **Black and White** (tel: 133 222; www.blackandwhitecabs.com.au) or **Swan** (tel: 131 330; www.swantaxis.com.au), for up to four passengers. Black and White also have maxicabs (up to 10 passengers) and a service for the disabled (tel: 133 222 for these). Rates are reasonable: a small flag fall charge followed by a rate per kilometre.

Hobart

Taxis can be hired in the street if their vacant sign is lit. All cabs use meters and tipping is not necessary. **United Taxis** (tel: 133 222; www.unitedtaxistas.com.au) will connect you to taxi companies in most of the major towns in Tasmania, including Hobart.

Motorcycles and bicycles

Both are available for hire throughout Australia. Thoughtfully designed systems of bicycle paths provide good views or access to tourist sites – a pleasant, healthy and environmentally friendly alternative to the city bus tour. Helmets are compulsory for bicycles and motorbikes.

Sydney

Bonza Bike Tours (www.bonzabiketours.com) offers 1- to 5-hour tours of the city from A\$29, as well as bike hire. A range of mountain, hybrid and children's bikes, including dragsters, choppers and tandems, can be hired at **Sydney Olympic Park** (www.sydneyolympicpark.com.au). *Cycling Around Sydney* by Bruce Ashley is a useful guide available from book and bike shops.

Canberra

Cycling is perhaps the most pleasant choice for sightseeing in Canberra, as the terrain is flat and bike paths are extensive. There's a **share-a-bike** operation (www.shareabike.com.au), or to hire a bike for a while, try **Cycle Canberra** (www.cyclecanberra.com.au/bikehirecanberra). Bicycles can be hired by the hour, by the day or by the week. If you intend hiring a bike, make sure to get a copy of the *Canberra Cycleways* map from the tourist office or bookshops.

Melbourne

Melbourne is fairly flat, which affords the cyclist a number of good long tracks. Bike paths lie along the Yarra River, the Maribyrnong and the Merri Creek. For general cycling information, contact **Bicycle Network Victoria** at 4/246 Bourke Street, tel: 03-8376 8888; www.bicyclenetwork.com.au. **Melbourne Bike Share** (www.melbournebikeshare.com.au) has docking stations around the city and, for a small fee, bikes are available for sightseeing. Helmets are compulsory, however, so go equipped or buy a cheap one from a local store.

Adelaide

Running alongside the Torrens River in Adelaide is the 35km (22-mile) Linear Park Bike and Walking Track, one of the best in Australia. You can hire bikes from **Linear Park Bike Hire**, tel: 08-7424 7677. The Adelaide Council provides a **free bike hire** service (tel: 08-8168 9999; www.bikesa.asn.au/adelaidefreebikes; daily during daylight hours).

Brisbane

Brisbane City Council has built more than 500km (310 miles) of cycleways across the city. The riverside Bicentennial Bikeway, from the CBD along Coronation Drive to Toowong, is one of the most pleasant. Maps of popular cycleways can be found on the council's website, www.brisbane. qld.gov.au. Grabbing a steed from the **CityCycle** (www.citycycle.com.au; courtesy helmets available) bike rental scheme is a good way to explore. Or hire a bike from **BikeObsession** (www.bikeobsession.com.au).

Darwin

Grab a **Spinway** (www.spinwaynt.com.au) bike from various locations. Bike tours can be arranged through **Darwin Bike Tours** (www.darwinbiketours.com). Some backpacker hotels, and a few five-star hotels offer their guests cycle hire. There are plenty of cycle tracks; especially good is the one to East Point around Fannie Bay. Or, if it's too hot to pedal, you can hire scooters. Try **Darwin Scooter Hire**, 9 Daly Street (tel: 08-8941 2434). Small 50cc scooters are very popular for running out to the beaches around Darwin.

Perth

Cycle paths have been developed all around Perth, alongside the freeway and coast, into the hills and cross-country. The **WA Bicycle Network** (www.transport.wa.gov.au/cycling) is a useful source of information. Maps are available from bike shops. **All About Bikes** (on the corner of Riverside Drive and Plain Street, tel: 08-9221 2665; www.aboutbikehire. au) rents bikes, electric bikes, tandems and quadcycles.

Hobart

Hobart Bike Hire (www.hobartbikehire. com.au) offers a wide range of bikes, including electric steeds. Tasmania's longest-dedicated cycleway is the 15km (9-mile) Intercity Cycleway in Hobart. The bike club **Bicycle Tasmania** (www.biketas.org.au) has all the information you'll need.

By car

Car hire

By international standards, renting a car in Australia is expensive. The big three rental companies are **Avis**, **Hertz** and **Budget**, whose rates are just about identical. **Thrifty** and **Europcar** are also players in the market. The small outfits are usually much cheaper and offer special deals, but they may not offer all the services of the major companies – which can be useful. These include discounts for pre-booking overseas,

and the ability to return the car to another city at no extra charge. Be aware that many rental cars have manual, rather than automatic, gears (the latter are pricier).

The big three have offices in almost every town, as well as at airports and rail terminals. They offer unlimited kilometre rates in the city, but when travelling in the Outback, rates are usually per kilometre. Compulsory third-party insurance is included in car rentals, but collision damage waiver is an add-on. More comprehensive insurance plans are available for an additional fee, or your travel insurance may cover them. Most companies have 25 as their minimum driver age, or will charge a premium for drivers aged between 21 and 25.

Since driving a conventional vehicle off sealed roads may invalidate your insurance, four-wheel drive (4WD) cars are expensive but worth considering for safe Outback touring. Camper vans are popular, especially in Tasmania; they aren't cheap, however, and it might work out more economical to rent a regular car and stay at budget hotels.

Motoring advice

If you do opt to explore Australia by car, keep in mind that distances are often huge and towns may be few and far between. Many visitors on short-term trips opt to fly between major cities.

The major highways linking capital cities are all sealed and of a good standard, but you don't have to go far to find yourself on dirt roads. In remote areas such as Cape York and the Kimberley, most 4WDs travel in pairs or teams, to assist one another when bogged.

If you're travelling around the Outback independently, you must constantly remind yourself that you're in frontier country. Do plenty of research and planning before you head off. Carrying adequate water, notifying people of your intentions,

⊘ Basic motoring rules

Australians drive on the left. The law requires you to keep your seat belt fastened at all times, whether driver or passenger.
Overseas licences are valid throughout Australia.

using reliable vehicles and protecting yourself from sunburn should be high on your list. If you do break down, always stay with your vehicle.

Independent travellers should be aware that significant tracts of the Outback are designated as Aboriginal land, and a permit may be required to enter them.

The speed limit in a built-up area is 60kph (37mph) and sometimes 50kph (31mph) or 40kph (25mph) in suburban residential areas; in the country it is usually 100kph (62mph), unless otherwise signposted. Darwin has the most open roads in the country. Beyond city limits there is a maximum speed limit of 130kph (81mph).

Drink driving is a major problem. There is random breath testing for alcohol in most states. If you exceed 0.05 percent blood-alcohol level, a hefty fine and loss of licence are automatic.

Fuel comes in super, unleaded, super-unleaded, LPG (gas) and diesel. It is becoming more expensive in remote country areas.

Each state has an Automobile Association that offers excellent maps and literature. For a small membership fee, they also provide a free, highly recommended, nationwide emergency breakdown service.

Automobile associations

Sydney: National Roads and Motorists' Association (NRMA), 74–6 King Street, tel: 132 132 or 02-9292 8292; www.nrma.com.au
Canberra: National Roads and Motorists Association (NRMA), ACT Woden, 6/17 Neptune Street, tel: 02-6285 2811 ACT 2600; road assistance 13 1111; www.nrma.com.au
Melbourne: Royal Automobile Club of Victoria (RACV), 501 Bourke Street, tel: 131 111 or 03-9944 8888; www.racv.com.au
Adelaide: Royal Automobile Association of South Australia (RAA), 41 Hindmarsh Square, Adelaide, tel: 131 111; www.raa.com.au
Brisbane: Royal Automobile Club of Queensland (RACQ), 2649 Logan Road, Eight Mile Plains, tel: 1319 05; www.racq.com.au
Darwin: Automobile Association of the Northern Territory (AANT), 2/14 Knuckey Street, Darwin, tel: 131 111 or 08-8925 5901; www.aant.com.au
Perth: Royal Automobile Club of Western Australia Inc. (RAC WA), 832 Wellington Street, West Perth, tel: 131 703; www.rac.com.au

A

Accommodation

The standard of accommodation in Australia is high. Note that Sydney's hotels are significantly more expensive than anywhere else in Australia, with the possible exception of Perth. Serviced apartments are popular, especially in the cities, as are Airbnb options.

Australia has been slow off the mark in developing ultra-luxury lodges on the New Zealand model. However, a number of signature properties have sprung up around the country, including Saffire in Tasmania's Freycinet region, Southern Ocean Lodge on Kangaroo Island, and Longitude 131° near Uluru. Expect rates somewhere north of A$1,000 a night.

At the opposite end of the scale, there is an excellent choice of backpacker budget accommodation available (for example, Darwin, NT). Victoria Street in Sydney's Kings Cross has a score of hostels; it's also the place to network with other travellers to arrange lifts, buy cheap flights, or buy a car for an extended road odyssey around Australia. Log onto www.tntmagazine.com for more information.

Over the past decade, the choice of accommodation available in wilderness areas has increased significantly. In addition to camping, properties such as Ramada Eco Beach outside Broome or Wildman Wilderness Lodge near Kakadu let you experience these pristine areas without sacrificing your creature comforts.

For a holiday with a difference, you can stay as a paying guest with Australian families in a private home or on a working farm.

B&Bs come and go, so the best source of current information is the

Bed and Breakfast and Farmstay Australia (BBFA); visit www.australian-bedandbreakfast.com.au covering more than 1,000 B&Bs and Farmstays. The Farmstays include everything from small dairy farms in the hills to vast grain farming and sheep- and cattle-grazing properties. Also check out options on **Airbnb** (www.airbnb.com.au).

Admission charges

Compared with the UK and USA, admission charges to sights and attractions are fairly low, and museums and galleries are often free, though you may find that they politely ask for a donation, or charge for entry to temporary exhibitions. The 'worlds' – including Dreamworld and Sea World in Queensland, for example – have some of the highest admission charges, but usually offer discounted family tickets, which can help keep a lid on costs if travelling with children. Concession prices are often available on production of a student or senior card.

For more information contact the relevant tourist office (see page 332), while contact information for Australia's National Parks and National Trust offices are listed under Useful addresses.

B

Budgeting for your trip

The cost of living in Australia has traditionally been lower than Europe and the USA (although manufactured goods tend to be more expensive in Australia). However, since the global financial crisis started in 2008, Australia's economy has outperformed most others and the Australian dollar has risen in value

(at time of print it is: A$1= US$0.71). These days, Australia feels relatively expensive to visitors from the US and Europe. Mind you, Sydney has always had property prices up there with cities like London and New York, and day-to-day expenses such as public transport and dining out tend to be noticeably higher than in other Australian cities. As you move away from the east coast, where most of Australia's population lives, to cities like Adelaide, Hobart and Darwin, the cost of living is lower again. However, there are exceptions such as Perth, where the mining boom sent prices skyrocketing, and the isolated towns and settlements of the Outback, where the cost of transporting supplies long distances drives petrol and food prices upwards.

In general accommodation can cost from A$50–60 for a double room in a country pub, A$100 for self-contained cabin-style accommodation in the country, A$120 for a basic hotel room and A$200 upwards per night for five-star hotels.

The variety of climates means Australia grows lots of fresh produce that is of a high quality, although the standard in supermarkets is generally lower than what you will find in markets and fruiterers. A takeaway or dine-in café meal costs anywhere from A$15 to A$25, a main in a restaurant ranges from A$25 to A$35 and a main in a fine dining restaurant costs A$40–50. In major cities, some of the most affordable and best-quality food can be found in Asian restaurants, particularly around Chinatown.

Travel tends to be expensive because of the distances involved and high fuel prices. Car hire can start from around A$70 per day including insurance, although significant discounted rates apply for longer rental periods. Budget airlines Virgin Australia, Jetstar and Tigerair continue to have price wars and you can pick up flights from Sydney to Cairns, some 2,500km (1,550 miles), for A$149 one way. An airfare between Sydney and Melbourne can cost as little as A$60 if you book a few weeks ahead. The train between Sydney and Melbourne can cost around A$100, but when you take into account the 12 hours' travel time versus only 1.5 hours on a plane, it's easy to see why most people prefer to fly.

C

Climate

The seasons in Australia are the reverse of the northern hemisphere's. September to November is spring, December to February summer, March to May autumn, and June to August winter. Since fine, mild weather occurs during all seasons, any time can be recommended for a visit to Australia – although some months are warmer and drier than others.

About 40 percent of the country lies in the tropical zone north of the Tropic of Capricorn. In the Top End around Darwin (the monsoon belt) and near Cairns, there are only two seasons: the dry (April–November) and the wet (December–March). In the dry, there are warm days, clear blue skies and cool nights. The wet is usually characterised by heavy rain alternating with sunny hot weather. On the Great Barrier Reef most rain falls in January and February.

In the southern temperate zone seasons are more distinct. Winter days in Sydney are usually sunny with a maximum of 15°C (60°F) – chilly enough to require an overcoat – while humid summer temperatures can regularly hit 30°C (90°F) and higher. Snow falls on the southern mountain ranges, but not in the cities (except Hobart). Melbourne is pleasant in spring, summer and autumn, but winter can be grey and miserable, especially in July and August. Tasmania, the island state off the southern tip of the continent, is the coolest: summers are by far the best time to visit here, as winters can be damp and depressing.

South Australia has a Mediterranean climate: summers are hot and dry with temperatures regularly above 30°C (85°F), and highs of 40°C (105°F) and above are not uncommon.

Western Australia also has a Mediterranean climate. There are four distinctive seasons and moderate temperatures in its southern parts, while the north is in the tropical zone, so Top End conditions prevail.

In central Australia, summer temperatures are generally too high for comfort. In winter, the nights may be cool, with clear warm days.

Visitors should also bear in mind the various Australian school holidays; Christmas coincides with the long summer school break, which lasts throughout January. Easter is another big break. If you are travelling during these seasons, book well in advance.

Crime and safety

When it comes to crime, Australia is a relatively safe country. That being said, you should use the same common sense and precautions as you would elsewhere regarding your possessions and personal security. Issues surrounding prostitution, drugs and drunken behaviour occur in all cities. However, these are unlikely to affect travellers. If an incident occurs, report it to the police or, for urgent attention, call the emergency services by dialling **000**.

When it comes to safety, non-human elements can pose more of a risk in Australia. Bushfires occur regularly each year and it is important to be aware of fire bans or restrictions. If you are out in the bush and notice smoke, it is important to take it seriously and head for the nearest open space.

It is also important you thoroughly prepare if you are bushwalking or exploring the Outback. Take plenty of water and supplies, a good map and let a friend or the local ranger know of your plans in case you get stranded. Daily temperatures can reach the extremes, with searing heat during the day and freezing nights.

In northern Australia saltwater crocodiles are a real danger and have been known to take humans. They can be found in rivers, creeks, waterholes and around the coast. In popular tourist areas, croc-inhabited waterholes are regularly signposted. However, if you are unsure whether a place is croc-free, it is best not to risk swimming at all.

Box jellyfish are another danger in the far north during the wet season (November to May). Their venomous sting is extremely painful and can be fatal. During these months make sure you wear a special 'stinger' suit.

Unsuspecting tourists can easily find themselves in trouble when swimming at Australian surf

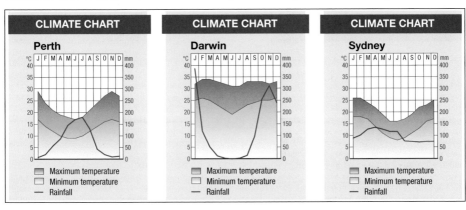

beaches. Lifesavers patrol popular beaches and put up red and yellow flags that swimmers should stay between. If an undertow or 'rip' drags you out, raise an arm if you need help and a surf lifesaver will come to your aid.

Customs regulations

Non-dutiable allowances are 25g (0.9oz) of tobacco goods (25 cigarettes) and 2.25 litres of beer, wine or spirits, and other dutiable goods to the total value of A$900, plus personal clothing, footwear and toiletries. Up to A$450-worth of dutiable goods, not including alcohol or tobacco, are allowed in the baggage of children under 18. Visit www.homeaffairs.gov.au for further information.

Strict quarantine regulations forbid the importation of foods, plants, animals and their by-products. Heavy jail penalties apply to the smuggling of drugs of any kind. Visitors are allowed to carry up to four weeks' supply of prescribed medications, but for larger supplies you should carry a doctor's certificate for customs purposes.

Laws strictly prohibit the export of protected Australian wildlife and products made from the skins, feathers, bones, shells, corals, or any part of protected species.

Quarantine

Australia is free of rabies, anthrax and foot-and-mouth disease, so all incoming animals are placed in quarantine. Cats and dogs (including guide dogs) are quarantined for up to 6 months, depending on the animal's country of origin – from the UK the period is 30 days. See www.agriculture.gov.au.

D

Disabled travellers

Most new buildings, public transport and tourist attractions have wheelchair access and other facilities for the disabled. The major rental car companies have a small number of cars with hand controls (reserve at least seven days in advance). Advance notice with relevant details of your disability will facilitate the best possible assistance from airlines, hotels or railway offices. Taxi fleets in state

capitals all have cars that can carry wheelchairs. Tourism Australia has further information on its website (www.australia.com). The following websites also offer good information: www.leisureoptions.com.au; www.accessibletourism.org; www.disabledtravelersguide.com; www.disabled-world.com.

The state automobile associations publish accommodation directories which include information on disabled access.

E

Electricity

The power supply is 220–240 volts AC. Sockets are three-pin flat plugs. You may be able to find adaptors in hardware stores or at some hotels.

Embassies and consulates

If you need help with matters such as legal advice or a stolen passport while in Australia, most countries have diplomatic representations, with embassies in major cities. A comprehensive list of every country represented in Australia is available on the Australia Department of Foreign Affairs and Trade website www.dfat.gov.au.

Canberra
Canada
Commonwealth Avenue, Yarralumla, tel: 02-6270 4000; www.canadainternational.gc.ca/australia-australie.
Ireland
20 Arkana Street, Yarralumla, tel: 02-6214 0000; www.dfa.ie/irish-embassy/australia
Japan
112–4 Empire Circuit, Yarralumla, tel: 02-6273 3244; www.au.emb-japan.go.jp.
Malaysia
7 Perth Avenue, Yarralumla, tel: 02-6120 0300; www.malaysia.org.au.
New Zealand
Commonwealth Avenue, Yarralumla, tel: 1300- 559 535; www.nzembassy.com/australia.
Singapore
17 Forster Cresent, Yarralumla, tel: 02-6271-2000; www.mfa.gov.sg/canberra.
UK
Commonwealth Avenue, Yarralumla, tel: 02-6270 6666; ukinaustralia.fco.gov.uk.

⊘ Canberra embassies

Over 60 countries have diplomatic representation in Canberra, and their buildings form a tourist attraction in their own right.

The embassies are mostly south and west of Capital Hill, scattered through the suburbs of Red Hill, Forrest and Yarralumla. Many of the buildings have been designed in the architectural style of the country the mission represents, such as the US Embassy in a red-brick Williamsburg Mission style and the Thai Embassy with its upswept roof corners and gold-coloured roof tiles.

USA
21 Moonah Place, Yarralumla, tel: 02-6214 5600; https://au.usembassy.gov/embassy-consulates/canberra.

Sydney
Canada
Consulate-General of Canada Level 5, Quay West, 111 Harrington Street, tel: 02-9364 3000; www.canadainternational.gc.ca/australia-australie.
China
Consulate General of the P.R. of China/Hong Kong, 39 Dunblane Street, St Camperdown, tel: 02-8595 8002 (9am–12.30pm); http://sydney.china-consulate.org/eng.
France
Consulate-General of France, Level 26, 31 Market Street, St Martin's Tower, tel: 02-9268 2400; www.amba-france-au.org.
Japan
Consulate-General of Japan, Level 12, 1 O'Connell Street, tel: 02-9250 1000; www.sydney.au.emb-japan.go.jp.
USA
Consulate-General of the United States of America, Level 10, MLC Centre, 19–29 Martin Place, tel: 02-9373 9200; https://au.usembassy.gov/embassy-consulates/sydney·

Melbourne
Japan
8/570 Bourke Street, tel: 03- 9679 4510; www.melbourne.au.emb-japan.go.jp.
UK
17th Floor, 90 Collins Street, tel: 03-9652 1600; http://ukinaustralia.fco.gov.uk.

USA

553 St Kilda Road, tel: 03-9526 5900; https://au.usembassy.gov/embassy-consulates/melbourne.

Adelaide

Germany
147/809 Pirie Street, tel: 08-8224 0682; http://germany.visahq.com.
Italy
398 Payneham Road, Glynde, tel: 08-8337 0777; www.consadelaide.esteri.it.
UK
444/446 Pulteney Street, tel: 08-8232-9817; http://ukinaustralia.fco.gov.uk.

Brisbane

China
Level 9, 79 Adelaide Street, tel: 07-3031 6300; http://brisbane.chinese-consulate.org.
Italy
Level 8, 199 George Street, tel: 07-3229 8944; www.consbrisbane.esteri.it.
UK
9/100 Eagle Street, tel: 07-3223 3200; http://ukinaustralia.fco.gov.uk.

Perth

Canada
Third Floor, 267 St George's Terrace, tel: 08-9322 7930; www.canadainternational.gc.ca/australia-australie.
UK
Adelaide Terrace, tel: 08-9224 4700; http://ukinaustralia.fco.gov.uk.
USA
4th Floor, 16 St George's Terrace, tel: 08-9202 1224; https://au.usembassy.gov/embassy-consulates/perth.

Darwin

British Consulate (emergencies only), tel: 07-3223 3200; www.british-consulate.net/uk/United-Kingdom-Consular-Assistance-Darwin·

Overseas missions

Canada – Ottawa
Australian High Commission, Suite 710, 50 O'Conner Street, Ottawa, Ontario, K1P 6L2, tel: 1 613-236 0841; www.canada.embassy.gov.au.
Toronto
Australian Consulate-General, Suite 1100 South Tower, 175 Bloor Street East, Toronto, Ontario, M4W 3R8, tel: 1 416-323 4280; www.dfat.gov.au/missions/countries/cato.html.
Vancouver
Australian Consulate, 1075 West Georgia Street, Vancouver, BC V6E 3C9, tel: 1 604-694 6160; www.dfat.gov.au/about-us/our-locations/missions/Pages/australian-consulate-in-vancouver-canada.aspx.
Hong Kong
Australian Consulate-General, 23/F Harbour Centre, 25 Harbour Road, Wan Chai, tel: 852-2827 8881; www.hongkong.china.embassy.gov.au.
Ireland
Australian Embassy, Cumberland Rd, Dublin, tel: 353 1-664 5300; www.ireland.embassy.gov.au.
Japan
Australian Embassy, 2-1-14 Mita, Minato-Ku, Tokyo 108-8361, tel: 81 35232 4111; https://japan.embassy.gov.au.
New Zealand – Wellington
Australian High Commission, 72 Hobson Street, Thorndon, Wellington, tel: 64 4473 6411; www.newzealand.embassy.gov.au.
Auckland
Australian Consulate-General, Level 7 PricewaterhouseCoopers Tower, 186–194 Quay Street, Auckland, tel: 64 9921 8800; www.newzealand.embassy.gov.au.
Singapore
Australian High Commission, 25 Napier Road, Singapore 258507, tel: 65 6836 4100; www.australia.org.sg.
UK
Australian High Commission, Australia House, The Strand, London WC2B 4LA, tel: 44 20-7379 4334; www.uk.embassy.gov.au.
USA – Washington DC
Australian Embassy, 1601 Massachusetts Avenue, Washington DC NW 20036-2273, tel: 1 202-797 3000; www.usa.embassy.gov.au.
New York
Australian Consulate-General, 150 East 42nd Street, 33rd floor, New York, NY 10017-5612, tel: 1 212-351 6500; www.newyork.usa.embassy.gov.au.
San Francisco
Australian Consulate-General, 575 Market Street, Suite 1800, San Francisco, CA 94105-2185, tel: 1 415-644 3620; www.usa.embassy.gov.au.
Atlanta
Australian Consulate-General, Atlanta Financial Center, 3353 Peachtree Road, NE, Suite 1140, Atlanta GA 30326, tel: 1 404-364-8560; www.usa.embassy.gov.au.

Emergencies

Call **000** for police, fire and ambulance assistance. This number is toll-free from any phone in Australia and can be made from public phones without a phone card or coins. **112** is the international standard

Painkillers Aussie-style.

emergency number that can be dialled from any mobile phone.

H

Health and medical care

Australian doctors, dentists and hospitals all have modern equipment, high-level training and extensive facilities. They are also expensive.

New Zealand, Belgium, Finland, Italy, Malta, the Netherlands, Norway, Slovenia, Sweden, the UK and Ireland have reciprocal health-care agreements with Australia, so visitors are entitled to free hospital treatment and Medicare (the Australian national health plan) benefits for GP treatment. Taking out a travel insurance policy that covers your health, before travelling to Australia, is recommended, however.

Vaccinations are not required if you are flying directly to Australia and have not passed through an epidemic zone or a yellow fever, cholera or typhoid-infected area in the six days prior to your arrival.

The sun in Australia has extremely strong ultraviolet rays, so extended exposure is not recommended, especially when the sun is at its fiercest – between 11am and 4pm. A wide-brimmed hat and adequate-strength sunscreen are essential.

I

Internet

Most hotels and hostels will have Wi-Fi, although you often need to pay to access it. Once ubiquitous, internet cafés can still be found, and many libraries have computer facilities.

L

LGBTQ travellers

Australia is popular with gay and lesbian travellers, although homophobic attitudes do exist, mostly in areas away from inner cities and popular tourist spots.

One of the main attractions is Sydney's annual gay and lesbian **Mardi Gras** (www.mardigras.org.au) each March, one of the greatest celebrations of its kind in the world. Sydney's Oxford Street is where all the action takes place, and outside Mardi Gras it remains a popular gay and lesbian hub, along with Newtown. **Midsumma** (www.midsumma.org.au), held each January/February, is the major gay and lesbian festival in Melbourne.

Major cities have gay and lesbian newspapers and magazines, available from many inner-city cafés, bars and pubs. Gay and Lesbian Tourism Australia (GALTA) is a network of gay-friendly tourism operators (www.galta.com.au).

M

Maps

Tourist information centres usually have free, quality local maps that also include useful tourism information. If you are travelling by car, many car-hire companies supply GPS devices. You can also pick up Australian road atlases from any good bookshop. Australia is a vast country and it is easy to get lost once you head to the Outback, so it is recommended you purchase maps that detail geography as well as road and track types for Outback travel and long-distance bushwalking.

The Tourism Australia website (www.australia.com) has a wide range of state, city and localised maps that can be useful for planning your itinerary.

Media

Each major city has one daily newspaper and in some cases two. The

Sydney Morning Herald (www.smh. com.au) and the Melbourne-based *The Age* (www.theage.com.au) are the two most important capital-city dailies, and can usually be found around Australia. The only national daily newspapers are *The Australian* and *The Financial Review*. Numerous weekly magazines are sold alongside local editions of international publications, such as *Newsweek* and *Time*.

The largest-selling papers are the tabloids in Sydney (the *Daily Telegraph*) and Melbourne (the *Herald-Sun*, online at www.heraldsun. com). There are about 120 newspapers catering to Australia's ethnic minorities, which are published in either English or one of 40 other languages.

Alternative views flourish online; www.crikey.com.au is one of the best for its take – generally scathing, often humorous – on politics, business, sport and other matters Australian. *The Conversation* (www.theconversation.com/au) is an independent, not-for-profit online media outlet with good in-depth articles about various issues, and the *Guardian Australia*, a dedicated Australia-focussed incarnation of the global online publication and British print newspaper, *The Guardian*, is also available online (www.theguardian.com/au).

Australia has a high readership of magazines: in addition to 1,200 magazine titles, airmail copies of overseas newspapers and journals are readily available at specialist newsagents and numerous bookstores in major cities.

The number of free-to-air television stations varies around the country. In some remote areas, the ABC (Australian Broadcasting Corporation; www.abc.net.au) may be the only station. This is the national, advertisement-free, television and radio network – the equivalent of Britain's BBC. The capital cities also offer three commercial stations and the excellent SBS (Special Broadcasting Service; www.sbs.com.au) multicultural station, with shows in many languages with subtitles. With the introduction of digital television, there are now 15 free-to-air stations available to suitably equipped households.

On radio, there is always ABC (FM and AM), plus a full spectrum of commercial and public broadcast stations, offering everything from rock to classical music.

Money

Australia's currency is in dollars and cents. The coins come in 5-, 10-, 20- and 50-cent silver pieces and 1- and 2-dollar gold coins. Notes are A\$5, 10, 20, 50 and 100. Amounts of over A\$10,000 must be declared on entering and leaving Australia.

The larger hotels will usually exchange cash and well-known traveller's cheques. Nearly all places accept major credit cards such as American Express, Visa, and MasterCard.

Banks The four big banks in Australia are the National (NAB), the Commonwealth, Westpac and ANZ. Trading hours are generally Monday–Thursday 9.30am–4pm, until 5pm on Friday. A few of the smaller banks and credit unions open on Saturday mornings.

Traveller's cheques in any currency can be readily cashed at international airports and banks. Bureaux de change offices are open seven days a week and are located throughout major cities – but usually charge a significant fee, so try to change money at banks when you can, despite limited opening hours.

Credit/Debit Cards and ATMs Carrying a recognised credit or debit card such as Visa, MasterCard or American Express is always a good idea when travelling. A credit card should provide access to EFTPOS (electronic funds transfer at point of sale), which is the easiest and often the cheapest way to exchange money – amounts are automatically debited from the selected account. Many Australian businesses are connected to EFTPOS.

Australian currency cash withdrawals can be made from automatic teller machines (ATMs) that are linked to overseas banks. Since some credit card companies start charging interest on cash withdrawals immediately, it is usually cheaper to withdraw cash using a debit card rather than a credit card. Some UK banks charge a fee for using debit cards overseas, so check this out before travelling to avoid any nasty surprises on your bank statement when you return home.

Some of the islands and the Outback towns have limited banking facilities, so make sure you have plenty of cash before heading into these less populated areas.

Tipping

Australia does not have a tipping tradition, as waiters are given a decent hourly wage. However, in cities especially, it is becoming customary to leave about 10 to 12 percent of the total bill.

Porters at luxury hotels once never received tips, but since many overseas visitors give them a dollar or two, there is an increasing look of expectancy. Porters at airports and taxi drivers do not expect to be tipped, but will hardly throw the money back if you do. 'It's up to you' has become the common advice from Australians. In other words: nobody really expects a tip, but it's always appreciated.

O

Opening hours

General retail trading hours for stores are Monday–Saturday 9am–5pm. Most shops open 10am–4pm on Sunday too. Late-night shopping (until 9pm) takes place at least one night a week in the capital cities – usually a Thursday or Friday.

Restaurants and snack bars, bookshops and local corner stores are open until later in the evening; at times all weekend. Australians still enjoy the tradition of the weekend holiday and most offices are closed on Saturday and Sunday.

Banks open Monday–Thursday 9.30am–4pm and until 5pm on Friday. Some selected branches are open on Saturday morning as well. All banks, post offices, government and private offices, and most shops close on public holidays (see Public holidays).

Phonebox in Melbourne's Chinatown.

P

Postal services

Post offices open Monday–Friday 9am–5pm, and the postal service is reasonably efficient. Post offices also provide fax services at urgent or ordinary rates, the cost depending on the rate selected and the destination.

The front pages of the telephone directory give further information on all postal services, including telephone interpreter service, community service and recorded information service.

Post Restante: post offices will receive and hold mail for visitors. American Express offices will also hold mail for members.

Public holidays

Public and school holidays affect availability of transport and hotel reservations, which often results in higher prices. The public holidays observed Australia-wide are as follows:

1 January **New Year's Day**
26 January **Australia Day**
mid-March or early October (varies in different states) **Labour Day**
late March/early April **Good Friday, Easter Saturday and Monday**
25 **April Anzac Day**
2nd Monday in June **Queen's Birthday**
25 December **Christmas Day**
26 December **Boxing Day**

In addition, the states have their own public holidays, such as Victoria's Melbourne Cup Day (first Tuesday in November).

R

Religion

Australia is a secular multicultural society and numerous religions are practised. In the major cities you will find all types of places of worship. Christianity has the most adherents and you won't be hard pushed to find church services for major denominations in cities and towns. The major cities have some magnificent cathedrals.

Buddhism, Islam, Judaism and Hinduism also have large followings in Australia. Muslim communities can be found in the western suburbs of Sydney, concentrating around Lakemba, and the northern suburbs of Melbourne around Broadmeadows. A strong Jewish community exists in Melbourne around St Kilda East.

S

Student travellers

Australia is popular with international students and backpackers so there is an abundance of budget tourism operators and accommodation providers. STA Travel (www.statravel.com.au) has offices in every state and offers a range of products and services aimed at students. Look out for free copies of *TNT Magazine* for budget travel tips and information. Universities also offer a range of services and local advice for international students, including affordable accommodation on campus.

T

Telephones

Emergency numbers: **police, ambulance, fire**, tel: **000**, or **112** from mobile telephones.

Australia has several telecommunication operators including Telstra, Optus and AAPT. Rates vary between companies for long distance, but local calls on all networks are untimed.

Toll-free phone calls

Toll-free or freecall numbers are common in Australian business. Numbers beginning with 13 (ie Qantas domestic 131 213) can be called from any phone in Australia at local-call rates; numbers starting with 800, 1300 or 1800 are freecall numbers (toll-free) when dialled from within Australia.

Making calls

Public telephones are located throughout cities and towns. Most public telephones take phonecards, which can be bought at newsagents and stores in various denominations. Dialling from hotel rooms is much more expensive than from a public or private phone.

Subscriber Trunk Dialling (STD) for calling long distance is available on all private and most public telephones. Dial the regional code (say 02 for NSW, 03 for Victoria, etc) followed by the local number. STD calls are cheapest between 7pm and 8am.

International calls

Direct-dialled international calls may be made from any ISD-connected private or public phone. International public phones are located at city GPOs, rail termini and airports. There are off-peak rates to most countries which generally apply all day Saturday and 11pm–6am Sunday to Friday. Dial 0011 followed by the relevant country code.

Time zones

Australia has three time zones: Eastern Standard Time for the east-coast states (Tasmania, Victoria, New South Wales, Queensland), 10 hours ahead of GMT; Central Standard Time (covering Northern Territory and South Australia), which is 30 minutes behind the east coast, or 9.5 hours ahead of GMT; and Western Standard Time (Western Australia), which is 2 hours behind the east coast, or 8 hours ahead of GMT.

During the summer most states introduce Daylight Saving Time, moving the clock forward by 1 hour. New South Wales and Australian Capital Territory run daylight saving October–March; Victoria, South Australia and Tasmania October–April. Neither Queensland nor Western Australia uses Daylight Saving Time.

Toilets

In their typical no-nonsense fashion, Australians manage without euphemisms for toilet. 'Dunny' or 'thunder box' is the Outback slang, but 'washroom', 'restroom', 'Ladies' and 'Gents' are all understood. Public toilets are often locked after certain hours, but you can generally use the facilities in any pub or cinema without making a purchase. Toilets are generally clean, even in the Outback.

For those who like to plan their rest stops, the government has produced the Toilet Map, available at www.toiletmap.gov.au, with details of the various public toilets in each of Australia's states.

Tourist information

Tourist information within Australia is handled principally by state tourist offices. These offices are generally open seven days a week, and will provide brochures, maps, price lists and other information. They can often book accommodation, tours and transport on your behalf. Most towns also have a local tourist information office.

ACT – Australian Capital Territory
Canberra and Region Visitors Centre
330 Northbourne Avenue, Dickson, ACT
Tel: 1300-554 114 or 02-6205 0044
www.visitcanberra.com.au
New South Wales
Sydney Visitor Centre
Corner Playfair and Argyle Streets, The Rocks, Sydney NSW
Tel: 1800-067 676 or 02-8273 0000
Also at Dickson Street, Chinatown
Tel: 02 9265 9333
www.sydneyvisitorcentre.com
Victoria
Melbourne Visitors Centre
Federation Square, Melbourne
Tel: 03-9658 9658
www.visitvictoria.com
South Australia
South Australian Visitor and Travel Centre
9 James Place, Adelaide
Tel: 1300-764 227 276 or 1300 588 276
www.southaustralia.com
Queensland
Visitor Information Centre
Queen Street Mall, Brisbane
Tel: 07-3006 6290
www.queensland.com
Northern Territory
Tourism Top End
6 Bennett Street, Darwin
Tel: 1300-138 886 or 08-8936 2499
www.travelnt.com
Western Australia
Western Australian Visitor Centre
55 William Street, Perth
Tel: 1800-812 808 351 or 08-9483 1111
www.westernaustralia.com
Tasmania
Tasmanian Visitor Information Centre
22 Davey Street, Hobart
Tel: 03-6238 4222
www.discovertasmania.com.au

U

Useful addresses

Tourist information abroad

Tourism Australia (www.australia.com) supplies excellent information for travellers wishing to plan their trip.
London
Australia House, 6th Floor, The Strand, London, WC2B 4LG
Tel: 020-7438 4600
Los Angeles
2029 Century Park E Ste 3150, Los Angeles, CA 90067
Tel: 310-695 3200
Hong Kong
Suite 6706, Central Plaza, 26 Harbour Road, Wanchai
Tel: 852-2531 3832
Singapore
101 Thompson Road, United Square 08-03, Singapore 307591
Tel: 65-6351 6323
Sydney
Tel: 02-9360 1111

National trust offices

The National Trust in Australia (www.nationaltrust.org.au) owns and preserves more than 180 historic properties. All of them are open to the public and Trust members are entitled to free entry. If you intend to visit a number of Australia's historic buildings it may be worth joining. Annual membership costs A$110 for an individual, A$140 for households. Non-members can pay to see particular properties. To join call toll-free in Australia 1800-246 766 or contact one of the state offices. A reciprocal arrangement exists with similar organisations in other countries, such as the National Trust in Britain, so members should bring cards to Australia in order to reap the benefits.
National
The Australian Council of National Trusts, 14/71 Constitution Avenue, Campbell, ACT 2612
Tel: 02-6247 6766
www.nationaltrustact.org.au
New South Wales
Observatory Hill, The Rocks, Sydney, NSW 2001
Tel: 02-9258 0123
www.nationaltrust.org.au/nsw
Australian Capital Territory
1st Floor, North Building, Civic Offices, Civic Square, Canberra, ACT 2608
Tel: 02-6230 0533

www.nationaltrust.org.au/act
Victoria
4 Parliament Place, East Melbourne,
Vic 3002
Tel: 03-9656 9800
www.nationaltrust.org.au/vic
South Australia
Beaumont House, 631 Glynburn
Road, Beaumont 5066
Tel: 08-8202 9200
www.nationaltrust.org.au/sa
Queensland
Ground Floor, 91–95 William Street,
Brisbane, Qld 4001
Tel: 07-3223 6666
www.nationaltrust.org.au/qld
Western Australia
The Old Observatory, 4 Havelock
Street, West Perth, WA 6005
Tel: 08-9321 6088
www.nationaltrust.org.au/wa
Tasmania
Franklin House, 413 Hobart Road,
Launceston, TAS 7250
Tel: 03-6344 6233
www.nationaltrust.org.au/tas

National parks

Some national parks require you
to purchase permits before entry.
Visitor centres and regional offices
where you can obtain information
and permits are located throughout
Australia and are often in or close to
popular parks. National parks infor-
mation can also be obtained from
these regional offices:
**NSW: National Parks and Wildlife
Service**
Level 14, 59 Goulburn Street, The
Rocks, Sydney, NSW 2000
Tel: 1300-072 757 or 02-9995 6500
www.nationalparks.nsw.gov.au
**ACT: Territory and Municipal
Services**
Tel: 13 22 81
www.tams.act.gov.au
Vic: Parks Victoria
Level 10/535 Bourke Street
Melbourne, Victoria 3000
Tel: 03-8627 4700; or 131 963
www.parkweb.vic.gov.au
SA: National Parks South Australia
Tel: 08-8204 1910
www.parks.sa.gov.au
Qld: Parks & Wildlife Service
160 Ann Street, Brisbane, Qld 4000
Tel: 137 468
www.nprsr.qld.gov.au
**NT: Parks & Wildlife, Northern
Territory**
Goyder Centre, 25 Chung Wah
Terrace, Palmerston, NT 0830
Tel: 08-8999 4555
https://nt.gov.au/leisure/parks-reserves

Tas: Parks and Wildlife Service
134 Macquarie Street, Hobart 7000
Tel: 1300-827 727
www.parks.tas.gov.au

Visas and passports

Visitors to Australia must have a
passport valid for the entire period
of their stay. All non-Australian
citizens also require a visa – except
for New Zealand citizens, who
are issued with a visa on arrival in
Australia. The visa you need depends
on what your visit is for and how long
you plan to stay.

Visitor visa (subclass 600, free
visa) allows you to stay in Australia
for up to three months. You are
not allowed to work. Electronic
Travel Authority ETA (subclass 601)
allows you to enter Australia as
many times as you want, for up to
three months at a time, for up to 12
months. The service fee is A$20.
EVisitor (subclass 651, free visa)
is for people who hold passports
from certain countries. You may
enter Australia as many times as
you wish, for up to three months,
for up to 12 months after the visa
is granted. Special category visa
(subclass 444) is for citizens of
NZ. Working holiday visa (subclass
417) is for young people between
18-31 years of age. You must apply
for it outside of Australia. You can
only work six months with one
employer. For more information
about other visa types see www.
border.gov.au.

Temporary residence Those
seeking temporary residence must
apply to an Australian visa office,
and in many cases must be spon-
sored by an appropriate organisation or employer. Study visas are
available for people who want to
undertake registered courses on a
full-time basis.

Entry requirements for
Australia are continually updated.
Information and applications for
visas should be made to the nearest Australian Government representative in your home country
well before travelling (see page
329), or visit www.border.gov.au,
which gives information on all the
different types of visas, and allows
online applications.

Weights and measures

Australia uses the metric system
of weights and measures. Despite
the change from the imperial to the
metric system in the 1970s, a 183cm
person is still frequently referred to
as being '6 feet tall' and some people
still give their weight in stones (14lb
to the stone).

The main conversions are as
follows:
1 metre = 3.28 feet
1 kilometre = 0.62 miles
1 kilogram = 2.2 pounds
1 litre = 2.1 pints (US)
1 litre = 1.8 pints (UK)
0°C (Centigrade) = 32°F (Fahrenheit)

What to wear

Generally, Australians are informal dressers, especially when the
weather is warm: comfort trumps
formality. However, for special occasions or dining in fine restaurants,
formal attire or neat casual dress
is appropriate. While a jacket and
tie are rarely required for men, the
more elegant establishments would
not welcome gym shoes or shorts.
In other words, dress more or less
as you would in other cosmopolitan
cities.

If you visit Australia during summer, include at least one warm gar-
ment for the occasional cold snap,
and a light coat. If travelling to the
southeastern states during winter,
include warm, waterproof clothing
– temperatures in Melbourne can
dip below freezing at night, and the
Southern Alps experience snow. The
weather in northern Queensland and
the Top End of the Northern Territory
is rarely chilly, even in August.

At any time of the year, solid,
waterproof walking shoes are essential if you intend to go bushwalking.
If exploring the Great Barrier Reef,
bring along an old pair of trainers for
reef walks. And always pack a hat.

Women travellers

Women are generally safe in
Australia, though the same degree
of caution should be used as you
would elsewhere. Some backpacker
hostels such as Base Backpackers
(www.stayatbase.com) offer women-
only dorms and floors.

FURTHER READING

GENERAL

The Australian Wine Annual by Jeremy Oliver. Rigorous guide to everything good in a bottle.
The Age/Sydney Morning Herald Good Australian Wine Guide by Nick Stock. Formerly branded as the Penguin guide.
Unreliable Memoirs by Clive James. Aussie expat and wit looks back at his formative years in Sydney and possibly finds rationale for being an expat.
The Sydney Morning Herald and **The Age Good Food Guides**. Definitive guides to eating out in, respectively, Sydney and Melbourne.
The Rise and Fall of Australia by Nick Bryant. A forensic look at the Lucky Country from an outsider's perspective.
Australia's Second Chance by George Megalogenis. The most important questions confronting Australia now – how to maintain the country's winning streak.

HISTORY

At Home in Australia by Peter Conrad. The pictures are the draw in this analysis of a nation.
Australia: A Biography of a Nation by Phillip Knightley. Wide-ranging history, particularly good in its snapshots of key individuals.
Australia: A New History of the Great Southern Land by Frank Welsh. Dependable assessment of the growth of a country.
Australians: Origins to Eureka by Thomas Keneally. The first of three volumes aimed at anatomising the people of the continent.
A Concise History of Australia by Stuart Macintyre. Reliable and thoroughly up-to-date account, including the Gillard ascent.
The Explorers edited by Tim Flannery. A compendium of accounts from the early days of European settlement.
The Fatal Shore by Robert Hughes. Landmark laying bare of convict transportation and its impact.
Gallipoli by Les Carlyon. Detailed account of the formative Anzac engagement of World War I.
Kokoda Spirit: In the Footsteps of Australia's World War Two Heroes by Patrick Lindsay. Analysis of searing experiences in Papua New Guinea.
A Secret Country by John Pilger. Provocative analysis of the political and commercial foundations of modern Australia.

⊘ Send us your thoughts

We do our best to ensure the information in our books is as accurate and up-to-date as possible. The books are updated on a regular basis using local contacts, who painstakingly add, amend and correct as required. However, some details (such as telephone numbers and opening times) are liable to change, and we are ultimately reliant on our readers to put us in the picture.

We welcome your feedback, especially your experience of using the book 'on the road'. Maybe you came across a great bar or new attraction we missed.

We will acknowledge all contributions, and we'll offer an Insight Guide to the best letters received.

Please write to us at:
Insight Guides
PO Box 7910
London SE1 1WE

Or email us at:
hello@insightguides.com

The Making of Australia by David Hill. The story of how a struggling convict settlement grew into six dynamic colonies and a remarkable nation.

NATURAL HISTORY

Country: A Continent, a Scientist and a Kangaroo by Tim Flannery. Palaeontology, natural history and memoir nicely combined.
Field Guide to the Birds of Australia by Ken Simpson and Nicolas Day. Comprehensive identification guide.
Green Guide: Mammals of Australia by T. Lindsey. Handbook to the country's weird and wonderful wildlife.
Green Guide: Snakes and Other Reptiles of Australia by G. Swan. As above but with more venom.
The Slater Field Guide to Australian Birds by Peter, Pat & Raoul Slater. Fully illustrated spotter's tool.
Wild Australia: A Guide to the Places, Plants and Animals by Graham Edgar, Robert Edgar and Allan Edgar. Extends to insects and aquatic life as well.

TRAVEL

Down Under by Bill Bryson. The urbane, breezy style is deceptive – some serious research has gone into this entertaining travelogue.
Explore Australia by 4WD by Craig Lewis and Cathy Savage. How to source the right equipment and find the right tracks.
Into the Blue: Boldly Going Where Captain Cook Has Gone Before by Tony Horwitz. Penetrative retracing of Cook's Pacific voyages.
One for the Road: An Outback Adventure by Tony Horwitz. One man's breezy journey and the people he encounters.
The Songlines by Bruce Chatwin. Remarkable outback journey into Aboriginal tradition and lore.
Tracks by Robyn Davidson. The adventures of a woman crossing the continent by camel.
Walks in Nature: Australia by Viola Design. Over 100 trails in and around major Australian cities.
Wild Swimming: Sydney Australia by Sally Tertini. Gorgeous outdoor swimming locations within reach of Sydney.

ABORIGINAL AUSTRALIA

Aboriginal Art of Australia by Carol Finley. Concise guide to art in all media, which includes a walk through some of the symbolism employed.
Aboriginal Australians by Richard Broome. An analysis of the impact of white settlement from 1788.
Aboriginal Myths, Legends and Fables by A.W. Reed. Straightforward retelling of some of the key stories.
The Artist is a Thief by Stephen Gray. Prize-winning detective story that delves into cultural clashes in modern Australia.
Balanda: My Year in Arnhem Land by Mary Ellen Jordan. A move from Melbourne to unfamiliar Arnhem Land with the predictable and unpredictable cultural collisions implicit in that.
The Hard Light of Day by Rod Moss. A moving, fascinating, occasionally hilarious, more-often heartbreaking story of a white artist's friendships in Arrernte Country, illustrated by extraordinary paintings.
My Place by Sally Morgan. Morgan's investigation of her family history reveals some wider truths of Aboriginal repression.
Wings of the Kite-Hawk: A journey into the heart of Australia by Nicholas Rothwell. Starting with the routes of early explorers and expanding to take in current issues.
Aboriginal Australians by Diana Marshall. Describes the history, culture and traditional and modern lifestyles of Aboriginal Australians.
Aboriginal Designs by Polly Pinder. The unique and vibrant artwork of Aboriginal people.

AUSTRALIAN LANGUAGE

The Dinkum Dictionary by Susan Butler. Bonzer stickybeak into Aussie lingo.
My Life As Me by Barry Humphries. Reminiscence of growing up in 1950s Melbourne, the genesis of his various characters and the path to a level of worldwide acclaim that saw Dame Edna Everage given the city keys.
Unpolished Gem by Alice Pung. Leaving the Cambodia of Pol Pot as a child, Pung's assimilation into

life in Footscray along with her family is the core of this revealing memoir.

FICTION

The Art of the Engine Driver by Steven Carroll. Suburban Melbourne post-World War II is the setting for this measured look at how progress distorts the lives of ordinary people.
All the Birds Singing by Evie Wyld. Centres on an Aussie woman who has fled trauma and is living in an unnamed wind and rain-swept English island.
Barracuda by Christos Tsiolkas. Shows the absurdity of the idea that Australia is a classless society, or a place in which anyone can succeed if only they try hard enough.
Breath by Tim Winton. The surf is as much the focus as the relationships in this accomplished novel.
The Broken Shore by Peter Temple. A sophisticated crime novel that reaches to the very heart of Australian society.
Capricornia by Xavier Herbert. Sweeping narrative from the 1930s that partly inspired Baz Luhrmann's film, Australia.
Carpentaria by Alexis Wright. Hefty and densely lyrical account of an Aboriginal community in the far north.
Cloudstreet by Tim Winton. A family saga in the West mirroring the growth of the nation in the 20th century.
Cocaine Blues by Kerry Greenwood. The first in a series of detective novels set in 1920s Melbourne.
Death of a River Guide by Richard Flanagan. A man drowning in Tasmania's Franklin River spools back through his family's history and struggle in this unforgiving land.
English Passengers by Matthew Kneale. Prize-winning novel about an 1857 voyage to Tasmania, by turns stark and hilarious.
Eucalyptus by Murray Bail. From its fairy-tale conceit, Eucalyptus evolves into a magical love story.
Fly Away Peter by David Malouf. Life on Queensland's bucolic coastal region plays counterpoint to the Great War.
For the Term of His Natural Life by Marcus Clarke. The great convict pot-boiler published in 1874.

A Fortunate Life by A.B. Facey. Rough-hewn yet classic autobiography of an outback farmer.
Gould's Book of Fish by Richard Flanagan. Tasmania's Sarah Island in the 1830s is the setting for this wildly ambitious freewheeling novel.
The Harp in the South by Ruth Park. Part of a trilogy of loved, if soapy, novels set in the slums of Sydney in the first half of the 20th century.
The Idea of Perfection by Kate Grenville. Beautifully honed romance in small-town New South Wales.
Illywhacker by Peter Carey. An expansive narrative by the 139-year-old self-confessed liar of the title takes us on a journey through history and the forging of the larrikin spirit.
It's Raining in Mango by Thea Astley. Saga stretching over a century and takes in gold-digging in Queensland and Aboriginal dispossession.
Last Drinks by Andrew McGahan. Multi-award-winning crime thriller.
Loaded by Christos Tsiolkas. Loaded unflinchingly sifts the problems of a gay Greek teenager coming to terms with both himself and a hostile city.
The Man from Snowy River by Banjo Paterson. Derring-do in the southern mountains has taken on mythical status in Australian literature.
Monkey Grip by Helen Garner. Captures the tedium of life with self-obsessed hippies and junkies in 1970s Melbourne.
Morgan's Run by Colleen McCullough. The tale of a man convicted and sentenced to prison on Norfolk Island.
My Brilliant Career by Miles Franklin. Feisty teenager grapples with the stifling constraints of early 20th-century Australia.
Of A Boy by Sonya Hartnett. The story of nine-year-old Adrian, adrift in 1977 without family anchors and when three other children have just disappeared.
On the Beach by Nevil Shute. Melbourne is the last redoubt of humanity as the fallout from nuclear annihilation in the northern hemisphere heads southward.
Oscar and Lucinda by Peter Carey. Booker winner, film and calling card for the precociously talented Carey.

Oyster by Janette Turner Hospital. The arrival of a cult-like community in a remote desert settlement is the catalyst for upheaval.

Picnic at Hanging Rock by Joan Lindsay. An eerie story of schoolgirls disappearing in the picturesque Macedon Ranges.

Remembering Babylon by David Malouf. Moving story of a white youth taken in by a Queensland Aboriginal community in the 1840s.

The Secret River by Kate Grenville. Deftly explores the ramifications of Aboriginal and white communities interacting with each other, this time in early 19th-century NSW.

The Slap by Christos Tsiolkas. Skewers suburban Melbourne values in this bestselling, Man Booker prize-nominated novel.

The Sound of One Hand Clapping by Richard Flanagan. A woman walks out into a snowstorm, leaving her family in the Tasmanian wilderness.

The Thorn Birds by Colleen McCullough. The romantic blockbuster of life on the station.

Tree of Man by Patrick White. Dissecting an Outback marriage.

The True History of the Kelly Gang by Peter Carey. The Kelly story in Ned's own words from 'newly discovered' letters.

The Vivisector by Patrick White. Sydney Nolan was the model for this dissection of an Australian artist.

CHILDREN'S BOOKS

The Complete Adventures of Blinky Bill by Dorothy Wall. Tales of a mischevious koala.

The Magic Pudding by Norman Lindsay. The absurd and amusing adventures of Bunyip Bluegum, Bill Barnacle, Sam Sawnoff and their pudding companion.

Possum Magic by Julie Vivas and Mem Fox. A beautifully illustrated children's classic.

Snugglepot & Cuddlepie by May Gibbs. One of Australia's best-loved children's books, first published in 1918.

Wombat Divine by Mem Fox and Kerry Argent. An endearing Christmas tale about a stage-struck wombat.

Wildlife by Fiona Wood. A book for young adults about friendship, love and identity.

Rivertime by Trace Balla. A tender tale of a boy and his bird-watching uncle on a paddling trip.

OTHER INSIGHT GUIDES

Insight Guide Australia is a top-selling title in the series, with superb photography and in-depth background reading on the history and culture of the Land Down Under. In addition, Insight Explore Guides provide illuminating walks and tours around a destination, showing you the smartest way to link the sights and taking you beyond the beaten tourist track. Titles in the Explore series include *Explore Sydney, Explore Melbourne, Explore Queensland, Explore Perth and West Coast Australia* and *Explore New Zealand*.

CREDITS

INSIGHT GUIDE CREDITS

Distribution
UK, Ireland and Europe
Apa Publications (UK) Ltd;
sales@insightguides.com
United States and Canada
Ingram Publisher Services;
ips@ingramcontent.com
Australia and New Zealand
Woodslane; info@woodslane.com.au
Southeast Asia
Apa Publications (SN) Pte;
singaporeoffice@insightguides.com
Worldwide
Apa Publications (UK) Ltd;
sales@insightguides.com
Special Sales, Content Licensing and CoPublishing
Insight Guides can be purchased in bulk quantities at discounted prices. We can create special editions, personalised jackets and corporate imprints tailored to your needs.
sales@insightguides.com
www.insightguides.biz

Printed in China by CTPS

All Rights Reserved
© 2019 Apa Digital (CH) AG and
Apa Publications (UK) Ltd

First Edition 1992
Ninth Edition 2019

Every effort has been made to provide accurate information in this publication, but changes are inevitable. The publisher cannot be responsible for any resulting loss, inconvenience or injury. We would appreciate it if readers would call our attention to any errors or outdated information. We also welcome your suggestions; please contact us at: hello@insightguides.com

www.insightguides.com

Editor: Sian Marsh
Head of DTP and Pre-Press: Rebeka Davies
Updated By: Patrick Kinsella
Managing Editor: Carine Tracanelli
Picture Editor: Tom Smyth
Cartography: original cartography Polyglott Kartographie, updated by Carte

CONTRIBUTORS

This new edition of Insight Guides Australia was thoroughly updated by **Patrick Kinsella**, a writer and dual citizen of Australia and the UK. It builds on the previous work of the following writers: **Ron Banks**, **Jerry Dennis, Ute Junker, Victoria Kyriakopoulos, Kerry McCarthy, Fran Severn, Tania Sincock, Dorothy Stannard** and **Hermione Stott**. The book was copy-edited by **Sian Marsh** and indexed by **Penny Phenix**.

ABOUT INSIGHT GUIDES

Insight Guides have more than 45 years' experience of publishing high-quality, visual travel guides. We produce 400 full-colour titles, in both print and digital form, covering more than 200 destinations across the globe, in a variety of formats to meet your different needs.

Insight Guides are written by local authors, whose expertise is evident in the extensive historical and cultural background features. Each destination is carefully researched by regional experts to ensure our guides provide the very latest information. All the reviews in **Insight Guides** are independent; we strive to maintain an impartial view. Our reviews are carefully selected to guide you to the best places to eat, go out and shop, so you can be confident that when we say a place is special, we really mean it.

Legend

City maps

	Freeway/Highway/Motorway
	Divided Highway
	Main Roads
	Minor Roads
	Pedestrian Roads
	Steps
	Footpath
	Railway
	Funicular Railway
	Cable Car
	Tunnel
	City Wall
	Important Building
	Built Up Area
	Other Land
	Transport Hub
	Park
	Pedestrian Area
	Bus Station
❶	Tourist Information
✉	Main Post Office
✚	Cathedral/Church
☾	Mosque
✡	Synagogue
⚲	Statue/Monument
	Beach
✈	Airport

Regional maps

	Freeway/Highway/Motorway (with junction)
	Freeway/Highway/Motorway (under construction)
	Divided Highway
	Main Road
	Secondary Road
	Minor Road
	Track
	Footpath
	International Boundary
	State/Province Boundary
	National Park/Reserve
	Marine Park
	Ferry Route
	Marshland/Swamp
	Glacier
	Salt Lake
✈	Airport/Airfield
∴	Ancient Site
⊖	Border Control
	Cable Car
	Castle/Castle Ruins
⋒	Cave
⌂	Chateau/Stately Home
✝	Church/Church Ruins
	Crater
	Lighthouse
▲	Mountain Peak
★	Place of Interest
✺	Viewpoint

INDEX

MAIN REFERENCES ARE IN BOLD TYPE

A

aboriginal people and sites 29
Aboriginal Cultural Centre and
Keeping Place (Armidale) 136
Anangu 266
Kata Tjuta 267
Uluru 266
Aboriginal people and sites 59,
65, 103, 141, 171, 253, 286, 289
Aboriginal Progressive
Association 65
Aboriginal Tent Embassy
(Canberra) 153
Anaiwian 136
Anangu 257
ancient sites 147, 148, 256, 261
art and crafts 65, 264, 274
Australian Aborigines
Advancement League 65
Bangarra Dance Company 73
Brambuk Aboriginal Cultural
Centre 177
Bunjilaka Aboriginal Centre
(Melbourne) 165
cliff carvings 122
corroboree 30
Dandiiri Maiwar Centre 216
Dreamtime 29
festivals 253
Freedom Rides 66
history 29, 33, 47, 272
Kata Tjuta 258
Kombumerri 218
land rights 48, 59, 65
Ngarrindjeri 204
rock paintings 30, 149, 177, 231,
261, 262, 290
Stolen Generation 66, 67, 152
Tandanya National Aboriginal
Cultural Institute (Adelaide)
195
Tiwi Islanders 265
tours 288
Uluru 20, 103, 257
Wilpena Pound 201
Abrolhos Islands 284
Absalom, Jack 147
accommodation 326
farm stays 59
in Aboriginal communities 288
AC/DC 74
Adelaide 103, 191
Adelaide Festival Centre 193
Adelaide Festival of Ideas 196
Adelaide Festival of the Arts
196
Adelaide Fringe 196
Adelaide Oval 193
Art Gallery of South Australia
194
Ayers House 194
Botanic Gardens 195
Central Market 195
Chinatown 195

Elder Park 193
Government House 194
Migration Museum 194
North Adelaide 192
North Terrace 194
Parliament House 193
Rundle Mall 195
South Australian Museum 194
State Library 194
St Peter's Cathedral 193
Tandanya National Aboriginal
Cultural Institute 195
taxis 324
transport 192, 321, 322, 323
University of Adelaide 194
Victoria Square 195
Womadelaide 196
Writers' Week 196
Adelaide Hills 197
Adelaide River 262
Admirals Arch (Kangaroo Island)
205
admission charges 326
Adventure Bay (Bruny Island) 308
Agnes Water 222
agriculture 58. See also farming
cotton 146
fruit 130, 145, 146
fruits 183, 204
sugar cane 132, 223
wheat 146, 177, 282
air travel 320
domestic flights 320
Albany 280
Australian Light Horse
memorial 281
Church of St John the
Evangelist 281
post office 281
Strawberry Hill 281
Whaleworld 280
Albury 182
Aldgate 197
Alice Springs 253
Alice Springs Desert Park 254
Alice Springs School of the Air
254
Anzac Hill 254
Araluen Cultural Precinct 254
Aviation Museum 255
Henley-on-Todd Regatta 255
Museum of Central Australia
257
Royal Flying Doctor Service
Visitors' Centre 254
Springs 253
Strehlow Research Centre 254
Telegraph Station 253
transport 322
Allenby, Robert 86
Allen, Peter 136
Alpine National Park 184
Alpine Village 307
American River (Kangaroo Island)
205

amusement parks. See theme and
amusement parks
Anakie 173
Fairy Park 173
Andamooka 203
Anglesea 174
Bells Beach 174
Angourie 132
animalparks 112
Antill, John 73
Anxious Bay 206
ANZAC 41
Apollo Bay 174
aquariums
AQWA (Hillary's Boat Harbour)
277
Melbourne Aquarium 167
National Zoo and Aquarium
(Canberra) 155
Oceanworld(Sydney) 112
Reef HQ (Townsville) 225
Seahorse World (Beauty Point)
305
SeaLifeSydney(Sydney) 115
Sea World (Gold Coast) 219
aquatic reserves
Fly Point 129
Halifax Point 129
Julian Rocks 133
Arakwal National Park 133
Ararat 178
Ardrossan 206
Argyle Diamond Mine 291
Argyle Downs Homestead 291
Arkaroola 201
Arltunga 255
Armidale 136
Aboriginal Cultural Centre and
Keeping Place 136
Armstrong, Gillian 75
Arnhem Highway 261
Arnhem Land 68, 261
artgalleries 112
arts, performing 48, 166. See
also theatres and concert
venues, casinos
Melbourne Theatre Company
167
arts, visual 73
Aboriginal art 68
Australian School 74
Heidelberg School 73
Atherton 227
Atherton Tableland 227
Aussie World 220
Australian Antarctic Division HQ
308
Australian Ballet 73
Australian Capital Territory 38
Australian Outback Spectacular
219
Australian Reptile Park 125
Australian Rules Football 85,
164
Grand Final 164

Tiwi Islands Football League Grand Final 264
Australia Zoo 220
Ayers Rock. *See* Uluru

B

Bairnsdale 184
  Botanic Gardens 184
  St Mary's Catholic Church 184
Balconies, The 177
Balgo Hills 68
Ballarat 37, 161, 178
  Ballarat Fine Art Gallery 178
  Botanic Gardens 178
  Eureka Centre 178
  Lake Wendouree 178
  Museum of Australian Democracy at Eureka 178
  Sovereign Hill 178
Ballina 132
Balranald 147
Bana, Eric 75
Banfield, E.J. 243
Bangarra Dance Company 73
Banks, Sir Joseph 31, 231
Banrock Station 200
Barcaldine 235
  Workers' Heritage Centre 235
Bardon, Geoffrey 68
Barkly Tableland 259
Barossa Valley 103, 196, 197
Barren Range 281
Barrow Creek 258
Barrow Island 287
BasinTrail 122
Bateman's Bay 142
Bathurst 36, 143
  Bathurst Goldfields 144
Bathurst island 265
Batman Bridge 305
Batman, John 161
Bay of Fires 303
Bay of Islands 175
beaches 8, 54, 103, 328
  Melbourne 169
  New South Wales 125, 127, 129, 131, 132, 140, 141, 143, 155
  Northern Territory 265
  Queensland 218, 220, 221, 223, 226, 228
  South Australia 197, 203, 207
  Sydney 54, 112, 118, 119
  Tasmania 302, 303, 313, 314, 305
  Victoria 187
  Victoria 184, 186
  Western Australia 277, 279, 281, 284, 285, 286, 289
Beaconsfield 305
  Beaconsfield Mine and Heritage Centre 305
Beagle Bay 288
Beaufort 178
Beauty Point 305
  Platypus House 305
  Seahorse World 305
Bedarra Island 243
Beechworth 183
  Post Office 183
  Robert O'Hara Burke Memorial Museum 183

Tanswell's Commercial Hotel 183
Bee Gees, The 74
Beer, Maggie 199
Bega 143
Belgrave 180
  Puffing Billy 180
Bellingen 131
Bell, John 73
Bell Shakespeare Company 73
Benalla 182
  Benalla Art Gallery 182
Ben Boyd National Park 143
Bendigo 179
  Central Deborah Goldmine 179
  Golden Dragon Museum 179
  Joss House 179
Ben Lomond National Park 307
Bermagul 142
Berri Estates 200
Berrima 137
Berry 140
Beswick Falls 253
Bicheno 303
Big Red 235
Big Tree Reserve 310
Binalong Bay 303
birdlife 93, 146, 229
  birdwatching sites 146
  bowerbird 93
  cassowaries 230
  cockatoos 93, 290
  emus 177, 205, 207
  mutton birds 176
  parrots 93
  pelicans 186
  penguins 142, 185, 205, 278, 308
Birdsville 235
Birdsville Track 201, 235
Blackheath 121
  Govett'sLeap 121
Blackwood 197
Blanchett, Cate 75
Bligh, Captain William 33, 232
Bliss 'n' Eso 74
Blowering Reservoir 138
Blue Lake 204
Blue Mountains 34, 103, 120
Blue Mountains National Park 120
Blundstone Arena 301
Boat Harbour Beach 313
boat trips and cruises 323. *See also* whale- and dolphin-watching
  Adelaide River 262
  Brisbane River 216
  Freycinet Peninsula 316
  Gippsland Lakes 184
  Huon Jet boat (Huonville) 309
  Katherine Gorge 260
  Lake St Clair 310
  Macquarie Harbour/Gordon River 311
  Murray River 179, 180, 205
  New South Wales 125
  Sydney 324
  Yardie Creek Gorge 286
  Yellow Water 261
Bodalla 142
  Big Cheese 142
Bond, Alan 273

Bonner, Neville 67
Boodjamulla National Park 233
Booti Booti National Park 129
Border Ranges National Park 133
Borroloola 259
Botany Bay 31
***Bounty* mutineers, descendants of** 134
Bourke 149
Bowral 136
Boyd, Ben 143
Boydtown 143
  Boyd's Tower 143
  Seahorse Inn 143
Brabham, Jack 87
Bradman, Don 84, 136, 137, 194
Breakaways 203
Breakers 283
Bridport 303
  Barnbougle Dunes Golf Links 303
  Bridestowe Estate Lavender Farm 303
Bright 184
Brisbane 33, 103, 213
  All Saints Church 216
  Anzac Square 214
  Brisbane Arcade 214
  Brisbane City Hall 213
  Brisbane Museum 214
  Brisbane Naval Stores 215
  Brunswick Street Mall 216
  Chinatown Mall 216
  City Botanic Gardens 215
  Fortitude Valley 216
  Gallery of Modern Art 75
  General Post Office 214
  Kangaroo Point 215
  nightlife 216
  Old Government House 215
  Old Windmill 216
  Parliament House 214
  Performing Arts Centre 217
  Queensland Art Gallery 216
  Queensland Cultural Centre 216
  Queensland Gallery of Modern Art 216
  Queensland Maritime Museum 217
  Queensland Museum 216
  Queen Street Mall 214
  Riverside Centre 215
  Roma Street Parkland 216
  South Bank 216
  South Bank Parklands 217
  State Library 217
  St John's Cathedral 215
  St Mary's Anglican Church 215
  Story Bridge 215
  St Stephen's Cathedral 214
  taxis 324
  The Mansions 214
  transport 321, 322, 323
  Treasury Building 214
  visitor information centre 213
  Wheel of Brisbane 217
Brisbane River 213, 215
BrokenBay 74
Broken Head Nature Reserve 133
Broken Hill 103, 147
  Pro Hart's 147

White's Mining Museum 147
Bronte Park 310
Brooklyn 125
Broome 20, 40, 62, 288
   Cable Beach 289
   Gantheaume Point 289
Bruny Island 308
Bryce, Quentin 49
Buccaneer Archipelago 290
Buchan 185
   Fairy Cave 185
Bunbury 279
   Dolphin Discovery Centre 279
   Koombana Beach 279
Bundaberg 222
Bungendore 155
Bungle Bungle Range 20, 291
Burke, Robert O'Hara 35, 202
Burleigh Heads 218
Burnie 313
   Burnie Regional Art Gallery
      313
   Burnie Regional Museum 313
   Fern Glade 313
Burrowa Pine Mountain National
   Park 183
bushfires 17, 180, 181, 327
bushrangers 37
bush, the 58, 91, 93
   tours 59
bushwalking 121
business hours. See opening
   hours
Busselton 279
bus travel
   long-distance 321
Byron Bay 128, 132

C

Cabramurra 139
Cairns 226, 242
   Cairns Historical Museum 227
   Esplanade 227
   Regional Art Gallery 227
Calcified Forest (King Island) 314
Caloundra 221
Calwell, Arthur 44
Cambewarra Lookout 141
Camden 122
   CamdenParkHouse 122
Campbell Town
   Red Bridge 307
Canberra 38, 103
   Aboriginal Tent Embassy 153
   Australian War Memorial
      Museum 154
   Captain Cook Memorial Water
      Jet 152
   Carillon 154
   High Court 153
   Lake Burley Griffin 152
   Museum of Australian
      Democracy 153
   National Arboretum Canberra
      155
   National Botanic Gardens 154
   National Capital Exhibition 153
   National Gallery 68, 153
   National Library 153
   National Museum of Australia

154
National Portrait Gallery 153
National War Memorial 91
National Zoo and Aquarium 155
Old Parliament House 153
Parliament House 152
Questacon – The National
   Science and Technology
   Centre 153
Tidbinbilla Nature Reserve 155
transport 321
Cape Arid National Park 281
Cape Bridgewater 176
Cape Bruny Lighthouse (Bruny
   Island) 308
Cape Byron Headland National
   Park 133
Cape du Couedic (Kangaroo
   Island) 205
Cape Grim 314
Cape Hawke 129
Cape Jervis 205
Cape Leeuwin 280
Cape Le Grand National Park 281
Cape Naturaliste 279
Cape Nelson 176
Cape Otway 174
   Lighthouse 174
Cape Range National Park 286
Cape Tourville 305
Cape Tribulation 229, 242
Cape Wickham Lighthouse (King
   Island) 314
Cape York Peninsula 231
Captains Flat 155
Carcoar 144
Carey, Peter 72
car hire 325
Carlton, Paddy 68
Carmody, Kev 67
Carnarvon 286
   Bibbawarra artesian bore 286
   Miaboolya Beach 286
   Pelican Point 286
Carnarvon Gorge National Park
   222
Carr Boyd Range 291
Carroll, Tom 87
Cash, Pat 86
casinos
   Crown (Melbourne) 167
   Sky City (Darwin) 263
   Star(Sydney) 115
Castlemaine 179
   Victorian Goldfields Railway 179
cathedrals 111
Cave, Nick 74
Cave of Hands 177
Caversham Wildlife Park 278
caves 185
   Cave of Hands 177
   Chillagoe-Mungana National
      Park 233
   Fairy Cave (Buchan) 185
   Hastings 309
   Jenolan 121
   Jewel 280
   Junee 310
   King Solomon's 312
   Lake 280
   Mammoth 280

Marakoopa 312
Naracoorte 204
Wellington 146
Yarrangobilly 138
Ceduna 207
Central Tilba 142
Chambers, Kasey 74
Chambers Pillar 256
Chapman Valley 285
Charleville 235
   Cosmos Centre 235
   Steiger Gun 235
Charlotte Pass 138
Charters Towers 225
Chifley, Ben 43
Childers 222
Chillagoe 233
Chillagoe-Mungana National Park
   233
Chiltern 182
   Lake View Homestead 182
Chudleigh 312
Chunky Move 73
churches and cathedrals
   All Saints (Brisbane) 216
   St David's Cathedral (Hobart)
      299
   St John's Cathedral (Brisbane)
      215
   St John the Evangelist (Albany)
      281
   St Mary's Anglican (Brisbane)
      215
   St Mary's Catholic (Bairnsdale)
      184
   St Paul's Cathedral (Melbourne)
      163
   St Peter (Paynesville) 184
   St Peter's Cathedral (Adelaide)
      193
   St Stephen's Cathedral
      (Brisbane) 214
churchesandcathedrals
   Garrison(Sydney) 111
Churchill Island Heritage Farm
   187
Cilento, Diane 229
cinema. See film and TV
cinemas 121
   openair 111, 117
Clare 199
Clarence River 131
Clarke, Marcus 72
Clarke, Rev. W.B. 36
Clark, Manning 56
Classen, Adolf 35
climate 21, 327
   cyclones 22
   El Niño 22
   Northern Territory 251, 259
   Outback 203
   South Australia 191
   Victoria 176
   Western Australia 288
Cloncurry 234
   Ernest Henry Mine 234
clothing and what to wear 333
Clunes 179
Coal Mines Historic Site 302
Cobar 149
   Great Cobar Heritage Centre

149
Cobourg Peninsula 265
Cockatoo Island 109, 290
AustralianConvictSites 109
Cockle Creek 309
Coffin Bay 206
Coffs Harbour 128, 130
Coles Bay 302
Collette, Toni 75
concertvenues 109
convicts 31, 32, 33, 34, 55, 107,
213, 272, 302
AustralianConvictSites(Cockato
olsland) 109
Coober Pedy 103, 203
Cook, Captain James 30, 31, 231
Cooktown 231
James Cook Historical Museum
231
Coolgardie 36, 281
Cooma 138
Coonawarra 200
Coorong National Park 203
Coral Bay 287
Corryong 182
Man From Snowy River Folk
Museum 182
Cossack 287
Cowra 144
Cowra Japanese Garden 143,
144
Cradle Mountain 103, 312, 315
Crafers 197
Crawford, Evelyn 67
Crescent Head 130
cricket 84, 136
Adelaide Oval 193
Ashes 164
Blundstone Arena (Hobart) 301
Melbourne Cricket Club 164
Tasmanian Cricket Museum
(Hobart) 301
crime and safety 54, 327
drugs 133
Croajingolong National Park 185
Croydon 233
cruises. See boat trips and cruises
Currie (King Island) 314
Currumbin Wildlife Sanctuary 219
Curtin, John 40
Curtin Springs 256
cycle hire 324

D

Daintree 229
Daintree Discovery Centre 230
Daintree National Park 103
Dale, Robert 283
Daly Waters Pub 259
Dampier Archipelago 287
Dampier Peninsula 288
tours 288
Dampier, William 29, 272, 287
dance 73
Dandenong Ranges 180
Darling Downs 219
Darlington 302
Darwin 40, 54, 103, 262
Aquascene 264
Beer Can Regatta 264

Botanic Gardens 264
Brown's Mart 263
Cyclone Tracy (1974) 263
Darwin Harbour 263
Fannie Bay 263
Fannie Bay Gaol 263
Fannie Bay Gaol Museum 264
Museum and Art Gallery of the
Northern Territory 264
Nightcliff 263
Old Navy Headquarters 263
Parap 263
Parliament House 263
Rapid Creek 263
Sky City Casino 263
taxis 324
transport 321, 322
Vestey's 263
Wharf Precinct 264
Daydream Island 241
Daylesford 179
de Heer, Rolf 75
Deloraine 312
Denham Sound 285
Denial Bay 207
Dennis, C.J. 72
Derby 290, 303
Derwent Bridge 310
Devil's Kitchen 302
Devil's Marbles Conservation
Reserve 258
Devonport 313
Bass Strait Maritime Centre 313
Dharug National Park 125
Dig Tree, The 35, 235
Dingo Fence 202
Dinner Plain 184
dinosaur footprints 20, 289
Dirk Hartog Island 285
disabled travellers 328
Discovery Bay Coastal Park 176
diving and snorkelling 243
effect on coral reef 239
Great Barrier Reef 242
New South Wales 129, 133, 134,
140, 141
Queensland 227, 228, 231
South Australia 206
Tasmania 308
Western Australia 277, 285, 287
Dog Line 301, 306
Dongara-Denison 284
Dorrigo 131
Dorrigo National Park 131
Douglas-Apsley National Park
303
Dove Lake 312
Dover 309
Doyalson 125
Dreamworld 219
Drewe, Robert 54
driving 288, 325
in the Outback 203
Dubbo 146
Old Dubbo Gaol 146
Western Plains Zoo 93, 146
Dudley Peninsula (Kangaroo
Island) 205
Duncan, Greg 311
Dunk Island 243
Dunstan, Don 192, 195

Dusty, Slim 74

E

Eaglehawk Neck 301, 306
Eastern MacDonnell Ranges 255
East Gippsland 184
eating out 76
Echuca 179
paddle steamer cruises 179
Sharps Magic Movie House and
Penny Arcade 179
economy 48, 46
Eddystone Point 303
Eden 128, 143
Eden Killer Whale Museum
143
Edithburgh 206
Eighty Mile Reach 288
Elands 129
electricity 328
Ellenborough Falls 129
Ellendale Bluffs 285
Elliott 259
Elsey National Park 260
embassies and consulates 328
Emerald 223
emergencies 329
Emily Gap 255
Emita (Flinders Island) 314
Furneaux Museum 314
environmental issues
climate change 239
conservation 92, 133
natural disasters 22
protecting the Great Barrier
Reef 246
Erskine Falls 174
Esperance 281
Pink Lake 281
Esson, Louis 72
Ettamogah Pub 220
Eureka Stockade. See Ballarat
Evandale 307
Brown's Village Store 307
Clarendon Arms 307
Ewaninga 256
Exmouth 286
Eyre Highway 207, 281
Eyre, John 206
Eyre Peninsula 206

F

Fairweather, Ian 74
Falls Creek 184
farming 58
cattle 146
dairy 122
horse stud farms 127
sheep 31, 122, 146
ferries 109, 112, 125, 323, 324
Sydney 109
festivals and events
Adelaide Festival of Ideas
(Adelaide) 196
Adelaide Festival of the Arts
(Adelaide) 196
Adelaide Fringe (Adelaide) 196
Avon River Descent (Northam)
283

Barossa Vintage Festival (Barossa Valley) 196
Barunga Festival 253
Beer Can Regatta (Darwin) 264
Birdsville Races 235
cherry blossom festival (Cowra) 143
country music festival (Tamworth) 135
Easter Fair (Bendigo) 179
Festival of the Falling Leaves (Tumut) 138
Gay and Lesbian Mardi Gras (Sydney) 55, 117
Gold Rush Festival (Gympie) 222
Henley-on-Todd Regatta (Alice Springs) 255
in Byron Bay 133
International Comedy Festival (Melbourne) 163
Motorcycle Grand Prix (Phillip Island) 186
National Penny Farthing Championships (Evandale) 307
Pier-to-Pub Swim (Lorne) 174
Rose and Rodeo Festival (Warwick) 220
Sculpture by the Sea (Sydney) 120
Shinju Matsuri – Festival of the Pearl (Broome) 289
Tulip Festival (Mittagong) 136
Walking with Spirits (Beswick Falls) 253
Wangaratta Jazz Festival (Wangaratta) 182
Womadelaide (Adelaide) 196
Writers' Week (Adelaide) 196
film and TV 75
soap operas 73
Finke Gorge National Park 256
fishing
New South Wales 129
Northern Territory 259
Tasmania 303, 310
Victoria 181, 182
Western Australia 281, 283, 284, 287, 288
Fitzgerald River National Park 281
Fitzroy Island 243
Fleurieu Peninsula 205
Flinders Chase National Park (Kangaroo Island) 205
Flinders Island 314
Flinders, Matthew 207, 280
Flinders Range National Park 200
Flinders Ranges 21, 200
Fluted Cape (Bruny Island) 308
Flynn, Rev. John 254
food and drink 76
boutique beers 169, 278, 280
bush tucker 79, 195
bush-tucker tours (Jervis Bay) 141
cheese 142, 143, 280, 314
Poachers Way 155
rum 222
wine 80
football. See Australian Rules

Football
Forrest, John 281
Forster 129
Fortescue River 288
fossicking 146, 148, 223
Fossil Downs 290
Fotheringate Beach (Flinders Island) 314
Franklin 309
Wooden Boat Centre 309
Franklin, Miles 72
Franklin River 311
Fraser, Dawn 86
Fraser, Eliza 224
Fraser Island 222, 224
Fraser, Malcolm 46
Freeman, Cathy 67
Fremantle 275, 277
Fremantle Markets 277
Fremantle Prison 277
Maritime Museum 275
Round House 275
Shipwreck Galleries 275
French Island 187
Frew's Ironside Ponds 259
Freycinet National Park 103, 302, 305
Freycinet Peninsula 302
Furphy, Joseph 71
further reading 334

G

Gammon Ranges National Park 201
gardens 112
Gardiner, Frank 37
Gascoyne River 286
gay culture 55
Geelong 173
Barwon Grange 173
Geeveston 309
Forest and Heritage Centre 309
Geikie Gorge 290
gem fields 223
Geographe Bay 279
geography and geology 19
Georgetown 233
Terrestrial Centre 233
George Town 305
Watch House Museum 305
Geraldton 284
Western Australian Museum 285
ghost towns
Cossack 287
Gwalia 282
Hill End 144
Kanowna 282
Silverton 148
Sofala 144
Gibson Desert 19
Gilbert, John 37
Giles, Ernest 257
Gillard, Julia 49
Gingin 283
Gippsland Lakes 184
Gippsland Lakes Coastal Park 184
Gipps, Sir George 36
Gladstone 222
Glass House Mountains 21, 220

Glenelg 197
Glen Helen Gorge 255
Glen Innes 136
Glenisla Shelter 177
Glenrowan 182
Glenrowan Inn 181
gliding 205
Gloucester Tree 280
Gold Coast 218
goldfields 36
New South Wales 144, 145
Queensland 225
Victoria 171, 178
Western Australia 281
gold rush 36, 144, 161
Queensland 225, 228, 231
Victoria 171, 178, 182, 183, 184
Western Australia 272, 274, 281
golf 86
New South Wales 130, 131
Northern Territory 259
Tasmania 303
Goolagong-Cawley, Evonne 67, 86
Gordon Dam 310
Gordon River 312
Gordon River Road 309
Gosford 125
Gosse, William 257
Gostwyck 135
Goulburn 137
Gould, Shane 86
government and politics 43
Aboriginal Development Commission (ADC) 66
Department of Aboriginal Affairs 66
Labor Party 44
Liberal Party 44
Goyder, G.W. 35
Grafton 131
Grampians National Park 177
Granite Island 205
Great Australian Bight 207
Great Barrier Reef 22, 93, 103, 228, 227
Great Dividing Range 20, 21, 103, 135, 171, 220, 227
Great Keppel Island 240
Great Lake 310
Great Northern Highway 290
Great Ocean Road 103, 171, 174
Great Otway National Park 174
Great Oyster Bay 317
Great Sandy Desert 19
Great Sandy National Park (Fraser Island) 224
Great Victoria Desert 19
Great Western 178
Great Western Highway 120, 143
Great Western Plateau 19
Green Island 243
Greenway, Francis 34
Greenwell Point 141
Greer, Germaine 45
Grennough Historical Hamlet 284
Grenville, Kate 72
greyhound racing 141
Grey River Scenic Reserve 174
Griffiths Island 176
Grindelwald 305
Guilderton 283

Guildford 278
Gulf of Carpentaria 20, 233
Gundagal 137
Gunlom 261
Gunn, Jeannie 261
Gurrumul Yunupingu, Geoffrey 67
Guyra 136
Gwalia 282
Gypsy Point 185

H

Hahndorf 197
Hall, Ben 37
Halls Creek 291
Halls Gap 177
Hamelin Pool 285
Hamersley Range 19
Hamilton 176
  Big Wool Bales 176
Hargraves, Edward 36
Hartog, Dirk 272
Hart, Pro 147
Hartz Mountains National Park
  309
Harvey 279
Hastings Caves and Thermal
  Springs 309
Hawke, Bob 47
Hawker 200
Hawkesbury 122
Hawkesbury River 125
Hawks Nest 129
Hay 146
Hayman Island 241
Hazards Beach 305
Healesville 181
  Healesville Sanctuary 93, 181
health and medical care 47, 329
  dangerous creatures 94
  Royal Flying Doctor Service 148,
    234, 254
Henbury Meteorite Craters 256,
  257
Henley Beach 197
Henty Dunes 312
Heron Island 240, 244
Hester, Joy 74
Hewitt, Lleyton 86
Highway 1 (Prince's Highway)
  139, 221
hiking and bushwalking 327
  New South Wales 129, 155
  Northern Territory 255, 256,
    258, 265
  Queensland 220, 227, 233
  South Australia 201
  Tasmania 301, 309, 310, 312,
    315
  Victoria 177, 184
  Western Australia 279
hikingandbushwalking
  Sydney and environs 121, 122
Hillary's Boat Harbour 277
Hill End 144
Hilltop Hoods 74
Hinchinbrook Island 226, 243
Hippo's Yawn 283
historic houses
  Argyle Downs Homestead 291
  Ayers House (Adelaide) 194

Barwon Grange (Geelong) 173
Camden Park House (Camden)
  122
Churchill Island Heritage Farm
  187
Como House (Melbourne) 169
Cooks' Cottage (Melbourne) 166
Cooma Cottage (Yass) 137
Lake View Homestead (Chiltern)
  182
Rio Vista (Mildura) 180
Runnymede (Hobart) 300
Vaucluse House (Sydney) 120
Werribee Park 173
Woolmers Estate (Longford) 305
history 26
  discovery and colonisation 31
  Federation 38
  Iraq war 49
  modern era 43
  Vietnam War 46
  World War I 38, 281
  World War II 40, 43, 144, 262
Hobart 103, 298
  Battery Point 298
  Bellerive 301
  Cascade Brewery 301
  Cenotaph 300
  Centre for the Arts 298
  Constitution Dock 298
  Elizabeth Street Mall 299
  Female Factory 301
  General Post Office 299
  Henry Jones Art Hotel 298
  IXL#19 Jam Factory\0039\
    DeletedText\3\6\ 298
  Kangaroo Bluff Battery 301
  Macquarie Street 299
  Maritime Museum of Tasmania
    299
  Mercury Newspaper Building
    299
  Moorilla Estate 300
  Museum of Old and New Art 75,
    300
  Narryna Heritage Museum 299
  North Hobart 300
  Parliament House 299
  Penitentiary Chapel and
    Criminal Courts 300
  Queens Domain 300
  Royal Botanical Gardens 300
  Runnymede 300
  Salamanca Place 298
  Salamanca Square 298
  St David's Cathedral 299
  Supreme Court 299
  Tasmanian Cricket Museum 301
  Tasmanian Museum and Art
    Gallery 299
  taxis 324
  Theatre Royal 299
  Town Hall 299
  transport 322
  Treasury Building 299
  Victoria Dock 298
Hogan, Paul 56
Horne, Donald 46
Horrock Beach 285
horse racing 87, 141
  Derby Day 164

Melbourne Cup 87, 164
Horsham 177
  Botanic Gardens 178
  Horsham Regional Art Gallery
    178
hotels See accommodation
Hotham, Sir Charles 37
Howard, John 48
Hughenden 235
  Flinders Discovery Centre 235
Hughes, Robert 45, 54
Hughes, William Morris 38
Hume, Hamilton 137
Humphries, Barry 45, 56, 160
Humps 283
Hunter Valley 125
Huon Valley 308
Huonville 308
Hyams Beach 140

I

Illawarra Plateau 139
immigrants 47, 55, 160, 262
  Arabs 53
  Asian 44, 62
  Chinese 40, 62, 179, 204, 227
  German 199
  Immigration Museum
    (Melbourne) 167
  Italian 168
  Migration Museum (Adelaide)
    194
  White Australia policy 44, 46, 62
immigration
  effect on cuisine 77
  post-war reforms 43
Indiana Cottesloe Beach 277
industry 45
Innamincka 202
Innisfail 226
Internet 330
INXS 74
Ipswich 219
  Workshops Rail Museum 219
Irwin, Steve 220

J

Jabiru 261
Jackman, Hugh 75
James, Clive 45
JenolanCaves 121
Jervis Bay 128, 141
  Booderee Botanic Gardens 141
Jesse Gap 255
Jewel Cave 280
Jim Jim Falls 261
Jindabyne 138
John Forrest National Park 292
Jones, Alan 87
Julian Rocks Aquatic Reserve 133
Junee Cave 310
Jurien 284

K

Kadina 206
Kakadu National Park 103, 261
  Bowali Visitor Centre 261
  Marrawuddi Gallery 261

Kalbarri National Park 285
  tours 286
Kalgoorlie 36, 272, 281
  Palace Hotel 282
  Super Pit 282
Kangaroo Island 205
Kangaroos rugby team 86
Kangaroo Valley 140
  Pioneer Museum Park 140
Kanowna 282
Karijini National Park 288
Kata Tjuta 266, 258
Katherine 260
Katherine Gorge 260
Katoomba 121
  EchoPoint 121
  RuinedCastle 121
  ScenicRailway 121
  ThreeSisters 121
Keating, Paul 47
Keep River National Park 260
Kellyland 181
Kelly, Ned 39, 164, 181, 182
Kelp Industries Centre (King Island) 314
Kempton 308
Kennett, Jeff 162
Kennett River 174
Keppoch 200
Kerr, Sir John 46
Kettering 308
Khancoban 139
Kiandra 139
Kidman, Nicole 75
Kimberley, The 19, 103, 288, 289
Kinchega National Park 148
King George Sound 280
King Island 314
  King Island Dairy 314
Kings Canyon 256
  Canyon Rim Walk 256
Kingscote (Kangaroo Island) 205
King Solomon's Cave 312
King Sound 290
Kingston 204
Kingston (Norfolk Island) 134
Klama Bay 140
Kngwarreye, Emily 68
Koolan Islands 290
Kosciuszko National Park 138
Kununurra 291
Kuranda 227
  Skyrail 227
Ku-ring-gaiChaseNationalPark 122

L

Lady Elliot Island 222, 240, 244
Lady Musgrave Island 240
Lake Bellfield 177
Lake Bonney 204
Lake Cave 280
Lake Eildon 181
Lake Eyre 20, 202
Lakefield National Park 231
Lake Hume 182
Lake Hutt 285
Lake Jindabyne 138
Lake Mackenzie 224
Lake MacLeod 286

Lake Macquarie 125
Lake Mountain 181
Lake Pedder 310
Lakes Entrance 184
Lakes National Park 184
Lake St Clair 310, 315
Lamington National Park 220
Lancelin 283
Larapinta Trail 256
Lark Quarry Dinosaur Trackways 235
Lasseter, Harold 255
Latrobe 313
Latrobe Valley 185
Launceston 303
  Boag's Brewery 304
  Brisbane Street Mall 304
  Cataract Gorge 304
  City Park 304
  Civic Square 304
  Cliff Grounds 305
  Design Centre of Tasmania 304
  Library 304
  Macquarie House 304
  National Automobile Association of Tasmania 304
  Old Umbrella Shop 304
  Quadrant Mall 304
  Queen Victoria Museum 304
  Queen Victoria Museum and Art Gallery 303
  Ritchies Mill 304
  Seaport 304
  Town Hall 304
  Yorktown Square 304
Laura 231
Laver, Rod 86
Lawlor, Ray 72
Lawn Hill Gorge 233
Lawrence, D.H. 17
Lawson, Henry 58, 71
Leichhardt, Ludwig 35
Lennox Head 132
Leura 121
  Everglades gardens 122
LGBTQ travellers 117, 330
Light, Colonel William 192, 197
Lilydale 303
  Bardenhagen's General Store 303
Lindeman Island 241
Litchfield National Park 265
literature 71. *See also* further reading, writers by name
Lithgow 121
  Zig-ZagRailway 121
Little Gravelly Beach 305
Little, Jimmy 67
Living Desert Reserve 148
Lizard Island 231, 243
Loch Ard Gorge 175
London Bridge 175
Longford 305
  Brickendon Estate & Historic Farming Village 307
  Brown's Big Store 305
  National Rose Garden 307
  Woolmers Estate 305
Long Island 241
Longreach 234
  Australian Stockman's Hall of

  Fame 234
  Qantas Founders Outback Museum 234
Lord Howe Island 134
Lorne 174
Lower Glenelg National Park 176
Low Head 305
  Maritime Museum 305
  Pilot Station 305
Luhrmann, Baz 75
Lyell Highway 310
Lyndoch 199

M

Macarthur, John 33
Macarthur, John 122
MacDonnell Ranges 253
Mackay 223
  Airlie Beach 223
  Shute Harbour 223
Mackellar, Dorothea 145
Macksville 130
Maclean 132
Macquarie Harbour 311
Macquarie, Lachlan 34
Macquarie Valley Irrigation Area 146
Maggie Beer's Farm Shop 199
Magnetic Island 225, 241
Mahogany Creek 283
Maitland 127
Malanda 227
Maldon 179
Mallacoota 185
Mallee 171
Malouf, David 72
Mammoth Cave 280
Mandurah 278
Mangrove Mountain 125
Manning Valley 129
Mansfield 181
maps 330
Marakoopa Cave 312
Marble Bar 20, 288
  Comet Gold Mine 288
Margaret River 103, 279
Maria Island 302
markets 9
  Barossa Farmers' Market 199
  Central (Adelaide) 195
  Fish Market (Sydney) 115
  Fremantle Markets (Fremantle) 277
  in Darwin 263
  Paddington Bazaar (Sydney) 117
  Prahan (Melbourne) 169
  Queen Victoria (Melbourne) 168
  Salamanca Place (Hobart) 298
  Sunday Bondi Markets (Sydney) 119
Marree 202
Maryborough 222
Marysville 181
Maslin Beach 197
Mataranka 259
  Mataranka Homestead Tourist Resort 260
  Mataranka Thermal Pool 260
Matilda Highway 234
McKenzie Falls 177

McKinlay 234
McLaren Vale 199
media 63, 330
Melbourne 55, 54, 103, 103
  Acland Street 169
  ANZ Bank Building 163
  Arts Centre 167
  Australian Centre for
    Contemporary Art 75
  Australian Centre for the
    Moving Image 163
  bars and pubs 166
  Birrarung Marr 163
  Block Arcade 163
  Bourke Street Mall 164
  Brunswick Street 168
  Carlton Gardens 165
  Chapel Street 169
  Chinatown 165
  clubs 166
  Collins Street 163
  Como House 169
  Cooks' Cottage 166
  Crown Casino 167
  Docklands 168
  Edge 163
  Etihad Stadium 168
  Eureka Tower 167
  Fairies Tree 166
  Federation Bells 163
  Federation Square 162
  Fitzroy Gardens 166
  Fitzroy Street 169
  Flemington Racecourse 87, 164
  Flinders Street Station 162
  Hamer Hall 167
  Heide Museum of Modern Art
    74
  Hopetoun Tearooms 164
  Ian Potter Centre 162
  Immigration Museum 167
  Little Italy 168
  Luna Park 169
  Lygon Street 168
  Melbourne Aquarium 167
  Melbourne Central 164
  Melbourne Cricket Ground
    (MCG) 163, 164, 166
  Melbourne Exhibition Centre
    168
  Melbourne Museum 165
  Melbourne Town Hall 163
  Melbourne Zoo 93, 168
  music venues 166
  National Gallery of Victoria 167
  National Sports Museum 166
  Old Melbourne Gaol 164
  Old Treasury 165
  Parliament of Victoria House
    165
  Prahan 169
  Princess Theatre 165
  Queen Victoria Market 168
  QV Centre 164
  Regent Theatre 163
  Royal Arcade 164
  Royal Botanic Gardens 167
  Royal Exhibition Building 165
  Scienceworks 169
  shopping 163
  Shrine of Remembrance 166

  South Yarra 169
  State Library of Victoria 164
  St Kilda 169
  St Paul's Cathedral 163
  taxis 324
  tours 165
  transport 163, 321, 322, 323
  Treasury Garden 166
  Tudor Village 166
  Upper Esplanade 169
  Victoria Harbour 168
  Webb Bridge 168
  Williamstown 169
  Young and Jackson's pub 163
Melville island 265
Men at Work 74
Menindee Lake 148
Menzies, Robert 40, 44
Mereenie Loop Road 256
Merimbula 143
Merredin 282
meteorite craters 291
Metung 184
Miallo 229
  Karnak Playhouse 229
Michôd, David 75
Middle Lagoon 288
Midland Highway 305
Midnight Oil 74
Mildura 180
  Mildura Arts Centre 180
  Rio Vista 180
  Workingmen's Club 180
Miles 235
  Historical Village 235
Millaa Millaa 227
Miller, George 75
Miller, Godfrey 74
Millstream-Chichester National
  Park 288
mining 145, 147, 148, 149, 233. See
  also gold rush
  coal 127, 186
  copper 206, 259
  diamonds 291
  gemstones 136
  gold 225, 259, 281
  iron ore 287
  mine tours 148, 178, 179, 186,
    234, 260
  opals 203
  quartz 178, 179
  uranium 261, 272
Minogue, Kylie 74
Mission Beach 226
Mittagong 136
  Tulip Festival 136
Moe 186
  Old Gippstown 186
Moffat, Tracey 74
Mogo Zoo 142
Mole Creek Karst National Park
  312
money matters 330
  budgeting for your trip 326
Monkey Mia 285
Montague Island 142
Moonlight, Captain 137
Moonta 206
Moreton Bay 218
Mornington Peninsula 187

Morton National Park 140
Moruya 142
Mossman Gorge 228
motorbike hire 324
motor racing 87, 144
  Motorcycle Grand Prix 186
Mount Baw Baw National Park 186
Mount Beauty 184
Mount Buffalo National Park 184
Mount Canobolas 145
Mount Conner 257
Mount Coot-tha Botanic Gardens
  217
Mount Field National Park 310
Mount Freycinet 305
Mount Gambier 204
Mount Gibraltar 136
Mount Gibraltar Reserve 137
Mount Graham 305
Mount Grenfell Aboriginal cave
  paintings 149
Mount Hotham 184
Mount Isa 233
  City Lookout 233
  Riversleigh Fossil Display &
    Interpretive Centre 233
Mount Kosciuszko 21, 138
Mount Ossa 315
Mount Panorama 144
Mount Richmond 176
Mount Strzelecki (Flinders
  Island) 314
MountVictoriavillage 121
Mount Warning 133
Mount William 177
Mount William National Park 303
Mout Buller 181
Mudgee 127
Mungo National Park 147
Murramarang National Park 141
Murray River 171, 179, 182
Murray Smith, Joanna 72
Murrurundi 135
museums and galleries 9, 68
  Araluen Cultural Precinct (Alice
    Springs) 254
  Art Gallery of New South Wales
    (Sydney) 111Australian
    Museum (Sydney) 113
  Art Gallery of South Australia
    (Adelaide) 194
  Art Gallery of Western Australia
    (Perth) 274
  Australian Centre for
    Contemporary Art
    (Melbourne) 75
  Australian Centre for the
    Moving Image (Melbourne)
    163
  Australian Democracy at
    Eureka (Ballarat) 178
  Australian Democracy
    (Canberra) 153
  Australian War Memorial
    Museum (Canberra) 154
  Ballarat Fine Art Gallery
    (Ballarat) 178
  Bass Strait Maritime Centre
    (Devonport) 313
  Benalla Art Gallery (Benalla)
    182

Brisbane Museum (Brisbane) 214
Burnie Regional Art Gallery (Burnie) 313
Burnie Regional Museum (Burnie) 313
Cadman's Cottage (Sydney) 110
Cairns Historical Museum (Cairns) 227
Central Australia (Alice Springs) 257
Chiverton House Museum (Northampton) 285
Contemporary Art (Sydney) 110
Cosmos Centre (Charleville) 235
Design Centre of Tasmania (Launceston) 304
Eden Killer Whale Museum (Eden) 143
Fannie Bay Gaol Museum (Darwin) 264
Flagstaff Hill Maritime Village 175
Fleet Air Arm Museum (Nowra) 140
Flinders Discovery Centre (Hughenden) 235
Furneaux Museum (Emita) 314
Gallery of Modern Art (Brisbane) 75
Galley Museum (Queenstown) 311
Gippsland Regional Maritime Museum (Port Albert) 186
Golden Dragon Museum (Bendigo) 179
Hawkesbury Regional Gallery (Windsor) 122
Heide Museum of Modern Art (Melbourne) 74
Horsham Regional Art Gallery (Horsham) 178
Hyde Park Barracks (Sydney) 55, 113
Ian Potter Centre (Melbourne) 162
Immigration Museum (Melbourne) 167
James Cook Historical Museum (Cooktown) 231
Kronosaurus Korner (Richmond) 235
Manly Art Gallery and Museum (Sydney) 112
Man from Snowy River Folk Museum (Corryong) 182
Maritime Museum (Fremantle) 275
Maritime Museum (Low Head) 305
Maritime Museum (Sydney) 114
Maritime Museum of Tasmania (Hobart) 299
Marrawuddi Gallery (Kakadu National Park) 261
Melbourne Museum (Melbourne) 165
Migration Museum (Adelaide) 194
Motor Museum (Whitman Park) 278

Museum of Contemporary Art (Sydney) 75
Museum of Sydney (Sydney) 113
Narryna Heritage Museum (Hobart) 299
National Automobile Museum of Tasmania (Launceston) 304
National Capital Exhibition (Canberra) 153
National Gallery (Canberra) 68, 153
National Gallery of Victoria (Melbourne) 167
National Motor Museum 197
National Museum of Australia (Canberra) 154
National Portrait Gallery (Canberra) 153
National Sports Museum (Melbourne) 166
Northern Territory (Darwin) 264
Old and New Art (Hobart) 75, 300
Old Gippstown (Moe) 186
Pioneer Museum Park (Kangaroo Valley) 140
Pioneer Settlement (Swan Hill) 179
Powerhouse (Sydney) 116
Pro Hart's (Broken Hill) 147
Qantas Founders Outback Museum (Longreach) 234
Queensland Art Gallery (Brisbane) 216
Queensland Gallery of Modern Art (Brisbane) 216
Queensland Museum (Brisbane) 216
Queen Victoria Museum and Art Gallery (Launceston) 303
Queen Victoria Museum (Launceston) 304
Questacon – The National Science and Technology Centre (Canberra) 153
Regional Art Galery (Cairns) 227
Riversleigh Fossil Display & Interpretive Centre (Mount Isa) 233
Robert O'Hara Burke Memorial Museum (Beechworth) 183
Rockhampton Art Gallery (Rockhampton) 223
Scienceworks (Melbourne) 169
Shipwreck Galleries (Fremantle) 275
South Australian Museum (Adelaide) 194
Sovereign Hill (Ballarat) 178
Strehlow Research Centre (Alice Springs) 254
Sydney Observatory (Sydney) 111
Tandanya National Aboriginal Cultural Institute (Adelaide) 195
TarraWarra Museum of Art 181
Tasmanian Cricket Museum (Hobart) 301

Tasmanian Museum and Art Gallery (Hobart) 299
Terrestrial Centre (Georgetown) 233
Wagga Wagga Art Gallery (Wagga Wagga) 144
Waltzing Matilda Centre (Winton) 234
Warrnambool Art Gallery (Warrnambool) 175
Watch House Museum (George Town) 305
West Coast Pioneers Museum (Zeehan) 312
Western Australian Museum (Geraldton) 285
Western Australian Museum (Perth) 275
Whaleworld 280
White's Mining Museum (Broken Hill) 147
Workers' Heritage Centre (Barcaldine) 235
Workshops Rail Museum (Ipswich) 219
music
country and western 74
didgeridoo 31
rock and pop 74
Mutawintji National Park 148
Myall Lakes 127, 129
Myrtleford 183

N

Namatijira, Albert 255
Nambung National Park 284
Nampitjin, Eubana 68
Naracoorte Caves 204
Nariel Creek 183
Narooma 142
Narromine 146
National Motor Museum 197
national parks 130, 230, 333
Alpine 184
Arakwal 133
Ben Boyd 143
Ben Lomond 307
Blue Mountains 120
Boodjamulla 233
Booti Booti 129
Border Ranges 133
Burrowa Pine Mountain 183
Cape Arid 281
Cape Byron Headland 133
Cape Le Grand 281
Cape Range 286
Carnarvon Gorge 222
Chillagoe-Mungana 233
Coorong 203
Croajingolong 185
Daintree 103
Dharug 125
Dorrigo 131
Douglas-Apsley 303
Elsey 260
entry fees 130
Finke Gorge 256
Fitzgerald River 281
Flinders Chase 205
Flinders Ranges 200

French Island 187
Freycinet 103, 302, 305
Gammon Ranges 201
Grampians 177
Great Otway 174
Great Sandy (Fraser Island) 224
Hartz Mountains 309
John Forrest 292
Kakadu 103, 261
Kalbarri 285
Karijini 288
Keep River 260
Kinchega 148
Kosciuszko 138
Ku-ring-gai Chase 122
Lakefield 231
Lakes 184
Lamington 220
Litchfield 265
Lower Glenelg 176
Maria Island 302
Millstream-Chichester 288
Mole Creek Karst 312
Morton 140
Mount Baw Baw 186
Mount Buffalo 184
Mount Field 310
Mount William 303
Mungo 147
Murramarang 141
Mutawintji 148
Myall Lakes 129
Nambung 284
New England 136
Nightcap 133
Nitmiluk 260
Noosa 221
Nullarbor 207
permit requirements 204
permits 308
Port Campbell 175
Purnululu 20, 291
Royal 118
Snowy River 184
Southwest 309
Stirling Range 280
Tunnel Creek 290
Uluru-Kata Tjuta 257
Uluru-Katja Tjuta 267
Walls of Jerusalem 312
Watarrka 256
West MacDonnell 255
Wilson's Promontory 171, 186
Windjana Gorge 290
Woodgate 222
Wyperfeld 177
Yalgorup 279
Yanchep 283
Yarra Ranges 181
National Trust 332
nature reserves 93, 130. See
    also aquatic reserves
Alice Springs Desert Park (Alice
    Springs) 254
Barrow Island 287
Big Tree 310
Broken Head 133
Currumbin Wildlife Sanctuary
    219
entry fees 130
Gippsland Lakes Coastal Park

184
Grey River Scenic Reserve 174
Mount Canobolas 145
Mount Gibraltar 137
Ningaloo Reef Marine Park 287
Tidbinbilla (Canberra) 155
Tower Hill State Game Reserve
    175
Tyagarah 133
Yumbarra Conservation Park
    207
N'dhala Gorge 255
Nelson 176
Nelson Bay 129
Newcastle 125
Newcastle Waters 259
Newcombe, John 86
New Engand Tableland 135
New England 135
New England National Park 136
New Norcia 283
New Norfolk 309
New South Wales
    climate 131
NewSouthWales 107
Nichols, Sir Doug 67
Nightcap National Park 133
Nimbin 133
Ninety Mile Beach 184
Ningaloo Reef Marine Park 287
Nitmiluk National Park 260
Nolan, Sidney 45, 74
Noonuccal, Oodgeroo 67
Noosa Heads 221
Noosa National Park 221
Norfolk Island 32, 134
Norman, Greg 86
Normanton 233
Norseman 281
Northam 283
Northampton 285
    Chiverton House Museum 285
Northern Territory 251
Nourlangie Rock 261
Nowra 140
    Fleet Air Arm Museum 140
    Nowra Raceways 141
Nowra, Louis 72
Nullarbor National Park 207
Nullarbor Plain 281
Nundle 135
Nuriootpa 199
Nymbolda River 131
Nyngan 146

O

Oatlands 307
    Callington Mill 307
Ochre Pits 255
oil and gas 262, 272, 287
Old Mogo Town 142
Olgas, The. See Kata Tjuta
Olinda 180
    National Rhododendron
        Gardens 180
opening hours 331
Opera Australia 71
Ophir Goldfields 145
Orange 145
Orbost 184

Orford 302
Ormiston Gorge and Pound 255
Orpheus Island 243
Otway Fly 174
Otway Ranges 174
Outback 53, 103
    Northern Territory 253, 258
    Queensland 232
    South Australia 200
    Western Australia 288
Overland Track 312, 315

P

Pacific Highway 124
Padthaway 200
    Padthaway Estate Homestead
        200
Pambula 143
Papunya 68
Parachilna Pass 201
parachuting
    Queensland 227
parasailing
    New South Wales 131
Parkes 145
    Observatory 145
Parkes, Sir Henry 136
Park, Ruth 72
parks and gardens. See
    also national parks
    Birrarung Marr (Melbourne) 163
    Booderee Botanic Gardens
        (Jervis Bay) 141
    Botanic Garden (Ballarat) 178
    Botanic Gardens (Adelaide) 195
    Botanic Gardens (Bairnsdale)
        184
    Botanic Gardens (Darwin) 264
    Botanic Gardens (Horsham) 178
    Botanic Gardens (Wagga
        Wagga) 144
    Carlton Gardens (Melbourne)
        165
    Centennial Park (Sydney) 117
    Chinese Garden (Sydney) 115
    City Botanic Gardens (Brisbane)
        215
    City Park (Launceston) 304
    Cliff Grounds (Launceston) 305
    Cowra Japanese Garden
        (Cowra) 143, 144
    Elder Park (Adelaide) 193
    Everglades gardens (Leura) 122
    Fitzroy Gardens (Melbourne)
        166
    Hyde Park (Sydney) 113
    Kings Park (Perth) 273
    Mount Coot-tha Botanic
        Gardens 217
    National Arboretum (Canberra)
        155
    National Botanic Gardens
        (Canberra) 154
    National Rhododendron
        Gardens (Olinda) 180
    National Rose Garden
        (Longford) 307
    Nielsen Park (Sydney) 112
    Roma Street Parkland
        (Brisbane) 216

Royal Botanical Gardens (Hobart) 300
Royal Botanic Gardens (Melbourne) 167
Royal Botanic Gardens (Sydney) 111
Salmon Ponds Heritage Hatchery and Garden 309
South Bank Parklands (Brisbane) 217
Stirling Gardens (Perth) 274
Treasury Garden (Melbourne) 166
Victoria State Rose Garden 173
Parramatta 112
Patterson, Banjo 58, 71, 146
The Man From Snowy River 58, 71, 183
Waltzing Matilda 71
Paynesville 184
Church of St Peter 184
Pearce, Guy 75
pearls 288
Pemberton 280
Pendulum 74
Penneshaw (Kangaroo Island) 205
people 53. See also Aboriginal people and sites
Perisher Blue 138
Perth 103, 271, 272
Art Gallery of Western Australia 274
Cloisters 274
Deanery 274
East Murray Street Precinct 274
Government House 274
His Majesty's Theatre 274
Horseshoe Bridge 274
King's Park 273
Kings Park 292
London Court 274
nightlife 275
Northbridge 275
Old Court House 274
Old Gaol 275
Perth Cultural Centre 274
Perth Mint 274
Stirling Gardens 274
Subiaco 275
Swan Bells 273
taxis 324
Town Hall 274
transport 273, 321, 322, 323
Western Australian Museum 275
Petyarre, Kathleen 68
Phillip, Arthur 32
Phillip, Captain Arthur 65, 107
Phillip Island 185, 186
Cowes 187
Penguin Parade 187
Summerland Beach 185
Picnic Bay 186
Picton 122
Pilbara, The 287
Pilbeam, Rex 223
Pimba 202
Pine Creek 261
Pine Gap 256
Pinnacles, The 284
plantlife 20, 93. See also rainforest

eucalyptus 20, 93
grass trees 293
Gympie vine 230
jarrah forests 93
Western Australia 282
wild flowers 292
Poachers Way 155
Point Labatt 207
Pokolbin 127
politics. See government and politics
polo 127
Pondalowie Bay 206
Pontville 308
Porcupine Gorge 235
Port Albert 186
Gippsland Regional Maritime Museum 186
Port Arthur Penal Settlement 103, 297, 302, 306
Port Augusta 200
Port Campbell National Park 175
Port Denison 284
Port Douglas 228, 242
Port Fairy 176
Caledonian Inn 176
Port Hedland 288
Port Kembla 140
Portland 171, 176
Port Lincoln 206
Port Macquarie 129
Port Phillip Bay 173
Port Stephens 128, 129
Port Victoria 206
Possession Island 31
postal services 331
Princes Freeway 173
public holidays 331
Purnululu National Park 20, 291
Pyengana 303
Pub in the Paddock 303
St Columba's Falls 303

Q

quarantine 328
Queenscliff 173
Queensland 211, 236
Queenstown 311
Galley Museum 311
Miners Siding 311
Quorn 200

R

Racecourse beach 130
Railbow Valley 256
rail travel 322
Ghan 200, 253, 322
Trans-Australian railway 207
rail travel, scenic & heritage lines 323
Pichi Richi Railway 200
Puffing Billy (Belgrave) 180
Scenic Railway (Katoomba) 121
Victorian Goldfields Railway (Castlemaine) 179
West Coast Wilderness Railway 311
Zig-Zag Railway (Lithgow) 121
rainforests 21, 115, 131, 133, 228, 230
Daintree Discovery Centre 230
Rasp, Charles 145
Ravenshoe 227
Ravenswood 225
Rayson, Hannie 72
Recherche Archipelago 281
Redbank Gorge 255
Red Centre 253
Reid Lookout 177
religion 44, 331
Remarkable Rocks (Kangaroo Island) 205
Renmark 204
Renner Springs 259
restaurants 326. See also eating out, food and drink
Richards, Mark 87
Richardson, Henry Handel 72, 182
Richardson's Beach 317
Richmond 122, 235, 301
Kronosaurus Korner 235
Old Hobart Town Model Village 301
Riverland 200
Riversleigh Fossils site 233
Riversleigh Fossil Display & Interpretive Centre (Mount Isa) 233
Roach, Archie 67
road trains 206, 207
Roberts, Tom 73
Rockhampton 223
Rockhampton Art Gallery 223
Rockingham 278
rodeo 234
Roebourne 287
Roma 235
Roses Gap 177
Ross 307
Rottnest Island 277, 278
Roxon, Lillian 45
Royal Flying Doctor Service 148, 234
Visitor's Centre (Alice Springs) 254
RoyalNationalPark 118
Rudd, Kevin 49, 67, 152
Rudd, Steele 72
rugby 85
Rush, Geoffrey 75
Rutherglen 182

S

Sale 185
Salmon Ponds Heritage Hatchery and Garden 309
Sandringham 187
San Remo 186
Sarah Island 311
Scarborough 277
School of the Air 234, 254
Schultz, Hugh 147
Scone 127
Scotts Head 130
Seal Rocks 129, 187
sea travel 323
Sea World 219
Seekers, The 74
Serpentine Gorge 255

Seven Spirit Bay 265
Seventy-Five Mile Beach (Fraser Island) 224
Shaffer, Anthony 229
Shark Bay 285
Sheffield 312
   Tazmania 312
   Village of Lower Crackpot 312
shopping 117
   Aboriginal art and crafts 69
Shute, Neville 253
Silverton 148
   Daydream Mine 148
Simpson's Gap 255
Singleton 127
Skenes Creek 174
skiing See winter sports
Sleepy Bay 305
snorkelling. See diving and snorkelling
Snowy Mountains 103, 138, 155
Snowy River National Park 184
soccer 86
Socceroos soccer team 86
society 43, 46, 54
   alternative culture 131, 133
   multiculturalism 61
   racial tension 53
   women's role 44, 48, 56
Sofala 144
Solander, Daniel Carl 31
Sorrento 187
South Australia 191
South Beach 219
South Cape Bay 309
South Coast Track 309
Southern Highlands 136
South Molle Island 241
Southwest National Park 309
South West Rocks 130
   Trial Bay Gaol 130
Spencer Gulf 200
Spiky Beach 302
sports 84, 164. See also individual sport names
   National Sports Museum (Melbourne) 166
Spring Hill 216
Squeaky Beach 186
Standley Chasm 255
Stanley 313
   Highfield 314
   Nut 21
Stead, Christina 72
St Helens 303
Stirling, Captain James 272
Stirling Range National Park 280
Stirling Ranges 292
St Matthews 309
Strahan 311
Strathgordon 310
Streeton, Sir Arthur 73
Strzelecki Track 201
student travellers 331
Sturt, Charles 34
Sturt Highway 204
Styx Valley 310
Summerland Coast 132
Sunshine Coast 220
Surfers Paradise 218
surfing

New South Wales 129, 130, **132**
Queensland 221
South Australia 207
Sydney 118, 119, 122
Victoria 174
Western Australia 277, 279, 281, 283
surfing, competitive 87
Swan Hill 179
   Pioneer Settlement 179
Swan River 273
Swansea 302
Swan Valley 278
swimming, competitive 86
Sydney 31, 55, 112, 103
   Anzac War Memorial 113
   Argyle Centre 111
   Argyle Cut 110
   Art Gallery of New South Wales 111
   Australia nMuseum 113
   Balmain 116
   Balmoral beach 112
   bars and pubs 111
   Blues Point Road 112
   boat trips and cruises 109, 324
   Bondi Beach 118
   Bronte 119
   Cadman's Cottage 110
   Campbell Parade 118
   Camp Cove 112
   Centennial Park 117
   Central Business District 113
   Chinatown 116
   Chinese Garden of Friendship 115
   Circular Quay 109, 110, 112
   Clovelly 119
   Coogee beach 119
   Cremorne Point 112
   Customs House 113
   Darling Harbour 114
   Double Bay 120
   Elizabeth Bay 117
   ferries 109, 112, 324
   FishMarket 115
   Garrison Church 111
   Gay and Lesbian Mardi Gras 55, 117
   Glebe 116
   Gordon's Bay 119
   Government House 110
   Harbour Bridge **109**
   history 32, 107
   Hyde Park 113
   Hyde Park Barracks 55, 113
   King's Cross 116
   Kirribilli 112
   Lady Jane beach 112
   Madam Tussaud's 115
   Manly 112
   Manly Art Gallery and Museum 112
   Maritime Museum 114
   McMahons Point 112
   Mrs Macquarie's Point 111
   Museum of Contemporary Art 75
   Museum of Contemporary Art 110
   Museum of Sydney 113
   Nielsen Park 112

nightlife 116
ObservatoryHill 111
Oceanworld 112
Open Air Cinema 111
Opera House 71,**109**
Oxford Street 117
Paddington 117
Paddington Bazaar 117
Palm Beach 122
Parliament House 113
Potts Point 117
Power house Museum 116
Pylon Lookout 109
Queen Victoria Building 114
River Cat 112
Rocks, The 110
Royal Botanic Gardens 111
Sea Life Sydney Aquarium 115
South Head 120
Star casino 115
State Library 113
Sunday Bondi Markets 119
Sydney Mint 113
Sydney Observatory 111
Sydney Tower 114
Tamarama 119
Taronga Park Zoo 93, 112
taxis 323
tourist information 115
transport 321, 322, 323
University of Sydney 116
Vaucluse 120
Vaucluse House 120
Victoria Street 117
water taxis 109
Watsons Bay 120
Wild Life Sydney Zoo 115
Sydney Harbour 109
Sydney Symphony 71
Sydney Theatre Company 72

T

Table Cape 313
Tahune Forest Air Walk 309
Tallangatta 182
Tamar Island 305
Tamar Valley 305
Tamar Valley Wine Route 305
Tamworth 135
Tanami Track 258
Tanunda 199
Taree 129
Taroona 308
   Shot Tower 308
Tarraleah 310
Tasman, Abel 297
Tasman Arch 302
Tasman Bridge 301
Tasmania 33, 103
   transport 322
Tasmanian Devil Park 302
Tea Gardens 129
telephones 331
Temper Trap 74
Tennant Creek 259
tennis 86
Tenterfield 136
Territory Wildlife Park 264
Tesselated Pavement 301
theatre 72

theatres and concert venues. *See also* arts, performing, casinos
Adelaide Festival Centre (Adelaide) 193
ARA Darling Quarter Theatre (Sydney) 115
Arts Centre (Melbourne) 167
Edge (Melbourne) 163
Gaiety Theatre (Zeehan) 312
Hamer Hall (Melbourne) 167
His Majesty's Theatre (Perth) 274
Karnak Theatre (Miallo) 229
Opera House (Sydney) 71, 109
Performing Arts Centre (Brisbane) 217
Princess Theatre (Melbourne) 165
Regent Theatre (Melbourne) 163
Tandanya National Aboriginal Cultural Institute (Adelaide) 195
Theatre Royal (Hobart) 299
theme and amusement parks
Aussie World 220
Australian Outback Spectacular (Gold Coast) 219
Dreamworld (Gold Coast) 219
Fairy Park (Anakie) 173
Kellyland (Victoria) 181
Luna Park (Melbourne) 169
Old Mogo Town 142
Warner Brothers' Movie World (Gold Coast) 219
Wet 'n' Wild (Gold Coast) 219
Whitewaterworld (Gold Coast) 219
Thomas, Rover 68
Thorpe, Ian 86
Thredbo 138
Thursday Island 232
Tidal River 186
Tidbinbilla 155
Deep Space Communications Complex 155
Tiddas 67
time zones 147, 332
Timor Sea 262
Tinderbox 308
tipping 331
Tiwi Islands 264, 265
tours 264
toilets 332
Tom Price 288
Toodyay 283
Toowoomba 220
Torquay 174
Torres Strait 232
Torres Strait Islands 232
tourist information 332
Tower Hill State Game Reserve 175
Town of 1770 222
Townsville 225
Museum of Tropical Queensland 225
Reef HQ 225
Towrang Stockade 137
Trangle 146
transport 320, 326
Trephina Gorge 255

Trigg 277
Trollope, Anthony 159
Trousers Point (Flinders Island) 314
Tucker, Albert 74
Tully Gorge 226
Tumut 138
Tunnel Creek National Park 290
Twain, Mark 17, 38, 161, 297, 301
Tweed Heads 133
Twelve Apostles 175
Twin Falls 262
Twofold Bay 143
Tyagarah Nature Reserve 133

U

Ubirr Rock 261, 262
Ulladulla 141
Uluru 20, 103, 103, **257**, 253
Uluru-Kata Tjuta National Park 257, 267
Ulverstone 313
Undara Lava Tubes 21, 233
Unesco World Heritage sites 109, 147
Upton, Andrew 73
Uralla 135
Urban, Keith 74
useful addresses 332
Utopia 68
Utzon, Jørn 109

V

Valley of the Winds 258
Van Diemen's Land 33, 297
Victor Harbour 205
Victoria 159
Victoria Range 177
Victoria State Rose Garden 173
vineyards and wineries 80
Barossa Valley 196, 197, 200
Clare Valley/Watervale 199
Great Western 178
Hunter Valley 127
Margaret River 279
Moorilla Estate 300
Mudgee 127
Rutherglen 182
Swan Valley 278
Tamar Valley 305
Yarra Valley 180
visas and passports 333

W

Waddy Point (Fraser Island) 224
Wagga Wagga 144
Wagga Wagga Art Gallery 144
Wahroonga 125
Waikerie 205
Walhalla 186
Long Tunnel Extended Gold Mine 186
Walker, Katch. *See* Noonuccal, Oodgeroo
Wallabies rugby team 86
Wallaroo 206
Walls of China 147
Walls of Jerusalem National Park

312
Wall, The 311
Walpa Gorge 267
Walpole 280
Waltzing Matilda 71
Wangaratta 182
Wangi Wangi 125
Warburton 181
Warner Brothers' Movie World 219
Warrnambool 175
Flagstaff Hill Maritime Village (Warrnambool) 175
Warrnambool Art Gallery 175
Warrumbungle Mountains 21
Warwick 220
Watarrka National Park 256
waterfalls
Ellenborough Falls 129
Erskine Falls 174
Horseshoe Falls 310
Jim Jim Falls 261
Lady Barron Falls 310
McKenzie Falls 177
Millaa Millaa Falls 227
Millstream Falls 227
Russell Falls 310
St Columba's Falls 303
Twin Falls 262
water sports
Victoria 181, 182
Western Australia 283
Wauchope 130
Timbertown 130
Waverley Heights 285
Wave Rock 20, 282, 283
Webber, Mark 87
weights and measures 333
Wellington 146
Wellington Caves 146
Wentworth 147
Wentworth, William Charles 121
Werribee Open Range Zoo 173
Werribee Park 173
West Coast Wilderness Railway 311
Western Australia 271
West MacDonnell National Park 255
West Wyalong 145
Wet 'n' Wild 219
Wet Tropics World Heritage area 230
whale- and dolphin-watching 128, 129, 143, 205
Wharton, Herb 67
Whispering Wall 199
White Cliffs 148
Whiteley, Brett 74
Whiteman Park
Motor Museum 278
Whitemark (Flinders Island) 314
White, Patrick 45, 53, 72
whitewater rafting
New South Wales 131
Queensland 227
Whitewaterworld 219
Whitlam, Gough 47, 66
Whitman Park 278
Whitsunday Island 241
Whitsunday Islands 241

Wilcannia 148
wildlife 91, 20, 230. *See also* birdlife, national parks, nature reserves
arachnids 54, 230
camels 256
crocodiles 54, 229, 230, 260, 262, 263, 290, 291, 327
dangerous creatures 94
dingoes 91, 202
dolphins 93, 128, 129, 279, 285
dugongs 286
echidnas 92
fish, freshwater 180
frogs and toads 92
goannas 230
jellyfish 93, 264, 327
kangaroos 91, 92, 139, 141, 145, 146, 174, 177, 207
koalas 92, 177
lizards 92
marine life 93, 134, 140, 242
marsupials 91
monotremes 92
of Kangaroo Island 205
platypuses 92, 227, 313
possums 54, 91, 137
potoroos 92
scorpions 95
seals 187, 207
sea turtles 286
sharks 93, 112, 207, 288
snakes 54, 92, 230
Tasmanian devils 92
termite mounds 259
thrombolites 279
wallabies 92, 287
whales 93, 128, 129, 175, 207, 280, 286
wombats 92, 137
Willandra Lakes World Heritage Site 147
William Ricketts Sanctuary 180
Williams, Fred 74
Williamson, David 72
Wills, John 202
Wills, W.J. 35
Wilpena Pound 200

Wilson's Promontory National Park 171, 186
Wimmera, The 177
Windich, Tommy 281
Windjana Gorge National Park 290
Windsor 122
HawkesburyRegionalGallery 122
Wineglass Bay 302, 305
Wineglass Bay Track 316
wineries. *See* vineyards and wineries
winter sports
New South Wales 155
Victoria 181, 184, 186
Winton 234
Waltzing Matilda Centre 234
Winton, Tim 72
Wiseman's Ferry 125
Wodonga 182
Wolfe Creek 291
Wolfmother 74
Wollongong 139
Wollumbin *See* Mount Warning
women travellers 333
Wonderland Range 177
Woodgate National Park 222
wool industry 146, 182
woolindustry 122
Woolnorth 314
Woomera 202
Wybalenna (Flinders Island) 314
Wynard 313
Wyndham 291
Wyperfeld National Park 177

Y

Yackandandah 183
Yalgorup National Park 279
Yamba 132
Yanchep National Park 283
Yarra Glen 181
Yarra Ranges National Park 181
Yarra River 159
Yarra Valley 180
Yarrongobilly Caves 138

Yass 137
Cooma Cottage 137
Yellow Rock Beach (King Island) 314
Yellow Water 261
Yerling Station vineyard 180
York 283
Yorke Peninsula 205
Yorketown 206
Yothu Yindi 67, 74
Younghusband Peninsula 203
Young, Nat 87
You Yang mountains 173
Yulara Resort 258
Yumbarra Conservation Park 207
Yungaburra 227

Z

Zeehan 312
Gaiety Theatre 312
West Coast Pioneers Museum 312
zoos and animal parks 93
Australian Reptile Park 125
Australia Zoo 220
Caversham Wildlife Park 278
Dolphin Discovery Centre (Bunbury) 279
Healesville Sanctuary (Healesville) 93, 181
Melbourne Zoo (Melbourne) 93, 168
Mogo Zoo 142
National Zoo and Aquarium (Canberra) 155
Platypus House (Beauty Point) 305
Taronga Park Zoo (Sydney) 93, 112
Tasmanian Devil Park 302
Territory Wildlife Park 264
Werribee Open Range Zoo 173
Western Plains Zoo (Dubbo) 93, 146
WildLifeSydneyZoo(Sydney) 115
Zumstein 177
Zumstein, Walter 177